DRYDEN: THE CRITICAL HERITAGE

THE CRITICAL HERITAGE SERIES

GENERAL EDITOR: B. C. SOUTHAM, M.A., B.LITT. (OXON.)
Formerly Department of English, Westfield College, University of London

For list of books in the series see back end paper

First published 1971
by Routledge and Kegan Paul Ltd,
Broadway House,
68–74 Carter Lane,
London, EC4V 5EL
© *James and Helen Kinsley 1971*
First published in the United States, 1971
by Barnes & Noble, Inc.
No part of this book may be reproduced
in any form without the permission from
the publisher, except for the quotation
of brief passages in criticism

ISBN 389 04126 2

Printed in Great Britain

DRYDEN

THE CRITICAL HERITAGE

Edited by
JAMES KINSLEY
Professor of English, University of Nottingham
and
HELEN KINSLEY

BARNES & NOBLE, Inc.
NEW YORK
PUBLISHERS & BOOKSELLERS SINCE 1873

General Editor's Preface

The reception given to a writer by his contemporaries and near-contemporaries is evidence of considerable value to the student of literature. On one side we learn a great deal about the state of criticism at large and in particular about the development of critical attitudes towards a single writer; at the same time, through private comments in letters, journals or marginalia, we gain an insight upon the tastes and literary thought of individual readers of the period. Evidence of this kind helps us to understand the writer's historical situation, the nature of his immediate reading-public, and his response to these pressures.

The separate volumes in the *Critical Heritage Series* present a record of this early criticism. Clearly, for many of the highly productive and lengthily reviewed nineteenth- and twentieth-century writers, there exists an enormous body of material; and in these cases the volume editors have made a selection of the most important views, significant for their intrinsic critical worth or for their representative quality—perhaps even registering incomprehension!

For earlier writers, notably pre-eighteenth century, the materials are much scarcer and the historical period has been extended, sometimes far beyond the writer's lifetime, in order to show the inception and growth of critical views which were initially slow to appear.

In each volume the documents are headed by an Introduction, discussing the material assembled and relating the early stages of the author's reception to what we have come to identify as the critical tradition. The volumes will make available much material which would otherwise be difficult of access and it is hoped that the modern reader will be thereby helped towards an informed understanding of the ways in which literature has been read and judged.

B.C.S.

Contents

CONTENTS

Note on the Text

Copy-texts and modern editions are identified in the head-notes to the texts. For pieces originally printed in italics the type has been reversed. Long 's' and merely typographical devices have been discarded. Errors of spacing and numbering, turned letters, wrong founts, obvious misprints, and irregularities in the use of 'æ' and 'œ' have been corrected silently; proper names in roman type have been italicized in some contexts; the distinction between italicized plurals in ——'s and possessives in roman ——'s has been regularized. The original punctuation has been preserved except in a few passages where it is misleading.

Original footnotes are indicated by a star(*), dagger(†), etc.

A late addition is No. 86, excerpted from transcripts of Lord Monboddo's papers generously supplied to us by Dr Emily Cloyd, University of Michigan.

Introduction

I

In his Dedication of *Examen Poeticum* (1693) Dryden wrote:

Thus the corruption of a Poet, is the Generation of a Critick: I mean of a Critick in the general acceptation of this Age: For formerly they were quite another Species of Men. They were Defendors of Poets, and Commentators on their Works: to Illustrate obscure Beauties; to place some passages in a better light, to redeem others from malicious Interpretations: to help out an Author's Modesty, who is not ostentatious of his Wit; and, in short, to shield him from the Ill-Nature of those Fellows, who were then call'd *Zoili*, and *Momi*, and now take upon themselves the Venerable Name of Censors . . .: what their Reputation was then, we know; and their Successours in this Age deserve no better.[1]

Harsh, but substantially true. Much of the seventeenth-century material in this book is of historical interest, and some of it is entertaining; but Dryden's identification of critics with libellers and poetasters is again and again justified. In his lifetime Dryden was his own best critic. In the century after his death good criticism of his work is surprisingly sparse; but it includes the prose essays of Dennis and Congreve, the verse tributes of Pope, Gray, and Churchill, some of Dr Johnson's most powerful critical writing, and (if we add a decade) the final Augustan assessment by Sir Walter Scott. I propose in this Introduction to look first at the evidence, in theatrical records and publishing history, for the early popularity of Dryden's work; to survey the course of criticism from his own prefaces and dedications down to Blake's rejection of Dryden and Pope *c.* 1810 (No. 85), with special reference to Johnson and Scott; and to give a summary account of criticism from Scott to the present time.

II

In 1754, a hundred years after the publication of Dryden's first poem, Thomas Gray was placing him just after Shakespeare and Milton in *The Progress of Poesy* (No. 69b); in 1808, a hundred years after his death, Walter Scott confirmed his place in that hierarchy (No. 83Aa). But what was the response of Dryden's contemporaries to his immense and varied work in poetry, drama, criticism and history, with Shakespeare only half a century dead and Milton still alive?

The most immediate response, and that on which he depended most for his living, came less from the small literary reading public than from the audiences and managers of the theatres. Dryden first made 'the Town [his] Judges' with *The Wild Gallant* at the Theatre Royal early in 1663, and 'the greater part condemn'd it' (Nos. 1 and 2a). But he pleased at least Pepys with *The Rival Ladies* in 1664 (No. 2d); and although this play turned out to be less influential than its dedicatory epistle (to the Earl of Orrery) on rhyme in drama, it was twice printed before the end of the decade. The printing of these early plays, however, and the revival of *The Wild Gallant* in 1667, followed on the success of other theatrical ventures—Pepys did not buy a copy of *The Rival Ladies* till 18 July 1666. Dryden and his brother-in-law, Sir Robert Howard, set the new fashion of the heroic play—rhetorical, extravagant, spectacular—with *The Indian Queen*, which drew both town and court in January 1664 (No. 2b, c). Dryden's own *Indian Emperour*, though its early run in the spring of 1665 was cut short by the plague, established itself at the Theatre Royal and at court in 1667 and was seen at least four times by Pepys, who bought it for his library;[2] Charles II saw it several times in 1666–7 and in 1674;[3] and it was reprinted nine times in Dryden's lifetime.[4] *Secret-Love, or The Maiden-Queen* had a comparable reception in March 1667: the king saw it twice within four days and commanded a court performance,[5] gracing it (says Dryden) 'with the title of His Play'; and Pepys loved it the more he saw it (No. 2e). But this was afterwards a less popular play, reprinting (after two editions) once in a decade until Dryden's death.

Pepys was at the second performance of Dryden's first comedy, *Sir Martin Mar-all, or The Feign'd Innocence* (the Duke of Newcastle's

2

'bare Translation' of Molière's *L'Etourdi* which Dryden had adapted for the Duke of York's company, 'curiously polishing the whole'[6]): it was

the most entire piece of mirth, a complete farce from one end to the other, that certainly was ever writ. . . . I laughed till my head [ached] all the evening and night with the laughing; and at very good wit therein, not fooling. The house full, and in all things of mighty content to me.[7]

John Downes, former prompter for the company, says that this play, with Etherege's *Love in a Tub* (1664), was the most profitable comedy they had so far presented. The Lord Chamberlain's records show two performances before royalty in August 1667, five in the next eight months, and others at Whitehall in 1672, 1673, 1674, and 1686.[8] The immediate popularity of *Mar-all* is reflected in the two 1668 printings; demand fell off thereafter.

The outrageous adaptation of Shakespeare's *Tempest* by Dryden and Davenant was first performed at the Duke's Theatre on 7 November 1667. Five performances before royalty are recorded by the Lord Chamberlain between November 1667 and April 1668, and two on 17–18 November 1674.[9] These, and Pepys's comments, are a sad reflection on the taste of the day:

forced to sit in the side balcone over against the musique-room at the Duke's house, close by my Lady Dorset and a great many great ones. The house mighty full; the King and Court there: and the most innocent play that ever I saw; and a curious piece of musique [III. iv.] . . . which is mighty pretty. The play [has] no great wit, but yet good, above ordinary plays. Thence home with [Sir] W. Pen, and there all mightily pleased with the play.[10]

Worse was to follow, in the operatic version attributed to Shadwell (1674),[11] which reprinted till the end of the century.

Dryden's publisher, Herringman, was rather slow to register the comedy, *An Evening's Love* (1668), and slower in publishing (1671). But then, though Pepys says that 'the world commends' this play, it provoked 'the little Criticks' and offended John Evelyn (see No. 9), displeased Mrs Pepys,[12] and seems to have attracted the king and queen but once;[13] and Dryden, busy over *Tyrannick Love* in early 1669, had a difficult defensive preface to write for *An Evening's Love* before he let it out into print. In the event, demand for the published play seems to have fallen off after the two editions of 1671. Herringman was prudently quicker with *Tyrannick Love*, entering it in the Stationers' Register three weeks after its opening in June 1669; he published two editions within three years, and three more by 1695. This ambitious tragedy (see No. 8) was costly to produce, and delays in preparing the elaborate set provoked a law-suit;[14] but in its first run of fourteen days it is said—admittedly by the scene-painter whom the company sued and who stood to gain by exaggeration—to have 'brought in £100 per day, whereas the ordinary play produced only £40 or 50 per day',[15] and it increased both Dryden's income and his financial interest in the King's company.

Another stage hit and best-seller followed in the heroic play, *The Conquest of Granada*. The First Part was acted in December 1670 and the Second Part in early January 1671 at the Theatre Royal, and both parts of 'the famous Play' were 'two days acted successively' at Whitehall on 10–11 February with 'indeede very glorious scenes and perspectives'.[16] Again Herringman registered with speed (25 February 1671) and published in early 1672 and 1673. The play reached six editions by 1704. Of the two comedies first acted in 1672, *Marriage à-la-Mode* (in the spring) and *The Assignation* (in the autumn), the first was Dryden's best, and the other an ill success 'at the representation ... whether the fault was in the Play itself, or in the lameness of the Action, or in the number of Enemies who came resolv'd to damn it'.[17] But both plays had shorter and slower histories in print: *Marriage à-la-Mode*, published in May–June 1673, did not reprint for ten years and reached only four editions by 1698; *The Assignation*, published at the same time, was reprinted in 1678 and 1692.

Dryden's worst dramatic work of the seventies, the tragedy of *Amboyna* (acted probably in spring 1673) and *The State of Innocence* ·.. *An Opera* (?1673; see Nos. 18 and 22), had notably different fates in print. *Amboyna*, political propaganda hurried through the press in the year of its first presentation, was reprinted only once, in 1691. *The State of Innocence*, written perhaps to celebrate the Duke of York's marriage in November 1673 but (says Dryden) never acted, did not lapse into merited obscurity. The public didn't share Marvell's distaste for Milton rhymed: Dryden says he had to publish in self-defence, 'many hundred Copies ... being dispersed abroad without my knowledge or consent'; and the thing ran to ten editions between 1677 and 1703.

The group of tragedies which followed illustrates the quality of the continuing taste for heroic drama both on the stage and in print. *Aureng-Zebe*, praised to Charles II by the Earl of Mulgrave and said by the king to be Dryden's best tragedy to date (No. 21), was first performed at the Theatre Royal on 17 November 1675, acted before royalty on 17 and 20 November and at court on 29 May 1676,[18] registered twelve days after opening, and seven times printed by 1704. *All for Love*, despite its high place in the estimation both of Dryden (No. 24) and of his modern critics, seems to have had much less general appeal. Published early in 1678, a few months after its first stage presentation, it was only twice reprinted in Dryden's lifetime.[19] On the other hand the bombastic violence of *Oedipus*, by Dryden and Nat Lee, was a scandalous success, with the Bettertons playing Oedipus and Jocasta. 'It took prodigiously,' says Downes, 'being *Acted* 10 Days altogether', and reached six editions by 1701. *Troilus and Cressida*, Dryden's second excursion into 'Shakespearean' tragedy, did not do even as well as *All for Love*; acted and published in 1679, it was reprinted only in the 1690s.

Despite the moral outrage of *The Kind Keeper*, first acted on 11 March 1678 and prohibited after three performances (see No. 23b), the play attracted little interest on its belated appearance in print in 1680. Dryden's pessimism ('if it live to a second Impression') was almost wholly justified; there was no reprint until 1690. *The Spanish Fryar*, first acted on 8 March 1680 at Dorset Garden, did deservedly better; its success on the stage, says Downes, brought 'vast Profit' to the Duke's company; royal attendances are recorded for 8 March 1680, 29 November 1684, 28 May 1689;[20] and there were five editions by 1704.

The Duke of Guise, doubtless in part because of its political theme, ran to four editions in Dryden's lifetime. The rest of the later plays did less well, as new dramatists and new fashions became established. The opera *Albion and Albanius* (1685) ran to three editions, but one of these was a fine and probably limited printing.[21] *Don Sebastian*, one of Dryden's best plays (see Nos. 41, 76f, 83Bd), was not a success in the acting and was reprinted only once. So was *King Arthur* (1691)— Purcell's music was published twice; but Dryden, not to offend the new regime in Whitehall, had been 'oblig'd so much to alter the first Design, and take away so many Beauties from the Writing, that it is now no more what it was formerly than the present Ship of the *Royal Sovereign* [is] the vessel it was at the first Building'. *Cleomenes* (1692), at first prohibited on political grounds, was published once; so was *Love Triumphant* (1694), according to a letter of 22 March 1694 'damned by the universal cry of the town, *nemine contradicente* but the conceited poet'.[22]

Among Dryden's early poems, only *Heroique Stanza's* (on the death of Oliver Cromwell) was much reprinted—and that for the most part by the poet's enemies—until the revised edition of *Annus Mirabilis* appeared in 1688. This printing includes *Astræa Redux*, *To His Sacred Majesty*, and *To My Lord Chancellor*, and is in effect the first collected edition of Dryden's poetry. *Absalom and Achitophel* stands alone: got out hurriedly in November 1681 (there are four 'states' of the first edition) presumably to prejudice the trial of Shaftesbury, it ran to three London editions before the end of the year, three more in 1682 together with a couple of translations into Latin verse, and two Dublin editions; it was reprinted with *Mac Flecknoe* and *The Medall* to form the opening section of Tonson's first *Miscellany Poems* in 1684 (reprinted in 1692 and reordered in 1702), again with the other satires to make a 'collected edition' in 1692, and from time to time during the eighteenth century. *The Medall*, in contrast, had only one separate London edition (one in Edinburgh and one in Dublin, all 1682). The Second Part of *Absalom and Achitophel* (in part by Dryden) ran to two editions between November and the end of 1682, and a Dublin edition, but it was not again reprinted before Dryden's death. *Mac Flecknoe*, pirated by 'D. Green' in 1682 and authoritatively published by Tonson in *Miscellany Poems* (1684), was reprinted only in the 1692 gathering already mentioned and in one or two miscellanies. Even in this age the theological poems do not appear to have been commercial successes. The second edition of *Religio Laici* in 1682 may well be evidence of a run on the poem, since we know that the first edition came out in late November of that year;[23] there was a third edition in 1683; but no further printings before 1700. There were five editions of *The Hind and the Panther*—a much more controversial poem, with political overtones—in 1687 (licensed 11 April); but one of these was Irish, and another an Edinburgh reprint by the King's Printer; and again there were no further editions before Dryden's death.

Ovid's Epistles, *Translated* by Dryden and others (1680) went to a second edition within a year, to a third in 1683, and to fourteen by 1748[24]—reflecting a persistent taste for classical romance, however bad the poetry. The great folio translations have a solid but less spectacular printing history. The *Satires* of Juvenal and Persius (1693) was reprinted in octavo in 1697 with engravings, again in 1702, 1711, 1713, 1726, and occasionally thereafter. A second edition of the *Virgil* appeared within a year (1698), revised; a third in three volumes octavo came out in 1709; and there were several reprints during the eighteenth century. The *Fables* (1700) was reprinted in octavo in 1713, and there were five other editions during the first half of the century. The Miscellanies published by Tonson with Dryden as literary adviser and editor had a shorter life, I suppose because much of the verse they contained was eventually absorbed in the folio translations or made obsolete by these, or was included in collected editions of the *Poems* from 1701 onwards. *Miscellany Poems* (1684) was reprinted in 1692 and (with omissions and additions) 1702; *Sylvae* (1685) was also reprinted in 1692 and (again with changes) 1702; *Examen Poeticum* (1693) was reprinted in 1706; *The Annual Miscellany* (1694) was reprinted in 1708. *Poetical Miscellanies: The Fifth Part* (1704) was not reprinted.[25]

Of the sixteen prose works wholly or partly by Dryden—mainly translation and historiography—only five reached more than one edition in a quarter-century: *Of Dramatick Poesie, An Essay* (1668, 1684, 1693), *The History of Polybius* (1693, 1698), *De Arte Graphica* (1695, 1716), *The Annals of Tacitus* (1698, 1716), and *Plutarch's Lives* (1683). The *Plutarch* was a popular translation, running to five editions by 1703 and often reprinted thereafter.

The posthumous collected editions are evidence of the status and the continuing vitality of Dryden's writing in the Augustan age. There had been a growing demand for gatherings of both plays and poems in the 1690s,[26] and in 1701 sets of the *Works* were made up in four folio volumes: two volumes of *Comedies, Tragedies, and Operas*, the 1698 edition of the *Virgil*, and *Poems on Various Occasions* (1701) together with *Fables Ancient and Modern*. The set had a general title and sold at £4 2s. The *Dramatick Works* probably in some degree edited by Congreve, and containing his Memoir (No. 66), were published in six volumes duodecimo by Tonson in 1717, and reprinted in 1725, 1735, and 1762. The *Poems and Translations* were edited for Tonson by Thomas Broughton and published in two volumes duodecimo in 1743; an independent Dublin edition appeared ten years later. Foulis of Glasgow reprinted the Tonson edition (omitting the translations) in 1756. Samuel Derrick, who helped Dr Johnson with his life of Dryden, edited the *Miscellaneous Works* for Tonson in four volumes octavo in 1760, with 'Explanatory Notes and Observations. Also an Account of his Life and Writings'; the edition was reprinted in 1767.

III

Criticism [says Professor Sutherland],

became an increasingly prominent activity in the literary world of the late seventeenth century. . . . That there was a serious interest in critical principles (as distinct from critical personalities) may be seen from the fact that much of the work of Boileau, Le Bossu, Rapin, Saint-Evremond, and other French critics was quickly made available for the English reader in translation. Native English criticism . . . was rapidly making up . . . lost ground. Not only did many of the poets and dramatists set forth their critical ideas in prefaces and dedications, but the last few decades of the century saw the emergence of such men as Rymer and Dennis, who were primarily critics rather than creative writers.[27]

This is well said, and it introduces an excellent survey of the main critical concerns of the age. But it may raise expectations which are not to be fulfilled. Of the authors listed in Professor Sutherland's bibliography—150 or so—only about a dozen were in any significant sense critics at any time in their careers, and only one or two are of permanent critical interest.

DRYDEN HIS OWN CRITIC

It is commonplace, following Dr Johnson, to speak of Dryden as the father of modern English criticism. But it is prudent not to expect too much modernity in him; for though we recognize in his essays something more familiar in tone, emphasis, and interest than we find in Elizabethan or Jacobean critics,[28] we have equally to struggle with outworn modes of thought, digressive antiquarianism, panegyrical excesses which (for us) detract from the seriousness of the literary operation, self-defence and self-commendation, raids and skirmishes against 'little Criticks' now almost forgotten. The didactic criticism of Dryden [says Scott],

is necessarily, at least naturally, mingled with that which he was obliged to pour forth in his own defence; and this may be one main cause of its irregular and miscellaneous form. What might otherwise have resembled the extended and elevated front of a regular palace, is deformed by barriers, ramparts, and bastions of defence; by cottages, mean additions, and offices necessary for personal accommodation. The poet, always most in earnest about his immediate task, used, without ceremony, those arguments which suited his present purpose (No. 83 As).

But I doubt whether Dryden had the architectural skill and concern to erect a 'regular palace'. There is no great intellectual or aesthetic system behind these essays of his, other than a diffused latter-day renaissance humanism. Most of them are introductions to translations from classical and other authors, or prefaces and dedications printed with his poems and plays; independent, self-sufficient general criticism is still (if we ignore the moribund tradition of the *Rhetoricks*) a good way off. Partly in imitation of Corneille's prefaces—and Ben Jonson's, earlier—Dryden's essays deal with matters which concerned him as a working dramatist and translator: blank verse and rhyme, the classical unities, the heroic poem, stage morality and diction, the histories of classical genres like epic and satire, fidelity to an ancient original and the art of making Roman poets speak like Englishmen. Few of the essays are academic, objective; many are designed in part to gain or reward a patron, pacify a critic, salvage an ill-fortuned piece of writing or sell a new one. And Dryden can pursue such aims with rare subtlety: much of his criticism is like 'the studio-talk of a successful artist who knows how to give away a little, but not much, whose revelations are always likely to be self-recommendations artfully disguised, and who in debate never hesitates to evade or suppress'.[29] These characteristics, inconvenient and distracting as they may be to a modern reader in pursuit of critical truth, are typical of Dryden and his time, and we have to adjust to them. On the credit side, it is this self-engagement, this apparent frankness about success and failure, this almost theatrical confiding in us, that makes Dryden the most readable early critic of his own work—indeed, until the publication of the brilliant burlesque *Rehearsal* (No. 10), the only critic of any interest. It may be argued that English Augustan criticism evolved round the writings of Dryden, explained, recommended, defended or apologized for by himself. There is perhaps a little in Swift's jibe, that 'great *Dryden* has often said to me in Confidence, that the World would have never suspected him to be so great a Poet, if he had not assured them so frequently in his Prefaces' (No. 61c); but Dryden was much more profoundly aware of the merits and weaknesses of his work than most of his contemporary critics were, and much better endowed with wit, sensibility, and style to express that awareness. We make no apology for what may at first seem an illicit procedure, bringing Dryden in from time to time to speak for himself—though we have tried to select passages that deal, not with the origin or purpose of a work, but with its quality. An anthology of seventeenth-century comment on Dryden is (whatever its primary aim) inevitably a documentation of English criticism in embryo and infancy, and to omit Dryden on himself is to throw the midwife and wet-nurse out with the bath-water.

There is another reason for including passages from Dryden. He often reports the oral criticism of court, salon, and coffee-house, which would otherwise be lost. Thus he tells us that 'a Royal Judg' approved *Secret-Love*, and what the arguments were about 'the Character of *Philocles*' (No. 4). He records the approval given to *Aureng-Zebe* by Charles II and the Earl of Mulgrave, and the objections made by 'some of the fair Ladies' (No. 21); audience-reaction to *Don Sebastian* (No. 41); and the lately-dead Charles's view of *Albion and Albanius*:

He had been pleas'd twice or thrice to command, that it should be practis'd before him, especially the First and Third Acts of it; and publickly declar'd more than once, That the Composition and Chorus's were more Just, and more Beautiful, than any he had heard in *England*. How nice an Ear he had in Musick, is sufficiently known; his Praise therefore has establish'd the Reputation of it, above Censure, and made it in a manner Sacred. 'Tis therefore humbly and religiously dedicated to his Memory.[30]

1660–1700

Dryden himself aside, there is almost no sustained and serious criticism until Dennis's essays at the end of the century. Yet there is a great deal of writing about, and allusion to, Dryden; some of it critical, much of it merely adulatory or abusive. That sort of satire, says Dryden,

which is known in *England* by the Name of Lampoon, is a dangerous sort of Weapon, and for the most part Unlawful. We have no Moral right on the Reputation of other Men. 'Tis taking from them, what we cannot restore to them. . . . More Libels have been written against me, than almost any Man now living: And I had Reason on my side, to have defended my own Innocence: I speak not of my Poetry, which I have wholly given up to the Criticks; let them use it, as they please; Posterity, perhaps, may be more favourable to me: For Interest and Passion, will lye bury'd in another Age: And Partiality and Prejudice be forgotten. I speak of my Morals, which have been sufficiently aspers'd: That only sort of Reputation ought to be dear to every honest Man, and is to me. But let the World witness for me, that I have been often wanting to my self in that particular; I have seldom answer'd any scurrilous Lampoon: When it was in my power to have expos'd my Enemies: And being naturally vindicative, have suffer'd in silence; and possess'd my Soul in quiet.[31]

That critical judgments should have to be disentangled from lampoons on the author's character is of course a startling novelty to modern readers. But Dryden's complaint, and his apologia, are fully justified. He confesses to being 'vindictive enough to have repell'd force by force, if I cou'd imagine that any of them had ever reach'd me',[32] and the way he retaliated upon Shadwell and Settle[33] is sufficient evidence of what he was capable of in obliteration. But a multitude of libellous scribblers was allowed to slither by, beneath his notice. Their heyday was the 1680s, when Dryden changed his role of master-dramatist to that of Tory apologist, hammer of the Whigs, and religious controversialist.

> Parties in *Wit* attend on those of *State*,
> And publick Faction doubles private Hate,
> *Pride*, *Malice*, *Folly*, against *Dryden* rose,
> In various Shapes of *Parsons*, *Criticks*, *Beaus*. . . .[34]

Their lampoons, says Scott, the 'fruits of incensed and almost frantic party-fury',

are marked by the most coarse and virulent abuse. The events in our author's life were few, and his morals, generally speaking, irreproachable; so that the topics for the malevolence of his antagonists were both scanty and strained. But they ceased not, with the true pertinacity of angry dulness, to repeat, in prose and verse, in couplet, ballad, and madrigal, the same unvaried accusations, amounting in substance to the following: That Dryden had been bred a puritan and republican; that he had written an elegy on Cromwell, (which one wily adversary actually reprinted;)[35] that he had been in poverty at the Restoration; that Lady Elizabeth Dryden's character was tarnished by the circumstances attending their nuptials; that Dryden had written the 'Essay on Satire,' in which the king was libelled;[36] that he had been beaten by three men in Rose–alley;[37] finally, that he was a Tory, and a tool of arbitrary power. This cuckoo song, garnished with the burden of *Bayes* and *Poet Squab*,[38] was rung in the ear of the public again and again, and with an obstinacy which may convince us how little there was to be said, when that little was so often repeated.[39]

We would, however, be mistaken in enforcing a simple distinction between criticism and libel, and letting these lampoons lie in obscurity. For in them the libellous and the critical are often inextricably tangled, and the literary comment is not always merely abusive by infection from the scandal: see the earliest reprinted here, by Rochester (No. 20); the reluctant recognition of Dryden's satiric power in the 'answers' to *Absalom and Achitophel* (No. 27); the curried hotch-potch (by Shadwell?) of pseudo-biography, literary criticism, politics, and scurrility in *The Medal of John Bayes* (No. 30); and Prior's general assault in *A Satyr on the modern Translators* (No. 35). Nor is the censure of the 'Rota' (Nos. 12 and 13) always tendentious, pedantically niggling, and far from the bone.[40]

There is, too, a vein of critical comment running through the adulatory verses prefixed to *Absalom and Achitophel* and other poems (Nos. 26, 28, 29); but it is thin and drossy, exposing a poverty of ideas, vocabulary, and imagery even in reputable men of letters; and the bias is often political rather than critical (*cf.* No. 33, a prose tribute). Critical quality improves in the commendatory verses written for the classical translations of the 1690s—e.g., of Persius (No. 46) and of Virgil (No. 53); partly because some of the panegyrists are better poets, Congreve and Addison among them.

The major assault on Dryden in his last years was made by Jeremy Collier in *A Short View of the Immorality, and Profaneness of the English Stage* (1698), which ran to two editions in a month and initiated a violent controversy.[41] But this is now little more than a literary curiosity: Collier's 'Malice infinitely surpassing his Ability,' said Dennis, 'his Performance is somewhat aukward':

In the beginning of his Book, he produces his own Reasons why the Stage reform'd ought to be encourag'd, and in the End of the same Book, he brings other Mens Opinions to shew, that every Stage ought to be abolish'd; and so endeavours to ruin his own Reasons by a long Scroll of other Peoples Author-ities, which is certainly a pleasant Condescension; but such is the fantastick Humility of pedantick Pride! And yet Mr. *Collier* is very right, and very sincere in his Reasons, and very wrong, and very corrupt in his Authorities. As if he were so great an Enemy to the Truth, that he would suborn the very Dead, to destroy the Force of what he himself had asserted.[42]

Collier's intentions are more honourable than those of Dryden's libellers in the 1680s had been, but his critical manners are little better. Dryden himself played almost no part in the controversy that followed Collier's book; he knew that although the conduct of the prosecution was unsophisticated, laborious, and comically grave, the moral charges were valid:

> O Gracious God! How far have we
> Prophan'd thy Heav'nly Gift of Poesy?
> Made prostitute and profligate the Muse,
> Debas'd to each obscene and impious use,
> Whose Harmony was first ordain'd Above

> For Tongues of Angels, and for Hymns of Love?
> O wretched We! why were we hurry'd down
>   This lubrique and adult'rate age,
>   (Nay added fat Pollutions of our own)
> T'increase the steaming Ordures of the Stage?[43]

Dryden himself, his theatre audiences, his verse libellers and adulators, with an occasional 'censor' or 'vindicator' in prose—these, then, are the main critics of his work before 1700. There are occasional touches of criticism elsewhere: in the King's Patent (No. 7), taking notice of Dryden's 'great skill and elegant style both in verse and prose'; the burlesques by Buckingham in *The Rehearsal* (No. 10), by Arrowsmith (No. 11), and by Prior and Montague (No. 36); the unexpected piece of 'practical criticism' from Rymer on *The Indian Emperour*, curiously abandoned 'to the Readers ingenuity' (No. 19); Cibber's delightful recollections of two leading actors (No. 42), with Kynaston making theatrical capital out of the ambivalent attitude to the heroic which underlies so much of Dryden's work; and the not unrelated comment of Farquhar on the 'farce and heroicks' of Dryden's funeral (No. 59). But one climbs with relief out of this tangled undergrowth of libel, trivial disputation, hollow panegyric and other sorts of para-criticism, to the clearer and firmer ground of the eighteenth century.

IV

1700–1800

Criticism of Dryden in the half-century or so following his death is sparse, and contributions from the major men of letters are disappointingly casual and undeveloped. Swift's comments are not much more than witty jeers (No. 61). The *Spectator* essayists drew heavily and with ease on Dryden's works for illustrations of imagery and rhetoric and for ornamental quotation (No. 63), but attempted no critique of him as they did of Milton. The enormous debts of Pope to Dryden are recorded in his editors' commentaries; Pope's admiration of him is rarely, briefly expressed in occasional remarks and in one fine triplet (No. 68). Gray (No. 69) follows Pope in setting Dryden with Shakespeare and Milton as 'great landmarks', and uses the same device of rhetorical imitation to praise him. The lines from Churchill's *Apology* (No. 73a) are an emphatic reminder that during

13

the life and after the death of Pope, Dryden continued to receive the veneration of neoclassical poets. With Jabez Hughes (No. 62), Sarah Fielding obliquely (No. 70), Joseph Warton (No. 71h), and Horace Walpole (No. 75),[44] Churchill shows (No. 73b) that the narrative and descriptive power of Dryden's *Fables*—their rhetoric and 'romance' —did not reassert itself in the Romantic age[45] but made a strong imaginative appeal to readers right through the eighteenth century.[46]

But the best prose criticism of Dryden in this half-century comes from Dennis, Congreve, and (in little) Garth (see Nos. 64, 65, 66). There is passion as well as admiration in Dennis's regard for Dryden's poetry. "Tis indeed impossible,' he wrote to Dryden on 3 March 1693,

that I should refuse to Love a Man, who has so often given me all the pleasure that the most Insatiable Mind can desire; when at any time I have been Dejected by Disappointments, or Tormented by cruel Passions, the recourse to your Verses has Calm'd my Soul, or rais'd it to Transports which made it contemn Tranquillity. . . . You with a breath can bestow or confirm Reputation; a whole Numberless People Proclaims the praise which you give, and the Judgments of three mighty Kingdoms appear to depend upon yours. . . . I had rather have your Approbation than the applause of Fame. Her commendation argues good luck, but Mr. Dryden's implies desert.[47]

If Dennis's loyalty to the memory of Dryden led him into an unreasonable and bitter attack on Pope (No. 64b), it also drew from him some of the earliest judicious *general* criticism of Dryden:

the Solidity of his Thought . . . the Spring, the Warmth, and the beautiful Turn of it . . . the Power, and Variety, and Fulness of his Harmony . . . the Purity, the Perspicuity, the Energy of his Expression . . . the Pomp and Solemnity and Majesty of his Style. . . . Mr. *Dryden*'s great Qualities . . . his Art, his Variety, his Passion, his Enthusiasm. . . .

But Dennis curiously failed to understand what Dryden says about the nature of satire and the delight of 'fine Raillery', transporting us to a region beyond that of moral instruction and reformation, in his Dedication of the *Juvenal*.[48] *Absalom and Achitophel*, *The Medall*, and *Mac Flecknoe* are not merely, as Dennis would have them, 'beautiful Libels' too full of 'Flattery or Slander' to be accounted 'just Satire'. Dennis's assessment of *All for Love* (No. 67) will strike readers as oddly perverse, too disconcertingly close to Jeremy Collier's for comfort; but tragedy was expected to give instruction as well as delight, to offer practical wisdom to the commonweal.[49]

The moving memorials by Garth and Congreve (Nos. 65, 66) are of course not primarily critical in intention; but Congreve notably draws attention to the virtues of Dryden's *prose*, and to the prologues and songs which were not to receive much appreciative attention until our own day; and in Garth's tribute there is dignified sympathy and melancholy sense.

These and other memoirs of Dryden were gathered up in a different literary form which, right into the nineteenth century, was to be the vehicle for sustained criticism of his work: the biography prefixed to an edition. The first true 'life' of Dryden is by Dr Thomas Birch in the *General Dictionary, Historical and Critical* (1734–41; iv (1736)); the next was by Samuel Derrick, an Irishman (1724–69), who published an edition of Dryden with a prefatory Life in 1760 and assisted Dr Johnson in preparing his Life of Dryden. Dr J. M. Osborn is surely right to 'see Derrick writing these words after sitting at the elbow of Samuel Johnson':[50]

What a prodigious field for admiration opens upon us in contemplating our author as a poet! Here, in whatever light we view him, he is sure always to excel; and if universality of genius gives a title to pre-eminence, perhaps we shall be scarcely excused for admitting any to rank above him. In elegy he was plaintive and tender; in panegyric he had the art of throwing a lustre round a character that sunk all its imperfections. In satire he was strong, bold, penetrating, and severe; in didactic or controversial writing, concise, clear, and persuasive. His epistles are familiar, easy, and entertaining. His prologues and epilogues abound with wit, pleasantry, and often excellent traces of criticism. In his songs the thoughts appear new; the phraseology unconstrained; and the conclusions pointed. ... In prose he was equally excellent, his words were always happily chosen, his periods round and flowing, his meaning clear, his arguments supported with masterly elocution, and his conclusions well deduced. In his prefaces, indeed, we find him sometimes a deserter, and opposing his own arguments in a manner to which Dryden only was equal; he has appeared unanswerable till he answered himself.

Johnson was, however, the first critic-biographer to write of Dryden's work on a level comparable with that of Dryden himself, and to make main statements about it which remain valid or at least provocative still. His Life of Dryden in *Prefaces, Biographical and Critical* (reprinted and commonly known as *Lives of the Poets*; see No. 76) consists of a biographical sketch, a personal 'character', a critical survey (in which some of the matters treated in the biography are taken up again), and a general literary analysis of Dryden. Dr

Osborn has weighed the strengths and weakness of the biography, and has drawn attention to the technical advance Johnson made in providing an 'intellectual character' of his subject—now 'a fundamental part of the biographer's craft'.[51] The critical sections are vintage Johnson: unsystematic but authoritative monologue, reading often (says T. S. Eliot) 'like the writing of a man who is more habituated to talking than to writing'; impressionistic, prejudiced, sternly moral, critically definitive. Johnson gives the first substantial and objective account of Dryden's essays, recognizing him as historically 'the father of English criticism'. He distinguishes his 'general', philosophical, and disinterested criticism from what is 'occasional', interested, even self-concerned; he sees that this is all 'the criticism of a poet' at work; he develops Congreve's hints of a subtly effective prose style; and he conveys, as Dryden habitually did, a lively sense of his own delight (No. 76j). Johnson begins to take a historical view of Dryden as a poet—his inheritance, innovations, and achievements (k). His is the first extended 'examen' of *Annus Mirabilis*, one of Dryden's 'greatest attempts' (n). He recognizes the variety and the stylistic *tour-de-force* in *Religio Laici* (q), and is apparently the first critic to understand the nature of *Absalom and Achitophel* as 'Varronian' satire. Dennis had called the poem a beautiful libel. But in the Dedication of the *Juvenal* Dryden says that whereas 'satire' is now used of 'invective Poems', the Romans gave the term a 'more general signification'. Thus Varro is said to have described his satire:

Notwithstanding ... that those Pieces of mine ... are sprinkled with a kind of mirth, and gayety: Yet many things are there inserted, which are drawn from the very intrails of Philosophy, and many things severely argu'd: Which I have mingl'd with Pleasantries on purpose, that they may more easily go down with the Common sort of Unlearn'd Readers.[52]

And thus, with insight, Johnson describes *Absalom and Achitophel*:

If it be considered as a poem political and controversial it will be found to comprise all the excellences of which the subject is susceptible: acrimony of censure, elegance of praise, artful delineation of characters, variety and vigour of sentiment, happy turns of language, and pleasing harmony of numbers; and all these raised to such a height as can scarcely be found in any other English composition. (o)

Johnson makes a powerful case for the *Virgil* (s). He gives us a first-rate demonstration of comparative criticism (w). Above all, he ends his Life of Dryden with the first attempt at a 'character' of Dryden

in depth, critical but finely perceptive, recognizing the bold, imaginative element in this poet who was soon to be labelled a 'classic
of our prose':

Next to argument, his delight was in wild and daring sallies of sentiment, in
the irregular and excentrick violence of wit. He delighted to tread upon the
brink of meaning, where light and darkness begin to mingle; to approach the
precipice of absurdity, and hover over the abyss of unideal vacancy. . . . (u

Comparison with Pope, started ill-naturedly by Dennis, became the
standard way of approaching Dryden—in, for example, Warton
(No. 71), Johnson (No. 76w), Cowper (No. 77), Hugh Blair (No. 78),
and Burns (No. 79). (It should be noted that, although Burns so often
echoes or alludes to Pope in his poems and letters, his probable debt
to Dryden is nearly as great.)
    Edmond Malone's Life, prefixed to his edition of Dryden's *Critical
and Miscellaneous Prose Works* and published almost exactly one
hundred years to the day after Dryden's death, is not only the first
major biography of the poet; it is also, as Dr Osborn claims, 'the
first great literary biography'.[53] But Malone's purpose was to
delineate life and character, not to evaluate critically, and his literary
comments seldom add or alter much. It is interesting, however, to
have a link made between Dryden and Burke (No. 80a).

V

SCOTT

The last and most splendid classical monument to Dryden was the
edition by Sir Walter Scott, educated in the Athens of the North
and (despite his prominent place among the 'new men' who were
creating the Romantic movement) in many respects an Augustan
who was much closer in temper, taste, and intellectual range to
Dryden than any of these earlier critics had been. It is impossible to
doubt, says Scott's biographer, Lockhart,

that the success of Dryden in rapidly reaching, and till the end of a long life
holding undisputed, the summit of public favour and reputation, in spite of
his 'brave neglect' of minute finishing, narrow laws, and prejudiced authorities,
must have had a powerful effect in nerving Scott's hope and resolution for
the wide ocean of literary enterprise into which he had now fairly launched

his bark. Like Dryden, he felt himself to be 'amply stored with acquired knowledge, much of it the fruits of early reading and application'; anticipated that, though, 'while engaged in the hurry of composition, or overcome by the lassitude of continued literary labour,' he should sometimes 'draw with too much liberality on a tenacious memory,' no 'occasional imperfections would deprive him of his praise'; in short, made up his mind that 'pointed and nicely-turned lines, sedulous study, and long and repeated correction and revision,' would all be dispensed with,—provided their place were supplied, as in Dryden, by 'rapidity of conception, a readiness of expressing every idea, without losing anything by the way,' 'perpetual animation and elasticity of thought'; and language 'never laboured, never loitering, never (in Dryden's own phrase) *cursedly confined*.'[54]

Scott's eighteen-volume edition appeared in the last week of April 1808, two months after the publication of *Marmion*. It is pleasant, though fortuitous, to pay tribute here to Scott the scholar and critic while, as his bicentenary approaches, so much is being made of Scott 'the Wizard of the North'.

Lockhart represents Dryden as at this time neglected, unattractive to the literary public. Negatively, because of 'the obsoleteness of the party politics which had so largely exercised the author's pen'; and positively, because of 'the indecorum, not seldom running into flagrant indecency, by which transcendent genius had ministered to the appetites of a licentious age'. George Ellis was to confess that he opened Scott's edition, when it appeared, 'with some trepidation':

but as soon as I became acquainted with your plan I proceeded boldly, and really feel at this moment sincerely grateful to you for much exquisite amusement. It now seems to me that your critical remarks ought to have occurred to myself. Such a passionate admirer of Dryden's fables, the noblest specimen of versification (in my mind) that is to be found in any modern language, ought to have perused his theatrical pieces with more candour that I did, and to have attributed to the bad taste of the age, rather than to his own, the numerous defects by which those hasty compositions are certainly deformed. I ought to have considered that whatever Dryden wrote must, for some reason or other, be worth reading; that his bombast and his indelicacy, however disgusting, were not without their use to any one who took an interest in our literary history; that—in short, there are a thousand reflections which I ought to have made and never did make, and the result was that *your* Dryden was to me a perfectly new book.[55]

Johnson's essay was the climax of Augustan *criticism* of Dryden, a Scott readily admitted (No. 83Aa); Malone had given a scholarly account of 'the *man*' Dryden: Scott emulated neither, but planned 'on these twin pillars ... a transcendent structure, comprehending no less than the whole of Restoration literature'.[56] Scott was by nature—as the Waverley Novels were soon to reveal—a panoramic social historian, deeply and creatively interested in the intellectual and cultural tensions in societies of the past. He saw that 'literary history is an important step in that of man himself'.

The Life of Dryden may be said to comprehend a history of the literature of England, and its changes, during nearly half a century. ... It is the object of this memoir to connect, with the account of Dryden's life and publications such a general view of the literature of the time, as may enable the reader to estimate how far the age was indebted to the poet, and how far the poet was influenced by the taste and manners of the age.

Historical criticism, and the critical biography, have arrived together. We have only to look at, for instance, the 'general view' of Eliza-bethan poetry in Thomas Warton's *History of English Poetry* (1774–81; sect. lxi), the great literary-historical achievement of the generation before Scott's, to see what an advance was made in the Life of Dryden. Warton describes a cultural pattern made up of 'vernacular versions of the classics, the ... translation of Italian novels, the visionary reveries or refinements of false philosophy ... superstition ... the machineries of romance, and ... allegoric exhibition in the popular spectacles'—a broad but still mainly literary picture. Scott's canvas, though it has but one central figure, is wider and much more varied: he takes account not only of literature and philosophy, but also of politics, science, social life, and the other arts. Yet he never abandons Dryden for historical divagations; he works out and round his central figure to bring out its particularity and distinction.

In the extracts given in this book he looks back, for example, from the early Dryden to Donne and Cowley (No. 83Ac); he relates *Annus Mirabilis* carefully to the work of Davenant, and beyond that to the metaphysical and Ovidian traditions of wit: 'when Dryden declares, that he proposes Virgil, in preference to Ovid, to be his model in the *Annus Mirabilis*, it sufficiently implies, that the main defect of the poetry of the last age had been discovered, and was in the way of being amended' (Ag). He is able to connect the debates on 'meta-physical passion' in the heroic play—'the metaphysical logic of amorous jurisprudence'—with the early parliaments of love and with the chivalric romances which he knew well, and he examines the moribund and hollow chivalry of the Restoration court (Ai; *cf.* Al,

'There is too much of the love-lorn knight-errant, and too little of the Roman warrior, in Dryden's [Antony]'). After some close criticism of the political poems of 1681–2 (Am) Scott relates Dryden to the satiric tradition of Hall and the 'metaphysical' poets and measures his achievement in 'elevated satire' (*cf.* the discussion of 'metaphysical' satire in As; p. 363). He sees the *historical* importance of Dryden's criticism, 'resisting the domination of Gallic criticism' which was becoming familiar in England through translations. His commentary contains some notable pieces of historical writing; we have reprinted (Bi) what seems to be the first consideration of the prologues and epilogues as occasional pieces for the theatre.

Scott has a stronger sense of history, and wider historical interests and knowledge, than Johnson. But how does he stand up to comparison with Johnson as a critic? How much originality *can* he show, since Johnson has sketched 'the general critical view of Dryden's works ... with unequalled felicity'? Scott does not often follow in Johnson's tracks for long. He makes no attempt, for instance, to emulate Johnson's long analysis of *Annus Mirabilis*, though he has a long note on the poem in his commentary (Be). He has little new to say on the prose essays, after Johnson's magisterial judgment. But he takes far more trouble over the plays, even the indifferent ones (*cf.* Ah, Ak, Al). In a long general discussion of the heroic play and its romance ancestry (Ai) he shows much deeper understanding of the genre, and (in spite of some mild satire) much more sympathy with it, than Johnson had: demonstrating that indeed 'something may be said for the heroic drama'. Compare his short critique of *The Conquest of Granada* (No. 83Ba) with Johnson's (No. 76c). Johnson is more judicial, Scott more responsive to the qualities the play really has; and Scott, less susceptible than Johnson to the intoxicating fumes of his own rhetoric, is more sensible. On *All for Love*, Johnson is ungenerous to Dryden's poetry and characterization, and stays content with Dennis's kind of stricture on the morality of the play (No. 76e); Scott, though critical of Antony, comes much closer to the drama (No. 83Al), and his general note on the treatment of the same theme by Shakespeare and Dryden (Bb) is a nice piece of comparative criticism. Johnson has nothing on—or even against—*The Spanish Fryar;* the still latent novelist in Scott responds with delighted horror to Father Dominic (Al) and with admiration to the structural subtlety of the play (Bc). Johnson looks briefly at *Don Sebastian,* 'commonly esteemed' one of Dryden's best plays, and gives it what Scott calls a 'meagre commendation'; Scott's general note (Bd) remains one of the best short discussions of it.

Nor does Johnson, despite the celebrity of his critique of Dryden, necessarily bear away the bell for what he has to offer on the non-dramatic verse. Scott's consideration of some of the minor poems is not only fuller (he had more space) but more humane: contrast Johnson's merely literary note on *Heroique Stanza's* (No. 76m) and Scott's comments on Dryden's generosity and truth (No. 83Ad). I have already noticed Johnson's discerning and comprehensive paragraph on the satire of *Absalom and Achitophel*; against his objections to the poem's structure Scott offers a commonsense defence (Bf) and justifies the poetic adaptation of the king's speech. Scott is the first critic to elucidate Dryden's art of satiric characterization—'the traits of praise are so qualified and artfully blended with censure, that they seem to render his faults even more conspicuous, and more hateful' (Am)—and the first to recognize this as 'fine raillery' (As; p. 364). Johnson notes only that *Mac Flecknoe* is 'exquisitely satirical' and a model for Pope's *Dunciad*;[57] Scott evaluates the satire, and compares the two poems to the advantage of *Mac Flecknoe* (Bj). On *The Hind and the Panther*, Scott attempts the historico–critical defence (Bh) of a fable which Johnson was content to call absurd (No. 76q), and is much more willing than Johnson to see excellence in Dryden's satire and versification.[58]

Scott follows Johnson in describing Dryden's ratiocinative faculty as his distinguishing characteristic (No. 83 As), and he is ready, despite Wordsworth's strictures on Dryden (see No. 81), to advance the Augustan view that this 'power of ratiocination' is central in a poet. Johnson had further noted what might appear a paradox in Dryden— that 'next to argument, his delight was in wild and daring sallies of sentiment, in the irregular and excentrick violence of wit' (No. 76u); but it was Scott who brought these two aspects of Dryden's genius together and resolved the paradox. (His implicit distinction between ratiocinative poetry and prose argument has become part of the modern reply to the Victorian charge that Dryden is a classic of our prose.) Dryden's 'sole object of consideration', he says,

was to maintain his present point; and that by authority, by declamation, by argument, by every means. But his philosophical powers are not the less to be estimated, because thus irregularly and unphilosophically employed. His arguments, even in the worst cause, *bear witness to the energy of his mental conceptions; and the skill with which they are stated, elucidated, enforced, and exempli-*

fied, ever commands our admiration, though, in the result, our reason may reject their influence.[59]

Reviewing Dryden's treatment of the passions, and indeed his whole 'poetical character', Scott provides a portrait in softer lines and warmer colours than Johnson's (No. 83 As; Johnson, No. 76u). Both critics deal briefly with the odes, despite the popularity of the St Cecilia pieces throughout the eighteenth century;[60] but while Johnson's comments (No. 76t) are those of a dominie with a red pencil—brisk marginalia—Scott's are considered criticism:

We listen for the completion of Dryden's stanza, as for the explication of a difficult passage in music; and wild and lost as the sound appears, the ear is proportionally gratified by the unexpected ease with which harmony is extracted from discord and confusion.

Johnson is curiously almost silent on the *Fables*. Scott's response is predictably 'romantic'; but he also takes the trouble which an editor, unlike an essayist, dare not shirk, of comparing these tales with their originals. And here, as in his discussion of Dryden's translations from the classics, he is excellent.

Scott has his shortcomings, as biographer and as critic. He wrote in the shadow of Johnson, and must have found this at times depressing. He is sometimes diffuse, repetitious, and heavy (though never as ponderous as Johnson). But his is still the best critical biography of Dryden, whether one looks for historical and literary context, or for sequence and relation, or for critical insight. 'Dryden the man', says Dr Osborn, 'lives in Scott's pages as he had never done in any other biography'; 'after three years of thinking about Dryden, Scott saw him steadily and saw him whole'. That is equally true of Scott's criticism. Dryden was enshrined; the great appraisal had been made. But critics were now caught up in great new issues and with great new poets, and the labours of Scott were not enough, says Lockhart, to restore Dryden to his rightful place in the favour of the intelligent public (with the men of letters, 'those who make literature the business or chief solace of their lives . . . he had never forfeited it'):

. . . nor have I observed among the numberless recent speculations of the English booksellers, a single reprint of even those tales, satires, and critical essays, not to be familiar with which would, in the last age, have been considered as disgraceful in any one making the least pretension to letters.

Now, in 1836, Lockhart transcribes Ellis's letters to Scott which I quoted earlier, in the hope 'of exciting the curiosity, at least of some of the thousands of young persons who seem to be growing up in contented ignorance of one of the greatest of our masters'.[61]

VI

AFTER SCOTT

Romantic and Victorian criticism of Dryden is spasmodic and casual. Apart from the collected editions with their biographical-critical introductions,[62] the more notable essays are by Hazlitt (*Lectures on the English Poets*, 1818; Dryden isn't among The English Comic Writers) and Macaulay (*Edinburgh Review*, xlvii, 1828). Both critics show a much narrower sympathy than Scott, despite Hazlitt's preference for Dryden's 'strength of mind' against Pope's 'refinement and delicacy', his awareness of the 'genius, vehemence, and strength of description' in *The Hind and the Panther*, and his sense that in satiric 'characters' Dryden grapples with real people while Pope 'seems to refine upon them in his own mind, and to make them out just what he pleases'.[63] Hugh Macdonald recorded just over a dozen articles on Dryden for the *Cambridge Bibliography*, between Hallam's review of Scott in 1809 and the end of the century; and there was no sustained discussion of Dryden after Scott until George Saintsbury's book appeared in the English Men of Letters series in 1881. This was an independent re-valuation in modern critical terms, rough on Macaulay, Christie, and prosy Victorian reiterators; freshly—sometimes brashly—written, and the most enjoyable general study of Dryden we have. Saintsbury claimed to practise the 'style of minute criticism' which had 'gone out of fashion . . . terribly little to do with "criticism of life" ' (how that merry-go-round keeps turning!); and he followed through Scott's earlier intention in estimating not only the influence of the age on the poet, but also the poet's contribution to his age and to posterity:

Not only did the immense majority of men of letters in his later days directly imitate him, but both then and earlier most literary Englishmen, even when they did not imitate him, worked on the same lines and pursued the same objects. The eighteen volumes of his works contain a faithful representation of the whole literary movement in England for the best part of half a century, and what is more, they contain the germs and indicate the direction of almost the whole literary movement for nearly a century more.[64]

Since Saintsbury's time Dryden studies have grown into an academic industry. S. H. Monk's *List* (1950) of 'critical studies' published between 1895 and 1948 runs to nearly 800 items; in the *Annual Bibliography of English Language and Literature* for the much shorter period 1949–66 there are an additional 400 items. Some of this work is biographical—Osborn's *Facts and Problems* and C. E. Ward's *Life* are substantial pieces of scholarship. Some of it is bibliographical, contributing to or deriving from the immense and devoted labour of Hugh Macdonald (1939). Some of it is editorial: we have had G. R. Noyes's one-volume student edition of the poems in modern spelling, incorporating much of Scott (1909; revised 1950); my four-volume Oxford edition in the original spelling (1958; one volume, 1962); a few good editions of plays, notably the two volumes by L. A. Beaurline and Fredson Bowers (1967); and the first volumes of the California edition which should eventually replace Scott's. But a great deal of recent work on Dryden has been critical. There has been perhaps too much specialized criticism in the periodicals—or rather, too little synthesis on any scale; for although there were some influential essays in the first half of this century (by T. S. Eliot, Bonamy Dobrée, E. M. W. Tillyard and others), Mark Van Doren's (1920) was the only general study of merit. The pattern, however, is changing. A new approach to Dryden's translations has been attempted by William Frost in *Dryden and the Art of Translation* (1955; see also Tillyard's *The English Epic and its Background* (1954) and my introduction to the *Virgil* (1961)); and there are a number of good recent books concerned with rhetoric, imagery, and ideas—among them A. W. Hoffman, *John Dryden's Imagery* (1962), K. G. Hamilton's *The Two Harmonies* (1963), Alan Roper's *Dryden's Poetic Kingdoms* (1965), Earl Miner's *Dryden's Poetry* (1968), and Phillip Harth's *Contexts of Dryden's Thought* (1968). But there must be a new synthesis when the large corporate labours in California on the texts, contexts, and meanings of Dryden's work are complete.

J.K.

NOTES

1. *The Poems of John Dryden* (1958), ed. James Kinsley, ii. 791.
2. *Diary*, 22 August and 11 November 1667; 28 March and 21 April 1668; 28 October 1667.
3. Allardyce Nicoll, *A History of English Drama. I: Restoration Drama*, 1952 edn., pp. 343–4, 345.

4. For early editions of Dryden's works, see *infra*, pp. 404–9.
5. Charles saw the play on 2 and 5 March.
6. John Downes, *Roscius Anglicanus* (1929), ed. M. Summers, p. 28.
7. *Diary*, 16 August 1667.
8. Nicoll, *op. cit.*, pp. 346–7, 348, 351.
9. *Ibid.*, pp. 346–7, 348.
10. *Diary*, 7 November 1667.
11. See Nicoll, *op. cit.*, p. 430.
12. *Diary*, 19 June 1668.
13. Nicoll, *op. cit.*, p. 344; 12 June 1668.
14. C. E. Ward, *Life of Dryden* (1961), pp. 68–9.
15. *Ibid.*, p. 69.
16. Evelyn, *Diary*, 9 February 1671. There was another performance of Part I before royalty on 21 December 1675; Nicoll, *op. cit.*, p. 346.
17. Dryden, Dedication.
18. Nicoll, *op. cit.*, pp. 345–6.
19. Ward suggests (*op. cit.*, p. 121) that the apparent lack of royal favour towards this play was due to poor acting. It is as likely to have been due to undiscriminating taste.
20. Nicoll, *op. cit.*, pp. 349, 352.
21. Hugh Macdonald, *John Dryden: A Bibliography of Early Editions and of Drydeniana* (1939), p. 129.
22. Edmond Malone, *Critical and Miscellaneous Prose Works of John Dryden* (1800), I. i. 217.
23. Luttrell's copy dated 28 November; Macdonald, *op. cit.*, p. 33.
24. A. E. Case, *English Poetical Miscellanies* (1935), No. 165.
25. There is nothing by Dryden in the Sixth Part (1709).
26. For details, see Macdonald, *op. cit.*, pp. 146–7.
27. James Sutherland, *English Literature of the Late Seventeenth Century* (1969), p. 393.
28. *Cf. Elizabethan Critical Essays* (1904), ed. G. G. Smith; *Critical Essays of the Seventeenth Century* (1908; 1957), ed. J. E. Spingarn.
29. George Watson, introduction to Dryden, *Of Dramatic Poesy and other Critical Essays* (1962), I. v.
30. *Comedies, Tragedies, and Operas* (1701), ii. 308 (Postscript).
31. *Poems*, ed. Kinsley, ii. 645–6 ('Discourse concerning Satire'). *Cf. ibid.*, ii. 605, on 'these dull Makers of Lampoons'; Dryden's *Letters* (1942), ed. C. E. Ward, pp. 72–3: 'we poor Poets Militant ... are at the Mercy of Wretched Scribblers: And when they cannot fasten upon our Verses, they fall upon our Morals. ... For my Morals, betwixt Man and Man, I am not to be my own Judge. I appeal to the World if I have Deceiv'd or Defrauded any Man: And for my private Conversation, they who see me every day can be the best Witnesses, whether or no it be Blameless and Inoffensive'.

32. *Poems*, ed. Kinsley, ii. 605.
33. *Ibid.*, i. 282–5.
34. Pope, *Essay on Criticism* (1711), ll. 456–9.
35. With a satirical postscript (1681). Other malignant reprints, 1682, 1687, and in *Poems on Affairs of State* (1689–).
36. *Cf.* p. 153.
37. *Cf.* p. 146.
38. 'How little Dryden valued these nicknames appears from a passage in the "Vindication of the Duke of Guise": "Much less am I concerned at the noble name of Bayes; that is a brat so like his own father, that he cannot be mistaken for any body else. They might as reasonably have called Tom Sternhold [the psalm-versifier] Virgil, and the resemblance would have held as well.'
39. Scott, *Works of Dryden* (1808), i. 257–8.
40. For 'libels' associated with *The Hind and the Panther*, see *ibid.*, x. 102 ff., and Macdonald, *op. cit.*, pp. 258 ff.
41. E. N. Hooker lists thirty publications for and against Collier between April 1698 and March 1700; Dennis's *Critical Works* (1939–43), i. 468–9.
42. *The Usefulness of the Stage* (1698), Introduction.
43. *To the Pious Memory of ... Mrs. Anne Killigrew* (1686), ll. 56–65. *Cf.* the closing paragraphs of Dryden's Preface to *Fables Ancient and Modern* (1700).
44. *Cf.* April 12th [1784]. Went to a *bas bleu* party. ... The chief thing I heard was a difference of opinion respecting Dryden. Mr. Walpole and Dr. Burney extolled him above all our poets (E. and F. Anson, *Mary Hamilton*, 1925, p. 174).
45. *Cf.* Byron, quoted in No. 71i, footnote.
46. *Cf.* H. G. Wright, 'Some Sidelights on the Reputation and Influence of Dryden's *Fables*', *Review of English Studies*, xxi (1945), 23–37.
47. Dryden's *Letters* (1942), ed. C. E. Ward, pp. 68–9.
48. Johnson was the first critic to see what Dryden was at in *Absalom and Achitophel*; *infra*, p. 297.
49. *Cf.* E. N. Hooker, *op. cit.*, ii. 472; Gildon, Preface to Langbaine's *English Dramatick Poets* (1698): 'the All for Love of Mr. Dryden, were it not for the false Moral, wou'd be a Masterpiece that few of the Ancients or Moderns ever equal'd.'
50. *John Dryden: Some Biographical Facts and Problems* (1940), revised edn., 1965, p. 18. Osborn is excellent on the early lives of Dryden.
51. *Ibid.*, p. 37.
52. *Poems*, ed. Kinsley, ii. 636.
53. *Op. cit.*, p. 39: 'Boswell's *Johnson* is the nearest exception to my generalization, but Boswell's aim was to write a personal biography, whereas Malone's was primarily scholarly.'
54. *Life of Sir Walter Scott* (1837–8), 1914 edn., ii. 7–8.

55. Lockhart, *op. cit.*, ii. 3–4; *cf.* No. 82, *infra*. The reader will notice the continuing prominence of the *Fables* in critical considerations of Dryden, however casual. *Cf.* Thomas Warton's comment on the Chaucerian 'fable' of Palamon and Arcite: Chaucer's numbers are 'so nervous and flowing: a circumstance which greatly contributed to render Dryden's paraphrase of this poem the most animated and harmonious piece of versification in the English language' (*History of English Poetry* (1774–81), 1824, ii. 203).

56. On Scott as biographer, see Osborn, *op. cit.*, pp. 72–87: 'this book is well on the way toward the "life and times", which has since dominated the field of scholarly biography. But to anyone who is conscious of literary form the chief impression it leaves is of the art with which his conceptions have been molded. Here is the work not only of a superior pen but also of a superior mind.'

57. *Lives* (1905), ed. G. B. Hill, i. 383.

58. As Pope had done: *ibid.*, i. 443.

59. As, p. 369; my italics. *Cf.* Maynard Mack's introduction to Pope's *Essay on Man*, Twickenham edn.

60. *Cf.* John Pinkerton, *Letters on Literature* (1785), p. 34: 'Dryden's wonderful ode; which is of itself worth all that Pindar has written, as a large diamond is worth a vast heap of gold' (alluding to *Alexander's Feast*).

61. *Life of Scott*, ii. 3.

62. By Robert Bell (1854) and W. D. Christie (1870).

63. Note also Coleridge to Godwin, 8 July 1801: 'You say—I ... will not allow your admiration of Hume, & the pleasure you derive from Virgil, from Dryden. ... Of Dryden I am and always have been a passionate admirer. I have always placed him among our greatest men' (*Collected Letters*, 1956, ii. 743).

64. pp. 31, 184–5.

1. The reception of Dryden's first play

1663

Dryden's Preface to *The Wild Gallant*, the first of his plays to be acted (Theatre Royal, Vere Street, 5 February 1663); published 1669. Text from Dryden's *Comedies, Tragedies, and Operas* (1701), i. 30.

It would be a great Impudence in Me to say much of a *Comedy*, which has had but indifferent success in the action. I made the Town my Judges; and the greater part condemn'd it. After which I do not think it my Concernment to defend it, with the ordinary Zeal of a Poet for his decry'd Poem. Tho' *Corneille* is more resolute in his *Preface* before his *Partherite*, which was condemn'd more Universally than this: For he avows boldly, That in spight of Censure his *Play* was well, and regularly Written; which is more than I dare say for mine. Yet it was receiv'd at Court; and was more than once the Divertisement of His Majesty, by His own Command. But I have more modesty than to ascribe that to my Merit, which was His particular Act of Grace. It was the first attempt I made in *Dramatick Poetry*; and, I find since, a very bold one, to begin with *Comedy*; which is the most difficult part of it. The Plot was not Originally my own: But so alter'd, by me (whether for the better or worse, I know not) that, whoever the Author was, he could not have challeng'd a Scene of it. I doubt not but you will see in it, the uncorrectness of a Young Writer: Which is yet but a small excuse for him, who is so little amended since. The best Apology I can make for it, and the truest, is only this; That you have since that time receiv'd with Applause, as bad, and as uncorrect *Plays* from other Men.

2. Pepys at the theatre

1662, 1663, 1664, 1667, 1668

(*a*) Extract from *Diary*, 23 February 1662–3: '. . . we took coach and to Court, and there got good places, and saw *The Wilde Gallant*, performed by the King's house, but it was ill acted, and the play so poor a thing as I never saw in my life almost, and so little answering the name, that from beginning to end, I could not, nor can at this time, tell certainly which was the Wild Gallant. The King did not seem pleased at all, all the whole play, nor any body else. . . .' (*Diary* (1893–9; 1949), ed. H. B. Wheatley, iii. 48.)

(*b*) Extract from *Diary*, 27 January 1663–4: '. . . my wife and I took coach and to Covent Garden . . . in the way observing the streete full of coaches at the new play, *The Indian Queene*; which for show, they say, exceeds *Henry the Eighth*.' (iv. 23.)[1]

(*c*) Extract from *Diary*, 1 February 1663–4: '. . . and so home to dinner, and took my wife out immediately to the King's Theatre, it being a new month, and once a month I may go, and there saw *The Indian Queene* acted; which indeed is a most pleasant show, and beyond my expectation; the play good, but spoiled with the ryme, which breaks the sense. But above my expectation most, the eldest Marshall[2] did do her part most excellently well as I ever heard woman in my life . . . we came home mightily contented.' (iv. 27–8.)

(*d*) Extract from *Diary*, 4 August 1664: 'Sir W. Pen . . . did carry me to a play and pay for me at the King's house, which is *The Rivall Ladys*, a very innocent and most pretty witty play. I was much pleased with it.' (iv. 194.)

---

[1] *Cf.* Evelyn, *Diary*, 3 February 1664: 'The *Indian Queene* a Tragedie well written, but so beautified with rich Scenes as the like had never ben seene here . . . on a mercenarie *Theater.*'

[2] Anne Marshall.

(*e*) Extracts from *Diary*, 2 March 1666–7 and 24 January 1667–8: 'After dinner, with my wife, to the King's house to see *The Mayden Queene*, a new play of Dryden's, mightily commended for the regularity of it, and the strain and wit; and, the truth is, there is a comical part done by Nell,[1] which is Florimell, that I never can hope ever to see the like done again, by man or woman. The King and Duke of York were at the play. But so great performance of a comical part was never, I believe, in the world before as Nell do this, both as a mad girle, then most and best of all when she comes in like a young gallant; and hath the motions and carriage of a spark the most that ever I saw any man have. It makes me, I confess, admire her. . . . *The Mayden Queene* . . . the more I see, the more I love, and think one of the best plays I ever saw. . . .[2] (vi. 192–3; vii. 273.)

(*f*) Extract from *Diary*, 16 August 1667: 'After dinner my wife and I to the Duke's playhouse, where we saw the new play acted yesterday, *The Feign Innocence, or Sir Martin Marr-all*; a play made by my Lord Duke of Newcastle, but, as every body says, corrected by Dryden.[3] It is the most entire piece of mirth, a complete farce from one end to the other, that certainly was ever writ. I never laughed so in all my life . . . and at very good wit therein, not fooling. The house full. . . .' (vii. 64–5.)

(*g*) Extract from *Diary*, 22 August 1667: 'After dinner with my Lord Bruncker and his mistress to the King's playhouse, and there saw *The Indian Emperour*; where I find Nell come again, which I am glad of; but was most infinitely displeased with her being put to act the Emperour's daughter; which is a great and serious part, which she do most basely. The rest of the play, though pretty good, was not well acted by most of them, methought; so that I took no great content in it.' (vii. 71–2.)

(*h*) Extracts from *Diary*, 19 June and 20 June 1668: '. . . by and by comes my wife and Deb. home, have been at the King's playhouse to-day, thinking to spy me there; and saw the new play, *Evening*

---

[1] Nell Gwyn.

[2] He had seen the play often by 24 May 1667; *cf. Diary*, 23 August 1667, 18 January 1667–8, 13 January 1668–9.

[3] The Duke gave Dryden 'a bare Translation of it, out of a Comedy of . . . *Moleire*: He Adapted the Part purposely for the Mouth of Mr. *Nokes*, and curiously Polishing the whole' (Downes, *Roscius Anglicanus*, ed. M. Summers, p. 28).

Love, of Dryden's, which, though the world commends, she likes not. ... Creed and I ... saw an act or two of the new play ... but like it not. Calling this day at Herringman's,[1] he tells me Dryden do himself call it but a fifth-rate play.' (viii. 50-51, 52.)

3. Dryden on *The Indian Emperour*

1667, 1679

(*a*) Extract from the Epistle Dedicatory of *The Indian Emperour, or, The Conquest of Mexico by the Spaniards* to the Duchess of Monmouth (12 October 1667): 'Under your Patronage *Montezuma* hopes he is more safe than in his Native *India*. ... His Story is, perhaps, the greatest which was ever represented in a Poem of this Nature; the Action of it including the Discovery and Conquest of a new World. In it I have neither wholly follow'd the Truth of the History, nor altogether left it: But have taken all the Liberty of a Poet, to add, alter, or diminish, as I thought might best conduce to the beautifying of my Work; it being not the bus'ness of a Poet to represent Historical Truth, but Probability. But I am not to make the Justification of this *Poem*, which I wholly leave to your Grace's Mercy. 'Tis an irregular Piece, if compar'd with many of *Corneille*'s, and, if I may make a Judgment of it, written with more Flame than Art; in which it represents the Mind and Intention of the Author. ... ' (Dryden's *Comedies, Tragedies, and Operas* (1701), i. 108.)

(*b*) Extract from the Preface to *Troilus and Cressida* (1679): "Tis necessary therefore for a Poet, who would concern an Audience by describing of a Passion, first to prepare it, and not to rush upon it all at once. ... The next necessary Rule is to put nothing into the Discourse which may hinder your moving of the Passions. Too many accidents, as I have said, incumber the Poet. ... There is yet another

---

[1] Dryden's publisher.

obstacle to be remov'd, which is pointed Wit, and Sentences[1] affected out of Season; these are nothing of kin to the Violence of Passion: no Man is at leisure to make Sentences and Similies, when his Soul is in Agony. I the rather name this Fault, that it may serve to mind me of my former Errors; neither will I spare my self, but give an Example of this kind from my *Indian Emperour*: *Montezuma*, pursu'd by his Enemies, and seeking Sanctuary, stands parlying without the Fort, and describing his danger to *Cydaria*, in a Simile of six Lines:

> *As on the Sands, the frighted Traveller*
> *Sees the high Seas come rowling from afar,* &c.[2]

My *Indian* Potentate was well skill'd in the Sea for an Inland Prince, and well improv'd since the first Act, when he sent his Son to discover it. The Image had not been amiss from another Man, at another time: *Sed nunc non erat hisce locus:*[3] he destroy'd the Concernment which the Audience might otherwise have had for him; for they could not think the danger near, when he had the leisure to invent a Simile.' (*Ibid.*, i. 207–8.)

---

[1] I.e. *sententiae*.
[2] Act V.
[3] Horace, *De Arte Poetica*, l. 19: 'But this was, at the moment, not the place.'

4. Dryden on *Secret-Love*

1668

Extract from Dryden's Preface to *Secret-Love, or The Maiden Queen* (1668; see p. 31, *supra*).

For what else concerns this Play, I would tell the Reader that it is regular, according to the strictest of Dramatick Laws, but that it is a commendation which many of our Poets now despise, and a beauty which our common Audiences do not easily discern. Neither indeed do I value my self upon it, because with all that symmetry of parts, it may want an air and spirit (which consists in the writing) to set it off. 'Tis a question variously disputed, whether an Author may be allowed as a competent judg of his own works. As to the Fabrick and contrivance of them certainly he may, for that is properly the employment of the judgment; which, as a Master-builder may determine, and that without deception, whether the work be according to the exactness of the model; still granting him to have a perfect Idea of that pattern by which he works: and that he keeps himself always constant to the discourse of his judgment, without admitting self-love, which is the false surveigher of his Fancy, to intermeddle in it. These Qualifications granted (being such as all sound Poets are presupposed to have within them) I think all Writers, of what kind soever, may infallibly judg of the frame and contexture of their Works. But for the ornament of Writing, which is greater, more various and bizarre in Poesie then in any other kind, as it is properly the Child of Fancy, so it can receive no measure, or at least but a very imperfect one, of its own excellencies or faillures from the judgment. Self-love (which enters but rarely into the offices of the judgment) here predominates. And Fancy (if I may so speak) judging of it self, can be no more certain or demonstrative of its own effects, then two crooked lines can be the adæquate measure of each other. What I have said on this subject, may, perhaps, give me some credit with my Readers, in my opinion of this Play, which I have ever valued above the rest of my Follies of this kind: yet not thereby in the least dissenting from their judgment who have concluded the writing of this to be much inferior to my *Indian Emperour*. But the Argument of that was much more noble, not having the allay of Comedy to depress it: yet if this be more perfect, either in its kind, or in the general notion of a Play, 'tis as much as I desire to have granted for the vindication of my Opinion, and, what as nearly touches me, the sentence of a Royal Judg. Many have imagin'd the Character of *Philocles* to be faulty; some for not discovering the Queen's love, others for his joining in her restraint. But though I am not of their number, who obstinately defend what they have once said, I may with modesty take up those answers which have been made for me by my Friends; namely, that *Philocles*, who was but a Gentleman of ordinary birth, had no reason to guess so soon at the Queen's Passion she being a person so much above him, and by the suffrages of all her people, already destin'd to *Lysimantes*: Besides, that he was prepossessed, (as the Queen somewhere hints it to him) with another inclination which rendred him less clear-sighted in it, since no man, at the same time, can distinctly view two different objects. And if this, with any shew of reason, may be defended, I leave my Masters the Criticks to determine whether it be not much more conducing to the beauty of my Plot, that *Philocles* should be long kept ignorant of the Queen's love, then that with one leap he should have entred into the knowledg of it, and thereby freed himself, to the disgust of the Audience, from that pleasing Labyrinth of errors which was prepar'd for him. As for that other objection of his joyning in the Queen's imprisonment, it is indisputably that which every man, if he examines himself, would have done on the like occasion. If they answer that it takes from the height of his Character to do it; I would enquire of my over-wise Censors, who told them I intended him a perfect Character, or indeed what necessity was there he should be so, the variety of Images, being one great beauty of a Play? It was as much as I design'd, to show one great and absolute pattern of honour in my Poem, which I did in the Person of the Queen: All the defects of the other parts being set to show, the more to recommend that one character of Vertue to the Audience. But neither was the fault of *Philocles* so great, if the circumstances be consider'd, which, as moral Philosophy assures us, make the essential differences of good and bad; He himself best explaining his own intentions in his last Act, which was the restauration of his

Queen; and even before that, in the honesty of his expressions when he was unavoidably led by the impulsion of his love to do it. That which with more reason was objected as an indecorum, is the management of the last Scene of the Play, where *Celadon* and *Florimell* are treating too lightly of their marriage in the presence of the Queen who likewise seems to stand idle while the great action of the *Drama* is still depending. This I cannot otherwise defend, then by telling you I so design'd it on purpose to make my Play go off more smartly; that Scene, being in the opinion of the best judges, the most divertising of the whole Comedy. But though the Artifice succeeded, I am willing to acknowledg it as a fault, since it pleas'd His Majesty, the best Judg, to think it so.

5. Dryden on his comedies

1668, 1671

(*a*) Extract from 'A Defence of an Essay of Dramatique Poesie' prefixed to *The Indian Emperour* (1668): 'I confess my chief endeavours are to delight the Age in which I live. If the humour of this, be for low Comedy, small Accidents, and Raillery, I will force my Genius to obey it, though with more reputation I could write in Verse. I know I am not so fitted by Nature to write Comedy: I want that gayety of humour which is required to it. My Conversation is slow and dull, my humour Saturnine and reserv'd: In short, I am none of those who endeavour to break Jests in Company, or make reparties. So that those who decry my Comedies do me no injury, except it be in point of profit: reputation in them is the last thing to which I shall pretend.' (*Dryden: Of Dramatick Poesie, An Essay* (1964), ed. J. T. Boulton, p. 130.)

(*b*) Extract from the Preface to *An Evening's Love, or The Mock Astrologer* (1671): 'Neither, indeed, do I value a reputation gain'd from

Comedy, so far as to concern my self about it any more than I needs must in my own defence: for I think it, in it's own nature, inferiour to all sorts of Dramatick writing. Low Comedy especially requires, on the Writer's part, much of conversation with the vulgar: and much of ill nature in the observation of their follies. But let all men please themselves according to their several tastes: that which is not pleasant to me may be to others who judge better: and, to prevent an accusation from my enemies, I am sometimes ready to imagine that my disgust of low Comedy proceeds not so much from my judgement as from my temper; which is the reason why I so seldom write it; and that when I succeed in it, (I mean so far as to please the Audience) yet I am nothing satisfi'd with what I have done; but am often vex'd to hear the people laugh, and clap, as they perpetually do, where I intended 'em no jest; while they let pass the better things without taking notice of them. Yet even this confirms me in my opinion of slighting popular applause, and of contemning that approbation which those very people give, equally with me, to the Zany[1] of a Mountebank; or to the appearance of an Antick on the Theatre, without wit on the Poet's part, or any occasion of laughter from the Actor, besides the ridiculousness of his habit and his Grimaces.'

---

[1] Attendant clown.

6. Flecknoe on Dryden

1670

One of the 'Theatrical Epigrams' in *Epigrams of all Sorts. Made at Divers Times on Several Occasions. By Richard Flecknoe* (1670; p. 70); confirming the justice of Dryden's choice of Flecknoe as Shadwell's poetical father.

Dreyden the Muses darling and delight,
Than whom none ever flew so high a flight.
Some have their vains so drosie, as from *earth*,
Their Muses onely seem to have tane their birth.
Others but *water-Poets* are,[1] have gon
No farther than to th' *Fount of Helicon*:
And they 'r but *aiery ones*, whose *Muse* soars up
No higher than to mount *Parnassus* top:
Whilst thou, with thine, dost seem to have mounted higher,
Then he who fetcht from *Heaven* Celestial fire:
And dost as far surpass all others, as
Fire does all other elements surpass.

[1] Like the prolific literary waterman John Taylor (*c.* 1578–1653).

7. Dryden's Patent

1670

Extract from Pat. 22 Car. II. 6. 6; Malone, *The ... Prose Works of John Dryden*, 1800, I. i. 553-9.

Charles the Second, by the grace of GOD, of England, Scotland, France, and Ireland, King, Defender of the Faith, &c. to the Lords Commissioners of our Treasury. ... Know yee, that wee, for and in consideration of the many good and acceptable services by John Dryden, Master of Arts, and eldest sonne of Erasmus Dryden, of Tichmarsh in the county of Northampton, Esquire, to us heretofore done and performed, and taking notice of the learning and eminent abilities of him the said John Dryden, and of his great skill and elegant style both in verse and prose, and for diverse other good causes and considerations us thereunto especially moving, have nominated, constituted, declared, and appointed, and by these presents do nominate, constitute, declare and appoint, him the said John Dryden, our POET LAUREAT and HISTORIOGRAPHER ROYAL; giving and granting unto him the said John Dryden all and singular the rights, privileges, benefits, and advantages, thereunto belonging, as fully and amply as Sir Geoffrey Chaucer, Knight, Sir John Gower, Knight, John Leland, Esquire, William Camden, Esquire, Benjamin Johnson, Esquire ... had or received. ... And for the further and better encouragement of him the said John Dryden, diligently to attend the said employment, we are graciously pleased to give and grant ... one Annuity or yearly pension of two hundred pounds. ...

8. Dryden on *Tyrannick Love*

1670, 1681

(*a*) Extract from the Preface to *Tyrannick Love; or The Royal Martyr. A Tragedy* (1670): '. . . In what else concerns the Play, I shall be brief; for the faults of the Writing and Contrivance, I leave them to the mercy of the Reader, for I am as little apt to defend my Errors, as to find those of other Poets: Only I observe, that the great Censors of Wit and Poetry, either produce nothing of their own, or what is more ridiculous than any thing they reprehend. Much of ill Nature, and a very little Judgment, go far in finding the mistakes of Writers. I pretend not that any thing of mine can be correct: This Poem, especialy, which was contrived and written in Seven Weeks, though afterwards hindred, by many Accidents, from a speedy Representation, which would have been its just excuse. . . . For the little Criticks,[1] who pleas'd themselves with thinking they have found a flaw in that line of the Prologue, (*And he who servilely creeps after Sense, is safe*, &c.)[2] as if I Patronized my own Nonsense, I may reasonably suppose they have never read *Horace, Serpit humi tutus*, &c. are his words:[3] He who creeps after plain, dull, common Sense, is safe from committing Absurdities, but can never reach any height, or excellence of Wit; and sure I could not mean that any excellence were to be found in Nonsense . . .' (Dryden's *Comedies, Tragedies, and Operas* (1701), i. 338–9.)

(*b*) Extract from the Dedication of *The Spanish Fryar, or, The Double Discovery* to Lord Haughton (1681): 'In a Play-House every thing contributes to impose upon the Judgment; the Lights, the Scenes, the Habits, and, above all, the Grace of Action, which is commonly the

---

[1] Added in the second edition, 1672.
[2] Poets, like lovers, should be bold and dare,
   They spoil their business with an over-care:
   And he who servilely creeps after sense
   Is safe, but ne're will reach an Excellence.
[3] *De Arte Poetica*, l. 28.

best where there is the most need of it, surprize the Audience, and cast a Mist upon their Understandings. ... But these false Beauties of the Stage, are no more lasting than a Rainbow, when the Actor ceases to shine upon them, when he gilds them no longer with his Reflection, they vanish in a twinkling. I have sometimes wonder'd, in the reading, what was become of those glaring Colours which amaz'd me in *Bussy Damboys*[1] upon the Theatre: but when I had taken up what I suppos'd, a fallen Star, I found I had been cozen'd with a Jelly ... to summ up all, uncorrect English, and a hideous mingle of false Poetry and true Nonsense; or, at best, a scantling of Wit which lay gasping for Life, and groaning beneath a heap of Rubbish. A famous modern Poet us'd to Sacrifice every Year a *Statius* to *Virgil's* Manes:[2] and I have Indignation enough to burn a *D'amboys* annually to the Memory of *Johnson*.[3] But now, My Lord, I am sensible, perhaps too late, that I have gone too far: for I remember some Verses of my own, *Maximin* and *Almanzor*,[4] which cry, Vengeance upon me for their Extravagance, and which I wish heartily in the same Fire with *Statius* and *Chapman*: All I can say for those Passages, which are, I hope, not many, is, that I knew they were bad enough to please, even when I writ them: But I repent of them amongst my Sins: and if any of their Fellows intrude by chance into my present Writings, I draw a stroke over all those *Dalilahs* of the Theatre; and am resolv'd I will settle my self no Reputation by the Applause of Fools. 'Tis not that I am mortified to all Ambition, but I scorn as much to take it from half-witted Judges, as I shou'd to raise an Estate by cheating of Bubbles.'[5] (*Ibid.*, ii. 257–8.)

[1] George Chapman's tragedy (1607), which survived on the Restoration stage.
[2] The poet was the Venetian Andrea Navagero (1483–1529); the sacrifice, Martial.
[3] Ben Jonson.
[4] The tyrant of *Tyrannick Love* and the hero of *The Conquest of Granada*.
[5] Delusive financial schemes.

9. Dryden on *An Evening's Love*

1671

Extract on the charges of immorality and plagiarism made against
this play, from the Preface to the first edition. 'The *Evening Lover*,
a foolish plot, and very prophane, so as it afflicted me to see how
the stage was degenerated and poluted by the licentious times'
(John Evelyn, *Diary*, 19 June 1668).

I have already acknowledg'd that this Play is far from perfect: but I
do not think my self oblig'd to discover the imperfections of it to
my Adversaries, any more than a guilty person is bound to accuse
himself before his Judges. 'Tis charg'd upon me that I make debauch'd
persons (such as they say my Astrologer and Gamester are) my Protagonists, or the chief persons of the *Drama*; and that I make them
happy in the conclusion of my Play; against the Law of Comedy,
which is to reward virtue and punish vice. I answer first, that I know
no such law to have been constantly observ'd in Comedy, either by
the Ancient or Modern Poets. *Chœrea* is made happy in the *Eunuch*,
after having deflour'd a Virgin: and *Terence* generally does the same
through all his Plays, where you perpetually see, not only debauch'd
young men enjoy their Mistresses, but even the Courtezans themselves rewarded and honour'd in the Catastrophe. The same may be
observ'd in *Plautus* almost every where. *Ben. Johnson* himself, after
whom I may be proud to erre, has given me more than once the
example of it. That in the *Alchemist* is notorious. . . . This being, then,
establish'd, that the first end of Comedie is delight, and instruction
only the second; it may reasonably be inferr'd that Comedy is not so
much oblig'd to the punishment of the faults which it represents, as
Tragedy. For the persons in Comedy are of a lower quality, the action
is little, and the faults and vices are but the sallies of youth, and the
frailties of humane nature, and not premeditated crimes: such to
which all men are obnoxious, not such, as are attempted only by few,

and those abandonn'd to all sense of vertue: such as move pity and
commiseration; not detestation and horror; such in short as may be
forgiven, not such as must of necessity be punish'd. But, lest any man
should think that I write this to make libertinism amiable; or that I
car'd not to debase the end and institution of Comedy, so I might
thereby maintain my own errors, and those of better Poets; I must
farther declare, both for them and for my self, that we make not
vicious persons happy, but only as heaven makes sinners so: that is by
reclaiming them first from vice. For so 'tis to be suppos'd they are,
when they resolve to marry; for then enjoying what they desire in
one, they cease to pursue the love of many. So *Chærea* is made happy
by *Terence*, in marrying her whom he had deflour'd: And so are
Wildblood and the *Astrologer* in this Play.

There is another crime with which I am charg'd, at which I am
yet much less concern'd, because it does not relate to my manners,
as the former did, but only to my reputation as a Poet: A name of
which I assure the Reader I am nothing proud; and therefore cannot
be very solicitous to defend it. I am tax'd with stealing all my Playes,
and that by some who should be the last men from whom I would
steal any part of 'em. There is one answer which I will not make;
but it has been made for me by him to whose Grace and Patronage
I owe all things.[1]

Et spes et ratio studiorum, in Cæsare *tantum.*[2]

And without whose command they shou'd no longer be troubl'd with
any thing of mine, that he only desir'd that they who accus'd me of
theft would always steal him Playes like mine. But though I have
reason to be proud of this defence, yet I should wave it, because I
have a worse opinion of my own Comedies than any of my Enemies
can have. 'Tis true, that where ever I have lik'd any story in a Romance,
Novel, or forreign Play, I have made no difficulty, nor ever shall, to
take the foundation of it, to build it up, and to make it proper for the
English Stage. And I will be so vain to say it has lost nothing in my
hands: But it alwayes cost me so much trouble to heighten it, for our
Theatre (which is incomparably more curious[3] in all the ornaments
of Dramatick Poesie, than the *French* or *Spanish*) that when I had

---

[1] Probably the Duke of Newcastle, to whom Dryden dedicated the play.
[2] 'All the hope and reward of our studies depend on Caesar' (Juvenal, *Sat.* vii. 1).
[3] Concerned with standards.

43

finish'd my Play, it was like the Hulk of *Sir Francis Drake*,[1] so strangely
alter'd, that there scarce remain'd any Plank of the Timber which
first built it. To witness this I need go no farther than this Play: It
was first *Spanish*, and call'd *El Astrologo fingido*; then made *French* by
the younger *Corneille*: and is now translated into *English*, and in print,
under the name of the *Freign'd Astrologer*. What I have perform'd in
this will best appear by comparing it with those: you will see that I
have rejected some adventures which I judg'd were not divertising:
that I have heightned those which I have chosen, and that I have
added others which were neither in the *French* nor *Spanish*. And
besides you will easily discover that the Walk[2] of the *Astrologer* is the
least considerable in my Play: for the design of it turns more on the
parts of *Wildblood* and *Jacintha*, who are the chief persons in it. I have
farther to add, that I seldome use the wit and language of any Romance,
or Play which I undertake to alter: because my own invention (as bad
as it is) can furnish me with nothing so dull as what is there. . . .

But these little Criticks do not well consider what is the work of a
Poet, and what the Graces of a Poem. The Story is the least part of
either: I mean the foundation of it, before it is modell'd by the art of
him who writes it; who formes it with more care, by exposing only
the beautiful parts of it to view, than a skilful Lapidary sets a Jewel.
On this foundation of the Story the Characters are rais'd: and, since
no Story can afford Characters enough for the variety of the *English*
Stage, it follows that it is to be alter'd, and inlarg'd, with new persons,
accidents, and designes, which wil almost make it new. . . .

But in general, the employment of a Poet, is like that of a curious
Gunsmith, or Watchmaker: the Iron or Silver is not his own; but
they are the least part of that which gives the value: The price lyes
wholly in the workmanship. . . .

But I have said more of this than I intended; and more, perhaps,
than I needed to have done: I shall but laugh at them hereafter, who
accuse me with so little reason; and withall contemn their dulness,
who, if they could ruine that little reputation I have got, and which
I value not, yet would want both wit and learning to establish their
own; or to be rememberd in after ages for any thing, but only that
which makes them ridiculous in this.

[1] The *Golden Hind* at Deptford.
[2] Action.

10. Dryden as Mr Bayes

1672

Extracts from *The Rehearsal* by George Villiers, second Duke of Buckingham (1628–87), and others; a dramatic satire on drama drafted about 1664 and first acted at Drury Lane on 7 December 1671. Dryden is represented as Bayes, an author. 'I answer'd not the *Rehearsall*,' he wrote in 1693, 'because I knew the Author sate to himself when he drew the Picture, and was the very *Bays* of his own Farce. Because also I knew, that my Betters were more concern'd than I was in that Satire: And lastly, because Mr. *Smith*, and Mr. *Johnson*, the main Pillars of it, were two such Languishing Gentlemen in their Conversation, that I cou'd liken them to nothing but to their own Relations, those Noble Characters of Men of Wit and Pleasure about the Town.' ('Discourse concerning Satire'; *Poems* (1958), ed. James Kinsley, ii. 605.)

(a) [Smith and Johnson ask Bayes the meaning of his last play.]

BAYES. Faith, Sir, the Intrigo 's now quite out of my head; but I have a new one, in my pocket, that I may say is a Virgin; 't has never yet been blown upon. I must tell you one thing, 'Tis all new Wit; and, though I say it, a better than my last: and you know well enough how that took. In fine, it shall read, and write, and act, and plot, and shew, ay, and pit, box and gallery, I gad, with any Play in *Europe*. This morning is its last Rehearsal . . . and if you, and your friend will do it but the honour to see it in its Virgin attire; though, perhaps, it may blush, I shall not be asham'd to discover its nakedness unto you.— I think it is o' this side.

[*Puts his hand in his pocket.*
. . . Yes, here it is. No, cry you mercy: this is my book of *Drama Common places*; the Mother of many other Plays.

JOHNS. *Drama Common places!* pray, what 's that?

BAYES. Why Sir, some certain helps, that we men of Art have found it convenient to make use of.

SMI. How, Sir, help for Wit?

BAYES. I, Sir, that 's my position. And I do here averr, That no man yet the Sun e'er shone upon, has parts sufficient to furnish out a Stage, except it be with the help of these my Rules.

JOHNS. What are those Rules, I pray?

BAYES. Why, Sir, my first Rule is the Rule of Transversion, or *Regula Duplex:* changing Verse into Prose, or Prose into verse, *alternative as* you please.[1]

SMI. How 's that, Sir, by a Rule, I pray?

BAYES. Why, thus, Sir; nothing more easie when understood: I take a Book in my hand, either at home, or elsewhere, for that 's all one, if there be any Wit in 't, as there is no Book but has some, I Transverse it. . . .

SMI. Well, Sir, and what d'ye do with it then?

BAYES. Make it my own. 'Tis so alter'd that no man can know it. My next Rule is the Rule of Record, and by way of Table-Book. Pray observe.

JOHNS. Well, we hear you: go on.

BAYES. As thus. I come into a Coffee-house, or some other place where wittie men resort, I make as if I minded nothing; (do you mark?) but as soon as any one speaks, pop I slap it down, and make that, too, my own.

JOHNS. But, Mr. *Bayes,* are not you sometimes in danger of their making you restore, by force, what you have gotten thus by Art?

BAYES. No, Sir; the world 's unmindful: they never take notice of these things.

SMI. But pray, Mr. *Bayes,* among all your other Rules, have you no one Rule for Invention?

BAYES. Yes, Sir; that 's my third Rule that I have here in my pocket.

SMI. What Rule can that be?

BAYES. Why, Sir, when I have any thing to invent, I never trouble my head about it, as other men do; but presently turn o'er this Book, and there I have, at one view, all that *Perseus, Montaigne, Seneca's Tragedies, Horace, Juvenal, Claudian, Pliny, Plutarch's lives,* and the rest, have ever thought, upon this subject: and so, in a trice, by leaving out a few words, or putting in others of my own, the business is done.

[1] *Cf.* pp. 167–73

JOHNS. Indeed, Mr. *Bayes*, this is as sure, and compendious a way of Wit as ever I heard of.

BAYES. I, Sirs, when you come to write your selves, o' my word you 'l find it so. But, Gentlemen, if you make the least scruple of the efficacie of these my Rules, do but come to the Play-house, and you shall judge of 'em by the effects. . . .

(The Rehearsal, ed. Edward Arber (1902), pp. 29–33.)

(*b*)

Enter BAYES

BAYES. Now, Gentlemen, I would fain ask your opinion of one thing. I have made a Prologue and an Epilogue, which may both serve for either: (do you mark?) nay, they may both serve too, I gad, for any other Play as well as this.

SMI. Very well. That 's, indeed, Artificial.

BAYES. And I would fain ask your judgements, now, which of them would do best for the Prologue? For, you must know, there is, in nature, but two ways of making very good Prologues. The one is by civility, by insinuation, good language, and all that, to—a—in a manner, steal your plaudit from the courtesie of the Auditors: the other, by making use of some certain personal things, which may keep a hank upon such censuring persons, as cannot otherways, A gad, in nature, be hindred from being too free with their tongues. To which end, my first Prologue is, that I come out in a long black Veil, and a great huge Hang-man behind me, with a Furr'd-cap, and his Sword drawn; and there tell 'em plainly, That if, out of good nature, they will not like my Play, why I gad, I'l e'en kneel down, and he shall cut my head off. Whereupon they all clapping—a—

SMI. But, suppose they do not.

BAYES. Suppose! Sir, you may suppose what you please, I have nothing to do with your suppose, Sir, nor am not at all mortifi'd at it; not at all, Sir; I gad, not one jot. Suppose quoth a!—

[Walks away.

JOHNS. Phoo! pr'ythee, *Bayes*, don't mind what he says: he 's a fellow newly come out of the Country, he knows nothing of what 's the relish, here, of the Town.

BAYES. If I writ, Sir, to please the Country, I should have follow'd the old plain way; but I write for some persons of Quality, and peculiar friends of mine, that understand what Flame and Power in writing is: and they do me the right, Sir, to approve of what I do.

47

JOHNS. I, I, they will clap, I warrant you; never fear it.

BAYES. I'm sure the design 's good: that cannot be deny'd. And then, for language, I gad, I defie 'em all, in nature, to mend it. Besides, Sir, I have printed above a hundred sheets of papyr, to insinuate the Plot into the Boxes:[1] and withal, have appointed two or three dozen of my friends, to be readie in the Pit, who, I'm sure, will clap, and so the rest, you know, must follow; and then pray, Sir, what becomes of your suppose? ha, ha, ha. .... (*Ibid.*, pp. 37–9.)

(*c*)

BAYES. Gentlemen, because I would not have any two things alike in this Play, the last Act beginning with a witty Scene of mirth, I make this to begin with a Funeral.

SMI. And is that all your reason for it, Mr. *Bayes*?

BAYES. No, Sir; I have a precedent for it too. A person of Honour, and a Scholar, brought in his Funeral just so: and he was one (let me tell you) that knew as well what belong'd to a Funeral, as any man in *England*, I gad.[2]

JOHNS. Nay, if that be so, you are safe.

BAYES. I gad, but I have another device, a frolick, which I think yet better than all this; not for the Plot or Characters, (for, in my Heroick Plays, I make no difference, as to those matters) but for another contrivance.

SMI. What is that, I pray?

BAYES. Why, I have design'd a Conquest, that cannot possibly, I gad, be acted in less than a whole week: and I'l speak a bold word, it shall Drum, Trumpet, Shout and Battel, I gad, with any the most warlike Tragœdy we have, either ancient or modern.

JOHNS. I marry, Sir; there you say something.

SMI. And pray, Sir, how have you order'd this same frolick of yours?

BAYES. Faith, Sir, by the Rule of Romance. For example: they divide their things into three, four, five, six, seven, eight, or as many Tomes as they please: now, I would very fain know, what should hinder me, from doing the same with my things, if I please.

JOHNS. Nay, if you should not be Master of your own works, 'tis very hard.

BAYES. That is my sence. And therefore, Sir, whereas every one makes

---

[1] The 'Connexion ... to the *Indian Queen*' circulated at the first performances of *The Indian Emperour* in 1665.

[2] Perhaps a reference to Henry Howard's *The United Kingdoms* (?1663).

five Acts to one Play, what do me I, but make five Plays to one Plot:
by which means the Auditors have every day a new thing.

JOHNS. Most admirably good, i' faith! and must certainly take, because
it is not tedious.

BAYES. I, Sir, I know that, there 's the main point. And then, upon
Saturday, to make a close of all, (for I ever begin upon a *Monday*) I
make you, Sir, a sixth Play, that sums up the whole matter to 'em,
and all that, for fear they should have forgot it.

JOHNS. That consideration, Mr. *Bayes*, indeed, I think, will be very
necessary.

SMI. And when comes in your share, pray Sir?

BAYES. The third week.

JOHNS. I vow, you'l get a world of money.

BAYES. Why, faith, a man must live: and if you don't, thus, pitch
upon some new device, I gad, you'l never do it, for this Age (take it
o' my word) is somewhat hard to please. There is one prettie odd
passage, in the last of these Plays, which may be executed to several
ways, wherein I'ld have your opinion, Gentlemen.

JOHNS. Well, what is 't?

BAYES. Why, Sir, I make a Male person to be in Love with a Female.

SMI. Do you mean that, Mr. *Bayes*, for a new thing?

BAYES. Yes, sir, as I have order'd it. You shall hear. He having passion-
ately lov'd her through my five whole Plays, finding at last that she
consents to his love, just after that his Mother had appear'd to him
like a Ghost, he kills himself. That 's one way. The other is, that she
coming at last to love him, with as violent a passion as he lov'd her,
she kills her self. Now my question is, which of these two persons
should suffer upon this occasion?

JOHNS. By my troth, it is a very hard case to decide.

BAYES. The hardest in the world, I gad; and has puzzled this pate very
much. What say you, Mr. *Smith*?

SMI. Why, truly, Mr. *Bayes*, if it might stand with your justice, I
should now spare 'em both.

BAYES. I gad, and I think—ha—why then, I'l make him hinder her
from killing her self. Ay, it shall be so. Come, come, bring in the
Funeral.

[*Enter a Funeral, with the two Usurpers and Attendants.*
Lay it down there: no, here, Sir. So, now speak.

K. USH. Set down the Funeral Pile, and let our grief
    Receive, from its embraces, some relief.

K. PHYS. Was 't not unjust to ravish hence her breath,
  And, in life's stead, to leave us nought but death?
  The world discovers now its emptiness,
  And, by her loss, demonstrates we have less.

BAYES. Is not that good language now? is not that elevate? It 's my *non ultra*, I gad. You must know they were both in love with her.

SMI. With her? with whom?

BAYES. Why, this is *Lardella*'s Funeral.

SMI. *Lardella!* I, who is she?

BAYES. Why, Sir, the Sister of *Drawcansir*. A Ladie that was drown'd at Sea, and had a wave for her winding-sheet.[1]

K. USH. *Lardella*, O *Lardella*, from above,
  Behold the Tragick issue of our Love.
  Pitie us, sinking under grief and pain,
  For thy being cast away upon the Main.

BAYES. Look you now, you see I told you true.

SMI. I, Sir, and I thank you for it, very kindly.

BAYES. Ay, I gad, but you will not have patience; honest Mr.—a— you will not have patience.

JOHNS. Pray, Mr. *Bayes*, who is that *Drawcansir*?

BAYES. Why, Sir, a fierce *Hero*, that frights his Mistriss, snubs up Kings, baffles Armies, and does what he will, without regard to good manners, justice or numbers.

JOHNS. A very prettie Character.

SMI. But, Mr. *Bayes*, I thought your *Heroes* had ever been men of great humanity and justice.

BAYES. Yes, they have been so; but, for my part, I prefer that one quality of singly beating of whole Armies, above all your moral vertues put together, I gad. You shall see him come in presently. . . .

              (*Ibid.*, pp. 91–7.)

(*d*)

Draw[*cansir*] . . . I drink, I huff, I strut, look big and stare,
  And all this I can do, because I dare.

SMI. I suppose, Mr. *Bayes*, this is the fierce *Hero* you spoke of?

BAYES. Yes; but this is nothing: you shall see him, in the last Act, win above a dozen battels, one after another, I gad, as fast as they can possibly be represented.

[1] An echo of Dryden's *The Conquest of Granada*, Part I, Act iv. *Drawcansir: cf.* Almanzor in that play.

JOHNS. That will be a sight worth seeing, indeed.

SMI. But pray, Mr. *Bayes*, why do you make the Kings let him use 'em so scurvily?

BAYES, Phoo! that is to raise the character of *Drawcansir*.

JOHNS. O' my word, that was well thought on.

BAYES. Now, Sir, I'l shew you a Scene indeed; or rather, indeed, the Scene of Scenes. 'Tis an Heroick Scene.

SMI. And pray, Sir, what is your design in this Scene?

BAYES. Why, Sir, my design is *Roman* Cloaths, guilded Truncheons, forc'd conceipt, smooth Verse, and a Rant: In fine, if this Scene does not take, I gad, I'l write no more. Come, come in, Mr.—a—nay, come in as many as you can. Gentlemen, I must desire you to remove a little, for I must fill the Stage.

SMI. Why fill the Stage?

BAYES. O, Sir, because your Heroick Verse never sounds well, but when the Stage is full.

(*Ibid.*, pp. 103–5.)

(*e*)

BAYES . . . the battel, Sir, [is] just coming in at door. And I'l tell you now a strange thing: though I don't pretend to do more than other men, I gad, I'l give you both a whole week to ghess how I'l represent this Battel.

SMI. I had rather be bound to fight your Battel, Sir, I assure you.

BAYES. Why, there 's it now: fight a Battel? there 's the common error. I knew presently where I should have you. Why, pray, Sir, do but tell me this one thing, Can you think it a decent thing, in a battel before Ladies, to have men run their Swords through one another, and all that?

JOHNS. No, faith, 'tis not civil.

BAYES. On the other side; to have a long relation of Squadrons here, and Squadrons there: what is that but a dull prolixity?

JOHNS. Excellently reason'd, by my troth!

BAYES. Wherefore, Sir, to avoid both those Indecorums, I sum up my whole battel in the representation of two persons only, no more: and yet so lively, that, I vow to gad, you would swear ten thousand men were at it, really ingag'd. Do you mark me?

SMI. Yes, Sir; but I think I should hardly swear, though, for all that.

BAYES. By my troth, Sir, but you would, though, when you see it: for I make 'em both come out in Armor, *Cap-a-pea*, with their Swords drawn, and hung, with a scarlet Ribbon at their wrists, (which, you know, represents fighting enough) each of 'em holding a Lute in his hand.

SMI. How, Sir, instead of a Buckler?

BAYES. O Lord, O Lord! instead of a Buckler? Pray, Sir, do you ask no more questions. I make 'em, Sir, play the battel in *Recitativo*. And here 's the conceipt. Just at the very same instant that one sings, the other, Sir, recovers you his Sword, and puts himself in a warlike posture: so that you have at once your ear entertain'd with Musick, and good Language, and your eye satisfi'd with the garb, and accoutrements of war. Is not that well?

JOHNS. I, what would you have more? he were a Devil that would not be satisfi'd with that.

SMI. I confess, Sir, you stupifie me.

BAYES. You shall see.

JOHNS. But, Mr. *Bayes*, might not we have a little fighting for I love those Plays, where they cut and slash one another, upon the Stage, for a whole hour together.

BAYES. Why then, to tell you true, I have contriv'd it both ways. But you shall have my *Recitativo* first. . . .

(Ibid., pp. 121–3.)

(*f*)

EPILOGUE

The Play is at an end, but where 's the Plot?
That circumstance our Poet *Bayes* forgot,
And we can boast, though 'tis a plotting Age,
No place is freer from it than the Stage.
The Ancients Plotted, though, and strove to please
With sence that might be understood with ease;
They every Scene with so much wit did store
That who brought any in, went out with more:
But this new way of wit does so surprise,
Men lose their wits in wond'ring where it lyes.
If it be true, that Monstrous births presage
The following mischiefs that afflicts the Age,
And sad disasters to the State proclaim;
Plays, without head or tail, may do the same.
Wherefore, for ours, and for the Kingdoms peace,

May this prodigious way of writing cease.
Let 's have, at least, once in our lives, a time
When we may hear some Reason, not all Rhyme:
We have these ten years felt its Influence;
Pray let this prove a year of Prose and Sence.

11. 'Tragedy I say 's my Masterpiece'

1673

Extract from Joseph Arrowsmith's comedy *The Reformation*, 1673, pp. 46–9. Dryden is represented as a tutor giving advice on the construction of heroic plays.

Antonio. . . . I hope Sir your heroick play goes on.
Tutor. As fast as a piece of that exactness can. I'le only leave a pattern to the world for the succeeding ages and have done. . . . I take a subject, as suppose the Siege of *Candy*, or the conquest of *Flaunders*, and by the way Sir let it alwayes be some warlike action; you can't imagine what a grace a Drum and Trumpet give a Play. Then Sir I take you some three or four or half a dozen Kings, but most commonly two or three serve my turn, not a farthing matter whether they lived within a hundred years of one another, not a farthing Gentlemen, I have tryed it. . . . Sir you must alwayes have two Ladies in Love with one man, or two men in love with one woman; if you make them the Father and the Son, or two Brothers, or two Friends, twill do the better. There you know is the opportunity for love and honour and Fighting, and all that. . . . Then Sir you must have a Hero that shall fight with all the world; yes, i'gad, and beat them too, and half the gods into the bargain if occasion serves. . . . When I have writ a play, I pick some Lady out of general acquaintance or favourite at the Court, that would be thought a wit, and send it in pretence for

to submit it to her judgment. This she takes for such a favour—and raises her esteem so much—she talks of nothing else but Mr. such a ones new play, and picks out the best on't to repeat, so half the town by this means is engag'd to clap before they come. . . .

12. *The Censure of the Rota*

1673

The first of a group of anonymous pamphlets (see also Nos. 13, 14, 15) published in the spring of 1673 in criticism or vindication of Dryden. The *Censure* is sub-titled *On Mr Driden's Conquest of Granada* and was published at Oxford.

Amongst severall other late Exercises of the *Athenian Vertuosi* in the *Coffe-Academy* instituted by Apollo for the advancement of *Gazett Philosophy Mercury's, Diurnalls,* &c: this day was wholly taken up in the Examination of the *Conquest* of *Granada*; a Gentleman on the reading of the *First Part,* & therein the Discription of the Bull-baiting, said, that *Almanzor's* playing at the Bull was according to the Standard of the *Greek Heroes,* who, as Mr *Dryden* had learnedly observ'd (*Essay of Dramatique poetry,* p. 25) were great Beef-Eaters. And why might not *Almanzor* as well as *Ajax,* or *Don Quixot* worry Mutton, or take a Bull by the Throat, since the Author had elsewhere explain'd himselfe by telling us the *Heroes* were more noble *Beasts of Prey,* in his *Epistle* to his *Conquest* of *Granada,* distinguishing them into *wild* and *tame,* and in his Play we have *Almanzor shaking his Chaine,* and *frighting his Keeper,* p. 28, broke loose, p. 64, and *tearing those that would reclaim his rage,* p. 135. To this he addes that his Bulls excell'd others *Heroes,* as far as his own *Heroes* surpass'd his Gods: That the *Champion Bull* was divested of flesh and blood, and made immortall by the poet, & bellow'd after death; that the fantastique Bull seem'd fiercer then the true, and the dead bellowings in Verse, were louder then the living; concluding with a wish that Mr *Dryden* had the good luck to have vary'd that old Verse quoted in his *Dramatique Essay*,

Atque Ursum, & Pugiles media inter Carmina poscunt
Tauros, & Pugiles prima inter Carmina posco,[1]

and præfixt it to the front of his Play, instead of

—Major rerum mihi nascitur Ordo,
Majus opus moveo.[2]

Another *Virtuoso* said he could not but take notice how ignorantly some charg'd *Almanzor* with transgressing the Rules of the *Drama*, vainly supposing that *Heroes* might be confin'd to the narrow walks of other common Mortals, not considering that those Dramatick Planets were Images of *Excentric Vertue*, which was most beautifull, when least regular: that *Almanzor* was no lesse maliciously tax'd with changing sides, then which charge what could be more unjust, if they look't on him as *Achilles* and *Rinaldos's*[3] countryman, and born with them in that *Poeticall Free-State*, (for Poets of late have form'd *Utopia's*) where all were Monarchs (without Subjects) and all swore Alleagiance to themselves, (and therefore could be Traytors to none else) where every man might invade anothers Right, without trespassing on his owne, and make, and execute what Lawes himself would consent to, each man having the power of Life and Death so absolutely, that if he kill'd himself, he was accountable to no body for the murder; that *Almanzor* was neither Mr *Drydens* Subject, *Boabdelins*,[4] but equally exempt from the Poets Rules, and the Princes Laws, and in short, if his revolting from the *Abencerrages* to the *Zegrys*, and from the *Zegrys* to the *Abencerrages* again had not equally satisfi'd both parties, it might admit of the same defence, Mr *Drydens* Outcries, and his Tumults did, that the Poet represented Men in a *Hobbian* State of War.[5] A third went on and told them that Fighting Scenes, and Representations of Battells were as necessary to a Tragedy, as Cudgells, and broken Pates to a Country Wake; that an Heroick

---

[1] 'The vulgar demand a bear and boxers in the midst of a play; I call for bulls and boxers at the beginning' (adapting Horace, *Epistles*, II. i. 185–6).
[2] *Aeneid*, vii. 44–5, 'a greater series of deeds appears to my mind; a greater task I attempt.'
[3] In the Charlemagne romances by Ariosto and Boiardo.
[4] The last king of Granada in Dryden's play.
[5] Hobbes, *Leviathan*.

Poem never sounded so nobly, as when it was heightned with Shouts, and Clashing of Swords; and that Drums and Trumpets gain'd an absolute Dominion over the minds of the Audience: (the Ladies, and Female Spirits.) Here an Acquaintance of the Authors interpos'd, and assur'd the Company, he was very confident, that Mr *Dryden* would never have had the Courage to have ventur'd on a Conquest had he not writ with the sound of Drum and Trumpet; and that if there was any thing unintelligible in his rants, 'twas the effect of that horrour those Instruments of War with their astonishing noise had precipitated him into, which had so transported him, that he writ beyond himselfe. But he was interrupted by a grave Gentleman *that us'd to sup in Apollo and could tell many Storys of Ben. Johnson*, who told them, that in his opinion Mr *Dryden* had given little proof of his Courage, since he for the most part combated the dead; and the dead—send no Challenges; nor indeed need they, since through their sides he had wounded himselfe; for he ever play'd the Critick so un-luckely, as to discover only his own faults in other men, with the advantage of this aggravation, that the *Grammaticall* Errors of older Poets, were but the Errors of their Age, but being made his, were not the Errors of this Age: since he granted this Age was refin'd above those *Solecismes* of the last: thus the *Synchæsis*, or ill placing of Words, a fault of *B. Johnsons* time,[1] was an usuall Elegancy in Mr *Drydens* writings, as in the Prologue to his *Indian Emperour*:

> Such easie Judges, that our Poet may
> Himself admire the fortune of his Play.

Himself in the second verse, which should have been plac'd before *may* in the first.

In the *Indian Emperour, Guyomar* say's,

> I for my Country fought, and would again,
> Had I yet left a Country to maintain.[2]

Left should not have preceded *Country*, but follow'd it.

In *Granada*, second part:

> The sooner trust th' Hyæna then your smile;
> Or then your Tears the weeping Crocodile.

And again:

> Yet then to change, 'tis nobler to despair.

[1] Says Dryden, in his 'Defence of the Epilogue' (1672).
[2] V. ii.

Thus the using *be* for *are*, the vice of those *dull* times, when *Conversation was so low*, that our Fathers were not taught to write and read good English, was frequent with Mr *Dryden* in this politer Age; In *Granada, second part*:

> ALMANZOR *Madam, your new commands I come to know,*
> *If yet you can have any where I goe,*
> *If to the Regions of the dead they be.*[1]

In the *Indian Emperour*:

> *Things good, or ill, by circumstances be.*[2]

In *Maximin*:

> *The Empress knows your worth, but, Sir, there be*
> *Those who can value it as high as she.*

And again:

> *And so obscene their Ceremonies be,*
> *As good men loath, and* Cato *blusht to see.*

In all these places he observ'd the Rhyme hid the false English. The placing of the Preposition at the end of a Verse or Sentence, Mr *Dryden* had confest was common to him with *Johnson*, but not discovering where, the Gentleman oblig'd the Company, by pointing at that in *Maximin*:

> *Your Brother made it to secure his Throne,*
> *Which this man made a step to mount it on;*[3]

And more conspicuously in his *Elegy* on *Oliver*, (one who was as great a contemner of Kings as *Almanzor*, and as great a defyer of the Gods as *Maximin*)

> *Fortune (that easy Mistresse of the young*
> *But to her ancient Servants coy and hard)*
> *Him at that Age her Favourites rank't among,*
> *When she her best lov'd* Pompey *did discard.*

To all which, he added that *ire* an obsolete word of *B. Johnson* was antiquated now, but *inthrall* and *oph*[4] in Mr *Dryden* were words

---

[1] II. ii, III. i, II. iii.
[2] IV. ii.
[3] *Tyrannick Love*, I. i, II. i, II. i.
[4] *Ouph*, goblin child.

antiquated in *Ben Johnsons* time, that *Johnson* only wrote English in good Latine, but Mr *Dryden* was so accomplish't as to write English fluently in all Languages, *Greek*, *Latin*, *Italian*, *Spanish*, and what not; in him he met with *Escapade*, *Mirador*, *Bizarre*, *torrents winding in volumes*, *Trumpets Clangors*, *Venus's Cestos*, besides *unthinking Crowd*, *bladder'd Air*, and such like *Poeticall Jargon*;[1] and to demonstrate that this Age (or Mr *Dryden*, which is the same) made some improvement in fals English as well as the last (if at least we have not received a newer *English Grammar* then *Ben. Johnsons*) he desired them to weigh these verses in his *Granada*:

> *Obey'd as Soveraign by thy Subjects he*
> *But know that I alone am King of me.*

Me, for my self.
Again,

> *I for her sake thy Scepter will maintain,*
> *And thou by me, in spight of thee, shall raign.*[2]

Thee, for thy self.
As for Mr *Drydens* cavill at the lines in *Catiline*,[3]

> *Go on upon the Gods, kiss lightning, wrest*
> *The Engine from the Cyclops, and give fire*
> *At face of a full Cloud—*

his mistaken Image of shooting (since the *Cyclops* Engine was a Thunderbolt) recoyl'd upon himself in his *Maximin*, where he suppos'd *Sulphur to rain down in fiery showers on Charinus*,[4] a clearer image perhaps of shooting, unknown as much in *Maximin*'s days, as *Catilin*'s. A Critick continuing on the discourse, said, he was sorry that Mr *Dryden* when he charg'd every page of *Shakespeer*, and *Fletcher* with some *Solecism* of speech, or notorious *flaw* in sence, did not read their writings and his own with the same spectacles, for had he, he would never have left so incorrect a line as this in that *Epilogue*, where he taxes the Antients so superciliously;

> *Then Comedy was faultless, but 'twas course.*[5]

[1] The only one of these probably introduced by Dryden is 'Mirador', a watchtower (*Conquest of Granada*, I. i.).
[2] I. i, Part II, III. i.
[3] In his criticism of Jonson in the 'Defence of the Epilogue'.
[4] *Tyrannick Love*, I. i.
[5] Epilogue to *The Conquest of Granada*, Second Part.

'Tis a favour to call this but a *flaw;* nay, in the threshold of his *Granada*:

> Thus in the Triumphs of soft peace I reign,
> And from my walls defie the pow'rs of Spain;

which two verses agree as ill, as if one were a *Moor,* and the other a *Spaniard.*

Again in the *First Part:*

> As some fair Tulip by a storm opprest,
> Shrinks up, and folds its silken arms to rest;
> And bending to the blast, all pale and dead,
> Hears from within the wind sing round its head.[1]

This *Tulip* that could hear the wind sing its *Epicedium,* after it was *dead,* you may be sure grew no where but in a Poets Garden.

In the *Second Part,*

> So two kind Turtles, when a Storm is nigh
> . . . . . .
> Pearch't on some dropping branch, they sit alone,
> And cooe, and hearken to each others moan.

Where because a *Turtle* was a solitary Bird, he made two of them sit alone.

Again, speaking of *Almanzor:*

> —a gloomy smile arose
> From his bent brows, and still the more he heard,
> A more severe, and sullen joy appear'd.[2]

Here is a *Smile* describ'd with so much Art, that the description may serve indifferently either for a *Smile,* or a *Frown;* any other *Smile,* but a *gloomy* one, rising from *bent Brows,* would have look't too effeminately pleasant in *Almanzor's* grim face; a clear proof this of the *Epistle,* that *dimples* may not mis-become the *stern beauty* of a *Heroe.*[3]

These he found in *Annus Mirabilis:*

> So sicken waning Moons too near the Sun,
> And blunt their Crescents on the edge of day.

[1] I. i. V. ii.
[2] I. ii, II. iii.
[3] Dryden's Dedication.

59

Compared with these in *Maximin*:

> *My flaming sword above them to display,*
> *All keen and ground upon the edge of Day.*[1]

From which he inferr'd, that the *Edge of Day* was capacitated indifferently either to *blunt*, or *sharpen*, according to the Poets pleasure, as from that verse in his *Astræa Redux*:

> *A horrid stilnesse first invades the Ear,*

he observ'd *that to invade the Ear* (in Mr *Drydens* Dictionary) signified any violence offer'd to the Ear, either from Noise, or Silence.

In another place in *Maximin*, he seems fully to have answer'd his Prologue, in not *servilely stooping so low as Sence*;

> *To bind* Porphyrius *firmely to the State,*
> *I will this day my Cæsar him create,*
> *And, Daughter, I will give him you for wife.*[2]

Here, in making *Porphyrius* a Bride, he has *reacht an excellence*, and justify'd his representation of *big-belly'd Men* in the *Wild Gallant*, a greater imposibility, then any *Shakespear* can be censur'd for (for imposybility's in Mr *Drydens* charge are sence, but in anothers nonsence) though he wants not these smaller *indecorum's* neither; such as his introducing *Donna Aurelia* in the *Mock-Astrologer*, retrenching her words, which how consistent 'tis with the *Spanish* Gravity, the great *Dons of Wit* can best resolve him, and such is that indecency, committed in his *Mayden Queen*, where the *Queen* and Courtiers stand still, to hear *Celadon* and *Florimell* with a great deal of cold mirth absurdly *usurp* the Queens Prerogative in making new Marriage-Laws.[3]

That Mr *Drydens* wit was as much advanc'd beyond that of the Ancients, as his sense & Language; was Evident from these Clenches (to omit that of Pulpit-Quibbling finding the *benefit of its Clergy* since he was so mannerly, as to leave to clench there) in his forecited *Elegy* on our English *Maximin*:

> *Though in his Praise, no Arts can liberall be.*[4]

[1] St. 125; *Tyrannick Love*, IV. i.
[2] *Ibid.*, I. i.
[3] *An Evening's Love*, III. i; *Secret-Love*, V. i.
[4] *Heroique Stanza's*, st. 3.

In his *Rivall Ladyes*, a Serving-man threatens to beat the Poet *with a staff of his own Rhymes.*

In his *Mayden Queen*,[1] little *Sabina* tells *Florimell*, *well my drolling Lady, I may be even with you*: to which *Florimell* wittyly, *not this ten years by thy growth yet*: and after, tells her taller sister *Olinda, she cannot affront her because she is so tall.* And to parallel *B. Johnson's,*

> Forty things more, dear Grand, *which you know true,*
> For which, or pay me quickly, or I'le pay you,

Celadon (in the same Play) tells *Florimell*; *I shall grow desperately constant, and all the tempest of my love will fall upon your head: I shall so pay you*: to which *Florimell* makes this reply; *Who you, pay me? you are a bankrupt, cast beyond all possibility of recovery.*[2] This when repeated by *Loveby* in that incomparable clenching Comedy, the *Wild Gallant*, Mr *Dryden*, and the *Taylors Wife* call'd a Jest, but is farr from Wit in all Languages. To be short, that his wit depended often on a ridiculous chiming of words, was evident from such instances as these,

> Under Almanzor *prosperously they fought,*
> Almanzor *therefore must with pray'rs be sought.*
>
> Know that as Selin *was not won by thee,*
> Neither will I by Selins *daughter be.*
>
> Forbear dear Father, *for your* Ozmyns *sake,*
> Do not such words to Ozmyns *father speak.*
>
> But what's the cause that keeps you here with me?
> That I may know what keeps me here with you.
>
> Would you your hand in Selins *bloud embrue,*
> Kill him unarm'd, who arm'd shund killing you?[3]

much after the rate of that old Tick-tack

> A Pye, a Pudding,
> A Pudding, a Pye,
> A Pudding-Pye.
> A Pye for me,
> A Pudding for thee,
> A Pudding for me,
> A Pye for thee,
>   A Pudding-Pye for me and thee.

[1] *Secret-Love*, IV. i.
[2] *Ibid.*, V. i.
[3] *Conquest of Granada*, First Part, V. i; Second Part, I. ii, IV. i.

A modern Poet stept up next, and said, he observ'd Mr *Dryden* pass'd no better a Complement on the Poets of this Age in his *Prologue* to his *Granada*, then on those of the former in his *Postscript* and *Epilogue;* for these he tax't as liberally with writing *dull sence*, as those with writing *incorrect;* and preferr'd his own *gay nonsence* equally to both. That his Play was the best comment on his *Prologue*, and his *Tulip* with *silken armes*, and two verses:

> But silk-wormlike, so long within have wrought,
> That I am lost in my own webb of thought,[1]

sufficiently displai'd his *gayety of nonsence*: and 'twas for this reason he suppos'd that he upbraided *Beaumont* and *Fletcher* with meannesse of expression in their *Scenes of Love*, because those *dull unthinking men* never had their thoughts so *well dres't*, as to transform their Lovers into such *gay* things, as *Silkwormes* and *Tulips*; but this was the unhappiness of their Education, they were not so well bred, nor kept so good Company as Mr *Dryden*; nay had *Johnson* (who was *more conversant in Courts*) converst (as our Poet) only with Persons of Honour, he had never disgrac'd the Stage with *Tib*[2] in her Rags, but attir'd her more like a modern Comœdian in a *broad-brim'd Hatt*, and *wast Belt:*[3] but 'twas plain, his Humor discover'd more of the Mechanique & the Clown, then the Gentleman; thus *Otters Horse*, and his *Bear*, and his *Bull*, might be entertaining to a Groom, or a Bear-ward, but nothing in nature and all that (to english *Tom. Otter's in rerum naturâ*) was more odious to a Man of Garniture and Feathers: in those days they regal'd their Audience with the *Acorns* of *Poetry*, and no marvell then if *Cobs Tankard* quench't their thirst no lesse then pure *Helicon*: in fine, *Johnson's* wit had too much *Alchymy*, and their beer too much allay to pass for that of the *Golden Age*, an honour only due to the Poets of these times, that bring *old Iron on the Stage*. The honour of the *Golden Age* (reply'd another) belongs justly to Mr *Dryden*, who ever return'd home richly fraught from *Spain* and *America*; to his Catholique Conquests Poetry ow's its *Indies*, and its *Plate-Fleets*:[4] and after such Voiages and Discoveries, he could not but wonder a little at his modest excusing his ignorance in Sea Terms in his *Annus Mirabilis;* since he was very confident that his Muse that

---

[1] *Ibid.*, Second Part, I. ii.
[2] Tib, Otter, and Cob: characters in Jonson's *Every Man in his Humor* and *Epicœne*.
[3] As Nell Gwyn in the Prologue to *Granada*, First Part.
[4] These brought American silver home annually to Spain.

had so often crost the Seas, and endur'd so many Storms and Ship-
wracks could not but be *Tarpawlin* sufficient enough to make an
Heroick Poem on *Star-board*, and *Lar-board*. His blustering Metaphors
would more then acquit him of *Horace* his Censure,

Serpit humi tutus, nimium timidusq: procellæ.[1]

The boldest of the old Poets never rais'd such Tempests as he,
though they labour'd to swell their Poetical Sails with all the four
winds blowing at once (as Mr *Cowly* ingeniously, on, *Una Eurusque;
Notusque ruunt, creberque procellis Africus,* &c.)[2] He was the man
Nature seem'd to make choice of to enlarge the Poets Empire, & to
compleat those Discovery's others had begun to *shadow: that Shakespear* and *Fletcher* (as some think) erected the *Pillars* of Poetry is a
grosse errour; this Zany[3] of *Columbus* has discover'd a Poeticall
World of greater extent then the Naturall, peopled with *Atlantick*
Colony's of *notionall creatures, Astrall Spirits, Ghosts,* & *Idols*, more
various then ever the *Indians* worshipt, and *Heroes*, more lawless than
their Savages. The already-discover'd habitable world (joyn'd with
Sr *Thomas Moor's*, and the Lord *Bacon's*)[4] was too narrow a com-
passe for his Geography of Thoughts, which would admit of no *un-
peopled Solitudes*, nor *Terra Incognita*; this Poeticall *Coryat*[5] would
travell beyond the Poles of Nature and Opinion; sometimes we have
him mounting his *Pegasus*, and taking a flight to the *Mountains of the
Moon*, and the Bed of *Nyle*, then (having *baited* first *at Heaven*) making
his Journey through the lower *Fields of Ayr*, to *Spencers Bower of
Bliss*, and *Tasso's Enchanted wood* (both lately discover'd in *Fairy-Land*)
there visiting such wandring Souls as *flagging flutter'd down from the
middle Sky*, and dispossessing the *Swallows* of their Winter Quarters,
lay leiger[6] for *Mortall frames* in Trunks of hollow Trees. Thus has he
out travall'd the Sun, and made his flights on the wings of his own
fancy without the assistance of *Ganza's*,[7] or *Bottles* of *May-Dew*. In
short, did Mr *Cowley*, or any others dislike this *Fairy* part of Poetry,
(though Mr *Cowly* had answer'd himself by making use of Angels

---

[1] *De Arte Poetica*, l. 28: 'he creeps on the ground, too careful and afraid of the gale.'
[2] *Aeneid*, i. 85–6, 'the east wind joined with the south, the south with the storm-laden
west. . . .'
[3] Clown's attendant.
[4] More's *Utopia* and Bacon's *New Atlantis*.
[5] Author of a travel-book, *Coryate's Crudities* (1611).
[6] Stationary.
[7] Wild swans which drew Gonsales to the moon in Godwin's *Man in the Moone* (1633).

[and] visions in his *Davideis*, where the Argument required it) the Poet had prettily excus'd his fantastique Scenes, & Visionary Pageants, in that Apologetick Verse,

> *Ast opere in tanto fas est obrepere Somnum.*[1]

With him joyn'd a *phlegmatick heavy Gownman*, who hoped that that Verse was a frank confession of the Poet, that he compos'd severall of his Raptures in a Dream, of which nature was this in his *Maximin*:[2]

> *Thou treadst th' Abyss of Light.*

Abyss is a word so inconsistent with *Light*, that 'tis scarce Bright enough for its Shadow. In *Granada*,

> *Heavens Out-cast, and the Dross of every Star.*

Compare this with another in *Maximin*,

> *—None, will be so bright,*
> *So pure, with so small allays of light,*

and you'l say 'tis all *pure refin'd* nonsense, without the least *allay* of *dull* Sence.

In another place in *Maximin*,

> *I reel, and stagger, and am drunk with light.*

This Verse the Poet made, when he was shut up in a *dark room* and not suffer'd to see the light.

Again,

> *So mayst thou live thy thousand years in peace,*
> *And see thy Aery Progeny increase.*

Here it may be a *Quære*, whether *Spirits* (since amongst them ther's no distinction of Sexes) get all *Sons*, or all *Daughters*. And following those,

> *So may'st thou still continue fresh and fair,*
> *Fed by the blast of pure Ætheriall Ayr.*

How the *Æther*, that yeelds a nourishment so thin (scarce distinguishable from none at all) that it would starve a *Cameleon*, should fatten

---

[1] 'But in so large a work it is allowable that sleep comes on' (Horace, *De Arte Poetica*, l. 360).

[2] Quotations in this paragraph from *Tyrannick Love*, IV. i and V. i; *The Conquest of Granada*, Second Part, I. ii.

a *Spirit*, seems a Paradoxe: now after all this, the World may judge whether the notions of Poets (the Fathers of his Church) concerning spirits and Specters, were more satisfactory, then those of Philosophers and Divines; and whether Mr *Dryden* was not stark Inspiration mad, and in one of his Enthusiastique fits, when he objected it as lazinesse, or dulnesse to the Clergy, that they did not preach in Verse; That Reformation this Age must not be so happy as to expect, since the Objector had alter'd his resolution of exchanging the Sock and Buskin for the Canonicall Girdle. Here a great Patron of Rhyme interpos'd, and said, he could heartily wish that not only Divines would preach, Lawyers plead, Philosophers dispute, and Councellers debate, but even our Ladys and Gallants would converse in Rhyme, for besides that this would take off the Argument of the unnaturallness of Rhyme, it would be a means of exalting our thoughts, and raising Conversation above the vulgar level, for what can be suppos'd more indecent then for Ladys and Persons of Quality to walk on foot in Prose with the Rabble? Without the sweetnesse and cadency of Rhyme our quick Repartees in discourse lose much of their Beauty, when as if he that spoke last be nick'd by another, both in wit and sound, nothing is left desireable. Nay, Mr *Dryden* that writ ill in Rhyme, would have writ worse without it, for such Redundancy's as this in *Granada, First Part*,

> This is my will, and this I will have done.[1]

Which is a handsome way of saying *this is my will* twice. Such mean Couplets as this in *Maximin*,

> O my dear Brother, whom Heav'n let us see,
> And would not longer suffer him to be!

and such precipitations from such heights, as,

> Say but he's dead, that God shall mortall be:
> See nothing, Eyes, henceforth, but Death and wo,
> You've done me the worst Office you can do,[2]

would never have been passable, were not many cozn'd with their sound; in a word, many things were charg'd upon the Poet, of which the Rhymer was no ways guilty, but there needed no greater Argu-

[1] V. i.
[2] *Tyrannick Love*, I. i.

ment for the efficacy of Rhime above Blank Verse, then that of blowing a Candle out, and blowing in again, in two Verses.

> GRANADA *Like Tapers new blown out the fumes remain,*
> *To catch the light, and bring it back again,*

where the snuff expires so sweetly, it cannot be offensive to the most critical Note. To this a Favourer of Blank Verse with some heat, reply'd, that these verses in *Granada, Second Part,*

> *You see Sir, with what hardship I have kept*
> *This precious gage which in my hands you left,*[1]

These in the *Indian Emperour,*

> *But I'me so far from meriting esteem,*
> *That if I judge, I must my self condemn,*[2]

and these in *Maximin,*

> PORPHYRIUS *Too long, as if Eternity were so.*
> BERENICE *Rise good* Porphyrius (*since it must be so.*)[3]

proclaim'd the Rhymer no less faulty then the Poet, and evidently prov'd that Mr *Dryden* enslav'd his sense as little to Rhyme, as elsewhere to Syllables; and both to sense. Who after this will deny that the way of writing in verse, is the most free and unconstrain'd? in which the Poet is not ty'd up to Language, sense, Syllables, or Rhyme, but even, sweet, and flowing numbers, and smart Repartees (in plain English, playing with words) attone for the want of all. With what impudence can the Adversaries of Rhyme object its difficultie? when those that are formed neither by Art nor Nature, may write whole plays, such as Mr *Dryden's* in it, without easing themselves on *pace and trot.* It is but framing the character of a Huff of the Town, one that from breaking Glass-windows, and combating the watch, starts up an *Heroe*: him you must make very saucy to his superiours, to shew he is of the same stamp with *Achilles* and *Rinaldo*; then tame the savage with the charming sight of the *Kings Daughter* (or wife) whom this *St. George* is to deliver from the *Dragon*, or greater dangers: to heighten his character the more, bring in a sheepish King with a Guard of poultrons to be kick't by him, as often as he thinks fit his

---

[1] II. ii.
[2] IV. iv.
[3] *Tyrannick Love,* I. i.

Miss. should be a witnesse of his Gallantry: if this be not enough, let him play prizes with Armies, still Tumults with one look, and raise Rebellions with another. The Language is no lesse easie then the characters, 'tis but stuffing five Acts with *Fate, Destiny, Charms, Charming fair, Killing fair, heavenly fair, the Fair and Brave, the Lover and the Brave, &c.*, an allusion to *two kind Turtles*, foisted in, an impertinent Simile from a Storm, or a Shipwrack, and a senslesse Song of *Phillis*, and the businesse is done: the descriptions may be borrowed from *Statius*, and *Montaigns* Essays, the Reason and Politicall Ornaments from Mr *Hobs*, and the Astrologicall (and if need be, the Language too) from *Ibrahim*, or the *Illustrious Bassa.*[1] To conclude all, he said, a barren Invention must ever be provided with such necessary helps, as the following Forms, to which he might have recourse on all occasions.

[The *Censure* ends (pp. 19–21) with an anthology from Dryden of:]

Some Forms and Figurative Expressions of so large an extent, that they are adjusted to all Characters in all Plays, Tragedys, Comedys, and Tragi-Comedys, whether written in Rhyme, Blank Verse, or Prose; suitable to all Prologues, Epilogues, and Dramatique Essays that are, or shall be written.

For magnifique Sound ... For gentle verses, that do not *shake* us in the reading ... For a Rant ... Or thus, higher ... For generous Love ... For sharpnesse of conceit ... For pleasant folly. ...

[1] A French romance (1641) by Madeleine de Scudéry.

13. Attack by vindication

1673

The second critical pamphlet on Dryden in 1673 (see No. 12), published at Cambridge anonymously with the title *The Friendly Vindication of Mr Dryden From the Censure of the Rota by His Cabal of Wits.*

The excellent Mr *Dryden* taking into serious consideration the Affairs of *Wit*, and having made an Assignation to that purpose with some flourishing *Ingenuities*, no less conscious than admirers of his Fame: One of the forwardest urged the immediate discussing the severe *Censure of the Rota of Oxford*; which, though seeming only to point at *Granada*, did collaterally reflect on all his *Plays* and *Poems* whatsoever. Mr *Dryden*, not a little surprized to hear of *Critical Engines* levelled at his *Sieges, Conquests,* and the like, was meekly falling into a swound almost past recovery by tweaking of his Nose; till one of his ingenious Friends putting him in mind how the King had made him his *Laureat*, and how his *Muse* had accomplished him for her *Hero*, in both which respects it did not become him to discover that she had placed her *Ensigns* of *Wit* in so unsteady and pusillanimous a *Brain* as his might appear to be, (did he not suddenly recollect his Spirit according to that Expression in his *Maiden-Queen*, spoken by her Handmaid *Astrea*, Act. I.)

> You were gay humour'd, and you are
> Now pensive—*
> Once calm and now unquiet—

Not to say that few Poets besides Mr *Dryden*, ever treated a Queen with so light and homely an Entertainment of Words, as *Gay-humour'd*, and the rest in these two ridiculous lines.

A *Knavish Wit* here, that had a good mind to have been nibling

---

* *Melancholick* in the first Impression.

68

at the fore-going Expression, which signified no more in all those
words, than to say that the Queen was at some one time in better
humour than at another: yet as he was of Mr *Drydens* Cabal, said, he
should rather infuse into his soul (in this Conjuncture) some Doses of
Maximins and *Almanzors* Heroical Bravery, and not give himself up
to his Pursuers; like that *simile* of the Hare in *Annus Mirabilis*, of
which two whole *Stanza's* are paraphrastically, and somewhat more
compendiously rendred thus,

[*Annus Mirabilis*, sts. 131-2, mangled in four lines]

The Reader may suppose that Mr *Dryden* was in almost as cold a fit
as the Hare he describes, wherefore not in a condition to be asked by
what reason he calls fearful, so timorous a Creature as a Hare naturally
is; since no man ever heard of a *valiant Hare*: or why he presumed to
apply this mean *simile* to Prince *Ruperts* Ship and some others, when
disabled in their fight with the *Dutch*; which if allowed, does rather
imply that the Prince and the rest, had run away like the Hare at
first, and would have done so afterwards, in imitation of a Hare, had
it been in their power; and not have encountred the Enemy with
that magnanimity that appeared throughout this action. But though
this *simile* squar'd so ill with the gallantry of the Action, a fault not
to be pardoned in Poetry, since its Illustrations and Metaphors should
not only suit, but endeavour to exalt, (and not depress, as it is observable in Mr *Dryden*) the greatness of the Subjects it treateth of; According to this of *Horace*,

[*De Arte Poetica*, ll. 14-16, quoted]

Yet this Gentleman who spake last was so indulgent to Mr *Drydens*
Repute, that he advised him, rather than yeild to any thing that could
be objected against his Poetry, to turn the line in his first Part of
Granada, mentioned by the *Rota*,[1] *This is my will*, &c. into

This is my wit, and this my wit shall be.

Adding, that he conceived his Muse had not made a more useful
conversion for him of any Verse of his. That he had proved they
had kindness enough to justifie what he had, or could write, though
they barked for his sake, at better Wit than any of his.

At which, some conflict passed betwixt the *Pale* and *Vermilion* of
his Cheek, (a thing very incident to such Complexions, when made

[1] *Supra*, p. 65.

Creatures of Fame) as also some melancholy puffs and swellings against the *Rota*, as if he had been inclinable to break silence with this pathetick and Courtly Expression delivered by his Maiden-Queen—

> *I must tell you, it is a sawcy**
> *Boldness thus to press on my Retirements.*

Here one made a *Querie*, whether *Sawcie* was not a pretty *Sawce-box* word annexed to boldness. Another of his Comrades, who had Authority enough over his Person and Muse, to pass his Raillery, said, that his restauration of spirit in this Issue of his Affairs, put him in mind of that Poeticall Expression of his in *Maximin*, Pag. 4:

> *Midst this was heard the shrill and tender crie*
> *Of well pleas'd Ghosts, which in the storm did flie,*
> *Danc'd to and fro, and skim'd along the ground,*
> *'Till to the Magick Circle they were bound.*

Here one took notice how excellently Mr *Dryden* had described the Voices, Musick, and Dancing of Ghosts; or if you please, an Anti-mask of Ghosts in the Air. But why shrill and tender should be the pleasing ornament of their Voices, since in it self no delightful way of speaking, or singing, was to be left to the discussion of Ghosts and Mr *Dryden* alone: though they could not but condescend, that Mr *Dryden* did deserve a tender Rebuke at least, for this harsh and gentle fiction, which his Pen had so musically bestowed on Ghosts. That it was true, that out of their respects to him, they had often endeavoured to blind the World from observing the incongruity of such Metaphors, (as sawcy boldness, shrill and tender, and the like,) not seldom used by him in this inconsistent manner of Expression, the better to wing his Muse to her height; or that she might flie in any storm, or dance to and fro, or skim along the ground, as he and she thought best: since he had merited that kindness from them, by his most ingenious converse and writing (besides some other more secret obligations) as also to cry up and preserve the honour of the Laurel conferred on him. Wherefore considering the Opposition which he and they have had, or may have; especially at this time, when his Muse is so perniciously attaqued by the *Rota*, and other malignant Criticks: they thought fit to desire him for the better strengthening

* Some say his first Copy had *consuming* in stead of *sawcy*, not much a better Epithet join'd to Boldness. [I. iii.]

of himself, to apply these Verses likewise of his *Maximin* to his present dangers,

> * *They coursing it, as he were fenc'd within*
> *And saw this dreadful Scene of Fate begin,*

which is his very conjuring expression, placing, *as he were*, in stead of, *while we were*.

Another said ingeniously enough, that the Censure of the *Rota*, or its Author, passed on his Poems and Plays, did very pertinently metaphor the volubility and rotation of Poetical fortune in neglect of his *Wit*; which it became him confidently to resent according to this in *Maximin*, where his Muse had often threatned bombast-vengeance on Gods and Men:

> *Provoke my rage no further, least I be*
> *Reveng'd at once, upon the Gods and Thee.*[1]

At this some could not chuse but smile (though his Entire Admirers) to think what a supreme Divinity Mr *Drydens* Muse was, that durst thus threaten all Powers, Divine and Human.

Mr *Dryden* being pretty well refreshed by swallowing these Cordials extracted from his Muses *Limbecks*, after he had cleared some drops of cold sweat from his forehead, and rubbed it to some Confidence, with due Obeysance made to these his Friends and Applauders, together with some pangs of thought, (not much unlike his Inspirations) Replied, That he must always acknowledge the support his *Wit* received from the Esteem and Vogue they allowed it; which though his Enemies called making his Party and Faction, it had been hitherto his good providence: nay added, That (among themselves) he had no reason to expect applause without it. That he still implored the same favourable Aspects from them, and that they would dare all Eyes which should observe or read his Writings with any reflections on their faults; though they may believe that it troubled not a little his Conference, that not withstanding their assignation of favour to his late New Play called *Love in a Nunnery*, the Town should conceive it Justice to condemn both his and their Endeavours. Upon which, he more instantly desired them for the future to *clap* and *bawl* more exceedingly for his sake, lest he sink by the Censure of the World, as well as the *Rota*'s: that whatsoever was his, might be reverenc'd

---

* *They Coursing it,* that is to say, the *Rota* coursing his Muse.
[1] I. i.

as a Play, and so voted, though without *Intrigue* or *Wit*. And since they had put him into a way to strengthen himself with his own Lines, he uttered these in *Maximin*, (a Play fruitful enough for such quotations) for their more kind memorial, using the word Plays, instead of Wars,

> *We are not sure tomorrow will be ours,*
> *Plays, have like Love, their favourable hours;*
> *Let us use all, for if we lose one day,*
> *That white one in the Crowd may slip away.*[1]

He desired them to forgive the large extent of his Petition, though perhaps the *Rota* might conceive it *Non-sense* amongst the rest; it being not usual in the *English* Tongue, to call a fair, serene, or prosperous day, a white day: That he desired them to impute this Inspiration to a Dream he had of white Money, to be shared in the Play-house. Adding, that nothing less could square with his profit, than wholly appropriating the fame and perquisits of *Wit*, (at least of one Play-house) to himself: for which purpose, he could not but with all humility, implore their Embargo on all other Poets that might possibly impair his repute, and Trade of Writing, though their Consciences were so guilty as to believe his Plays the worst.

That the *Drama* did require too many drams of *Wit* (he hoped they would excuse his Clinch) to be compounded by his *Genius*; which in the beginning of his undertaking he sufficiently observed, as was evident to them and the World, in his Practises to gain Proselytes to his Muse. As also his humble and supplicant Addresses to *Men* and *Ladies of Honour*, to whom he presented the most of his Plays to be read, and so passing through their Families to comply their Censures before-hand: confessing ingeniously, that had he ventured his *Wit* on the *Tenter-hooks of Fortune*, (like other Poets, who depended more on the merit of their Pens,) he had been more severely intangled in his own Lines long ago.

To this, one of his Associate *Wits* replied, That he thought it reasonable (were his profit not too deeply concerned) to perswade him to desist from Writing, as some Poets had discreetly and timely observed; like that of *Juvenal*,

> *Frange Miser Calamos—*[2]

since he was as egregious already as black and white could make him.

---

[1] *Tyrannick Love*, I. i; *white*, fortunate, a Latinism.
[2] *Sat.* vii. 27, 'Wretched man, break your pens.'

But however, if he were taken for no good Comick-Poet, or Satyrist; he had found a way of much easier License, (though more remarkable in the sense of some) which was, not only to Libel mens persons, but to represent them on the Stage too: That to this purpose he made his observations of men, their words and actions, with so little disguise, that many beheld themselves acted for their Half Crown: yet after all, was unwilling to believe, that this was not both good Comedy, and no less good Manners. Besides, that he had been so frankly obliging as (where he could not use a Character, or apprehended the License) to assign it to some other Poet of his Cabal, or exchange one Part for another, it may be *Club Wit* too, the better to set men forth: That this was a *Sir Positive Truth*[1] Mr *Dryden* had not fore-head enough to denie.

At which, there being observed a guilty variety in his Countenance —A certain Gallant stept forth and said, that what was past, was past: besides, that Mr *Dryden* had made his submissions and recantations most ingeniously both by word and writing: that he conceived a person of Honour, had a Letter dedicated to the Fire, even by the Hangmans hands, if the injur'd should think it necessary; therefore what was done was candid enough as to that particular. If Mr *Dryden* courted more his security than honour, he was not to be blamed, if his temper found it convenient: Or it might be interpreted his Kindness, in not being willing to put so much *Wit* as his own to hazard, especially since he proved it so dear to his Admirers. That it was enough to Cajole the fiercest Hector, imployed on any such account to him; as perhaps it succeeded with Sir *Fretchevil Hollis*, from this Verse in *Annus Mirabilis*,

> *Young* Hollis, *on a Muse by Mars begot.*[2]

No less than *Youth*, *Wit*, and *Valour*, chained together in one line; besides such a way to beget a *Hero* as is not to be found in any Poet; except that of his *Almanzor*, as extraordinarily begot by Mr *Dryden* on his Muse.

Here he extolled the *charming Wit* of Mr *Dryden*, that could so prepossess the hearts of men.

In a word, where he had figured any on the *Scene*, or *Press*, he was no less plyant to take them off as dexterously again: That it was Mr

---

[1] Sir Robert Howard was ridiculed as Sir Positive Attall in Shadwell, *The Sullen Lovers* (1668).

[2] St. 175.

Dryden's Bizarre in Wit, and Poets must be allowed so much variety, as sometimes to exceed the limits of Moderation and regular Characters.

Mr *Dryden* was in some disorder here, as indeed the mention of Regular parts and Characters could not but concern all his Plays, and did most especially at this time put him in mind of his dear beloved *Almanzor;* in honour to whom, he adorned the Frontispiece of *Granada* with,

—*Major rerum mihi nascitur Ordo,*
Majus opus moveo,[1]

and was now no less inwardly lamented by him, as suffering by the *Academick Rota*, not only as an abominated *Hero*, but as one who with his unruly Lines had broke most scornfully the Right Reverend *Priscians*[2] head, with some other deformities—he was going to add, *a gloomy smile arose*, but that it appeared by Mr *Dryden*,

—**That the more he heard,*
A more severe and sullen Joy appear'd.

Another was saying that Mr *Dryden's Wit* could be both blunt and sharp; and that the edge of day might possibly have this operation on his Muse when she awak'd his Verse too early, or out of humour; wherefore he advised Mr *Dryden* to trie what Effect the edge of Night would have on his Imagination; and perhaps the Metaphor might be better allowed *going to Bed*, or *Drunk*: desiring him to re-collect what time of the natural Day it was, that he writ the Prologue before the *Maiden Queen*, beginning thus,

He that writ this, not without pain and thought,
From French and English *Theatres has brought*
The exactest Rules, by which a Play is wrought.

Whether Mr *Dryden* was not confident enough, in putting such a *Panegyrick* of himself before a Play written with so feminine an *Intrigue* and *Genius*, as may be perceived by what hath been instanced already, in stead of troubling the Brain with further Remarques.

At which another replied briskly, that it was Mr *Dryden's* Interest to be allowed to speak, write, censure of Men and Wit as he pleased; that he had done it hitherto fortunately enough, and that for his

---

* Cited by the *Rota* out of the *Granada* [*supra*, p. 59].
[1] *Supra*, p. 55.
[2] An Athenian grammarian.

sake they must so applaud him, which was well enough hinted before by himself.

That it must be granted on all sides that Mr *Dryden* has *Wit*, or was to be thought *witty*—

Here one of his *Comrade-wits* cried, *Hold*, That it was not good to proceed on that ground, because it was fallacious, and would be answered by many, in saying, That he never had that Judgment or Wit he pretended to, for a Reason mentioned by the *Rota*, and such a one as Mr *Dryden* could not deny.

Wherefore the Logick of the Argument being in effect no more but this,

> *Either you have a Gig, or have lost a Gig,*

Which may be answered by saying,

> *You never had a Gig.*

But he forebore to apply it to Mr *Dryden*. He proceeded to shew, That whatsoever was Mr *Dryden*'s Wit, it was well enough proportioned to receive what praises they could bestow upon it; or what could be given by himself, to himself: To which purpose, his dealing with *Ben Johnson* (though dead, and of Immortal Fame with the Judicious) was very observable, in that Mr *Dryden*, who had at one time thought fit to call his Comedy, with the rest of his Time, mean, low, or as you have it in this hobling Verse of his mentioned by the *Rota*,

> *Then Comedy was faultless, but 'twas course,*[1]

(not to examine the consistency of *course* and *faultless*,) at another time had otherwise sung a Parallel of his Muses Fame with *Ben. Johnson*'s, as in his Prologue to the *Maiden Queen*, where he vaingloriously enough calls that Play

> *—a mingled Chime*
> *Of* Johnsons *humour, and* Corneille's *Rhime.*

But how *Johnsons* humour, could make such Musick with *Corneille*'s rhyme, is not to be understood otherwise, than as Mr *Dryden* hath made his own Commendation and it chime together. Which may be called another *Bizarre* in Mr *Dryden*.

As for his Comedy, it was objected by some, that it was as great

---

[1] *Supra*, p. 58.

an offence to good Morality, as his *Maximin* was to Christianity. That his *Marriage à la Mode*, and his *Love in a Nunnery*, were most excellent Collections of *Bawdery*. But the wonder was, how Mr *Dryden* came to conceive his fulsome Conceits to be refin'd Wit; as he had suggested to his Friends, since *Bawdery* had never that repute, before Mr *Dryden* writ it. That in good Comedy, there were innumerable Excellencies relating to *Wit* and *Manners*, to which there was some fear that his *Genius* would never arrive: which shews, that if his Invention be not free and airy enough for that purpose, his Imagination (whatsoever his person is) was sufficiently lascivious. But perhaps Mr *Dryden* conceives of the success of Plays, as *Martial* did of some licentious Writings of his:

Non possunt sine mentula placere,[1]

or which is all one, the *Dildo* of Mr *Drydens* Muse, so neatly applied to the females of the Town.

He that said this, though a great favourer of Mr *Dryden*, could not but grant that there were a great many Contradictions and Mistakes in the management of his *Muse*.

Here another took up the Discourse, saying, That since they were now met thus, it was not unfriendly to proceed to some Reformation of Mr *Drydens Wit* and *Manners* together; as well as they had hitherto in a headlong manner vindicated him to the World. In order to which, it was to be told Mr *Dryden* that he in the sense of some, with no less Arrogance and Ignorance, taxed *Virgil* the Prince of *Latine* Poets, then he had injured *Ben Johnson* the best of *English*; that in his Preface to his *Annus Mirabilis*, notwithstanding to adorn that miraculous Poem he had transversed many things of the incomparable *Virgils*, (as may be seen by his acknowledgment, and Marginal Notes to that purpose,) yet he there says thus of him:

Though he describes his Dido *well and naturally, in the violence of her passions, yet he must yield to* Ovid *in that of* Myrrha, *the* Biblis, *the* Althea *of* Ovid.

And a little later,

That if I see not more of their souls, then I see of Dido's, *at least I have a greater concernment for them.*

He added, That he could not chuse but reprehend this solœcism of commendation in Mr *Dryden:* wondring with what Brow he could

---

[1] VI. xxiii. 2, 'they cannot please without a penis.'

say, that if he saw not more of their souls then he saw of *Dido*'s, yet he had a greater concernment for them. How this would pass, or could quadrate with any favourable allowance of sense, he could not imagine. For to say that *Dido*'s was the more large, the more heroick, the more passionate Soul, yet must not concern Mr *Dryden*'s Ingenuity so far as the others, he thought fit to understand it amongst the rest of Mr *Dryden*'s *Bizarrs* in Wit and Judgment. And that he would not chuse his *Panegyricks* of most Poets, since they were either Impertinent, or Contradictory to what he could wish in him. Wherefore he would mind him of what some Criticks may retort upon him, (who though they take it not well, yet do not judge it worth their labour to vindicate the matchless Wit of *Virgil*) that if they see not more of his Love, than was to be seen in his *Eliza* the *Maiden Queen*, or what they saw in his *St. Catherine*, or his *Light buskin'd Queen Almahide*;[1] (that made *Boabdalin* her Cully, though her King and Husband, in order to the Embrace of her more strenuous *Almanzor*,) or if they perceived the same effects of his Muse in *Maximin* and *Almanzor*, as also throughout those Plays convertibly varied, he was not to believe they could be much concerned with his Characters, or that most of his Friends would not wish that Mr *Dryden* would either improve his Muse, or give over writing.

At this Mr *Dryden* began to be in a cold Sweat again; till promised that the discussion of *Maximin* and *Granada* should be deferred to a farther debate, if his concern required it.

Which a forward Wit of his Party perceiving, said, That the Gentleman that spoke last (though he could not contradict his Judgment) had mistaken the *Intrigue* that Mr *Dryden* endeavours to hold with the World: that Mr *Dryden* writ as well as any man that could write no better; and was no less himself in his last Play, called *Love in a Nunnery*; the fate whereof had occasioned him to confess, that he sometimes by their help had slurred a Play on the Audience, and that it was his utmost expectation and desire, that they would continue still so kind as to question nothing of his; that it had been likewise acknowledged by him, that he intended the same, for this last Catholick *Intrigue* of his, which he called *pawming of a Play on the Town*.

The Expression was something odd, it was yielded, and represented his hearers no less than *Sots* and *Gulls*, to be bubbled thus of their Understandings by him. That Mr *Dryden*'s Education was not so exact, as that no mixture was to be found in his *Manners* as well as

[1] *Tyrannick Love; The Conquest of Granada.*

77

Wit: that he was a Poet in *Olivers* time, and something more subservient to his Principality; but these were things to be handled at
another meeting, if Mr *Dryden* thought fit: adding that he did write
more for Profit than Reputation, or collaterally for both. The first of
which, he allowed to be the more absolute Mistress of his Muse, as
was hinted by himself before: though it is true that as an Ambidexter
in Wit, he intended to engross both solely to himself. But he was to
know that Mr *Dryden's* words did not always declare his meaning,
and were varied as best served his turn; sometimes for money, sometimes for both money and fame; another time for fame* above all
things, who by no means must be allowed other than the best Poet
in *England*, and had so caused himself to be given out by his Friends;
which cannot but be acknowledged another *quaint* variety in Mr
Dryden.

One asked whether upon the before-mentioned diversities observed
in Mr *Dryden*, he might not heroickly describe himself by saying
this Verse in *Maximin*,

I reel and stagger, and am drunk with light.[1]

That it must be acknowledged, that Mr *Dryden* could not deserve less
than to be soberly blamed; and so they had done and should do farther,
as occasion offered. He said, that it had been granted already that Mr
Dryden had been held an odd man enough always, by some who had
proved him. Notwithstanding, if his merit was small, they were sorry
he had taken so much pains to divulge it; which they did unwillingly
instance to him at this time, considering he was something pensive
and indisposed, as being under a *gloomy sullen* Censure of the *Rota's*;
and his Muse to undergo a severe penance for his assignations of *Love
in a Nunnery*; all which it was hoped he would suffer with a *shrill
tender* calmness of mind, if she could not inspire him with a more
proper and secure remedy. As likewise, not to be enraged from these
gentle stroakings of his Friends, or hope from thence more safely to
kick at their Counsels, like this of *Horace*,

Hunc male si palpere, recalcitrat, undique tutus.[2]

When on the other side, it is but taking advice from his own Verse,

---

* See the conclusion of his Letter to Sir *R. H[oward]* before his *Ann. Mirab.*
[1] See *supra*, p. 64.
[2] *Sat.* II. i. 20, 'if you stroke him awkwardly he will kick back at you, being wholly
on his guard.'

and receive this noise and hubbub about his Wit, no more disturbed then if

A horrid stillness did invade his Ear.[1]

For his Plays, it was unanimously accorded, that though they wished them well, they resolved henceforth to be more just to his failings than they had hitherto appeared, and not endeavour the pawming of them on the Town, if his Wit had no better a trick to thrive by.

Asking some pardon of the World for so long concealing his defects, or mistaking his Wit, to the neglect of better: That if he did imploy some vacant hours of his Muse for his vindication against the *Rota*, they thought it not amiss (at least before he writ any more Plays) since his Audience was resolved to construe his sense a little better than yet they had done.

And since Mr *Dryden* and his Muse, are best extolled by his own Pen, it was thought fit to annex this honourable and pacifick Wish to his future Productions of Wit; (taken out of his *Maximin*) using only the word *Writing* in stead of *Thousand*.

Thus,

> *So may'st thou live thy* Writing *years in Peace.*
> *And see thy Airy Progeny increase.*[2]

FINIS or not FINIS
As Mr *Dryden* pleaseth.

---

[1] *Astræa Redux*, I. 7.
[2] *Cf. supra*, p. 64.

14. *Mr. Dreyden Vindicated*

1673

Mr. Dreyden Vindicated, in a Reply to The Friendly Vindication of
Mr. Dreyden. *With Reflections on the Rota* (1673). Anonymous;
attributed to Dryden's Whig friend, Charles Blount (see *infra*,
No. 33).

Sir,

Casting my eyes upon the Title of your Pamphlet, I promised my
self a Diversion I have much coveted, that is, a Vindication of Mr.
Dreyden, whose Pen at present is one of the most Ingenious and
Innocent Recreations *England* enjoys; when proceeding to satisfie my
Curiosity in the Discourse as before in the Title, I perceiv'd 'twas my
Destinie to share with Mr. *Dreyden* in his Abuse; onely with this
difference: His Reputation, and my lost time were the Preys. As for
my Injury, I had let it sleep, in respect that it was not onely mine, but
a general Calamity: But when I found Mr. *Dreyden* so coursly handled,
fearing such Discourses might be of ill consequence, (as Presidents who
make it a Mode to decry all Ingenuity) the Zeal and Reverence I had
for Learning, Wit, and Innocent pleasure, urg'd me (in this ensuing
Treatise) to vindicate *him*, who is so great a Patron of all those three
Virtues.

The world is now so over-run with *Wits*, that *Poets* have as hard a
Task as Women's Parsons or Taylors, not one in ten pleases. So
numerous are the Criticks, so frequent is Wit, and so elevated are their
Fancies, that as a *great Lady* did, they forget Common Notions, and
cry to their servants, *Give me, give me, give me, I think ye call it a Pin.*

Nay, your stomachs are now grown so squeamish, that good solid
Sense will not take; no, it must have Wit: But if you hear a sentence
which is a Jest with no Sense in it, then away you run with that; 'tis
Wit, 'tis Wit; no matter for Sense. Now of this latter sort of Wit is
the *Rota* fill'd with, from whence sprung your Pamphlet as Branches

from the Root of a tree: neither are you less severe; but as the Greatest Treasons are generally Masqueraded, and acted privately, so is yours, who meets him with a kiss, and then stabs him; Reprieves him in your Title, and Condemns him in your Book.

As on Mr. *Dreydens* behalf I cannot but be exceeding sorrowful that the *Rota* so surpriz'd him, as to put him in a Swound, (*with his Critical Engines levell'd against his Sieges and Conquests:*) so on the Publicks behalf I greatly rejoyce that you have found out such an easie Expedient to recover one out of a Trance, as you say *Tweaking by the Nose* is. Had you been Contemporary with *Mahomet*, and of his Cabal, you must either have conceal'd that Expedient, or you had confounded him for a Prophet. But howsoever, I hope you'll be so good a Commonwealths-man as to put it in *Culpeper's* Dispensatory[1] at the Next Impression.

I am altogether Ignorant whether your Expectation is of succeeding Mr. *Dreyden* in his Lawrel. If so, your War is Lawful. But the world is apt to censure it may be with you as with some University-professors of Wit, who having learnt one or two Sentences of Latine, or Divine Clinches,[2] make Discourses on purpose to extend them. Some Authors are as thrifty of their Jests, as Chancery-Clerks of their words, who allow but three a peny in their Writings. But you are as free of your Wit and Jests, as Citizens of Macquerel when they are Twenty a Groat; that you may winde the house (where they are) before you see it.

Those Objections you raise against Mr. *Dreyden*, are observ'd to be collected not so much out of Mr. *Dreyden* as out of the *Rota*; which makes your Readers conjecture you to be some Itinerant Pastor, that takes Breviates at *London*-Sermons, and then in the Country vents them for his own, and makes them fit any Text, though the Foppery be the same.

> *You were gay-humour'd, and you are*
> *Now pensive;*
> *Once calm; and now unquiet.*

Here you have borrow'd an Objection from the *Rota*, and for want of French fallen into their Mistake: for *Gay-humour'd* is nothing else but *Gayeté du Cœur*, and an expression that may be apply'd without forfeiture of Respect to any person how great soever. Besides, if this

---

[1] Nicholas Culpeper (1616–54), *A Physicall Directory* (1649).
[2] Puns.

expression were not refin'd enough for a Privie Counsellor to salute his Soveraign with, yet it were for a Chamber-maid, she never being bred up at the University.

> Ev'n as the fearful Hare when cours'd on Plain,
> and longer can't her flight maintain;
> By the fierce Dog, with flix turn'd up does lie,
> Who though not kill'd, yet cannot flie.[1]

Here I finde the main scruple which troubles his Conscience is, why Mr. *Dreyden* calls *fearful, so timerous a creature as a Hare naturally is?* To which I Reply: Why do we say, *Cruel Tyrant,* or *Wicked Rogue?* since a Tyrant naturally is so Cruel, and a Rogue so Wicked: for a Tyrant hath as little mercy, and Rogue goodness, as an Hare valour. *Pavidumque; Leporem,* says *Horace,* Epist. 2.[2] Also this Simile was appli'd onely to the Ship, and not to the Prince; wherefore it injures not him: and I believe the Ship never askt for Justice against Mr. *Dreyden's* Simile.

Methinks the Gentleman who was so Indulgent to Mr. *Dreydens* Reputation should have a little consider'd his own, and retain'd that Wit for himself which he so freely bestows on Mr. *Dreyden,* when he turns *This is my Will,* &c. into *This is my Wit, and this my Wit shall be.* He might e'en as well have said, *I love Wit, but Wit loveth not me.* As Sir *Roger* saith of Tobacco in the Play, when it makes him sick: *I love it, but it loveth not me: this is my will, and this I will have done.*

In the Descant upon these words, I finde the Author of the *Rota* goes a little beyond our Vindicator, and quarrels with the Chiming of the two words *Will* and *Will*; whereas that Ingemination addes a further grace and force to the Authority of the Resolution. Neither can it properly be call'd a Tautologie, the inculcating of a Command; as if a man should say, *You shall, you shall, I say you shall do 't*; where 's the Chime or the Absurdity of the same thing again? But here we have reason to imagine that worthy Gentleman (who was so indulgent to Mr. *Dreyden's* Repute) had more experience in Limning then Poetry, by his discourse of Mr. *Dreyden's* pale and Vermilion cheeks; which terms of Art are to hint you of his skill in Polygraphy. He does like a Country-Justice in a Coffee-house, that brings in Henry the 8's Statutes, or *Dalton,*[3] upon all occasions, to shew his Reading; or as

---

[1] A garbled version of *Annus Mirabilis,* sts. 131–2.
[2] *Epode* ii. 35, 'the timid hare.'
[3] Michael Dalton (d. 1648?), author of *The Countrey Justice* (1618).

some Apothecaries, that will run you over all the Titles of their Gally-pots, to be thought Doctors. Again, the same indulgent party complains of the conjunction of *Sawcie* with *Boldness*, in the *Maiden-Queen*: *I must tell you it is a sawcie Boldness thus to press on my Retirements.*

Nay, and to make these words seem more Ridiculous, he says that *Saucie-Boldness* is a pretty Sawcebox-word. Truly a very ingenious Quibble: A man would almost swear this Gentleman to be the Poetaster that, in a Reply upon Doctor *Wild's Poems*,[1] Christen'd him the *Wild Poet*. But for his better Information, the Epithet of *Sawcie* serves very well to distinguish an *Impudent* or an *Insolent Boldness*, from a *generous*: as put the case, A man should take the freedom to pass a Judgement upon the *Boldness* of the *Vindicator*; there is a *Boldness* in censuring the Style of a man that writes better than himself; and that's an *Arrogant Boldness*: there is a *Boldness* of censuring a man that lives better than himself; and that's a *Scandalous Boldness*: and then there's the *Boldness* of *Blind Bayard*,[2] that makes a man run his head against Stone-walls; and that's a *Bruital Boldness*. I shall leave the *Vindicator* to take his Choice: for my Business is onely to prove that *Boldness* requires an *Epithet* to clear it. Another of your Comerades condemns Mr. *Dreyden's* Fiction in *Tyrannick Love*, pag. 4:

> *Midst this was heard the* Shrill *and* Tender *cry*
> *Of well-pleas'd Ghosts which in the storm did fly,*
> *Danc'd to and fro, and skim'd along the Ground,*
> *Till to the Magick Circle they were bound—*

Upon these Lines I perceive the Worthy Gentleman is offended that Mr. *Dreyden* permits his Ghosts to *Sing and Dance*: which is no great matter to him, so long as he is at no Charge either for *Singing-master* or *Dancing-master*. But his chief Cavil is at the words *Shrill* and *Tender* as inconsistent; which most ingeniously he illustrates by *Harsh* and *Gentle*. Now if Ghosts in general may be admitted, I beseech you let us imagine withal, that there is something for them to do; and it shall be all one to me whether they *sing* and *dance*, or play on the Sackbut or the Jews-trump. But to justifie the Congruity of the words *Shrill* and *Tender*, the former relates properly to the exility of the Sound, and the other with the softness of the voice denotes also a gentleness of Disposition or Affection. Who knows but that Ghosts may sing and dance as well as when they were Men and Women? I am sure if

---

[1] Dr Robert Wild (1609–79) wrote *Iter Boreale* (1660) and poems.
[2] Proverbial. *Bayard:* a bay horse.

Valeria's Ghost, in *Tyrannick Love*, speaks truth, they do: for she says,

> —*That after death we Sprights have just such Natures*
> *We had for all the world when Humane creatures.*—

Your next Quarrel is at these Lines in *Maximin*:

> —*They* Coursing *it as* He *were fenc'd within,*
> *And saw this dreadful Scene of Fate begin.*—

Your Asterism* upon *They*, and then your Marginal Comment upon it, *viz. The Rota Coursing his Muse*, has left us more in the Dark then we were before: for I hope you do not intend to make a pack of Curs of the Cabal, or that his Muse is brought upon the Stage to be baited to death, as the Primitive Christians were upon the Theatre. But your main Criticism lies upon placing *as he were* in stead of *while we were*: whence arise two difficulties, *viz.* upon *as* in stead of *while*; and then *he* for *we*. The *latter* was manifestly the Printers mistake; the *former* seems to me to be none at all: for *as* and *while* are very commonly and warrantably us'd to the same purpose; for Instance, *As* I was in my Chamber, *&c.* Why not *As* as well as *while*? But some people love to play with words, as a Cat with a Feather, or an Ape with a pair of Breeches; sometimes with his head out at the Knee-tyes, sometimes at the Codpiece, sometimes at the Waste-band; when the Breeches are the same still, which way soever he turns them. Again, I perceive you are much disgusted with those Lines of *Maximin*:

> —*Provoke my Rage no further, lest I be*
> *Reveng'd at once upon the Gods and thee.*—

Where you accuse Mr. *Dreyden* for Profaneness. This Nicety perchance may advance the sale of your Book among the pretended Zealots; yes, and your Reputation too; although it were as absurd to make an Atheist speak piously, as a pious man Atheistically: but the sound of Religion goes a great way with those that place it rather in the Accent than in the Practice. And methinks your Scruple at the Expression, might have done as well, if it had been season'd with a little Charity for the Author. But we'll Compound that Point, if you please; and Mr. *Dreyden*'s next *Pagan* shall enter the Stage with a *Pater Noster*. A man might make Remarques pleasant enough upon the Remainder of your sixth page, where you are pleas'd to sport your self with Mr. *Dreyden*'s Conscience, and the *Equivogue*[1] of *Assignation*

---

[1] Equivocation, ambiguity.

upon *Love in a Nunnery*: but it is all Bubble, and breaks with the blowing upon. Here now you must permit me to say, You are too severe to Railly upon this last new Play so suddenly, before you can have the opportunity of Reading it: which makes some apprehend it with you, as with Fruit-women, who are so eager of venting[1] the earliest fruit, that they bring onely Trash to the Market. And truly 'tis observed in your weak Objections, that you are Cautious what Devils you raise, lest you should not be able to lay them again. We'll now pass to somewhat more material, and that is, your grand Exception to the *Whiteday*, in these Lines of his *Maximin*:

> —*Let us use all, for if we loose one day,*
> *That White one in the Crowd may slip away.*

You urge, that it is not usual in the English Tongue to call a *prosperous day* a *White day*. Where you must give me leave to minde you of a whole Nest of Mistakes one within another. First, Mr. *Dreyden* does not intend a *prosperous day*, but a *day* that might have been *Prosperous*, if the Opportunity then offer'd had been improv'd; and advises the watching of all Opportunities that no Occasions slip. Secondly, you argue, *that it is not Current, because it is not Common*: which rate of Reasoning will destroy all things that are excellent. And thirdly, that *White day is not good in English*. As if a Roman Emperour had been to be treated in the English Tongue. But it is very Elegant Latine. See the two first lines of the second Satyr of *Perseus* . . . alluding to the Custom of casting a White stone into a Box upon every fortunate day, and a Black one on the contrary. . . . Nor will it avail at all, your conceit of the *Dream of White money* that put this *White day* in the Authors head; when it was in effect this *White day* which put a great deal of White money in the Authors Pocket.

You have another fling at him for his *Observations upon Men, their Words, and Actions*; and in short, *for bringing Humane nature upon the Stage*: Whereas you should rather have commended him for it, as the main End, Business, and Perfection of Comedy.

> *Quicquid agunt Homines, Votum, Timor, Ira, Voluptas,*
> *Gaudia, discursus nostri est farrago libelli.*[2]

This was *Juvenals* Theme, and may without any disparagement be Mr. *Dryden*'s. But the poor man, it seems, is fallen under a miserable

---

[1] Selling.

[2] *Sat.* i. 85–6, 'Whatever men do—their wish, fear, anger, pleasure, joys, their running to and fro—is the hotch-potch theme of our little book.'

Dilemma; either he must represent on the one side what was never said or done, (and so make himself Ridiculous) or fall under the scandal of a Libeller for the contrary on the other. But as to what you charge upon him for falling upon persons, it is neither prov'd by you, nor justifi'd by me.

Another Objection you collect from the *Rota*, upon the *Contradiction* in a *severe and sullen Joy*. Seneca tells you, *Res est severa Gaudium*.[1] And then for your *Gloomy smile* too, which gives so much offence; I think *A Gloomy smile and sullen joy appear'd*, is as proper a form of speech, as *A Gloomy or Waterish sunshine*, when the Sun appears through a Cloud or Mist.

For Mr. *Dreydens* Prologue to his *Maiden-Queen*, wherein *you tax him with Confidence*; this may be his excuse, *that Confidence as well becomes those that write well, as Silence those that write ill.* Now (for all your severe Censures) however Mr. *Dreyden* is highly oblig'd to you, in giving your self the trouble *to finde out whether he was a Wit or no*; which is a very great trouble, I can assure you Sir: for all Philosophers are not Harefinders: the pains being equal, as if you had gone to Mr. *Lilly*,[2] or Cast his Ingenuity[3]: for you prov'd it by as infallible a Signe, as any Privie Counsellor to the Planets could have certifi'd you by his Calculation, that is, by Logick, as thus:—*Either you have a Gig, or you have lost a Gig.*—Which may be answer'd,—*You never had a Gig.*— Truly, a very Learned way of Conjuring and Arguing, much after the rate that some Soph-wits prove the Moon to be made of Green-cheese; whose Arguments are these:

> The Moon is made of Green-cheese, or something else.
> Now Custard is something else; and it is not made of Custard.
> Ergo, 'tis made of Green-cheese.

Another Accusation against Mr. *Dreyden* is, that his presumption extends to the defaming of his Predecessors, as *Ben Johnson*, &c. by saying,—*Then Comedy was faultless, but 'twas course.*—This is the Commendation of a fresh Country-girl, that she is sound, but hard-favour'd: and it was a true definition of our predecessors Plays. The *Drama* and Poetical Methods were most accurately observ'd, as the Plot, &c., but view the Lines, apprehend the Sence, and compare the Language with those of this present Age, and then you'll perceive the difference.

[1] *Ep.* xxiii. 4, '[True] joy is a serious matter.'
[2] William Lilly, the astrologer (1602–81).
[3] Calculated his wit astrologically.

For Mr. *Dreyden's* Prologue to his *Maiden-Queen*, where you *tax him with Again for Boasting*; he does but confess his Little Theft honestly; and therefore justly merits a Pardon:

> —*A mingled Chime*
> *Of* Johnson's [*humour, with*] Corneille's *Rhime.*—

But if you condemn the Boldness of Poets, how comes *Ben Johnson* to scape you? who when his *Sejanus* was hiss'd, comes himself on the Stage, and speaks thus to the Audience:

> *Gentlemen,*
> *This in my Plays behalf I boldly say,*
> *By God 'tis good; and if you like 't, you may.*

The next Impeachment you bring against Mr. *Dreyden* is for the obscenity of his Comedies; where you term them all *downright Bawdery*, when the worst of them is but Implicite. Now against such Reports, he may plead that every Poet must strive to please the Humour of the Age wherein he writes; and so does Mr. *Dreyden*, and so did his Predecessors. See *The Heiress, Alchemist*, and *Bartholomew-Fayr*.[1] Besides, as a supple Courtier ought not to write against Flattery, so ought not you against Obscenity,

> *Whose Railing Style is so obscene and loud,*
> *As if your very Muse it self went Proud.*

'Tis a receiv'd Opinion amongst all your Readers, that Mr. *Dreyden* did Prophetically railly upon you in his Epilogue to *Granado*, 1 Part;[2] where he says,

> —*They who write Ill, and they who ne'er durst write,*
> *Turn Criticks out of meer Revenge and Spite.*

By your Writing, you do appear to be one of those Spiteful Criticks, who, like old crabbed-fac'd Maids, wish there were no such things as Beauty and Husbands, because they have none; and do so malice those who have, that they will Paint and Patch at Threescore years old to get them Beauty and Husbands; making themselves Baboons on Earth, for fear of leading Apes in Hell. The onely Defence I can make for you, is the same Quibling Excuse your Generosity conferr'd on

---

[1] The first not identified; the others by Ben Jonson.
[2] In fact, the Prologue to Part II.

Mr. *Dreyden*, which was—*That he writ as well as any man*—*that could write no better.*

Now as for Mr. *Dreyden*, all these Errours wherewith he hath been tax'd, are so few and inconsiderable, that nothing but a self-conceited Envie could have spy'd: which implies, either that he never committed great Crimes, or that you had not the Wit to finde them; to whom Mr. *Dreyden* makes this Application, in his Prologue to *Maximin*:

> *They* [then] *who of each Trip the advantage take,*
> *Finde but those Faults which they want wit to make.*

15. The Athenian Virtuosi answered

1673

Another defence of Dryden against the *Rota* (see Nos. 12, 13, 14), published anonymously in London with the title, *A Description of the Academy of the Athenian Virtuosi: With a Discourse held there in Vindication of Mr. Dryden's Conquest of Granada; Against the Author of the Censure of the Rota.*

No sooner does any person merit the bewitching name of a good Author, but he has the happiness to meet with envy; yet every one who will not spare the perishing paper deserves not this title, though he caress his Reader with those flattering Epithets of *gentle*, and *candid*, since even the Stationer sometimes circumvents your good opinion with the same appellatives. But such an Authour who seems to command his fame rather than receive it from the world, he like moral vertue (which is plac'd between two opposites of excess and defect) shall be sure to find a Parallel opposition from two sorts of vitious Criticks. I may justly stile them so, the one a poor dwindled Critick, who is in that defect of wit and judgement, that his endeavour is only to be thought to have a small portion, by the detracting of them in

another. The other is in that excess of conceit that he cannot forbear
to discover by his own vanity his judgement to be illegitimate. Now
no place abounds with more witty writers, and worse judges than this
City of *London*, whilst true Criticks are more moderate, being conscious of those peccadilloes, that every Writer as man must be subject
to. They know that expert *Homer* sometimes may be took napping;
therefore they willingly allow Poets with Painters to rove in a large
field of fancy, often repeating,

—*hanc veniam petimusque damusque vicissim*,[1]

and as wise men think themselves generally too green to fall on and
Criticize, remembering that Maxime of Longinus, a better judge sure
than any of these dare ever aspire to be, ἡ τῶν λόγων κρίσις πολλῆς
ἐστι πέιρας τελευταῖον ἐπιγέννημα,[2] that Criticisme must be the
deliberation of much experience. But these bastard Criticks without
any examination convict any Author and presently suspend him: but
who gave them this authority? I am sure they were never qualified
for the place by Nature, or by Art; how then can any one expect the
least justice from them, when their Justice only holds a sword in her
hands without any scales, and may be accounted blind from her
ignorance, and not from impartiality? Since then I am to speak to the
Athenian Virtuosi, I hope it may be lawful to borrow two Greek words
which will more emphatically denote them. There be some that damn
a book οὐκ ἑρμηνέυσαντες, that is, not interpreting or understanding
the Author, and these in our English tongue are called *Fopps*, Persons
whose judgement lyes alwayes in the ear never in the brain, who hear
what others say, and then speak like them: they are just like an Eccho,
a reiterating voice, and nothing else: as Poets are painted licking up
what old *Homer* let fall, so these lap up the Critical vomit which another has ejected. What judgement can they give of a book whose
palat is solely Critical, and they were never at any time stil'd judges,
unless when with the cusp of their tongue they could determine of the
virtue or vice of a glass of *Burgundy*, and as one said well when he
forbad any one to read his book with prejudice, or after dinner, these
very persons, for these two reasons since their heads are alwaies fill'd
with prejudice, and the fumes of a full stomach, by all sober men are
thought unfit to be of a Jury.

The other sort are παρερμηνέυσαντες, or as they are called by others

---

[1] 'This indulgence we beg and give in turn' (Horace, *De Arte Poetica*, l. 11.).
[2] *On the Sublime*, vi: 'Judgment in literature is the last fruit of mature experience.'

ὑπερπερικριτικοί, persons which do not only interpret badly, which they do, but also doe it wilfully. I can only fancy them a sort of vermin with very little eyes, but many teeth, and nailes, who though they cannot doe much harm, by reason of their weakness, yet strive to make up that want with their malice. These creatures for the most part live by knawing of books, and never leave nibling, till they can make some hole to discover some imperfection, whilst they deface the book of its native beauties, and expose those faults which themselves have made. Thus having show'd you the malignity of these animals, being inclin'd by a strong habit to inhumanity, they are like butchers, not to be permitted to sit upon the life and death of an Author. Such as these who think themselves Criticks, but are not so, have endeavour'd to traduce the writings of Mr. *Dryden*, when true Criticks, if they would, are asham'd to decry them, whilst others that are more modest than to be pretenders, justly admire them. As for my self, I never had the satisfaction of his acquaintance, which frees me from the suspicion of an *officious vindication*, yet I do know him, though far better in his Playes, and what has been my misfortune to want in the society of the father, has been some way made up in the ingenious and pleasant company of the children.

Some weeks ago there came out the *Censure of the Rota on Mr. Dryden's Conquest of Granada*, which I lightly read over, for it deserv'd little consideration. Indeed I was surpriz'd at the indiscretion of the Author to venture his poor thinn Off-spring to seek its Fortune in cold winter weather, but especially in such a dangerous time, when there was great need of wast Paper. Alas, how could he help his weak book, though it made sad moan, crying out,

Deferor in vicum vendentem thus & odores.[1]

Poor Author he imagin'd no harm, he only made use of the *Saturnalia*, as servants used to doe, make bold with his betters, and so forth. Thus much I did then argue for his simplicity, finding him to be so obliging to Mr. *Dryden* as to pick excellencies out of his Play, on purpose to affront him, that many Readers believ'd, it design'd by one of his best freinds for a complement to show the world, that if any one attempted to wound his honour, the Archers vanity did not so much lye in abusing his time to split an hair, as to hit a thing out of his reach.

[1] 'I am carried into the street where they sell frankincense and spices' (Horace, *Epist.* II. i. 269).

The Author of the *Rota*
    — & est mihi saepe vocandus
    Ad partes,[1]

has show'd in his censure so little conversation with Greek and Latin, nay English Poets, as I shall prove by and by, that it is disputed by some, whether it was simplicity or madness provoked him to paint himself in colours so ridiculous. In all reason Mr. *Dryden* will give me little thanks, since the goodness of an ominous cause may lose much of its lustre by the badness of the Orator; yet let Mr. *Dryden* look on with some diversion, since he would not be himself should he seem at the least concern'd, whilst his laurel which he deservedly wears has sufficient virtue to defend it self from the *bruta fulmina*[2] of any loose tongue.

Now give me leave to tell you, that having read the *Censure*, I had a great desire to find out the place where this *Cabal* sat: so one day meeting with one of my acquaintance, I ask'd him if he had read such a Pamphlet, he told me, he had lost so much time as to read it, and if I would goe with him he would bring me to their *Academy* which was a large room in a Coffee-house kept for them, where thrice a week they met retir'd from company, but of late since the Printing of the *Censure*, they find none so hardy as to answer it, they have admitted a free access, with design, I believe, that they telling the threats of the *Virtuosi*, and with what severity the Answerer is sure to be handled, might deterr the Writer from any further proceeding, and make him consult his safety in the throwing away of his pen. I very gladly embrac'd this newes, and bid him lead the way. We came soon to the place, and somewhat too soon, for the *Athenian Virtuosi*, to give them their beloved title, were not yet come, and the door-keeper said he durst not let any in, before the *Virtuosi* came, lest the room should be crowded, and several curiosities by handling be misplac'd; but I knew what the Fellow drove at, so gently tickling him in the hand, he let us in, where we prov'd him a lyar, by finding some company expecting, and one man with a goose-quill in his ear very busily marshalling books, paper, and pens: Asking one of the company who he was, I was answer'd he was *Secretary* to the *Society*; a worthy employment, thought I, and without doubt a worthy person; I presently made my address to him, desiring to know how long it would be before the

[1] [Who] has often to be called to his lessons.
[2] Heavy thunderbolts.

Athenian Virtuosi met? The clean beast, after much chewing of the cud, answer'd, it would be *Thirty minutes*. I admir'd at the periphrasis of the Secretary of the Criticks, but I left him, fearing to disgust the man, having more mind to view the Academy. The first thing I beheld, was o'r the chimney instead of a chimney-peice a Label held up in the beakes of two Owles, and in it these words written,

> The *Coffee-Academy of the Athenian Virtuosi*
> *instituted by* Apollo *for the advancement*
> *of Gazet-Philosophy, Mercurie's Diurnals, &c.*

and underneath these words written,

> Οἱ τῶν κριτικῶν κριτικώταγοι.[1]

Having read the Label I told my Friend the design of the Owles was very natural, because they were birds sacred to *Minerva*, and the *Virtuosi* went under the notion of *Athenians*; but that their Academy should be under the patronage of *Apollo*, I thought was not regular to the traditions of poetry, nor any way agreeing with history; and I wondred that these Criticks in poetry should be so over-seen. My Friend told me he admired at the absurdity, but who must judge the Criticks? He proceeded with the belief, that these were not Owles, but two of the *Virtuosi*, since they resembled the nature of those birds, being afraid to come abroad and spy faults fairly by the light of reason, lest they should be peckt at by every puny writer, and prosecuted with all the scorn, and derision imaginable, but love to flutter about in the dark, and make a noise in the twilight of prejudice. I then askt him, why the Academy thought it fit, to place it self in a Coffee-house, since it was instituted by *Apollo*; it had been more agreeable to have been in a Tavern; O, said he, that may be for many reasons, first, as well to hinder expences, as to vindicate the sober inclinations of the persons; since they intended to tax the manners of a poet as well as his writings, it was convenient at least to be hypocrites, and to disguise their own; and Coffee being esteem'd by its admirers a suppresser of fumes, and a great friend to the memory, they might be so simple to hope, it would put *idæas* into their heads, that were never there before: he added that they were inventing a drink for their own use of Helle-bore, and other ingredients, which will so refine their gross conceptions, that at length they should be rendred so acute as to make faults in the writings of any man. Or perhaps another reason is for the better

---

[1] 'The critic-commanders of the critics.'

divulging the fame of the *Virtuosi*, since persons of all qualities from all parts resorted to such places. I told him that could be no great reason, for they might hire a poor fellow for a small matter who would soon call the multitude together with a trumpet, or they might steal the Tablet from the Scriveners shop, wherein is written, The Office of Intelligence, and hang it at their street door, where when any poet shall come in he may be certified whether any longer he shall have fame or no fame, whether that shall live or die after death, whether poetry should be to him a rich wife or a poor wife, or whether he should have many children by her, and all this, without the help of *judicial Astrology*: and I further told him, I should rather call this place a *Lottery* than an *Academy*, since that was more usual in a Coffee-house, and a good poet in this place might draw twenty blanks before one prize; and I wisht that speaking of false wit, as well as false newes, had been lyable to the punishment of the proclamation. Having paraphras'd a little upon this inscription, we look't about, and beheld that on one side of the room were set up the heads of many Grammarians, and Criticks, and on the other side the heads of Greek and Latin and some English poets, amongst whom I wondred at these mighty three, *Hopkins*, *Sternhold*, and *Wild*, DD,[1] but I was soon pacified when I found *Chœrilus* amongst the Greeks, and *Bathyllus*[2] amongst the Latins; and why should any good Author repine, that he is excluded, may not the *Virtuosi* set up whom they please, may they not set up their own heads, nay upon poles, if they please, in their own room? But I ask'd my Friend why Dr. *Wild* wore a different wreath from all the rest; when every one else had one of *Bayes*, he had one of *Herrings*? My Friend told me he heard the reason of a Gentleman that was here the other night. The Author of the Censure of the *Rota*, you must know, is very intimate with Dr. *Wild*, and was with him eating of Herrings, when his Spouse run out with a herrings tail bobbing in her mouth, to receive the Letter from the Post which brought the joyful newes of his Majesties toleration. Now this Academy being instituted, and several poets heads being to be set up, a Letter was dispatched to Dr. *Wild* to invite him to be Prolocutor to the *Virtuosi*, (since it is well known, he writes as malitiously and as poorly as any of them) but in the close they ask'd him, since 'twas the honour the Academy intended him, whether his head should be set amongst the

---

[1] Sternhold and Hopkins, Tudor versifiers of the Psalms; and the broadsheet poetaster Dr Robert Wild (1609–79).
[2] Bad classical poets.

Criticks, or the Poets, (and indeed he might very well be either) he
return'd them great thanks for the great honour they design'd him,
but as for that weighty place to be Prolocutor, he begg'd some time to
consider on it: As to the other favour of being set up, either as Poet or
Critick, he told them plainly, he was ambitious of both, and did not
much care if his head was divided, and half set amongst the Poets, and
half amongst the Criticks; but on second thoughts, he referr'd all
to their better Judgments, with this *proviso*, if they should see him
amongst the Poets, he might wear a wreath of *Herrings*, since they
alwayes brought him good luck, when he had any thing to do with
them, wondring why *Will. Lilly*[1] could never find good omens hoarded
up for him in the house of *Pisces*. So in fine he kiss'd their hands with
this resolution, that he did not doubt but they would become him
better than his *Bayes*. For this reason you see him thus adorn'd, and I
was told last night that the Academy finds him more pliant than ever,
and are in great hopes of obtaining that malitious person to strengthen
their party. Since he hates innocent ceremonies, and beauty in the
Church, why may he not abhorr them in any thing? Having wearyed
our eyes with these objects, we turn'd about, and at the end of the
room were three *presses*, without any *books* in them, with *Optimi*
written upon the first, *Mediocres* upon the second, and *Mali* upon the
third, which presses I soon imagin'd to be the *Thecæ*[2] for books, as
they were esteem'd of by the *Virtuosi*. I laughing ask'd my Friend
which he thought the worst (with leave from the Criticks) either
Mediocres, or *Mali*? But he told me it were better to let this paradox
alone now, and pass on, lest we should be prevented by their coming.
So walking up the room we found whole rowes of *teeth*, and many
nailes sow'd upon cloath, and pinn'd to the hanging; and looking more
earnestly, I perceiv'd that most of them were such as we call doggs
teeth.[3] I could not imagine at present that these were meant to make
good my simile, I apply'd to them; nor did I think that the *Virtuosi*
were Toothdrawers. Yet they would be glad that their adversaries
teeth and nailes were drawn, for even then a lyon would be an innocent
beast. But a little further we beheld many engins of torture: here indeed
was the scene of death, here was one book suspended, another torn
upon a tenterhook, a third dead from a stab receiv'd from a cruel
Penknife; drawing nearer I found them all belonging to Mr. *Dryden*.

[1] The astrologer.
[2] Cases.
[3] Canines, fangs.

Here lay *Almanzor* stretcht upon the rack, that pain might force out words far distant from his thoughts; here the *Maiden Queen* lay deflowr'd, and there the *Indian Emperour* was defac'd with the scratches of a barbarous stile. Whilst my Friend and I were finding a name fit to decry these most unjust proceedings, we heard the door unlock, and the door-keeper cry out, Make room there for *Aristarchus, Scribonius,* and *Opilius,* make room I say for *Hyginus, Palæmon,* and *Orbilius.* I was amaz'd at these thundring names, considering whether or no, the Academy design'd this for an exemplary distich; at last I remembred these were great Criticks, and Grammarians, and that *Orbilius* was *Horace*'s School-master, and had whipt him often for not learning his lesson in old *Livius Andronicus,* wherefore he was stil'd by him *plagosus.*[1] Now thought I, these *Virtuosi* imitate the Popes, As they assume the gentle names of *Innocent, Clement,* and *Pius,* when they are *bloody, unmerciful,* and *irreligious,* so these wear the names of great Grammarians, whilst they all deserve with naked posteriors to tremble under the falling rod of the fierce *Orbilius.* They had scarce plac'd themselves, when more came in, but were Anonymous, 'twas no matter, I could tell who and what they were, by this gleek[2] of circumstances, the shrug, the shaking of the head, and tossing back the peruke with indignation: they had just reacht the table, when the door-keeper with a great deal of breath cry'd out, *Make room for Cassus the Author of the Censure of the Rota*; bless me, said I to my Friend, why is he called *Cassus*? Why, said he, I will tell you, he affects that name being delighted with the story of a certain poet called *Cassus,* who writ so much, that his very papers suffic'd to burn him when he was dead; he has vow'd to scribble so much if he lives. Alas, he values not the quality, so there be quantity, he is resolv'd to keep his vow, and to write any thing against any body: he has many general Pamphlets ready, that as soon as any new book is out with a little alteration, whip, he carryes them to the bookseller, he is a perfect *Stubbist,*[3] who though he must for ever despair to have those parts, and that learning, yet has attain'd to that likeness in his will to contradict every one. I smil'd at the strangeness of his humour, and whilst he was held in some serious discourse, by one as he was coming on, I wondred at the elocution of his gestures, he would so knit his browes, and work the

[1] *Epist.* II. i. 70.

[2] Set of three cards; hence, trio.

[3] After Philip Stubbes, Puritan pamphleteer and author of *The Anatomie of Abuses* 1583).

muscles of his mouth. I assur'd my self he was in labour, and us'd that midwifery to bring his imaginations to the birth: when he was delivered, he was a great enemy to the mans buttons, and would so stare in his face, forcing him to a smile, which he took for approbation, when the poor man did it only to be rid of him. Being sat down he bid the Secretary bring the teeth and the nailes; at this I concluded that these Criticks really us'd them in biting, and tearing other mens works; and I was confirm'd in this opinion, when I perceiv'd every one busy, but most of all *Cassus*, setting some of the sharpest of them into his upper jaw, where I presume he had lately broke some of them out in medling with some piece of Mr. *Dryden's Conquest of Granada*, that prov'd too hard for his teeth. Now every one having fitted himself with tusks, and talons, *Aristarchus* rose up, and made a short speech. It was an *Encomium* upon the *Virtuosi*, and the happiness of this age, wherein such judicious persons had taken the great trouble, for the benefit of mankind, to give each Poet that desert which their examination should allow him. After this *Scribonius* told them, that Mr. *Dryden* derided their *Censure*, and held the *Virtuosi* in that contempt, as if they were not; Does he so, sayes *Cassus*, does *Almanzor* despise those that would reclaim his rage? I would Mr. *Dryden* were here, or any of his admirers to speak for him; Secretary, bring hither his *Conquest of Granada*, and there I could show him innumerable Errataes; with that he opened the Play, and scratching the leaves very carelesly, cry'd out, here 's a fault, and there 's a fault, where is there not a fault, if we will make them so, dares he, or any one deny it? At this dull impertinency, I could not forbear smiling; which *Cassus* perceiving, ask'd me, if I would be so bold as to defend him? I told him, if he would draw up Mr. *Dryden's* faults under some heads that I might make my plea, I would endeavour to take off his objections. Why then, said he, if you have perpended my *Censure*, as I cogitate you have, you may there animadvert, that the Author Scholastically prosecutes Mr. *Dryden dupliciter*. *Primò*, for the irrationality of the transcendentality of his *Idæa's*. *Secundò*, for his superbosity, in prostrating the fame of defunct, and breathing Authors. I was so startled to hear *Cassus* alter his stile, that turning about to ask what tongue he spoke in, my Friend imagining my surprize told me in my ear, that *Cassus* was a great *Term-driver*, and had two wayes of speaking, the one more moderate, as I had heard, and this last was in use, when he would stupify a shopkeeper, confound a chambermaid, or puzzle his antagonist. Having now consider'd the meaning, I told him, if I might obtain a patient ear, I would make some answer. At this, Cassus called for his breast-plate, on which was writ, *The Author of the Censure of the Rota*: it serv'd both for pride and for defence, I wish he would wear it alwayes in the streets, for then if he should chance to lose his way, he would never be lost, but be sent home by a Bedle safe to the Academy. Having arm'd himself, *Eja age*,[1] said he, if you will act in any *Hypothesis* dissentaneous to this famous Circle, I my self provocate you to a contrary ratiocination, and *Cassi gratiâ* the *Virtuosi* will give you auscultation. After I had blow'd my nose, I thus began. Your first objection (O *Virtuosi Athenian*) is in the language of *Cassus* against the irrationality of the transcendantality of Mr. *Dryden's Idæas*, which for my contrymens sake, I thus faithfully render into English, against the unreasonable extravagance of Mr. *Dryden's* conceptions, which ye have strove with much labour to find in his *Conquest of Granada*: so whilst I am defending that, I shall all the while vindicate an Heroick poem, which must be by showing you, what the Masters of Poetry esteem to be its latitude, in what consists its grandeur, and what renders it uncapable of that title. As for its latitude, I must lay down before you the definition of its subject, which is Heroick vertue. By *Aristotle* it is called divine, not because it was peculiar to the Gods, but when a man was endued with this vertue, it elevated him above mankind, and as much as humane nature could be, it rendred him like a Deity; therefore it is defin'd by the best Moralists, a habit of mind not attain'd by humane industry, but inspir'd from above, to undergo great actions with an irresistable violence, and a most happy success, which other mortals were not able to perform. Without doubt Mr. *Dryden* made his *Almanzor* after this original, making him to do things above nature though not against it, placing in his soul humanity and fierceness mingled together, and him in a sphere rather nearer the *Hero* of *Homer*, than of *Scudery*.[2] Not so much a Greek as to imitate *Achilles* in his ferity, nor so Frenchified as to admire the stupidity of *Oroondates* in weeping at the feet of his Mistress. Since Mr. *Dryden* in this description has followed the precepts of Philosophy, all unprejudic'd Men with reason must speak for *Almanzor*, that with *Achilles* Mr. *Dryden* has rendred him invulnerable, unless his detractors by wounding him in the heel, will discover as much their fear as their baseness. I think there is no need to urge this clear point any further, but to pass on and to tell you, in what consists its grandeur. It is plac'd by all in a lofty stile, and in the rapture of a Poet. Look up

---

[1] 'Come on then!'

[2] Madeleine de Scudéry (1607–1701), romance-writer.

(O *Athenian Virtuosi*) and see my witnesses! O *Homer* dost thou hear this illiterate Censure,

> *Nec labra moves, cum mittere vocem*
> *Debueras, vel marmoreus vel aheneus?*[1]

Were ye but acquainted with him he would tell ye, that he makes his *Achilles* speak ἔπεα πτερόεντα, winged words. Ask but *Pindar*, he will assure you that he never adorns his Heroes but he must let fly expressions, which he calls (*Olymp.* 9) ὀϊστοὺς, arrowes, which do in another place κελαδέονη, make a noise. Surely if we had not lost his pæans, his dithyrambicks, or his tragedies, we should have found in them far bolder flights. Yet the generous *Thebans* thought his numbers only lofty, never extravagant. The divinity of such well built lines crown'd him even whilst he liv'd, and sav'd his house when he was dead. This mighty spirit of Poetry is admir'd in *Alcæus*, and stil'd by *Dion. Halicarnasseus* in as mighty words,

> Ἀλχαίου σκόπει τὸ μεγαλοφυὲς, [&c.]

Consider the mighty spirit of *Alcæus*, what sweetness there is even in its terrour. This is that which *Virgil* aimes at, when he sayes,

> —*Paulo majora canamus.*[2]

And *Lucan* when he sayes,

> *Surgat mihi carminis ordo.*[3]

This is that which *Horace* names (*Serm.* 10. *lib.* 1. [l. 43]) *Forte epos*, a strong Heroick verse. For this, *Martial* praises *Virgil* calling him *Cothurnatus*, and his Heroick Poem (*lib.* V. [v. 8] *Grande opus.*) *Juvenal* describes such a Poet with the title of *egregius*, and with *Sat.* 7. [ll. 53–7, 70] *qualem nequeo monstrare, & sentio tantùm*, he knew not how to express him, this made him fancy *Virgil* like a fury, and tells us that if he had been poor,

> —*caderent omnes à crinibus hydri.*[4]

'Twas in this the critick *Longinus* said *Juvenal* excell'd τῇ πομπικῇ λέξει,

---

[1] 'Marble or bronze, you do not move your lips when you are obliged to speak.'
[2] *Ecl.* iv. 1, 'let us sing in a loftier strain.'
[3] '[I am uncertain where] the order of the poem I write should start' (*Laus Pisonis*, l. 1, formerly attributed to Lucan. We owe the reference to Mr G. R. Watson).
[4] An 'excellent' poet, 'such as I cannot describe but only feel'; 'all the symbols of poetry would have dropped from his locks.'

a pompous expression; And this is that which the judicious Greeks call'd πάν ἐκ διαθέσεως γράφειν οὐκ ἀπὸ τῶν χειλῶν, [to write] with a resolution, and not superficially.

My last design is to lay before you what renders an Heroick Poem uncapable of its title.

Pindar will tell you (*Olymp.* 9) that if he would delineate an *Hero*, he must abstain from Χαμαιπετέων λόγων, from words that are flat and creeping upon the earth. *Virgil* sayes in his sixth Eclog, that *Apollo* admonish'd him in his ear as unfit to sing of Kings and battels, having used himself in his Pastorals to a humble verse,

—*Pastorem Tityre pingues*
Pascere oportet oves, deductum dicere carmen.[1]

Horace is then exalted when he speaks *Nil parvum, aut humili modo. lib. 3. Ode 25.*[2] And in his *Arte Poetica* laughs at that Poet for not continuing his heroick Poem with the same gallantry; and for his obedience brands him with,

Quid dignum tanto feret hic promissor hiatu?[3]

Juvenal allowes a flat verse no better name than *Carmen triviale. Sat. 7.* [l. 55.]. And *Martial* hates it, calling it *carmen supinum. lib. 2.* [86] and presently after, *Mollem debilitate Galliambon,* a Languid verse fit only for the mouth of *Cybele's* effeminate Priests. Sure what the Epigrammatist thinks unfit for himself, an Heroick Poet must be asham'd to use.

These few Testimonies out of a crowd, I have produced to complement the Academy, but if I have spoke in an unknown tongue I wish I had been better inform'd of your ignorance, that I might not have given my self the trouble. Therefore to speak to your capacities, I will bring all these witnesses in one, I mean the immortal *Cowley*, than whom none knew better to make or judge a Poem. In praising of Sr. *Wm. Davenants Gondibert,* he seems to characterize Mr. *Dryden's* Conquest of *Granada*:

> *Thy mortals do their Gods excel,*
> *Taught by thy Muse to fight, and love so well.*
> *So God-like Poets do past things rehearse,*
> *Not change, but heighten Nature, by their Verse.*

---

[1] 'A shepherd should feed fat sheep, Tityrus, and sing slender songs.'
[2] 'No trivial or low song (for me).'
[3] l. 138, transl. Roscommon, 'In what will all this Ostentation end?'

Thus I have with hasty touches drawn out the masculine beauty of an Heroick Poem; now if this censur'd play of Mr. *Dryden*'s be of it self exact and true, if it is fram'd by the rules of art, and keeps it self strict to the laws and canons of ancient Poets, as many of his envious enemies acknowledge, if you tear off the title page, and represent it without any relation to him, then this impertinent Censure without any violence will of it self fall to the ground, being supported by so weak a foundation as prejudice. When Criticks shall be found to be like foolish Parishioners, who in themselves commend what they hear, untill they look up, then they mistake the man, and by their consequence the Sermon. Thus the Conquest of *Granada*, as Conquest of *Granada*, is a very good play, but as made by Mr. *Dryden* fit to be exploded, when all Poets from *Homer* down to *Ben*, were esteem'd good, if their Judges could ascribe to them *Ciceroes* commendation *Pro Archia Poeta; mentis viribus excitari, & quasi divino quodam spiritu afflari.*[1] But Mr. *Dryden* because he goes by his own name, must not have the essence of a Poet, that is fiction, nay he must lose the portion of a son, and with quiet render up, or else those goodly fields of fancy, the uninterrupted inheritance of his forefathers must be confiscated because he has offended this Committee. His Muse must turn Quaker, or else be accounted light; she must have nothing to do with that goodly pride of figures, conceits, raptures, and sentences, without which gawdy retinue Mr. *Cowley*'s Muse never took the air.

I know the sons of the Poets have far less revenues, than their forefathers enjoy'd. The Greek Poets besides the other five, had a whole dialect appropriated to themselves, they might sound out ἄρες ἄρες[2] without offence. This made *Martial* complain in his time, that they could not renew the same lease, but had lost many of their priviledges; yet it was very well with them, if we consider the inconveniencies of their children, whilst the barbarous Criticks of these times are so whimseycal, and so unjust, as to allow some their own freedomes, and some none. If Mr. *Dryden* upon necessity uses *Enallage numeri*[3] when Greek and Latin commanded it, and English Poets very often make use of it, since the idiom of our tongue will bear it in prose, but better in verse, it is put down for an unpardonable enormity. I will

---

[1] [The poet] is aroused by mental activity, is infused with a supernatural inspiration (adapting *Pro Archia* viii. 18).

[2] Ares, given both long and short quantities by Homer, *Iliad* v. 31; *cf.* Martial, *Epi.* IX. xii. 15.

[3] A change of words.

forbear quotations to prove this known point, lest I prove my self Pedantick, and you more absurd.

If Mr. *Dryden*, as *Persius, librat in Antithetis*,[1] that is, use a seeming contradiction, which in all poets is and must be esteem'd wit, shall nevertheless wilfully be damned by the Academy, as in your Censure,

> *Thus in the triumphs of soft peace I reign,*
> *And from my walls, defie the powers of Spain*,[2]

O the stupidity of the *Virtuosi*! it would puzzle any one to imagine what they aime at here: these Cricks sure have pick'd them out for some default, so that I am forc'd to imagine this.

Pray observe this kind of excellency in two of the best Poets, *Virg.* [*Aen.*] II. speaking of *Camilla* [ll. 694–5]:

> *Orsilochum fugiens, magnumque agitata per orbem*
> *Eludit gyro interior, sequiturque sequentem.*[3]

Mr. *Cowley* in his *Dav*[*ideis*] *lib.* I. speaking of writing, and as it were prophesying what this Academy, and *Cassus* especially intends to do;

> *And with her spurious brood loads now the press,*
> *Laborious effects of idleness.*

I will add no more, though these great Poets delight much in them, yet be it spoken to your folly, that 'tis your unhappiness to light upon an accurate verse to vilifie your selves, not him, and since 'tis drawn out, may it be apply'd to you all, that there were more hopes of Triumphs by peace, than by this unsuccessful war.

If Mr. *Dryden* applyes an happy Epithete 'tis traduc'd, as in these excellent verses, speaking of *Almanzor*,

> *A gloomy smile arose*
> *From his bent browes, and still the more he heard,*
> *A more severe, and sullen joy appear'd,*[4]

which I am certain is in imitation of *Virgil*, where fierce *Mezentius* stands,

> *Olli subridens, mixta Mezentius ira,*[5]

[1] *Sat.* i. 86.
[2] *Conquest of Granada*, First Part, I. i.
[3] 'She fled Orsilochus and, wheeling in a great sweep, eluded him by taking the inner circle, and pursued the pursuer.'
[4] *Supra*, p. 59.
[5] *Aen.* x. 742.

which Mr. *Cowley* renders finely, *with half a smile, and half a frown,* or as it is in *Claudian IV. Cons. Honorii.*

> —*Torva voluptas*
> *Frontis,*[1]

and in many places of this Poet; but I shall hasten. If Mr. *Dryden* makes his verse run musically, or fills it with an argument, it is call'd tick-tack, as thus:

> *Know that as* Selin *was not won by thee,*
> *Neither will I, by* Selins *daughter be.*
> *Would you your hand in* Selins *blood embrue,*
> *Kill him unarm'd, who arm'd shunn'd killing you,*[2]

whilst you are ignorant he imitates *Ovids* humour in these neat numbers, *Met. lib.* 10. [ll. 317–8]:

> *Ex omnibus unum*
> *Elige Myrrha virum, dum non sit in omnibus unus;*[3]

and again in his 9. *lib.* [ll. 487–8]:

> *Quam bene Caune tuo poteram nurus esse parenti,*
> *Quam bene Caune meo poteras gener esse parenti;*[4]

and in his Epistles,

> *O Jove digna viro, ni Jove nata fores.*[5]

The Original is esteem'd by all good judges, and why do you condemn the true copy, but because you are bad? If Mr. *Dryden* heightens the sence with a simile, it is not like to pass, when all Poets ever use it, and an Heroick proclaims with *Pindar, Olymp.* XI, he cannot be without it.

> Ἔστι ἀνθρώποις ἀνέμων χρῆσις, ἔστι δ' οὐρανίων
> ὑδάτων &c., εἰ δὲ σὺν πόνῳ τὶς εὖ πράσσοι.

That in such cases as these, men must use the descriptions of winds, and waters &c. if they do labour to bring their work to a good effect.

---

[1] 'the grim pleasure of the brow.'

[2] *Supra,* p. 61.

[3] 'Choose one man from all these, Myrrha, so that among them all there shall not be one man'—[your father].

[4] 'How happily, Caunus, I could become the daughter-in-law of your father; how happily, Caunus, you could become the son-in-law of my father!'

[5] *Heroides,* xvi. 272: 'O worthy to have Jove as a husband, if you were not born from Jove.'

If Mr. *Dryden* illustrates his Poems, with spirits and immaterial beings, this cannot disgust any one, but the *Sadduces* of the age, who believe they have none, since as a Poet he may lawfully make use of them: for what Heroick Poet is there either Greek or Latin, that does not introduce very often θεὸν ἀπὸ μηχανῆς[1]: yet as a philosopher he will be defended by the Pythagorical, and Platonical opinion, which held these regions of the air under the concave of the Moon to be inhabited by *Dæmons*. If Mr. *Dryden* keeps the signification of words within their limits, you will venture to call him vagabond, though you declare your selves absolutely unacquainted with authors, or grammar, as in this fragment of a verse,

Thou treadst the abyss of light.[2]

You assert here that abyss is so inconsistent with light, that 'tis scarce bright enough for its shadow, whilst by proving the contrary let the world judge, if the darkness of your understanding, does not advantage the lustre of Mr. *Dryden*'s glory. Abyss properly signifies extream deep waters, *quasi* ἄνευ βύσσου,[3] an Ionick word for βύθον. This *Favorinus* and *Hesychius*, this *Minshæus* and *Vossius* with others, account the truest etymologie of the word, yet with *Calepine* grant, that it may be usurped, as it is by the Greeks, for an epithete to signifie any thing that is endless, which is prov'd by several Synonymous expressions of Scripture, and from St. *Chrysostome* who calls infinite labours πόνων ἄβυσσον.

This shall suffice O *Cassus* to prove thy ignorance, and little familiarity with classick authors, whilst this discovers thy malice, in making *Porphyrius* an Hermaphrodite by this verse,

And Daughter, I will give him you, for wife:[4]

Where as you please *Porphyrius* by misplacing the notional *comma* is either a man or a woman.

Thus like the Divel you æquivocate in your oracles, but at last like him you are found a lyar. I would willingly leave off defending Mr. *Dryden*, when he needs it not, was he not impeach'd with such animosity, for his strange flights, and that it may not be lawful for him to mount lest his wings be clipt, whilst *Horace* tells judicious *Mecænas*, he is turn'd into a Swan, and mounts and leaves these things below.

[1] *Deus ex machina*, a god by a theatrical device.
[2] *Supra*, p. 64.
[3] Without bottom.
[4] *Supra*, p. 60.

Whilst *Virgil* is sweetly Hyperbolical in many places, but especially in his description of *Camilla* . . .

[quotes *Aeneid* vii. 807–11]

And *Claudian Raptu Proser. lib.* 2. sayes . . .

[quotes ll. 198–9]

I will mention but one verse more of this Poet (though he is very luxuriant) in the end of the first book . . .

Ægra soporatis spumant oblivia linguis.[1]

Which I would beg the *Academy* if it can to translate hansomely into English. Yet *Julius Scaliger* gives this censure of him: *Fœlix in eo calor, temperatum judicium, dictio candida, numeri non affectati.*[2] I have the rather taken these Testimonies because as *Virgil* follow'd *Homer*, so Mr. *Cowley* has thought it fit to imitate them all, *Horace* in his Extasie, *Virgil* and *Claudian* in his description of *Asahel* . . .

[quotes *Davideis*, iii. 79–86]

I am in hast, and will forget *Seneca*'s Tragedies, historical *Lucan* and *Statius*, because Mr. *Dryden* is said to borrow many things from him, lest I should seem to produce him a witness for himself; let me only bring up the rear of my witnesses with one Testimony more of the much admir'd Mr. *Cowley* in his *Pindarick* call'd the Muse, he tells her,

Whatever God did say
Is all thy plain, and smooth uninterrupted way.
Nay even beyond his works thy voiages are known,
Thou hast thousand worlds too of thine own.
Thou speak'st great Queen, in the same stile as He,
And a new world leaps forth when thou say'st, let it be.

Sure he is more fit to set the bounds of Poetry than you, since all allow a Poet the same, what he allowes to *Mercury*, wings at head, and heel. The Poet is permitted by all to be

Commune profundis
Et superis numen, qui fas per limen utrumque
Solus habet, geminoque facit commercia mundo.[3]

[1] *De Raptu Proserpinae*, i. 281, 'let wretched oblivion foam from their slumbrous lips.'
[2] 'In him a happy ardour, restrained judgment, pure diction, unstudied numbers.'
[3] 'A spirit common to both the lower and upper worlds, who alone has the right to cross both thresholds and traffics with both worlds.'

Now who are ye (O *Athenian Virtuosi*) that dare set these narrow limits? must the Poet like *Alexander* repine there are no more worlds but this of yours to move in, where he shall soon lose his feet for want of exercise? If Mr. *Dryden* passes your little *Rubicon*, must he be proclam'd an enemy by this Senate, must his verses be like *Pliny's Acephali*, or rather resemble his judges, all feet, and excrement, and no head? I will stop here, ye have prov'd your selves, I will not make you any more ridiculous, only appealing to you whether or no this Academy does not represent an *Hobbian* state of nature,[1] in presuming to have as great a share in wit and judgment as others.

I am at last come to my second objection, which is Mr. *Dryden's* superbosity in prostrating the fame of defunct, and breathing Authors, which I shall thus translate, Mr. *Dryden's* pride in contemning dead, and living Authors. To which I shall not speak much, because I am so great a stranger to him, therefore I can only produce his own words to vindicate their Master, and if he wrongs them no more in his thoughts than in his writings he may safely plead Not guilty. In his Essayes and prefaces, as he payes veneration to the dead, so he payes submission to the living: though he cannot admire any of them blindly. And it is so unjust a calumny to urge that he labours to pluck leaves from the Baies of *Ben. Johnson*, when he adds to them by stiling him incomparable, one to be admir'd for many excellencies. In his preface to *Maximin*, he does not pretend any thing of his own to be correct, but submits his faults to the mercy of the Reader, being as little apt to defend his own errours, as to find those of others. In his defence of his Epilogue he ascribes to dead Authors their just praises in those things where they have excell'd us; and in those where we contend with them for preheminence, he acknowledges the advantage to the age, and not to wit. There might be produc'd many places which do strongly pronounce his judicious modesty: if he discovers any faults in other Poets, 'tis because his are too severely handled by others, and the reason why he does disturb the dead, is only that they would rise, and plead for him, as he professes in his Epilogue to the *Conquest of Granada*:

> *'Tis not to brand them that their faults are shown,*
> *But by their errours to excuse his own.*

If in the feaver of his writing he has discover'd any passion, the impertinency of the age is to be blam'd for troubling him, otherwise he

---

[1] Opposed to a state of grace; and by Hobbes defined as a state of war in which 'every Man is Enemy to every Man'.

is more to be esteem'd for his judgment than censur'd for his heat. If he tells us that *Johnson* writ by art, *Shakespeare* by nature; that *Beaumont* had judgment, *Fletcher* wit, that *Cowley* was copious, *Denham* lofty, *Waller* smooth, he cannot be thought malitious, since he admires them, but rather skilfull that he knows how to value them.

Mr. *Dryden* shall answer in *Horace*'s words, when he had offended many in medling with *Lucilius*,

> *Tu nihil in magno doctus reprendis Homero?*
> *Nil comis tragici mutat Lucilius Atti?*
> *Non ridet versus Enni gravitate minores,*
> *Quum de se loquitur, non ut majore reprensis?*[1]

Martial makes a distich on *Homer*, for patching up his verses with τὸν δ' ἀπαμειβόμενος,[2] though this was done grinning, yet any one may give his censure of another, so it produces nothing but candour, and judgment, as *Persius* gives his opinion of *Horace* . . .

[quotes *Sat.* i. 116–18]

But not like you (O *Athenian Virtuosi*) make faults where there are none. If the *Fopps* of the age are stung, that they kick up dirt, no person can blame Mr. *Dryden* for lashing them, since it would grieve any one, nay it would raise the choler of any ingenious man to that degree against them, when such will be so inconsiderate, nay so absurd, to censure a Poet, whilst they themselves cannot write, and perhaps not read, with commendation. This stirr'd up many antient Poets, and what Poet ever escaped such sinful examiners? It vex'd *Martial*, that at last he told them his verses were bad, yet he challeng'd them to mend them,

> *Haec mala sunt, sed tu non meliora facis.*

After this manner Mr. *Dryden* has provok'd the miserable jury of this age, but much hansomer,

> *You blame those faults, which you want wit to make.*[3]

Mr. *Dryden* having rebated the edge of all objections that can be

---

[1] *Sat.* I. x. 52–5: 'Do you, a scholar, find no fault in great Homer? Does the facetious Lucilius make no changes in Accius's tragedies? Doesn't he laugh at verses of Ennius which are too slight for the weight of the theme? When he speaks of himself, it isn't as superior to what he finds fault with.'

[2] 'Then answering him. . . .'

[3] Prologue to *Tyrannick Love* (incorrectly quoted).

brought to defend your assertion, it would appear very inconsistent
with modesty to alledge the arguments for my own; since he has
found so good, and I can find no better, and 'tis to himself he must
give the thanks, that he stands arm'd cap-a-pee. I will no longer give
my humanity the trouble, in reclaiming, if it were possible, your folly;
but only acquaint you that Mr. *Dryden* salutes you in a Semistanza of
your much honour'd *Hopkins*:[1]

> From all the sins that I have done,
> Lord quit me out of hand:
> And make me not a scorn to fools,
> That nothing understand.

At this *Cassus* started up, and told me, I was sawcy, not in observing
that decorum, which the gravity of the place requir'd. After some
whispering the door-keeper was commanded to clear the room, and
to take special notice of me, that I might be let no more into the
Academy, with the assurance that I should upon occasion be severely
dealt with for this rudeness. My Friend and I departed much pleas'd
with this scene of mirth: at his lodging we found a hypocritical
pamphlet against Mr. *Dryden* left by his book-seller; after a short view
I perceiv'd the needy Author plaid the plagiary, having transcrib'd all
those objections from *Cassus*, which *Cassus* had borrow'd from the
Rehearsal, whence 'tis easy to gather, that it is difficult to find fault with
Mr. *Dryden*, when his enemies are forc'd to tautologize. Indeed the
Burlesque way of writing is the most hopeful to abuse a good Author,
since the fantastick dress tickles the Reader, and makes him laugh
whether he will or no; and that the good old *Axiom* would hold here,
corruptio optimi fit pessima.[2] My Friend told me he was sorry we must
part so soon, having appointed to meet some persons hard by, amongst
whom he expected Mr. *Dryden*, promising me to find some other time
(if I thought it fit) to descant upon that book before us, and to divertise
me with some beloved fancies of *Cassus*. At this I took my leave,
desiring him to take his *Horace* with him, and to turn to *Serm*. 10. *lib*. 1.
where Mr. *Dryden* might read these verses out of his intimate acquaintance.

[quotes ll. 78–83; 'shall that insect Pantilius have any effect on
me ...']

---

[1] Versifier of the Psalms.
[2] 'The corruption of the best is the worst corruption.'

A Postscript.

Two things may here be inquir'd after, why Mr. *Dryden* is defended, since the unsavoury breath which proceeds from the fore-door of those windy Criticks, is to be regarded no more than that of the back-door, since they are both doom'd to the same date, to live for a moment and then to expire; but if he is defended, why so late, when delay will argue heaviness, or fear; indeed I neither bit my nailes nor scratch'd my head for this, nor will I conceit my Antagonist, like *Hercules*, a conquerour in his cradle, but rather, one of those Lapwing-writers, who venture to run with the shell on their backs,[1] the conscience of which rashness has alwaies so much deterr'd me, that this which was drawn up long agoe for my own diversion, should have slept in quiet, if the compliance to some had not been a motive to the contrary. Yet in this skirmish, I hope his presumption may be sufficient to keep me from despair.

[1] The new-hatched lapwing was said to run about with its head in the shell (*cf. Hamlet*, V. ii. 192).

16. Ravenscroft requites Dryden

1673

From the Prologue to *The Careless Lovers: A Comedy* (1673) by Edward Ravenscroft (1644–1707) of the Middle Temple, whose comedy *The Citizen turn'd Gentleman* (1672) had been ridiculed by Dryden in the 'Epilogue to *Secret-Love* Spoken by the Women' (*Covent Garden Drolery*, 1672) and the Prologue to *The Assignation* (1673). Ravenscroft says in his 'Epistle to the Reader' that his lines were 'Written in Requital to the *Prologue*, before the *Assignation*. ... But Devils of Wit are not very dangerous, and so we both sleep in whole Skins.'

They that observe the Humors of the *Stage*,
Find *Fools* and *Heroes* best do please this Age;
But both grown so extravagant, I scarce
Can tell, if *Fool* or *Hero* makes the better Farce,
As for Example, take our *Mamamouchi*,[1]
And then *Almansor*,[2] that so much did touch ye;
That Bully *Hero*, that did kill and slay,
And conquer ye *Ten Armies* in one day:
He that from side to side play'd *Runnegade*,
That Fought and Lov'd as if he had been mad.
He that gain'd Victory at ev'ry Stroke,
And made Kings tremble at each word he spoke; }
He that could Kill and Damne you with a Look. }
 Such are the *Heroes*, that with you are taking,
But such as never were of Heavens making:
Thus, whether *Grave* or *Comick* Scenes we write,
All 's turn'd to *Farce*, by *Hero*, or by *Knight*.

---

[1] The 'Paladin', played by Nokes to the delight of king and court, in Ravenscroft's *Citizen turn'd Gentleman*.

[2] In Dryden's *Conquest of Granada*. *Cf.* p. 50.

Without one of these Two it is decree'd
By all of you, that no *Play* shall succeed.
　An *Author* did to please you, let his Wit run
Of late, much on a *Serving-Man* and *Cittern*,
And yet you would not like the *Cerenade*,
Nay, and you Damn'd his *Nunns* in *Masquerade*.[1]
You did his *Spanish* Sing-Song too abhor,
Ayeque locura con tanto rigor.
In fine, the whole by you so much was blam'd,
To act their Parts, the *Players* were asham'd;
Ah! how severe your Malice was that Day,
To Damne at once, the *Poet* and his *Play*;
But why, was your Rage just at that time shown,
When what the *Poet* writ, was all his own?
Till then he borrow'd from *Romance*, and did Translate,
And those *Playes* found a more Indulgent Fate. ...

17. Wits and pedants

1673

From Dryden's Dedication of his comedy, *The Assignation* (1673),
to his friend Sir Charles Sedley (1639?–1701), dramatist and court
wit (Dryden's *Comedies, Tragedies, and Operas* (1701), i. 515–16).

Certainly the Poets of that [*Augustan*] Age enjoy'd much Happiness in
the Conversation and Friendship of one another. They imitated the
best way of Living, which was to pursue an innocent and inoffensive

[1] The sub-title of *The Assignation* is *Love in a Nunnery*. The first entry in the play is
made by Aurelian's servant Benito: 'There 's not a Street in all *Rome* which he does not
nightly disquiet with his villanous Serenade: with that Guitar there, the younger Brother
of a Cittern, he frights away the Watch. ...'

Pleasure; that which one of the Ancients called *Eruditam voluptatem*.[1]
We have, like them, our Genial Nights; where our Discourse is
neither too serious, nor too light; but always pleasant, and, for the
most part, instructive: the Raillery neither too sharp upon the Present,
nor too censorious on the Absent; and the Cups only such as will raise
the Conversation of the Night, without disturbing the Business of
the Morrow. And thus far not only the Philosophers, but the Fathers
of the Church have gone, without lessening their Reputation of good
Manners, or Piety. For this reason I have often laugh'd at the ignorant
and ridiculous Descriptions which some Pedants have given of the
Wits (as they are pleas'd to call them:) which are a Generation of Men
as unknown to them, as the People of *Tartary*, or the *Terra Australis*
are to us. And therefore as we draw *Giants* and *Anthropophagi* in those
Vacancies of our *Maps*, where we have not Travell'd to discover
better; so those Wretches paint Lewdness, Atheism, Folly, ill-Reason-
ing, and all manner of Extravagances amongst us, for want of Understanding what we are. Oftentimes it so falls out, that they have a
particular Picque to some one amongst us; and then they immediately
interest Heaven in their Quarrel; as 'tis an usual Trick in Courts, when
one designs the ruine of his Enemy, to disguise his Malice with some
Concernment of the King's; and to revenge his own Cause, with
Pretence of vindicating the Honour of his Master. Such Wits as they
describe, I have never been so unfortunate to meet in your Company:
But have often heard much better Reasoning at your Table, than I
have encounter'd in their Books. The Wits they describe, are the
Fops we banish. ... I am made a Detractor from my Predecessors,
whom I confess to have been my Masters in the Art. But ... I will be
no more mistaken for my good Meaning: I know I honour *Ben
Johnson* more than my little Critiques, because without Vanity I may
own, I understand him better. As for the Errors they pretend to find
in me, I could easily show them that the greatest part of them are
Beauties: And for the rest, I could recriminate upon the best Poets of
our Nation, if I could resolve to accuse another of little Faults, whom
at the same time I admire for greater Excellencies. But I have neither
Concernment enough upon me to write any thing in my own Defence,
neither will I gratifie the Ambition of two wretched Scriblers, who
desire nothing more than to be answer'd.[2] I have not wanted Friends,

[1] Quintilian, I. xii. 18: 'instructed pleasure'.
[2] The authors of *The Censure of the Rota* and *The Friendly Vindication* (see *supra*, Nos.
12 and 13).

even amongst Strangers, who have defended me more strongly, than my contemptible Pedant cou'd attack me. For the other, he is only like *Fungoso* in the Play, who follows the Fashion at a distance, and adores the *Fastidius Brisk* of *Oxford.* . . .[1]

[1] In Ben Jonson, *Every Man out of his Humour* (1600).

18. Marvell on *The State of Innocence*

1674

'On *Paradise Lost*', ll. 1–26 and 45–54; printed above the fore-
word on 'The Verse' in the second edition of *Paradise Lost* (1674).

'John Dreyden, Esq., Poet Laureate, who very much admires
[Milton], went to him to have leave to putt his *Paradise Lost* into
a Drame in rythme. Mr. Milton recieved him civilly, and told him
he would give him leave to tagge his Verses' (Aubrey, *Brief Lives*,
ed. O. L. Dick (1950), p. 203). The result was *The State of Innocence,
and Fall of Man: An Opera, Written in Heroique Verse*, probably
intended for the wedding celebrations of James, Duke of York,
and Mary of Modena at the end of 1673. It was not acted, says
Dryden; but 'many hundred Copies of it' were 'dispers'd abroad
without my knowledge or consent; so that every one gathering
new faults, it became at length a Libel against me' ('The Authors
Apology for Heroique Poetry', in the first edition of the opera,
1677).

Dryden and Andrew Marvell (1621–78) had both been in the
service of Cromwell's government; but they followed different
courses after the Restoration. In the Preface to *Religio Laici* (1682)
Dryden writes of the Elizabethan 'Martin Marprelate' as 'the
Marvel of those times ... the first Presbyterian Scribler, who
sanctify'd Libels and Scurrility to the use of the Good Old Cause'.

When I beheld the Poet blind, yet bold,
In slender Book his vast Design unfold,
Messiah Crown'd, *Gods* Reconcil'd Decree,
Rebelling Angels, the Forbidden Tree,
Heav'n, Hell, Earth, Chaos, All; the Argument
Held me a while misdoubting his Intent,
That he would ruine (for I saw him strong)
The sacred Truths to Fable and old Song

(So *Sampson* groap'd the Temples Posts in spight)
The World o'rewhelming to revenge his sight.
   Yet as I read, soon growing less severe,
I lik'd his Project, the success did fear;
Through that wide Field how he his way should find
O're which lame Faith leads Understanding blind;
Lest he perplex'd the things he would explain,
And what was easie he should render vain.
   Or if a Work so infinite he spann'd,
Jealous I was that some less skilful hand
(Such as disquiet always what is well,
And by ill imitating would excell)
Might hence presume the whole Creations day
To change in Scenes, and show it in a Play.
   Pardon me, Mighty Poet, nor despise
My causeless, yet not impious, surmise.
But I am now convinc'd, and none will dare
Within thy Labours to pretend a Share.

     .   .   .   .

   Well mightst thou scorn thy Readers to allure
With tinkling Rhime, of thy own sense secure;
While the *Town-Bayes*[1] writes all the while and spells,[2]
And like a Pack-horse tires without his Bells:
Their Fancies like our Bushy-points[3] appear,
The Poets tag them, we for fashion wear.
I too transported by the Mode offend,
And while I meant to Praise thee must Commend.[4]
Thy Verse created like thy Theme sublime,
In Number, Weight, and Measure, needs not Rhime.

[1] Dryden. See p. 45.
[2] Studies, ponders.
[3] Tasselled points for fastening hose.
[4] I.e. in order to complete the rhyme.

19. Rymer on *The Indian Emperour*

1674

The close of Thomas Rymer's Preface to his translation of Rapin's *Reflections on Aristotle's Treatise of Poesie* ... *with Reflections on the Works of the Ancient and Modern Poets, and their Faults noted.* Dryden's lines, 'All things are hush'd ...', are in *The Indian Emperour, or The Conquest of Mexico by the Spaniards* (1667), III. ii; 'made famous' (Dr. Johnson) by Rymer's criticism, they were often quoted and parodied (*cf.* Pope, *Dunciad*, ii. 418) during the eighteenth century.

Rymer (1643?–1713) was born near Northallerton and educated at Cambridge and Gray's Inn; seems not to have depended for his living on the practice of law; succeeded Shadwell as historiographer-royal in 1692. His other main critical works are *The Tragedies of the Last Age Consider'd* (1678) and *A Short View of Tragedy* (1692).

Any further *Reflections*, or more examples would be superfluous. What has been noted, rather concerns the Niceties of *Poetry*, than any the little trifles of *Grammar*. We have seen what the noblest Wits both ancient and modern, have done in other Languages, and observ'd that in their very Master-pieces they sometimes trip, or are however liable to Cavils. It now remains that our *English* be expos'd to the like impartial Censure.

> *All things are hush'd, as Nature's self lay dead,*
> *The Mountains seem to Nod their drowsie head,*
> *The little Birds in dreams their Songs repeat,*
> *And sleeping flowers beneath the Night-dew sweat,*
> *Even Lust and Envy sleep.*
> [In the Conquest of *Mexico*.]

In this description, four lines yield greater variety of matter, and more choice thoughts than twice the number of any other Language.

Here is something more *fortunate* than the boldest fancy has yet reached, and something more *just*, than the severest reason has observed. Here are the *flights* of *Statius* and *Marino* temper'd with a more discerning judgment, and the *judgment* of *Virgil* and *Tasso* animated with a more sprightly Wit. Nothing has been said so expressive and so home[1] in any other Language as the first Verse in this description. The second is *Statius* improv'd.

> *Et simulant fessos curvata cacumina somnos.*[2]

Saith *Statius*, where *simulant* is a bold word in comparison of our *English* word *seem*, being of an active signification; and *cacumina* may as well be taken for the tops of Trees, as the tops of Mountains, which doubtful meaning does not so well content the Reader, as the certainty.

In the *third* Verse, 'tis not said that the Birds sleep, but what is more new, and more Poetical, their sleep is imply'd by their dreams. Somewhat like the *Fourth* we have in *Marino*.

> —*E languidetti i fiori*
> *Giaceano a l' herba genitrice in seno.*
> [*Adonis* Canto 20.]

Which is a pretty image, but has not so near a resemblance with truth, nor can so generally be apply'd to all flowers. Our Author here dares not say directly that the flowers sleep, which might sound a little harsh, but slurs it over in the *participle*, as taken for granted, and affirms only that they *sweat*, which the *Night-dew* makes very easie.

In the last Half-verse, we may see how far our Author has out-done *Apollonius*.[3] 'Twas no such strange thing in the sorrowful Woman when she had spent her tears, for sleep to close her eyes: but here we have the most raging and watchful passions *Lust* and *Envy*. And these too instead of the lustful and the envious, for the greater force and emphasis, in the *abstract*.

Some may object, That the *third* Verse does contradict the *first*. How can *all things be hush'd, if Birds in dreams repeat their Songs?* Is not this like the indiscretion of *Marino*, who says, *That the Winds and all things are husht, and the Seas so fast asleep, that they snore.* [Canto 20.]

It may be answer'd, That in this place 'tis not the Poet that speaks, but another person; and that the Poet here truly represents the nature

[1] Effectively.
[2] *Sylvae*, V. iv. 3–6.
[3] Apollonius Rhodius, *Argonautica*, iii. 744–51.

of man, whose first thoughts break out in bold and more general terms, which by the second thoughts are more correct and limited. As if one should say, all things are silent, or asleep however; if there is any noise, 'tis still but the effect of sleep, as the dreams of Birds, &c. This comparison might be much further improved to our advantage, and more observations made, which are left to the Readers ingenuity.

20. Rochester on Dryden

1675-7

Extracts from *Poems on Several Occasions: By the Right Honourable, the E. of R——* (Antwerp, 1680).

John Wilmot, second Earl of Rochester (1647–80), was a libertine, wit, satirist and lyrist of Charles II's court, and arguably its best poet after Dryden.

The third extract is from one of numerous 'Sessions of the Poets' written in the seventeenth and eighteenth centuries in imitation of Boccalini's *De' Ragguagli di Parnaso* (1612; translated into English, 1656); see *A Journal from Parnassus* (1937), ed. Hugh Macdonald.

(a) '*An Allusion to* Horace The 10th Satyr of the 1st Book', ll. 1–17 (*Poems*, 1680, p. 40).

> Well Sir, 'tis granted, I said *D[ryden's]* Rhimes,
> Were stoln, unequal, nay, dull many times:
> What foolish *Patron*, is there found of his,
> So blindly partial, to deny me this?
> But that his *Plays*, embroider'd up, and down, }
> With *Wit* and *Learning*, justly pleas'd the *Town*, }
> In the same *Paper*, I as freely own. }
> Yet having this allow'd, the heavy *Mass*,

That Stuffs up his loose *Volumns*, must not pass:
For by that Rule, I might as well admit
Crown's[1] tedious *Scenes*, for *Poetry* and *Wit*.
'Tis therefore not enough, when your false sense
Hits the false Judgment of an *Audience*:
Of clapping *Fools*, assembled a vast Crowd,
Till the throng'd *Play-house* crack with the dull load;
Though ev'n that *Talent*, merits in some sort,
That can divert the *Rabble*, and the *Court*. . . .

(b) *Ibid.*, ll. 71–97.

D[*ryden*], in vain try'd this nice way of wit,
For he to be a tearing *Blade*, thought fit;[2]
But when he wou'd be sharp, he still was blunt,
To frisk his frollique fancy, he'd cry C**t,
Wou'd give the *Ladies*, a dry *Bawdy* bob,
And thus he got the name of *Poet Squab*.
But to be just, 'twill to his praise be found,
His *Excellencies* more than faults abound;
Nor dare I from his sacred Temples tear
That *Lawrel*, which he best deserves to wear.
But does not *D—* find ev'n *Johnson* dull?
Fletcher and *Beaumont*, uncorrect, and full
Of Lewd *Lines* as he calls 'em? *Shake-spears* stile
Stiff and affected;[3] to his own the while,
Allowing all the justness, that his Pride
So Arrogantly had to these deny'd?
And may not I, have leave impartially,
To search, and censure *D— Works*, and try,
If those gross faults, his choice *Pen* does commit,
Proceed from want of Judgment, or of Wit?
Or if his lumpish fancy does refuse
Spirit and Grace, to his loose slattern *Muse*?
Five hundred Verses ev'ry *Morning* writ,
Proves you no more a *Poet*, than a *Wit*:

[1] John Crowne (?1640–1712), minor dramatist.
[2] In the early 1670s, when he was intimate with several of the court wits.
[3] *Cf.* the Epilogue to *The Second Part of the Conquest of Granada, Defence of the Epilogue,* the Preface to *An Evening's Love,* and *Of Dramatick Poesie.*

Such scribling *Authors*, have been seen before;   ⎫
Mustapha, the *English Princess*,[1] Forty more,   ⎬
Were things perhaps compos'd in half an hour. ...   ⎭

(c) 'A Session of the Poets', ll. 1–16 (*Poems*, 1680, p. 111).

Since the *Sons* of the *Muses* grew num'rous, and loud,
For th' appeasing so factious, and clam'rous a Crowd,
Apollo, thought fit in so weighty a cause,
T' establish a Government, *Leader*, and *Laws*.
The hopes of the *Bays* at this summoning call
Had drawn 'em together, the *Devil* and all;
All thronging and listning, they gap'd for the Blessing,
No *Presbyter Sermon*, had more crowding, and pressing.
   In the Head of the Gang *J— D—* appear'd,
That Antient grave Wit, so long lov'd, and fear'd;
But *Apollo* had heard a Story ith' Town,
Of his quitting the *Muses*, to wear the Black *Gown*;[2]
And so gave him leave now his *Poetry* 's done,
To let him turn *Priest*, now *R[eeve]* is turn'd *Nun*.[3]
   This Reverend Author was no sooner set by,
But *Apollo* had got gentle *George*,[4] in his Eye. ...

[1] Roger Boyle's *Tragedy of Mustapha* (1665) and John Caryll's *English Princess* (1667).
[2] *Cf.* the unfinished 'Session of the Poets' by Prior (1688; *Works* (1959), ed. H. B. Wright and M. K. Spears, i. 63).
[3] The actress Anne Reeve, reputedly Dryden's mistress, entered a nunnery *c.* 1675.
[4] Sir George Etherege (?1634–91), author of *The Man of Mode* (1676) and other comedies.

21. Comedy and tragedy

1676

From Dryden's Epistle Dedicatory of *Aureng-Zebe: A Tragedy* (1676) to John, Earl of Mulgrave. Dryden's *Comedies, Tragedies, and Operas* (1701), ii. 2–3.

The Truth is, the consideration of so vain a Creature as Man, is not worth our Pains, I have Fool enough at home without looking for it abroad; and am a sufficient Theatre to my self of ridiculous Actions, without expecting Company, either in a Court, a Town, or Play-House. 'Tis on this account that I am weary with drawing the Deformities of Life, and Lazars of the People, where every Figure of Imperfection more resembles me than it can do others. If I must be condemn'd to Rhime, I should find some ease in my change of Punishment. I desire to be no longer the *Sysiphus* of the Stage; to rowl up a Stone with endless Labour (which to follow the Proverb, *Gathers no Moss*) and which is perpetually falling down again. I never thought my self very fit for an Employment, where many of my Predecessors have excell'd me in all kinds; and some of my Contemporaries, even in my own partial Judgment, have out-done me in *Comedy*. Some little hopes I have yet remaining, and those too, considering my Abilities, may be vain, that I may make the World some part of amends, for many ill Plays, by an Heroick Poem. Your Lordship has been long acquainted with my Design. . . .

In the mean time, my Lord, I take the confidence to present you with a Tragedy; the Characters of which are the nearest to those of an Heroick Poem. 'Twas dedicated to you in my Heart, before 'twas presented on the Stage. Some things in it have pass'd your Approbation, and many your Amendment. You were likewise pleas'd to recommend it to the King's Perusal, before the last Hand was added to it, when I receiv'd the Favour from him, to have the most considerable Event of it modell'd by his Royal Pleasure. It may be some Vanity in me to add this Testimony then, and which he graciously confirm'd afterwards, that it was the best of all my Tragedies; in which he has made Authentick my private Opinion of it; at least, he has given it a Value by his Commendation, which it had not by my Writing.

That which was not pleasing to some of the fair Ladies in the last Act of it, as I dare not vindicate, so neither can I wholly condemn, till I find more Reason for their Censures. The Procedure of *Indamora* and *Melesinda*, seems yet, in my Judgment, natural, and not unbecoming of their Characters. If they who arraign them fail not more, the World will never blame their Conduct: And I shall be glad for the Honour of my Country, to find better Images of Vertue drawn to the Life in their Behaviour, than any I could feign to adorn the Theatre. I confess, I have only represented a practicable Virtue, mix'd with the Frailties and Imperfections of Humane Life. . . .

22. Excellent imaging?

1677

Extract from 'The Authors Apology' prefixed to Dryden's opera, *The State of Innocence* (1677; Dryden's *Comedies, Tragedies, and Operas* (1701), i. 593).

I wish I could produce any one Example of excellent Imaging in all this Poem: Perhaps I cannot; but that which comes nearest it, is in these four Lines, which have been sufficiently canvas'd by my wellnatur'd Censors.

> Seraph *and* Cherub, *careless of their Charge,*
> *And wanton, in full ease now live at large;*
> *Ungarded leave the Passes of the Sky,*
> *And all dissolv'd in Hallelujah's lie.*

I have heard (says one of them) of Anchovies dissolv'd in Sauce, but never of an Angel in *Hallelujah's*. A mighty Witticism! (if you will pardon a new Word.) But there is some difference between a Laugher and a Critick. He might have burlesqu'd *Virgil* too, from whom I took the Image:

> *Invadunt Urbem, somno vinoq; sepultam.*[1]

A City's being buried, is just as proper on occasion, as an Angel's being dissolv'd in Ease, and Songs of Triumph. Mr. *Cowley* lies as open too in many places:

> *Where their vast Courts the Mother Waters keep,*[2] *&c.*

For if the Mass of Waters be the Mothers, then their Daughters, the little Streams, are bound in all good manners to make Curt'sie to them, and ask them Blessing. How easie 'tis to turn into ridicule the best Descriptions, when once a Man is in the humour of laughing till he wheezes at his own dull Jest! But an Image which is strongly and beautifully set before the Eyes of the *Reader*, will still be Poetry when the merry Fit is over; and last when the other is forgotten. . . .

---

[1] *Aeneid*, ii. 265, 'they rush upon the city buried in sleep and wine'.
[2] *Davideis*, i. 79 (parodied by Dryden in *Mac Flecknoe*, ll. 72–3).

23. Dryden on *The Kind Keeper*

1677, 1680

Extracts from (a) Dryden's letter to Lord Latimer, July 1677 (*Letters* (1942), ed. C. E. Ward, pp. 11–12); (b) the Epistle Dedicatory of *The Kind Keeper; or, Mr. Limberham: A Comedy* (1680) to Lord Vaughan (Dryden's *Comedies, Tragedies, and Operas* (1701), ii. 108).

(a) '... The Kings Comedy lyes in the Sudds till you please to send me into Northamptonshyre: it will be almost such another piece of businesse as the fond Husband,[1] for such the King will have it, who is parcell poet with me in the plott; one of the designes being a story he was pleasd formerly to tell me; and therefore I hope he will keep the jeast in countenance by laughing at it.'[2]

(b) 'It remains, my Lord, that I should give you some account of this Comedy, which you have never seen. . . . 'Twas intended for an honest *Satyr* against our crying sin of *Keeping*;[3] how it would have succeeded, I can but guess, for it was permitted to be acted only thrice. The Crime for which it suffer'd, was that which is objected against the *Satyrs* of *Juvenal*, and the *Epigrams* of *Catullus*, that it express'd too much of the Vice which it decry'd. . . .

'I ... have taken a becoming care, that those things which offended on the Stage, might be either alter'd, or omitted in the Press: For their Authority is, and shall be ever sacred to me, as much absent as present, and in all alterations of their Fortune, who for those Reasons have stopp'd its farther appearance on the *Theatre*. And whatsoever hindrance it has been to me, in point of Profit, many of my Friends can

---

[1] Tom D'Urfey's comedy (1676).
[2] The King, doubtless under pressure from someone at Court who thought himself libelled, commanded the withdrawal of the play after three performances.
[3] I.e., maintaining mistresses.

123

bear me witness, that I have not once murmur'd against that Decree. . . .
I will be bold enough to say, that this *Comedy* is of the first Rank of
those which I have written, and that Posterity will be of my Opinion.
It has nothing of particular *Satyr* in it: for whatsoever may have been
pretended by some Criticks in the Town, I may safely and solemnly
affirm, that no one Character has been drawn from any single Man;
and that I have known so many of the same humour, in every folly
which is here expos'd, as may serve to warrant it from a particular
Reflection. . . .

24. Dryden on *All for Love*

1678

Extract from Dryden's Preface to *All for Love: or, The World well
Lost. A Tragedy . . . Written in Imitation of Shakespeare's Stile* (1678).

All reasonable men have long since concluded, That the Heroe of the
Poem, ought not to be a character of perfect Virtue, for, then, he
could not, without injustice, be made unhappy; nor yet altogether
wicked, because he could not then be pitied: I have therefore steer'd
the middle course; and have drawn the character of *Anthony* as favour-
ably as *Plutarch*, *Appian*, and *Dion Cassius* wou'd give me leave: the
like I have observ'd in *Cleopatra*. That which is wanting to work up
the pity to a greater heighth, was not afforded me by the story: for
the crimes of love which they both committed, were not occasion'd
by any necessity, or fatal ignorance, but were wholly voluntary; since
our passions are, or ought to be, within our power. The Fabrick of the
Play is regular enough, as to the inferior parts of it; and the Unities of
Time, Place and Action, more exactly observ'd, than, perhaps, the
English Theater requires. Particularly, the Action is so much one, that
it is the only of the kind without Episode, or Underplot; every Scene

in the Tragedy conducing to the main design, and every Act concluding with a turn[1] of it. The greatest errour in the contrivance seems
to be in the person of *Octavia*: For, though I might use the priviledge
of a Poet, to introduce her into *Alexandria*, yet I had not enough
consider'd, that the compassion she mov'd to her self and children,
was destructive to that which I reserv'd for *Anthony* and *Cleopatra*;
whose mutual love being founded upon vice, must lessen the favour
of the Audience to them, when Virtue and Innocence were oppress'd
by it. And, though I justified *Anthony* in some measure, by making
Octavia's departure, to proceed wholly from her self; yet the force of
the first Machine still remain'd; and the dividing of pity, like the
cutting of a River into many Channels, abated the strength of the
natural stream. But this is an Objection which none of my Critiques
have urg'd against me; and therefore I might have let it pass, if I could
have resolv'd to have been partial to my self. The faults my Enemies
have found, are rather cavils concerning little, and not essential
Decencies; which a Master of the Ceremonies may decide betwixt us.
The *French* Poets, I confess, are strict Observers of these Punctilio's:
They would not, for example, have suffer'd *Cleopatra* and *Octavia* to
have met; or if they had met, there must only have pass'd betwixt
them some cold civilities, but no eagerness of repartée, for fear of
offending against the greatness of their Characters, and the modesty of
their Sex. This Objection I foresaw, and at the same time contemn'd:
for I judg'd it both natural and probable, that *Octavia*, proud of her
new-gain'd Conquest, would search out *Cleopatra* to triumph over her;
and that *Cleopatra*, thus attacqu'd, was not of a spirit to shun the
encounter: and 'tis not unlikely, that two exasperated Rivals should
use such Satyre as I have put into their mouths; for after all, though the
one were a *Roman*, and the other a Queen, they were both Women. . . .

. . . In my Stile I have profess'd to imitate the Divine *Shakespeare*;
which that I might perform more freely, I have disincumber'd my self
from Rhyme. Not that I condemn my former way, but that this is
more proper to my present purpose. I hope I need not to explain my
self, that I have not Copy'd my Author servilely: Words and Phrases
must of necessity receive a change in succeeding Ages: but 'tis almost
a Miracle that much of his Language remains so pure; and that he
who began Dramatique Poetry amongst us, untaught by any, and, as
Ben Johnson tells us, without Learning, should by the force of his own
Genius perform so much, that in a manner he has left no praise for

[1] I.e., for better for worse.

any who come after him. . . . Since I must not be over-confident of my own performance after him, it will be prudence in me to be silent. Yet I hope I may affirm, and without vanity, that by imitating him, I have excell'd my self throughout the Play; and particularly, that I prefer the Scene betwixt *Anthony* and *Ventidius* in the first Act, to any thing which I have written in this kind.

25. Dryden on *The Spanish Fryar*

1681

From the Dedication of *The Spanish Fryar: or, The Double Discovery* (1681) to Lord Haughton (Dryden's *Comedies, Tragedies, and Operas* (1701), ii. 257–8).

When I first design'd this Play, I found, or thought I found somewhat so moving in the serious part of it, and so pleasant in the Comick, as might deserve a more than ordinary Care in both: Accordingly I us'd the best of my endeavour, in the management of two Plots, so very different from each other, that it was not perhaps the Talent of every Writer, to have made them of a Piece. Neither have I attempted other Plays of the same Nature, in my Opinion, with the same Judgment; though with like Success. And though many Poets may suspect themselves for the fondness and partiality of Parents to their youngest Children, yet I hope I may stand exempted from this Rule, because I know my self too well, to be ever satisfied with my own Conceptions, which have seldom reach'd to those *Ideas* that I had within me: and consequently, I presume I may have liberty to judge when I write more or less pardonably, as an ordinary Marks-man may know certainly when he shoots less wide at what he aims. Besides, the Care and Pains I have bestowed on this beyond my other Tragi-Comedies, may reasonably make the World conclude, that either I can do nothing tolerably, or that this Poem is not much amiss. Few good Pictures have been finish'd at one sitting; neither can a true just Play, which is to bear the Test of Ages, be produc'd at a heat, or by the force of Fancy, without the maturity of Judgment. . . .

I had not said thus much, if some young Gallants, who pretend to Criticism, had not told me that this Tragi-Comedy wanted the dignity of Style: but as a Man who is charg'd with a Crime of which he thinks himself innocent, is apt to be too eager in his own defence, so perhaps I have vindicated my Play with more partiality than I ought, or than such a Trifle can deserve. Yet, whatever Beauties it may want, 'tis free at least from the grosness of those Faults I mention'd:[1] What Credit it has gain'd upon the Stage, I value no farther than in reference to my Profit, and the satisfaction I had in seeing it represented with all the justness and gracefulness of Action. But as 'tis my interest to please my Audience, so 'tis my Ambition to be read; that I am sure is the more lasting and the nobler Design: for the propriety of Thoughts and Words, which are the hidden beauties of a Play, are but confus'dly judg'd in the vehemence of Action: All things are there beheld, as in a hasty motion, where the Objects only glide before the Eye and disappear. The most discerning Critick can judge no more of these silent Graces in the Action, than he who rides Post through an unknown Country can distinguish the situation of Places, and the nature of the Soil. . . .

---

[1] In Chapman's *Bussy D'Ambois*, Statius, and some plays of his own. See No. 8b.

26. Verses on *Absalom and Achitophel*

1681, 1682

From *Absalom and Achitophel. A Poem. The Fourth Edition: Augmented and Revised* (1682). The first two poems were published in the second London edition (1681); the third was added in the third London edition (1682). The authors were the dramatist Nathaniel Lee (1649?–92); Richard Duke (1658–1711), poet, collaborator with Dryden in translations, and later chaplain to Queen Anne; and Nahum Tate (1652–1715), Irish dramatist, author of most of *The Second Part of Absalom and Achitophel*.

To the Unknown Author of this Excellent Poem

Take it as Earnest of a Faith renew'd,
Your Theam is vast, your Verse divinely good:
Where, tho the Nine their beauteous stroaks repeat, ⎫
And the turn'd Lines on Golden Anvils beat,   ⎬
It looks as if they strook 'em at a heat.   ⎭
So all Serenely Great, so Just, refin'd,   ⎫
Like Angels love to Humane Seed enclin'd,   ⎬
It starts a Giant, and exalts the Kind.   ⎭
'Tis Spirit seen, whose fiery Attoms roul,
So brightly fierce, each Syllable 's a Soul.
'Tis minuture of Man, but he 's all heart;
'Tis what the World woud be, but wants the Art:
To whom ev'n the Phanaticks Altars raise,
Bow in their own despight, and grin your praise.
As if a *Milton* from the dead arose,
Fil'd off his Rust, and the right Party chose.
Nor, Sir, be shock'd at what the Gloomy say,
Turn not your Feet too inward, nor too splay.
'Tis Gracious all, and Great: Push on your Theam,

Lean your griev'd head on *David*'s Diadem.
David that rebel *Israels* envy mov'd,
David by God and all Good Men belov'd.

   The beauties of your *Absalom* excel:
But more the Charms of Charming *Annabel*;[1]
Of *Annabel*, than *May*'s first Morn more bright,
Chearful as Summer's Noon, and chast as Winter's Night.
Of *Annabel* the Muses dearest Theam,
Of *Annabel* the Angel of my dream.
Thus let a broken Eloquence attend,
And to your Master-piece these Shadows send.

To the Unknown Author of this Admirable Poem

I thought, forgive my Sin, the boasted fire
Of Poets Souls did long ago expire;
Of Folly or of Madness did accuse
The Wretch that thought himself possest with Muse;
Laugh'd at the God within, that did inspire
With more than humane thoughts, the tuneful Quire;
But sure 'tis more than Fansie, or the Dream
Of Rhimers slumbring by the Muses stream.
Some livelier Spark of Heav'n and more refin'd
From Earthly dross, fills the great Poet's Mind.
Witness these mighty and immortal Lines,
Through each of which th' informing Genius shines.
Scarce a diviner Flame inspir'd the King,
Of whom thy Muse does so sublimely sing.
Not *David*'s self could in a nobler Verse
His gloriously offending Son rehearse,
Tho in his Breast the Prophet's Fury met
The Father's Fondness, and the Poet's Wit.

Here all consent in Wonder and in Praise,
And to the Unknown Poet Altars raise.
Which thou must needs accept with equal joy,
As when *Æneas* heard the Wars of *Troy*,
Wrapt up himself in darkness and unseen,
Extoll'd with Wonder by the *Tyrian* Queen.

[1] In *Absalom and Achitophel*, the Duchess of Monmouth.

Sure thou already art secure of Fame,
Nor want'st new Glories to exalt thy Name:
What Father else would have refus'd to own
So great a Son as God-like *Absalon*?

R. D.

To the Conceal'd Author of this Incomparable Poem

Hail Heav'n-born Muse! hail ev'ry Sacred page!
The Glory of our I'le and of our Age.
Th' inspiring Sun to *Albion* draws more nigh,   ⎫
The North at length teems with a Work to vie   ⎬
With *Homer*'s Flame and *Virgil*'s Majesty.   ⎭
While *Pindus* lofty Heights our Poet sought,   ⎫
(His ravisht Mind with vast *Idea*'s fraught)   ⎬
Our Language fail'd beneath his rising Thought: ⎭
This checks not his Attempt, for *Maro*'s Mines   ⎫
He dreins of all their Gold t' adorn his Lines;   ⎬
Through each of which the *Mantuan Genius* shines. ⎭
The Rock obey'd the pow'rfull *Hebrew* Guide,
Her flinty Breast dissolv'd into a Tide:[1]
Thus on our stubborn Language he prevails,
And makes the *Helicon* in which he sails.
The Dialect, as well as Sense, invents,
And, with his Poem, a new Speech presents.
Hail then thou matchless Bard, thou great Unknown,
That give your Countrey Fame, yet shun your own!
In vain—for ev'ry where your Praise you find,
And not to meet it, you must shun Mankind.
Your Loyal Theam each Loyal Reader draws,   ⎫
And ev'n the Factious give your Verse applause,   ⎬
Whose Lightning strikes to ground their Idol Cause. ⎭
The Cause for whose dear sake they drank a Floud
Of Civil Gore, nor spar'd the Royal-bloud:
The Cause whose growth to crush, our Prelates wrote
In vain, almost in vain our *Hero's* fought.
Yet by one Stabb of your keen Satyr dies:
Before your Sacred Lines their Shatter'd *Dagon* lies.

---

[1] Exodus xvii.

Oh! If unworthy we appear to know
The Sire, to whom this Lovely Birth we owe:
(Deny'd our ready Homage to express,
And can at best but thankfull be by guess:)
This hope remains,—May *David*'s God-like Mind,
(For him 'twas wrote) the Unknown Author find:
And, having found, show'r equal Favours down
On Wit so vast as cou'd oblige a Crown.

N. T.

27. Some responses to *Absalom and Achitophel*

1681, 1682

Extracts from (*a*) *Absolon's IX Worthies: or, A Key to a late Book or Poem, Entituled A.B. & A.C.*, 1681–2 (text in Dryden's *Works*, 1808, ed. Walter Scott, ix. 216); (*b*) *Poetical Reflections on a late Poem entituled, Absalom and Achitophel. By a Person of Honour*, 1681 (text, *ibid.*, ix. 272–4); (*c*) Samuel Pordage, *Azaria and Hushai, A Poem*, 1682 (text, *ibid.*, ix. 372); (*d*) Elkanah Settle, *Absalcm Senior: or, Achitophel Transpros'd. A Poem*, 1682 (text, *ibid.*, ix. 377–8).

(*a*)   To the Author of that Incomparable Poem . . .

Homer, amazed, resigns the hill to you,
And stands i' the crowd, amidst the panting crew:
Virgil and Horace dare not shew their face,
And long admired Juv'nal quits his place;
For this one mighty poem hath done more
Than all those poets could have done before.
Satyr, or statesman, poet, or divine,

Thou any thing, thou every thing that's fine,
Thy lines will make young Absalon relent;
And, though 'tis hard, Achitophel repent;
And stop—as thou has done—
Thus once thy rival muse, on Cooper's hill,
With the true story would not Fatme[1] kill.
No politics exclude repentance quite;
Despair makes rebels obstinately fight;
'Tis well when errors do for mercy call;
Unbloody conquests are the best of all.
   Methinks I see a numerous mixed croud
Of seduced patriots crying out aloud
For grace, to royal David. He, with tears,
Holds forth his sceptre, to prevent their fears,
And bids them welcome to his tender breast:
Thus may the people, thus the king be blest.
Then tunes his harp, thy praises to rehearse,
Who owes his son and subjects to thy verse.

(b)   To the Reader

... To epitomize which scandalous pamphlet, unworthy the denomination of poesy, no eye can inspect it without a prodigious amazement, the abuses being so gross and deliberate, that it seems rather a capital or national libel, than personal exposures, in order to an infamous detraction. For how does he character the King, but as a broad figure of scandalous inclinations, or contrived into such irregularities, as renders him rather the property of parasites and vice, than suitable to the accomplishment of so excellent a prince. Nay, he forces on king David such a royal resemblance, that he darkens his sanctity, in spite of illuminations from holy writ.

Next, to take as near our king as he could, he calumniates the Duke of Monmouth, with that height of impudence, that his sense is far blacker than his ink, exposing him to all the censures that a murderer, a traitor, or what a subject of most ambitious evil can possibly comprehend.

As to my Lord Shaftesbury, in his collusive Achitophel, what does he other than exceed malice itself, or that the more prudent deserts of

[1] A character in Sophy (1642), a tragedy by Sir John Denham (1615–69), who was also author of Cooper's Hill (1642).

that Peer were to be so impeached before hand by his impious poem,
as that he might be granted more emphatically condign of the hang-
man's axe, and which his muse does in effect take upon her to hasten . . .

> When late Protector-ship was cannon proof,
> And, cap-a-pe, had seized on Whitehall roof;
> And next on Israelites durst look so big,
> That, Tory-like, it loved not much the Whig;
> A poet there starts up of wondrous fame,
> Whether Scribe, or Pharisee, his race doth name.
>
> .   .   .   .   .
>
> A grace our mighty Nimrod late beheld,
> When he within the royal palace dwelled;
> And saw 'twas of import, if lines could bring
> His greatness from usurper to be king;*
> Or varnish so his praise, that little odds
> Should seem 'twixt him and such called earthly gods;
> And though no wit can royal blood infuse,
> No more than melt a mother to a muse,
> Yet much a certain poet undertook,
> That men and manners deals in without book,
> And might not more to gospel truth belong,
> Than he if christened does by name of John.
>
> .   .   .   .   .
>
> Fame's impious hireling, and mean reward,
> The knave that in his lines turns up his card;
> Who, though no Raby thought in Hebrew writ,
> He forced allusions that can closely fit;
> To Jews, or English, much unknown before,
> He made a talmud¹ on his muses score;
> Though hoped few critics will its genius carp,
> So purely metaphors king David's harp;
> And, by a soft encomium, near at hand,
> Shews Bathsheba embraced throughout the land. . . .²

(c)   Shimei, the poet laureat of that age,
       The falling glory of the Jewish stage,

---

* See his poem on Cromwell.
¹ Literally, compilation of Jewish oral teaching.
² Charles's mistress, the Duchess of Portsmouth.

Who scourged the priest, and ridiculed the plot,
Like common men, must not be quite forgot.
Sweet was the muse that did his wit inspire
Had he not let his hackney muse to hire:
But variously his knowing muse could sing,
Could Doeg[1] praise, and could blaspheme the king;
The bad make good, good bad, and bad make worse,
Bless in heroics, and in satires curse.
Shimei to Zabed's[2] praise could tune his muse,
And princely Azaria[3] could abuse.
Zimri,[4] we know, he had no cause to praise,
Because he dubbed him with the name of Bayes:[5]
Revenge on him did bitter venom shed,
Because he tore the laurel from his head;
Because he durst with his proud wit engage,
And brought his follies on the public stage.
Tell me, Apollo, for I can't divine,
Why wives he cursed, and praised the concubine;
Unless it were, that he had led his life
With a teeming matron, ere she was a wife;[6]
Or that it best with his dear muse did suit,
Who was for hire a very prostitute. . . .

(d)   But Amiel[7] had, alas! the fate to hear
An angry poet play his chronicler;
A poet raised above oblivion's shade,
By his recorded verse immortal made.
But, sir, his livelier figure to engrave,
With branches added to the *bays* you gave,[8]
No muse could more heroic feats rehearse;
Had with an equal, all-applauding verse,
Great David's sceptre, and Saul's[9] javelin, praised,

[1] Unidentified.
[2] Cromwell.
[3] Monmouth.
[4] Buckingham.
[5] See *supra*, No. 10.
[6] Lady Elizabeth Dryden was roughly treated by lampooners and gossips.
[7] Buckingham.
[8] See *supra*, No. 10.
[9] Cromwell.

A pyramid to his saint, Interest, raised:
For which, religiously, no change he mist,
From commonwealth's man up to royalist;
Nay, would have been his own loathed thing, called priest;
Priest, which with so much gall he does describe,
'Cause once unworthy thought of Levi's tribe.[1]
Near those bright towers, where Art has wonders done,
And at his feet proud Jordan's waters run,
Where David's sight glads the blest summer's sun,
A cell there stands, by pious founders raised,
Both for its wealth and learned rabbins praised;[2]
To this did an ambitious bard aspire,
To be no less than lord of that blest choir;
Till wisdom deemed so sacred a command
A prize too great for his unhallowed hand.
Besides, lewd Fame had told his plighted vow
To Laura's cooing love, perched on a drooping bough;
Laura,[3] in faithful constancy confined
To Ethiop's envoy, and to all mankind;
Laura, though rotten, yet of mould divine,
He had all her —, and she had all his coin.[4]

    .   .   .   .   .

And if at last his nature can reform,
As weary grown of love's tumultuous storm,
'Tis age's fault, not his, of power bereft, —
He left not whoring, but of that was left. . . .[5]

---

[1] The priesthood.

[2] Eton College, of which Dryden, it was said, aspired to be Provost.

[3] Unidentified. Dryden's supposed liaison with the actress Anne Reeve belongs (if anywhere) to the 1670s, his supposed Etonian ambition later; and his name was not associated with any other woman of town or stage.

[4] Parodying Dryden's portrait of Buckingham, *Absalom and Achitophel*, ll. 562, 567–8.

[5] *Ibid.*

28. Verses on *The Medall*

1682

From the 1692 printing of *The Medall. A Satyre against Sedition. By the Authour of Absalom and Achitophel*—part of the first collected edition of Dryden's satires. The first poem is by Nahum Tate (*cf. supra*, p. 128), the second by T. Adams.

(a)   Once more our awfull Poet Arms, t' engage
The threatning Hydra-Faction of the Age:
Once more prepares his dreadful Pen to wield,
And ev'ry Muse attends him to the Field:
By Art and Nature for this Task design'd,
Yet modestly the Fight he long declin'd;
Forbore the Torrent of his Verse to pour,
Nor loos'd his Satyre till the needfull Hour;
His Sov'reign's Right by Patience half betray'd,
Wak'd his Avenging Genius to its Aid.
Blest Muse, whose Wit with such a Cause was Crown'd,
And blest the Cause that such a Champion found.
With chosen Verse upon the Foe he falls,
And black Sedition in each Quarter galls;
Yet, like a Prince with Subjects forc'd t' engage,
Secure of Conquest he rebates his Rage;
His Fury not without Distinction sheds,
Hurls mortal Bolts but on devoted[1] Heads:
To less infected Members gentle found,
Or spares, or else pours Balm into the Wound.
Such gen'rous Grace th' ingratefull Tribe abuse,
And trespass on the Mercy of his Muse;
Their wretched dogrell Rhimers forth they bring
To snarl and bark against the Poets King;

[1] Doomed.

136

A Crew, that scandalize the Nation more
Than all their Treason-canting Priests before!
On these he scarce vouchsafes a scornfull Smile,
But on their Pow'rfull Patrons turns his Style.
A Style so keen, as ev'n from Faction draws
The vital Poyson, stabs to th' Heart their Cause.
Take then, great Bard, what Tribute we can raise;
Accept our Thanks, for you transcend our Praise.

(b)   To the Unknown Authour of the Following Poem, and
that of *Absalom* and *Achitophel*

Thus pious ignorance, with dubious praise,
Altars of old to Gods unknown did raise;
They knew not the lov'd Deity, they knew
Divine effects a cause Divine did shew;
Nor can we doubt, when such these Numbers are, ⎞
Such is their cause, tho' the worst Muse shall dare ⎬
Their sacred worth in humble Verse declare. ⎠

   As gentle *Thames* charm'd with thy tunefull Song,
Glides in a peacefull Majesty along;
No rebel Stone, no lofty Bank does brave
The easie passage of his silent wave;
So, sacred Poet, so thy Numbers flow,
Sinewy, yet mild as happy Lovers woe;
Strong, yet harmonious too as Planets move,
Yet soft as Down upon the Wings of Love:
How sweet does Vertue in your dress appear?
How much more charming, when much less severe?
Whilst you our senses harmlessly beguile,
With all th' allurements of your happy Style;
Y' insinuate Loyalty with a kind deceit,
And into sense th' unthinking Many cheat:
So the sweet *Thracian* with his charming lyre
Into rude Nature virtue did inspire;
So he the savage herd to reason drew,
Yet scarce so sweet, so charmingly as you:
Oh, that you would with some such powerfull Charm,
Enervate Albion to just valour warm!

Whether much suffering *Charles* shall Theme afford,
Or the great Deeds of God-like *James*'s Sword. . . .

No more, fond Isle! no more thy self engage,
In civil fury, and intestine rage;
No rebel Zeal thy duteous Land molest,
But a smooth Calm sooth every peacefull breast,
While in such Charming notes Divinely sings,
The best of Poets, of the best of Kings.

29. Verses on *Religio Laici*

1682, 1683

The first (anonymous) poem and the second, by Thomas Creech
(1659–1700), who became a Fellow of All Souls in 1683, were
published in the first edition of *Religio Laici or A Laymans Faith.
A Poem* (1682). The third piece, by Wentworth Dillon, 4th Earl
of Roscommon (1633?–85), appeared with the anonymous fourth
one in *Miscellany Poems . . . By the most Eminent Hands* (Tonson,
1684), pp. 190–6.

(*a*)   To Mr. Dryden, on his Poem, called *Religio Laici*

Great is the task, and worthy such a Muse,
To doe Faith right, yet Reason disabuse.
How chearfully the Soul does take its flight,
On Faith's strong wings guided by Reason's light?
But Reason does in vain her beams display,   ⎫
Shewing to th' place, whence first she came, the way, ⎬
If *Peter*'s Heirs must still hold fast the Key.   ⎭
The house which many Mansions shou'd contain,
Form'd by the great wise Architect in vain,

Of Disproportion justly we accuse,
If the streight-gate still entrance must refuse.
The onely free enriching Port God made ⎫
What shamefull Monopoly did invade? ⎬
One Factious Company ingross'd the Trade. ⎭
Thou to the distant Shore hast safely sail'd,
Where the best Pilots have so often fail'd.
Freely we now may buy the Pearl of price, ⎫
The happy Land abounds with fragrant Spice, ⎬
And nothing is forbidden there but Vice. ⎭
Thou best *Columbus* to the unknown World!
Mountains of Doubt that in thy way were hurld,
Thy generous Faith has bravely overcome,
And made Heaven truly our familiar home.
Let Crowds impossibilities receive,
Who cannot think, ought not to disbelieve.
Let 'em pay Tithes, and hud-wink'd go to Heaven,
But sure the *Quaker* cou'd not be forgiven,
Had not the Clerk who hates Lay-policy ⎫
Found out, to countervail the Injury, ⎬
Swearing, a trade of which they are not free. ⎭
Too long has captiv'd Reason been enslav'd,
By Visions scar'd, and airy Phantasms brav'd,
Listning t' each proud Enthusiastick Fool,
Pretending Conscience, but designing Rule;
Whilst Law, Form, Interest, Ignorance, Design,
Did in the holy Cheat together joyn.
Like vain Astrologers gazing on the Skyes,
We fell, and did not dare to trust our Eyes.
'Tis time at last to fix the trembling Soul,
And by thy Compass to point out the Pole;
All men agree in what is to be done,
And each Man's Heart his Table is of Stone,
Where he the God-writ Character may view:
Were it as needfull, Faith had been so too.
Oh, that our greatest fault were humble Doubt!
And that we were more Just, though less Devout;
What reverence shou'd we pay thy sacred Rhimes,
Who in these Factious too-believing Times
Hast taught us to obey, and to distrust:

Yet to our selves, our King, and God, prove just.
Thou wantst not Praise from an ensuring Friend,
The Poor to Thee on double Interest lend.
So strong thy Reasons, and so clear thy Sense,
They bring, like Day, their own bright Evidence:
Yet whilst mysterious Truths to light you bring, ⎫
And heavenly things in heavenly numbers sing, ⎬
The joyfull Younger Choir may clap the Wing. ⎭

(b)   **To Mr. *Dryden*, on *Religio Laici*.**

'Tis nobly done, a Layman's Creed profest,
When all our Faith of late hung on a Priest;
His doubtfull words like Oracles receiv'd,
And when we could not understand, believ'd.
Triumphant Faith now takes a nobler course,
'Tis gentle, but resists intruding force:
Weak Reason may pretend an awfull sway,
And Consistories charge her to obey;
(Strange Nonsense to confine the sacred Dove, ⎫
And narrow Rules prescribe how she shall love, ⎬
And how upon the barren Waters move.) ⎭
But she rejects and scorns their proud Pretence,
And whilst those groveling things depend on Sense;
She mounts on certain wings and flys on high, ⎫
And looks upon a dazling Mystery, ⎬
With fixt, and steddy, and an Eagle's Eye. ⎭
Great King of Verse, that dost instruct and please,
As *Orpheus* soften'd the rude Savages:
And gently freest us from a double Care,
The bold Socinian, and the Papal Chair:
Thy Judgment is correct, thy Fancy young,
Thy Numbers, as thy generous faith, are strong:
Whilst through dark Prejudice they force their way,
Our Souls shake off the Night and view the Day.
We live secure from mad Enthusiasts Rage,
And fond Tradition now grown blind with Age.
Let factious and ambitious Souls repine, ⎫
Thy Reason's strong, and generous thy Design, ⎬
And allways to doe well is onely thine. ⎭

(c)   On Mr. *Dryden's Religio Laici.*

Begone you Slaves, you Idle Vermin go,
Fly from the Scourges, and your Master know;
Let free, impartial men from *Dryden* learn
Mysterious Secrets, of a high concern,
And weighty truths, solid convincing Sense,
Explain'd by unaffected Eloquence.

What can you (*Reverend Levi*) here take ill?
Men still had faults, and men will have them still;
He that hath none, and lives as Angels do
Must be an Angel; But what's that to you?

While mighty *Lewis* finds the *Pope* too Great,
And dreads the Yoke of his imposing Seat,
Our Sects a more Tyrannick Power assume,
And would for Scorpions change the Rods of *Rome*;
That Church detain'd the Legacy Divine;
Fanaticks cast the Pearls of Heaven to Swine:
What then have honest thinking men to doe,
But chuse a mean between th' Usurping two? . . .

(d)   To Mr. *Dryden* on his *Religio Laici.*

Those Gods the pious Ancients did adore
They learn'd in Verse devoutly to implore,
Thinking it rude to use the common way
Of Talk when they did to such Beings pray.
Nay They that taught Religion first, thought fit
In Verse its sacred Precepts to transmit:
So *Solon* too did his first Statutes draw,
And every little Stanza was a Law.
By these few Precedents we plainly see
The Primitive Design of Poetry;
Which by restoring to its Native use,
You generously have rescu'd from Abuse.
Whilst your lov'd Muse does in sweet Numbers sing,
She vindicates her God, and God-like King.
Atheist, and Rebel too, She does oppose,
(God and the King have always the same Foes).

Legions of Verse you raise in their defence,
And write the Factious to Obedience.
You the bold *Arian* to Arms defie,
A conquering Champion for the Deity
Against the Whigs first Parents, Who did dare
To disinherit God-Almighty's Heir.
And what the hot-brain'd *Arian* first began ⎫
Is carried on by the *Socinian*, ⎬
Who still Associates to keep God a Man. ⎭
But 'tis the Prince of Poets Task alone
T' assert the Rights of God's, and Charles his Throne.
Whilst vulgar Poets purchase vulgar Fame
By chaunting *Cloris*, or fair *Phyllis* Name;
Whose Reputation shall last as long,
As Fops and Ladies sing the amorous Song.
A Nobler Subject wisely they refuse,
The Mighty Weight would crush their feeble Muse.
So Story tells, a Painter once would try
With his bold hand to limn a Deity:
And He, by frequent practising that part,
Could draw a Minor-God with wondrous Art:
But when great *Jove* did to the Workman sit,
The Thunderer such horrour did beget,
That put the frighted Artist to a stand,
And made his Pensil drop from 's bafl'd Hand.

30. *The Medal of John Bayes: A Satyr against Folly and Knavery*

1682

From the edition of 1682; Thomas Shadwell, *Complete Works* (1927), ed. M. Summers, v. 246–62. Credibly attributed to Dryden's political and poetic adversary, Shadwell, this is the fullest and most vigorous of the attacks made on Dryden.

The prefatory 'Epistle to the Tories' presents them with 'a Medal of an *Heroick Author*, which most properly belongs' to them. 'No body else will take him. We cannot say his Portraicture is done at the full length, or has all its Ornaments. ... But we dare say, these rough strokes have made the lineaments and proportions so true, that any one that knows him, will find there is a great resemblance of him.'

How long shall I endure, without reply,
To hear this* *Bayes*, this Hackney-rayler lie?
The fool uncudgell'd, for one Libel swells,
Where not his Wit, but Sawcinesss excels;
Whilst with foul Words and Names which he lets flie,
He quite defiles the *Satyr*'s Dignity.
For Libel and true *Satyr* different be;
This must have *Truth*, and *Salt*, with *Modesty*.
Sparing the Persons, this does tax the Crimes, ⎫
Gall's not great Men, but Vices of the Times, ⎬
With Witty and Sharp, not blunt and bitter rimes. ⎭
Methinks the Ghost of *Horace* there I see,
Lashing this *Cherry-cheek'd Dunce* of Fifty three;
Who, at that age, so boldly durst profane,
With base hir'd Libel, the free *Satyr*'s Vein.

* *His Name in the* Rehearsal. [See p. 45.]

Thou stil'st it Satyr, to call Names, Rogue, Whore,
Traytor, and Rebel, and a thousand more.
An Oyster-wench is sure thy *Muse* of late,
And all thy *Helicon*'s at *Billingsgate*.
A Libellers vile name then may'st thou gain,
And moderately the Writing part maintain,
None can so well the beating part sustain.
Though with thy Sword, thou art the last of Men,
Thou art a damn'd *Boroski*[1] with thy Pen.
As far from *Satyr* does thy Talent lye,
As far from being cheerful, or good company.
For thou art **Saturnine*, thou dost confess;
A civil word thy Dulness to express.
An old gelt Mastiff has more mirth than thou,
When thou a kind of paltry Mirth would'st show.
Good humour thou so awkwardly put'st on,
It sits like Modish Clothes upon a Clown;
While that of Gentlemen is brisk and high,
When Wine and Wit about the room does flie.
Thou never mak'st, but art a standing Jest;
Thy Mirth by foolish Bawdry is exprest;
And so debauch'd, so fulsome, and so odd,
As—
Let's Bugger one another now by G–d.
(When ask'd how they should spend the Afternoon,
This was the smart reply† of the Heroick Clown.)
He boasts of Vice (which he did ne'r commit)
Calls himself *Whoremaster*, and *Sodomite*;
Commends *Reeve's*[2] Arse, and says she Buggers well,
And silly Lyes of vitious pranks does tell.
This is a Sample of his Mirth and Wit,
Which he for the best Company thinks fit.
In a rich Soyl, the sprightly Horse y' have seen,
Run, leap, and wanton o're the flow'ry green,
Praunce, and curvet, with pleasure to the sight;

---

* *In his Drammatick Essay.* ['A Defence', 1668.]

† *At* Windsor, *in the company of several persons of Quality,* Sir G[eorge] E[therege] *being present.*

[1] A Pole executed in March 1682 for assassinating the Whig, Thomas Thynne of Longleat.

[2] The actress, Ann Reeve, said to have been Dryden's mistress.

But it could never any eyes delight,
To see the frisking frolicks of a Cow;
And such another merry thing art Thou.
In Verse, thou hast a knack, with words to chime,
And had'st a kind of Excellence in Rime:
With Rimes like leading-strings, thou walk'dst; but those
Lay'd by, at every step thou brok'st thy Nose.
How low thy Farce! and thy blank Verse how mean!
How poor, how naked did appear each Scene!
Even thou didst blush at thy insipid stuff,
And laid thy dulness on poor harmless Snuff.
No Comick Scene, or humour hast thou wrought; ⎫
Thou 'st quibling Bawdy, and ill breeding taught; ⎬
But Rime's sad downfal has thy ruine brought. ⎭
No Piece did ever from thy self begin;
Thou can'st no web, from thine own bowels, spin.
Were from thy Works cull'd out what thou 'st purloin'd,
Even D—*fey* would excel what 's left behind.
Should all thy borrow'd plumes we from thee tear,
How truly *Poet Squab would'st thou appear!
Thou call'st thy self, and Fools call thee, in Rime
The goodly *Prince of Poets*, of thy time;
And Sov'raign power thou dost usurp, *John Bayes*,
And from all *Poets* thou a Tax dost raise.
Thou plunder'st all, t' advance thy mighty Name,
Look'st big, and triumph'st with thy borrow'd fame.
But art (while swelling thus thou think'st th' art Chief)
A servile Imitator and a Thief.†
All written Wit thou seizest on as prize;
But that will not thy ravenous mind suffice;
Though men from thee their inward thoughts conceal,
Yet thou the words out of their mouths wilt steal.
How little owe we to your Native store,
Who all you write have heard or read before?
Except your Libels, and there 's something new;
For none were ere so impudent as you.
Some Scoundrel Poetasters yet there be,
Fools that Burlesque the name of Loyalty,

* *The Name given him by the Earl of* Rochester. [See p. 118.]
† Oh imitatores servum pecus!

145

Who by reviling Patriots, think to be
From louziness and hunger ever free:
But will (for all their hopes of swelling bags)
Return to Primitive nastiness and rags.

These are blind Fools: thou hadst some kind of sight,
Thou sinn'st against thy Conscience and the Light.
After the *drubs, thou didst of late compound,
And sold for th' weight in Gold each bruise and wound,
Clear was thy sight, and none declaim'd then more
'Gainst *Popish Plots*, and *Arbitrary Power*.
The *Ministers* thou bluntly wouldst assail,
And it was dangerous to hear thee rail.
(*Oh may not* England *stupid be like thee!*
Heaven grant it may not feel before it see.)
Now he recants, and on that beating thrives; ⎫
Thus *Poet Laureats*, and *Russian Wives*, ⎬
Do strangely upon beating mend their Lives. ⎭
But how comes *Bayes* to flag and grovel so?
Sure your new *Lords* are in their payments slow.
Thou deserv'st whipping thou 'rt so dull, this time,
Thou 'st turn'd the *Observator*[1] into Rime.
But thou suppliest the want of Wit and Sense,
With most malitious Lies, and Impudence.
At *Cambridge* first your scurrilous Vein began,
When sawcily you traduc'd a †*Nobleman*,
Who for that Crime rebuk'd you on the head,
And you had been Expell'd had you not fled.
The next step of Advancement you began, ⎫
Was being Clerk to *Nolls* Lord *Chamberlain*, ⎬
A Sequestrator and Committee-man.[2] ⎭
There all your wholesome Morals you suckt in,
And got your Gentile Gayety and Meen.
Your Loyalty you learn'd in *Cromwels* Court,
Where first your Muse did make her great effort.
On him you first shew'd your Poetick strain,

---

* *In* Rose-Alley. [Dryden was assaulted there in December 1679.]
† *A Lords Son, and all Noblemens Sons, are called Noblemen there.*
[1] Sir Roger L'Estrange's periodical.
[2] Dryden probably owed his post in Cromwell's administration to his influential cousin german, Sir Gilbert Pickering.

*_And prais'd his opening the Basilick Vein._
And were that possible to come agen,
Thou on that side wouldst draw thy slavish Pen.
But he being dead, who should the slave prefer,
He turn'd a Journey-man t' a †Bookseller;
Writ Prefaces to Books for Meat and Drink,
And as he paid, he would both write and think.
Then by th' assistance of a ‡Noble _Knight_,
Th' hadst plenty, ease, and liberty to write.
First like a _Gentleman_ he made thee live;
And on his Bounty thou dist amply thrive.
But soon thy Native swelling Venom rose,
And thou didst him, who gave thee Bread, expose.
'Gainst him a scandalous Preface didst thou write,
Which thou didst soon expunge, rather than fight.[1]
(When turn'd away by him in some small time)   ⎫
You in the Peoples ears began to chime,   ⎬
And please the Town with your successful Rime.   ⎭
When the best Patroness of Wit and Stage,
The Joy, the Pride, the wonder of the Age,
Sweet _Annabel_[2] the good, great, witty, fair;
(Of all this Northern Court, the brightest Star)
Did on thee, _Bayes_, her sacred beams dispence,
Who could do ill under such influence?
She the whole _Court_ brought over to thy side,
And favour flow'd upon thee like a Tide.
To her thou soon prov'dst an §_ungrateful Knave_;   ⎫
So good was she, not only she forgave,   ⎬
But did oblige anew, the faithless Slave.   ⎭
And all the Gratitude he can afford,
Is basely to traduce her Princely Lord.[3]

---

* _See his Poem upon_ Oliver.—_And wisely he essay's to stanch the Blood by breathing of a Vein._

† _Mr._ Herringman, _who kept him in his House for that purpose._

‡ _Sir_ R[obert] H[oward] _who kept him generously at his own House._ [Dryden married Howard's sister.]

§ _When he had thrice broken his Word, Oath, and Bargain with Sir_ William Davenant, _he wrote a Letter to this great Lady to pass her word for him to Sir_ William, _who would not take his own; which she did._ . . .

[1] Only the 'Defence of an Essay', a literary answer to Howard.

[2] Anne, Duchess of Monmouth, to whom Dryden dedicated _The Indian Emperour._

[3] As Absalom in _Absalom and Achitophel._

A *Heroe* worthy of a God-like Race,
Great in his Mind, and charming in his Face,
Who conquers Hearts, with unaffected Grace.
His mighty Vertues are too large for Verse,
Gentle as billing Doves, as angry Lions fierce:
His Strength and Beauty so united are,
Nature design'd him *Chief*, in Love and War.
All Lovers Victories he did excel,
Succeeding with the beautious *Annabel*.
Early in Arms his glorious course began,
Which never *Heroe* yet so swiftly ran.
Wherever danger shew'd its dreadful face,
By never-dying acts, h' adorn'd his *Royal Race*.
Sure the three Edwards Souls beheld with Joy,
How much thou outdidst Man, when little more than Boy.
And all the *Princely Heroes* of thy Line,
Rejoyc'd to see so much of their great Blood in thine.
So good and so diffusive is his Mind,
So loving too, and lov'd by Humane kind,
He was for vast and general good design'd.
In 's height of Greatness he all eyes did glad,
And never Man departed from him sad.
Sweet and obliging, easie of access,
Wise in his Judging, courteous in address.
Ore all the Passions he bears so much sway,
No *Stoick* taught 'em better to obey.[1]
And, in his Suffering part, he shines more bright,
Than he appear'd in all that gaudy light;
Now, now, methinks he makes the bravest show,
And ne're was greater *Heroe* than he 's now.
For publick good, who wealth and power forsakes,
Over himself a glorious Conquest makes.
Religion, Prince, and Laws to him are dear;
And in defence of all, he dares appear.
'Tis he must stand like *Scæva*[2] in the breach,
'Gainst what ill Ministers do, and furious Parsons preach.
Were 't not for him, how soon some *Popish* Knife
Might rob us of his *Royal* Fathers Life!

[1] Contradicting Dryden's 'character' of Monmouth.
[2] A heroic soldier in Caesar's army (Lucan, *Phars*, vi. 144).

We to their fear of thee that blessing owe: }
In such a Son, happy Great King art thou, }
Who can defend, or can revenge thee so. }
Next, for thy Medal, *Bayes*, which does revile
The wisest *Patriot*[1] of our drooping Isle,
Who *Loyally* did serve his Exil'd *Prince*,
And with the ablest Councel blest him since;
None more than he did stop *Tyrannick* Power, }
Or, in that *Crisis*, did contribute more, }
To his Just Rights our Monarch to restore; }
And still by wise advice, and Loyal Arts,
Would have secur'd him in his Subjects Hearts.
You own the Mischiefs, sprung from that Intrigue,[2]
Which fatally dissolv'd the *Tripple-League*.
Each of *your Idol mock-Triumv'rate knows*,
Our *Patriot* strongly did that Breach oppose.
Nor did this Lord a *Dover*-Journey go,
From thence our tears, the Ilium *of our woe.
Had he that Interest follow'd, how could he
By those that serv'd it then discarded be?
The *French* and *Papists* well his Merits know;
Were he a friend, they 'd not pursu'd him so:
From both he would our beset King preserve,
For which he does Eternal wreaths deserve.
His Life they first, and now his Fame would take,
For Crimes they forge, and secret Plots they make.
They by hir'd Witnesses the first pursue,
The latter by vile Scriblers hir'd like you.
Thy Infamy will blush at no disgrace,
(With such a harden'd Conscience, and a Face)
Thou only want'st an *Evidences*[3] place.
When th' *Isle* was drown'd in a Lethargick sleep,
Our vigilant *Heroe* still a watch did keep. . . .[4]

Go, *Abject Bayes!* and act thy slavish part;
Fawn on those *Popish Knaves*, whose Knave thou art:

* *Bayes his own expression*, Medal [l. 67].
[1] Shaftesbury.
[2] The secret Treaty of Dover (1670).
[3] Informer's, spy's.
[4] There follows a long defence of Shaftesbury the protestant champion.

'Tis not ill writing, or worse Policy,
That can enslave a Nation, so long free. . . .

Now farewel wretched Mercenary *Bayes*,
Who the *King* Libell'd, and did *Cromwel* praise.
Farewel, abandon'd Rascal! only fit
To be abus'd by thy own scurrilous Wit.
Which thou wouldst do, and for a Moderate Sum,
Answer thy Medal, and thy *Absolom*.
Thy piteous Hackney-Pen shall never fright us,
Thou 'rt dwindl'd down to *Hodge*, and *Heraclitus*.[1]
Go, *Ignoramus*[2] cry, and *Forty One*,[3]
And by *Sams Parsons* be thou prais'd alone,
Pied thing! half Wit! half Fool! and for a Knave, ⎫
Few Men, than this, a better mixture have: ⎬
But thou canst add to that, Coward and Slave. ⎭

---

* *A coffee-house where the Inferiour Crape-gown-men [clergy] meet with their Guide Roger* [L'Estrange], *to invent Lies for the farther carrying on the Popish-Plot.*

[1] The Tory paper *Heraclitus Ridens* (1 February 1681–22 August 1682).

[2] The endorsement by which the jury rejected the charge of high treason made against Shaftesbury on 24 November 1681.

[3] The rebellion against Charles I, 1641. A Whig complained in 1680: 'It hath been all the clamour of late, *forty-one, forty-one* is now coming to be acted over again.'

31. Dryden, the Tory poet

1682

Extracts from *The Tory-Poets: A Satyr*, 1682; attributed on inadequate evidence to Shadwell (*Complete Works* (1927), ed. M. Summers, v. 273-87). I 'heartily wish', says the author in his 'Epistle to the Tories', 'I had some of Mr. *Bays* his confidence, that I might speak in the praise of my own Poem, as he doth of his, indeed a rotten Post covered with Brass goes through all weathers, but I am no fond fool of my own Issue.' Other poets attacked in the poem are Otway, D'Urfey, and Aphra Behn.

> Now for a Cordial all begin to strive,
> To fetch their dying *Plot*[1] again to life:
> Their former *Evidences*[2] were dull tools,
> And all their subtle *Jesuites* were but fools.
> But next to the keen *Wits* they do address,
> And they must Charm it up again in Verse.
> The first they do Petition 's Mr. *Bays*,[3]
> So much extoll'd by Fools and vulgar Praise;
> By lewd lascivious Verses, bawdy Rhymes,
> Dubb'd the sweet singing Poet of the times;
> He the black Paths of Sin had travell'd o're
> And found out Vices all unknown before,
> To sins once hid in shades of gloomy Night,
> He gave new Lustre and reduc'd to Light.
> His *Muse* was prostitute upon the Stage,
> And 's *Wife* was Prostitute to all the age:
> The Wife is rich although the Husband Poor,
> And he not honest, and she is a Whore,

---

[1] The Popish Plot, attributed in 1678 to the Jesuits by Titus Oates.
[2] Witnesses.
[3] Dryden.

An ill, deformed, senceless earthly load,
And he the Monster of the *Muses* road;
His shapeless Body hangs an hundred ways,
The Poet looks just like a heap of Plays;
You shall not find through all the buzzing Town
So Ungentile, Unmannerly a Clown:
Though ugly, yet he vents a pleasing strain
For Nature never made a thing in vain.
If not for Priest, for States-man he may do;
Bless us! are Poets Politicians too?
Or are the *Muses* mad and in their Heat
Send out their Poets Officers of State?
Or are the Lawyers Drunk and think it fit
That reason yeild to that lewd thing, *a Wit*?
But private factious Plotters never heed
If their designs go on, who do the deed:
So engine *Bays*, the *Tory-Plot* to save
He first turns *Fool*, and then commences *Knave*:
But yet (methinks) I hear him e're he chuse
In private parley with his Fustian *Muse*.
Base *Muse*! he says, with impudence can'st sing?
In scornful lines can'st thou revile a King?
With inky Clouds of lyes, can'st thou obscure
An Hero's Glory infinitely pure?
Can'st thou call Politicians Fops and Fools?
Can'st ridicule the Arts of learned Schools?
Can'st dress up folly in a Garb so fit
That amongst Madmen it may pass for wit?
His *Muse* accustom'd to such tricks as these
Gave her consent by holding of her Peace.
But he replied, —
Base abject slave to any of the Town,
Who e're but Fops and Fools gave thee renown?
Can'st thou abuse that youthful *Hero's*[1] fame
That wide as the vast World hath spread his name?
When he from *Mastricht* warlike Trophies bore,
Vollies of Praises eccho'd on the Shoar;
Then every *Brave* his Offering did prepare

[1] Monmouth.

And Sacrifices to this God of War,
Then *Jo Peans* by our Swains were sung,
And Peals of Triumph through our Cities rung;
But now his honour 's sullied and forgot
And all his Glory poyson'd with a Plot.
Here hold, ingrate, recal his love to thee,
When fleg'd with Guynies he did let thee fly,
Impt with his favour thou didst dare the brave
And every other Poet was thy Slave;
Think! with indulgent Grace 'tis he hath been
The only Patron of thy *Maximin*;[1]
Were then thine accents lies or didst thou feign,
And only complement to draw in Coin;
So when to *Damn* was in her *graces*[2] power,
She kindly smil'd on th' *Indian Emperor*
Though drest in silly Fustion he did go
In ugglier Cloaths then e're at *Mexico*;
So basely scratcht by thy corroding Pen,
The *Indians* would scarce know their Prince again.
Poor *Montezuma* in no hands secure
Creeps to her *Alcove* for a perfect cure;
There having Scan'd the sence of every line
She hug'd the nasty *Indian* 'cause 'twas thine.
Then cheering up he ended the dispute;
Muses like Monarchs still are absolute;
Tempted by Gold, he lets his Satyr fly,
And swears that all within its Tallons dye;
He Huffs, and Struts, and Cocks an hundred ways,
And damns the *Whiggs* 'cause they did damn his Plays.
So raging once 'twas thought himself he'd stab'd
'Cause *Rochester* Baptis'd him *Poet Squab*.[3]
And he had don 't, but that he 'd vow'd before
After *Rose-alley* drubs[4] he 'd ne're use weapon more.
When Coin is spent he sooths the baser Cit;[5]

[1] The chief character in Dryden's *Tyrannick Love* (1670), dedicated to Monmouth.
[2] The Duchess of Monmouth, to whom Dryden dedicated *The Indian Emperour* (1667).
[3] See p. 118 *supra*.
[4] An anonymous *Essay upon Satyr* (?by Mulgrave) was circulated in the autumn of 1679, and widely attributed to Dryden, who was in consequence assaulted by hired ruffians in Rose Alley on the night of 18 December.
[5] Citizen.

And lives on his old stock, his mother wit;
Rubs up his rusty Muse and looks as big
As Crow in Gutter or ten penny Pig.
A Common-wealth he cryeth up to day,
To morrow Preacheth Arbitrary sway;
Lampoons the *Prince*, praises a *Tyrants* Laws
And giveth Lust and Zeal the same applause;
And in one Breath, so quick his fancies be ⎫
He can speak Treason, and fart Loyalty; ⎬
From such fleet wills kind Heav'n deliver me! ⎭
Read but his *Plays* and what else e're he writ
You'l find but little Judgment and less Wit;
If he dull *Ravenscroft*[1] by chance excel
Thanks to old *Nokes*[2] that humours it so well;
Thanks to the Scenes and Musick for his Wit,
Thanks to the Whores lie squeeking in the Pit,
That Bullies cannot hear, yet praise the Fact
And bravely Clap the *Actor*, not the *Act*.
Shadwel and *Settle*[3] are both Fools to *Bays*,
They have no bawdy Prologues to their Plays;
These silly Villains under a pretence
Of wit, deceive us and like men write sence.
Alas! says *Bays*, what are your Wits to me?
Chapman's a sad dul Rogue at *Comedy*;[4]
Shirley's an Ass to write at such a rate,[5]
But I excel the whole *Triumverate*:
In all my worthy Plays shew if you can
Such a rough Character as *Solyman*;[6]
But though I have no Plot, and Verse be rough,
I say 'tis Wit, and that sure is enough.
The Lawrel makes a Wit; a Brave, the Sword;
And all are wise men at a Councel Board;

---

[1] Author of *The Citizen turn'd Gentleman* (1672).

[2] The comedian James Nokes, who played in Ravenscroft's *Citizen* and in several of Dryden's comedies.

[3] Elkanah Settle (1648–1724), dramatist, attacked by Dryden and Shadwell in *Notes . . . on The Empress of Morocco* (1674), and ridiculed with Shadwell (as Doeg and Og) by Dryden in *The Second Part of Absalom and Achitophel*.

[4] *Cf.* Dedication of *The Spanish Fryar.*

[5] *Cf. Mac Flecknoe*, ll. 29 and 102.

[6] In Settle's *Ibrahim* (1676).

S——*le* 's a Coward, 'cause fool *Ot*—*y* fought him,[1]
And *Mul*——*ve* is a Wit because I taught him.
   So Hectors *Bay*, 'til one would think 'twas fit
That none but Fools should write or judge of Wit;
His pigmie wit, and little infant sence
Rightly defin'd is nought but impudence;
His lines are weak, though of lewd Catches full, ⎫
And naught is strong about him but his Scull,   ⎬
The brave defensive headpeice of a Fool.   ⎭
Of all mean Hackney Jades, 'de never use
This Mercenary party couler'd Muse;
Who e're beholds he strait must needs confess
She 's clad at once in home and forreign dress.
Read *Dry*—*ns* plays, and read *Corneille*'s too,
You'l swear the *Frenchman* speaks good *English* now.
'Mongst borrowed Sense some airy flashes drop,
To please the feeble Females and the Fop,
So soft and gentle flourishes do move
The weak admiring Maid, and fire [with] Love.
Quickens the dizzy Soul with Love beset,
And tamely draws it to the Golden Net,
Stupid it lies, and senceless of its pain,
And kindly kisses the bewitching Chain.
Cupid 's the God; and Love is all the Song,
The blest *Elysium* of the sportful young;
But eas'd of this so kind, so grateful pain,
And brought unto it's former sense again,
The glimmering Lamp is lustre once so bright,
Looks like the Torches of eternal night,
The amorous paths with sweets inchanted strown,
Looks like *Acyna* when her paint was gone:
That wit upon the Stage cry'd up to day,
To morrow in the Closet 's thrown away;
Wit, tho with glory it may chance to rise,
And mounting seem to kiss the very skies,
Yet if above the bounds of Sense it get,
It is all wind, and is no longer wit.
But *Bay* in all his wit is stanch and sound,

---

[1] The dramatist Otway, 'a man of the Sword', challenged Settle to a duel for lampooning him in a 'Session of the Poets'.

Tho in it all there 's no proportion found:
But what he speaks or writes, or does amiss,
It is all wit; but why? because 'tis his;
'Tis wit in him, if he all Sense oppose,
'Twas wit in D'avenant too to lose his Nose;[1]
If so, then Bays is D'avenants wisest Son,
After so many claps to keep his on.

32. Shadwell on *The Duke of Guise*

1683

Extract from Shadwell's *Some Reflections upon the Pretended Parallel in the Play called The Duke of Guise. In a Letter to a Friend* (1683; *Complete Works* (1927), ed. M. Summers, v. 385–400).

The Duke of Guise. A Tragedy, by Dryden and Nathaniel Lee, was completed by July 1682; but because of political obstruction it was not performed until November. In *The Vindication: or The Parallel of The French Holy-League, and The English League and Covenant* (1683; written in reply to attacks by Shadwell and others), Dryden says that this was his first attempt in drama, laid aside but revived in 1682 by himself and Lee 'to make ... a Parallel, betwixt the *Holy League* plotted by the House of *Guise* and its *Adherents*, with the *Covenant* plotted by the *Rebels* in the time of King *Charles* the First, and those of the *new Association*, which was the Spawn of the *old Covenant*'.

SIR,
According to your Commands, I went several times to see the so long expected, and so much talk'd of Play, called, the *Duke of Guise*, in order to give you my Opinion of it: and (thô I was very much wearied

[1] The dramatist Sir William Davenant (1606–68) lost his nose through venereal infection.

with the dulness of it, and extreamly incensed at the wicked and barbarous Design it was intended for) yet the obedience to your Commands, made me throughly observe it, even to every Line. And certainly, never was Mountain delivered of such a Mouse, nor was ever the Expectation of the People more deceived; insomuch that even the fiercest *Tories* (notwithstanding the violence of their Humours, and the rashness and insolence of their present Tempers) have been ashamed to defend this Piece. Yet there are few Follies, and Villanies, that seem to contribute to their Wicked Ends, which they will not publickly and most audaciously vindicate. . . . Yet still they who have any sparks of Wit amongst them, are so true to their Pleasure, that they will not suffer Dulness to pass upon them for Wit, nor Tediousness for Diversion: which is the Reason that this Piece has not met with the expected Applause. And truly, if I may be allowed to Judge, (as Men that do not *Poetise* may be Judges of Wit, Humane Nature, and Common Decencies) I never saw any thing that could be called a Play, more deficient in Wit, good Characters, or Entertainment, than this is.

This Play, at first (as I am inform'd by some who have a nearer communication with the Poets and Players than I have) was written by another, intending to expose that unparallel'd Villany of the *Papists* in the most horrid *Parisian Massacre*. And *Bayes*[1] himself, as I am also told, expressed then an intention of writing the Story of the *Sicilian Vespers*, to lay open the treacherous, inhumane, bloody Principles of the *Disciples of that Scarlet Whore*.

But he is since fallen from all Modesty and common Sense, and is not content with his own devil-like Fall, but like *old Satan*, he tempts his Friend, poisons and perverts his good Intentions, and by his wicked Management of the Play, turns it from the honest Aim of the first Author, to so diabolical an End, as methinks it should make a Civil Government blush to suffer it, or not to put the highest mark of Infamy upon it. But 'tis observable, though this could not be acted as it was first written against the *Papists*, yet when it was turn'd upon Protestants it found Reception.

I cannot believe the first Author of himself guilty of such evil Intentions, because I have heard better things of him; but the *old Serpent Bays* has deluded him, as he would have done of the Reputation, if any had been gotten by it; for so as I am told he did endeavour to do in Discourse with all his own Friends, when he joyn'd with him in

[1] Dryden.

Oedipus,[1] which deserved Applause: and since he hath found that this hath gotten little or no Esteem in the Town, he renounces all he can of it, and endeavours to cast the greatest *Odium* upon his Partner.

But Reproaches are thrown away upon this Wretch, who is hardned in his Folly and Wickedness, as much as any *Irish* Witness, therefore I shall as little as I can, touch him hereafter. But at present I shall fall upon the Consideration of this Parallel, (as he impudently calls it in his Prologue as I take it) and it is publickly known he intended to have had it acted by that Name, before it was forbidden to be acted by the *Lord Chamberlain*'s Order.

And 'tis not enough when he meets some of his old Acquaintance (whom he knows to be of an Opinion which he once profess'd to be of, and much different from what he now pretends) *that he thinks as they do still, but he must write as he does, he is put upon it*, &c. For certainly most exemplary Punishment is due to him for this most devilish Parallel; and methinks Magistrates (that respect their Oaths and Office) should put the Law in Execution against this lewd Scribler.

First, I shall consider in his pretended Parallel, the City of *Paris* in the time of *Hen*. 3 of *France*. . . .

I shall shortly send you some Observations upon the Faults of the Play, considering it as a Play. But it appears to me, that *Bays* did not intend it for a Diversion, but for a Direction and Advice what was to be done; and has more mind to recommend himself as a Counsellor, than a Poet, in this. 'Tis a fine Age, when Mercinary Poets shall become Politicians, and their Plays business of State.

[1] A tragedy by Dryden and Lee (1679).

33. A deist's tribute

1683

The Epistle Dedicatory of *Religio Laici*. *Written in a Letter to John Dryden* (1683) by Dryden's Whig friend, the deist Charles Blount (1654–93). See No. 14.

To His Much Honoured Friend JOHN DRYDEN Esq.

SIR,

The Value I have ever had for your Writings, makes me impatient to peruse all Treatises that are crown'd with your Name; whereof, the last that fell into my Hands, was your *Religio Laici*; which expresses as well your great Judgment in, as Value for, Religion: a thing too rarely found in this Age among *Gentlemen* of your Parts; and, I am confident, (with the Blessing of God upon your Endeavours) not unlikely to prove of great Advantage to the Publick; since, as Mr. *Herbert* well observes,

> *A Verse may find him, who a Sermon flies,*
> *And turn Delight into a Sacrifice.*[1]

We read in Ancient Times, before the Institution of *Moral Philosophy* by *Socrates*, that *Poets* in general were to the People in stead of their *Sacred Writ*, from whom they received their *Divinity*, and Opinion concerning the *Gods*; as, who, and how, to be worshipped, how pleased and pacified, by what *Prayers* and *Ceremonies*, together with such *Rites* and *Ceremonies* as were the *Dionysiaca, Cybeliaca, Isiaca, Eleusiniaca*, and the like, Instituted by *Orpheus*. All which were built upon this Ground, That there could be no true *Poet* but must be Divinely inspired; and if Divinely inspired, then certainly to be believed. This we find largely disputed and asserted even by *Philosophers* of best Account in those Days. But the two main Arguments [that] induced them to that

---

[1] George Herbert, *The Temple* (1633), 'The Church-Porch', st. 1.

Belief, were; *First*, That extraordinary Motion of Mind wherewith all good *Poets* in all Ages have been possessed and agitated: And, *secondly*, The Testimony of *Poets* themselves, who professing themselves Inspired, have made particular Relations of strange Visions, Raptures, and Apparitions to that purpose: So that as the Beginning, Growth, and Confirmation of Idolatry may be ascribed (as by many it is) to *Poets*, and their Authority; so also to supposed *Enthusiasms* and *Inspirations*, upon which that Authority was chiefly grounded. Hence it is, that many Ancient Authors, as *Aristotle*, *Strabo*, and others, affirm, That *Poetry* (in matter of *Writing* and *Composition*) was in use long before *Prose*: which might seem strange, if not incredible, did we judge by the Disposition of later Times; but of those *Enthusiastick Times*, not less probable, than certain, as our Learned *Casaubon* well observes. And this I thought fitting to premise, in Answer to that Objection which your Modesty is so apprehensive of, *viz*. That being a *Laick*, you interpose in Sacred Matters.

Rapin (in his *Reflections*)[1] speaking of the necessary Qualities belonging to a *Poet*, tells us, *He must have a* Genius *extraordinary, great Natural Gifts, a Wit just, fruitful, piercing, solid, and universal; an Understanding clean and distinct; an Imagination neat and pleasant; an Elevation of Soul, that depends not only on Art or Study, but is purely a Gift of Heaven, which must be sustained by a lively Sense and Vivacity; Judgment, to consider wisely of Things; and Vivacity, for the beautiful Expression of them, &c.* Now this *Character* is so justly *yours*, as I cannot but think that he described what a great *Poet* should be, by hearing what *you* were; and the rather, since I have been informed by some *English* of his Acquaintance, That *Monsieur Rapin* was studious in our Language, only for your sake: Nor would his Pains be lost.

'Tis a Question not easily to be decided, Whether you have been more serviceable to the Peace of the *State* in your *Absolom and Achitophel*, or to the *Church* in your *Religio Laici*, or to the *Nobility* and *Gentry* in the innocent Recreation of your *Plays*? A Country-Retirement, like that of *Ovid*'s, to one that has led the Spring of his Age, and Vigour of his Youth, among the Noise and Pleasures of the Town, is certainly a Transformation no less disagreeable, than that which the *Poets* feign of *Acteon*, or *Sacred Writ* of the *Assyrian Monarch*, who grazed with the *Beasts* of the Field;[2] and to abandon a *Covent-Garden* Society for the Insipid Dull Converse of a Country Village (where the

---

[1] René Rapin, *Réflexions sur la Poëtique d' Aristote;* transl. Thomas Rymer, 1674.
[2] Nebuchadnezzar; Daniel, iv. 33.

Nomination of New Healths is the heighth of their Invention) would render a *Rural Life* to be no less than a *Civil Death*, were it not for Mr. *Dryden's* Writings, which keep us still alive, and, by a most Natural Representation of the Humours of the Town, make us flatter and fansie our selves (like the Enjoyment of a Lover's Dream) to be still there.

But I shall wave these Acknowledgments to you, as things too general to be engrossed by me alone: And will now spend the Remainder of this *Epistle* in informing you of the Occasion of my troubling you with this small *Piece*, which I Entitle by the Name of *Religio Laici*, from a Treatise of the *Lord Herbert* of *Cherburie's* so called; whose *Notions* I have often made use of, and grounded the Chief of my Discourse upon his *Five Catholick* or *Universal Principles*: Wherein my only aim is, to assert an *Universal Doctrine*, such as no ways opposeth the Religion Established among us, and which may tend both to the Propagation of Vertue, and Extirpation of Vice, as well as to the Reconciliation of those *Dissenters* now in *England*, who have of late so disturbed the Quiet of this Realm, and who, under the Pretence of Religion, would exclude all *Governours* but *themselves*. For, as a late *Author* well observes, *Every Opinion makes a Sect; every Sect, a Faction; and every Faction (when it is able) a War: and every such War is the Cause of God; and the Cause of God can never be prosecuted with too much Violence: So that all Sobriety is Lukewarmness; and to be Obedient to Government, Carnal Compliance*.[1] Which are the Opinions of those that would rob *Cæsar* of his Due, as well as remove the Peoples *ancient Land-marks*.

But for my part, as in *Civil Politicks*, I would not, in this so *Ancient* and so *Lineal* a *Monarchy*, abandon the Beams of so fair a *Sun*, for the dreadful Expectation of a divided Company of *Stars*; so neither, in *Ecclesiasticks*, do I covet to be without the *Pale* of the *Church*: since, though I will not *Dogmatically* affirm, (as some do) That *Episcopacy* is *Jure Divino*; yet (with the *Lord Bacon*) I say, and think *ex Animo*, That it is the nearest to *Apostolical Truth*, and the most coherent with *Monarchy*: Wherein, I know, you will not differ from me.

And therefore, *Sir*, at this time, when the *Name* of *Christ* is made use of to palliate so great Villanies and Treasons, under the Pretext of *God's Cause*, against both *King* and *Government*, I thought I could do no less than snatch up all *Weapons* that might defend the *Publick*, and hope I have not lighted upon one with a *double Edge*.

[1] Not identified.

I have endeavoured that my Discourse should be onely a Continuance of yours; and that, as you taught Men how to *Believe*, so I might instruct them how to *Live*. For, as Dr. *Donne* well observes, Though *Christianity* is the *Fort* or *Citadel*, yet *Vertue* and *Moral Honesty* are its *Fences* and *Out-works*, whereby alone it is teneable.[1] Wherefore, I designed this Treatise of mine to be onely an *Addition*, or rather the *Consequence* of yours; encouraging Men to Live up to the *Vertue* of that *Doctrine* you teach. Which, with your Pardon for the present, and Friendship for the future, is the highest *Ambition* of,

SIR,

Your most Faithful Friend, and Servant,

C. B.

34. Dryden on his *History of the League*

1684

The opening of a letter to Tonson, Dryden's publisher (British Museum Egerton MS. 2869, f. 30), written in the autumn of 1684. Dryden's *History of the League. Written in French by Monsieur Maimbourg. Translated into English According to His Majesty's Command* had been published by Tonson in late July.

The two Melons you sent I receivd before your letter, which came foure houres after: I tasted one of them, which was too good to need an excuse; the other is yet untouchd. You have written diverse things which gave me great satisfaction; particularly that the History of the League is commended: and I hope the onely thing I feard in it, is not found out. Take it all together, and I dare say without vanity 'tis the best translation of any History in English, though I cannot say 'tis the best History; but that is no fault of mine. I am glad my Lord Duke of Ormond has one. . . .

[1] Letter of 4 October 1622.

35. *Odi imitatores servum pecus*, &c.[1]

1685

The first part of *A Satyr on the modern Translators* (1685) by Matthew Prior (1664–1721; see also *infra*, No. 36). The poem was provoked by the publication of *Ovid's Epistles*, *Miscellany Poems* (1684), and *Sylvae* (1685), all miscellanies for which Dryden was responsible. 'Let our translators know', said Prior in a letter, 'that Rome and Athens are our territories; that our Laureate might in good manners have left the version of Latin authors to those who had the happiness to understand them' (Prior, *Literary Works* (1959), ed. H. B. Wright and M. K. Spears, ii. 823; for the complete text of the *Satyr*, which was published in *Poems on Affairs of State* (1697), see *ibid.*, i. 19–24).

Since the united cunning of the Stage,
Has balk'd the hireling Drudges of the Age:
Since *Betterton* of late so thrifty 's grown,
Revives old Plays, or wisely acts his own:[2]
Thum'd *Rider*[3] with a Catalogue of Rhimes,
Makes the compleatest Poet of our Times:
Those who with nine months toil had spoil'd a Play,
In hopes of Eating at a full third Day,[4]
Justly despairing longer to sustain
A craving Stomach from an empty Brain,
Have left Stage-practice, chang'd their old Vocations,
Atoning for bad Plays, with worse Translations,
And like old *Sternhold*,[5] with laborious spite,

[1] 'I hate imitators, the servile herd, &c.'; Prior's epigraph, adapted from Horace, *Epistles*, I. xix. 19.
[2] Thomas Betterton (*c.* 1635–1710), actor-manager. The two theatre companies united in 1682, with Betterton at the head.
[3] John Rider (1562–1632), Bishop of Killaloe, author of a Latin-English dictionary.
[4] The dramatist usually took the third day's profits.
[5] Thomas Sternhold and John Hopkins rendered the Psalms in metre (1547–62).

Burlesque what nobler Muses better write:
Thus while they for their Causes only seem
To change the Channel, they corrupt the Stream.

·　　　　　·　　　　　·

In the head of this Gang too *John Dryden* appears,
But to save the Town-censure and lessen his Fears,
Join'd with a Spark whose Title makes me civil,[1]
For *Scandalum Magnatum* is the Devil:
Such mighty Thoughts from *Ovid*'s Letters flow,
That the Translation is a work for two;
Who in one Copy joyn'd their shame have shewn,
Since *T—e*[2] could spoil so many, though alone:
My Lord I thought so generous would prove,
To scorn a Rival in affairs of Love:
But well he knew his teeming pangs were vain,
Till Midwife *Dryden* eas'd his labouring Brain;
And that when part of *Hudibras*'s Horse
Jogg'd on, the other would not hang an Arse;[3]
So when fleet *Jowler* hears the joyful halloo,
He drags his sluggish Mate, and *Tray*[4] must follow.
But how could this learn'd brace employ their time?
One construed sure, while th' other pump'd for Rhime:
Or it with these, as once at *Rome*, succeeds,
The *Bibulus* subscribes to *Cæsar*'s Deeds:[5]
This, from his Partners Acts, ensures his Name,
Oh sacred thirst of everlasting Fame!
That could defile those well cut Nails with Ink,
And make his Honour condescend to think:
But what Excuse, what Preface can atone,
For Crimes which guilty *Bayes*[6] has singly done?
Bayes, whom *Rose Alley* Ambuscade[7] injoyn'd,
To be to Vices which he practic'd kind,

---

[1] John Sheffield, Earl of Mulgrave, with whom Dryden translated one of Ovid's epistles.

[2] Nahum Tate, who translated three of the epistles.

[3] Butler, *Hudibras*, I. i. 447–50.

[4] *Jowler . . . Tray:* hounds.

[5] Bibulus was so ineffectual a colleague of Julius Caesar's that their consulship was derided as that of Julius and Caesar (59 B.C.).

[6] Dryden; see *supra*, No. 10.

[7] See footnote 4 on p. 153.

And brought the venome of a spitefull *Satyr*
To the safe innocence of a *dull Translator.*
Bayes, who by all the Club was thought most fit ⎫
To violate the *Mantuan Prophet's*[1] wit,   ⎬
And more debauch what loose *Lucretius* writ.[2] ⎭
When I behold the rovings of his Muse,   ⎫
How soon *Assyrian* Ointments she would lose   ⎬
For Diamond Buckles sparkling at their Shoes.[3] ⎭
When *Virgil's* height is lost, when *Ovid* soars, ⎫
And in Heroics *Canace* deplores   ⎬
Her Follies, louder than her Father roars,[4]   ⎭
I'd let him take *Almanzor* for his Theme;   ⎫
In lofty Verse make *Maximin* blaspheme,   ⎬
Or sing in softer Airs St. *Katharine's* Dream.[5] ⎭
Nay, I could hear him damn last Ages Wit,
And rail at Excellence he ne'er can hit;[6]
His Envy shou'd at powerfull *Cowley* rage,[7]
And banish Sense with *Johnson* from the Stage:[8]
His Sacrilege should plunder *Shakespear's* Urn,[9]
With a dull Prologue make the Ghost return[10]
To bear a second Death, and greater pain,
While the Fiend's words the Oracle prophane;
But when not satisfy'd with Spoils at home,
The Pyrate wou'd to foreign Borders roam;

---

[1] Virgil; Dryden translated an eclogue for the 1684 *Miscellany Poems* and three passages from the *Aeneid* for *Sylvae*.

[2] 'Lucretius the Fourth Book, concerning the Nature of Love', in *Sylvae*.

[3] Prior adapts Dryden's 'Lucretius . . . concerning the Nature of Love', ll. 99–100, mocking the extravagance of lovers.

[4] Canace, daughter of Aeolus, god of the winds, is the heroine of an Ovidian epistle translated by Dryden.

[5] The hero of *The Conquest of Granada*, and the tyrant and heroine of *Tyrannick Love*.

[6] *Cf.* the Epilogue to *The Conquest of Granada*, the Second Part, and Dryden's 'Defence of the Epilogue. Or, An Essay on the Dramatique Poetry of the last Age' (published with the play).

[7] Presumably at this date a reference to Dryden's discussion of Cowley's free rendering of Pindar (Preface to *Ovid's Epistles*); though Dryden recognizes that 'a Genius so elevated and unconfin'd as Mr. *Cowley*'s, was but necessary to make *Pindar* speak *English*, and that was to be perform'd by no other way than Imitation.'

[8] Again a reference mainly to 'Defence of the Epilogue', but a misrepresentation of Dryden's critical attitude to Jonson.

[9] Dryden's adaptations of Shakespeare (1670, 1678, 1679).

[10] Prologue to Dryden's *Troilus and Cressida*, 'Spoken by Mr. *Betterton*, Representing the Ghost of *Shakespear*'.

May he still split on some unlucky Coast,
And have his Works, or Dictionary lost;
That he may know what *Roman* Authors mean,
No more than does our blind Translatress *Behn*.[1] . . .

---

[1] Aphra Behn (1640–89), author of 'Oenone to Paris' in *Ovid's Epistles*, done (says Dryden) 'in Mr. *Cowley*'s way of Imitation only. I was desir'd to say that the Authour who is of the *Fair Sex*, understood not *Latine*. But if she does not, I am afraid she has given us occasion to be asham'd who do.'

36. Prior parodies
The Hind and the Panther
1687

Extracts from *The Hind and the Panther Transvers'd to the Story of The Country Mouse and the City-Mouse* (1687), by Matthew Prior (1664–1721) and Charles Montague (1661–1715; created Baron Halifax in 1700). Prior wrote later in a letter:

Mr. Dryden turning R. C. wrote a Poem which he called the H. and the P. By the H. he means the Church of R. and the C. of E. by the P. . . . The main Objection against it was that the matter of it was false and inviduous, and the way of its writing ungentile and rayling; but Billings-gate Manners in better Language, and Far below even the dignity of Satyr, for which the Author has formerly been beaten. . . . The second Objection was that this piece contradicted the known rules of Poetry and even common Sense, for the whole being a Fable, the Beasts who speak should have reference to the Characters of the Persons they represent. . . . To make the thing yet more rediculous we took the same humour the D. of B. had some years since in his play, the Rehearsal [see p. 45 *supra*]; that is we Bring in B. by whom we mean D. defending (as his way is) the foolishest things in his Poem, and Smith and Johnson by whom we mean any two Gentlemen of Tolerable Sense and judg-ment finding those faults which are most obvious.

(Prior, *Literary Works* (1959), ed. H. B. Wright and M. K. Spears, ii. 832–3; for the complete text of the parody see *ibid.*, i. 35–57). *Cf.* Dr. Johnson, p. 300, *infra*.

(*a*)

SMI. Here 's the *Kings* Health to thee—Communicate.

BAYES. Well, Gentlemen, here it is, and I'le be bold to say, the exactest Piece the world ever saw, a *Non Pareillo* I'faith. But I must bespeak your pardons if it reflects any thing upon your perswasion.

JOHNS. Use your Liberty, Sir, you know we are no *Bigots*.

BAYES. Why then you shall see me lay the *Reformation* on its back, I'gad, and justifie our Religion by way of *Fable*.

JOHNS. An apt contrivance indeed! what do you make a *Fable* of your *Religion*?

BAYES. Ay I'gad, and without *Morals* too; for I tread in no mans steps; and to show you how far I can out-do any thing that ever was writ in this kind, I have taken *Horace*'s design, but I'gad, have so out-done him, you shall be asham'd for your *old friend*. You remember in him the *Story* of the *Country-Mouse*, and the *City-Mouse*; what a plain simple thing it is, has no more life and spirit in it, I'gad, than a Hobby-horse; and his *Mice* talk so meanly, such common stuff, so like *meer Mice*, that I wonder it has pleas'd the world so long. But now will I undeceive *Mankind*, and teach 'em to *heighten*, and *elevate a Fable*. I'le bring you in the very same *Mice* disputing the depth of *Philosophy*, searching into the fundamentals of *Religion*, quoting *Texts*, *Fathers*, *Councils*, and all that, I'gad, as you shall see either of 'em could easily make an Asse of a *Country Vicar*. Now whereas *Horace* keeps to the dry naked story, I have more copiousness than to do that, I'gad. Here, I draw you general *Characters*, and describe all the *beasts* of the *Creation*; there, I launch out into long *Digressions*, and leave my *Mice* for twenty Pages together; then I fall into *Raptures*, and make the finest *Soliloquies*, as would ravish you. Won't this do, think you?

JOHNS. Faith, Sir, I don't well conceive you; all this about two *Mice*?

BAYES. Ay, why not? is it not great and Heroical? but come, you'l understand it better when you hear it; and pray be as severe as you can, I'gad I defie all *Criticks*. Thus it begins.[1]

> *A milk-white* Mouse *immortal and unchang'd,*
> *Fed on soft Cheese, and o're the* Dairy *rang'd;*
> *Without, unspotted; innocent within,*
> *She fear'd no danger, for she knew no* Ginn.

JOHNS. Methinks Mr. *Bayes*, soft Cheese is a little too coarse Diet for an *immortal Mouse*; were there any necessity for her eating, you should have consulted *Homer* for some *Cœlestial Provision*.

BAYES. Faith, Gentlemen, I did so; but indeed I have not the *Latin* one, which I have mark'd by me, and could not readily find it in the Original.

> *Yet had She oft been* scar'd by bloody Claws
> *Of winged* Owls, and stern *Grimalkins* Paws

---

[1] Parodying the opening of *The Hind and the Panther*.

> *Aim'd at her* destin'd Head, which made her *fly*,
> Tho She was *doom'd to Death*, and *fated not to dye.*

SMI. How came She that *fear'd no danger* in the line before, to be scar'd in this, Mr. *Bayes?*

BAYES. Why then you may have it *chas'd* if you will; for I hope a Man may run away without being *afraid*; mayn't he?

JOHNS. But pray give me leave; how was She *doom'd to Death*, if She was *fated not to dye*; are not *doom* and *fate*, much the same thing?

BAYES. Nay *Gentlemen*, if you question my skill in the Language, I'm your humble Servant; the *Rogues* the *Criticks*, that will allow me nothing else, give me that; sure I that made the Word, know best what I meant by it; I assure you, *doom'd* and *fated*, are quite different things.

SMI. Faith, Mr. *Bayes*, if you were *doom'd* to be hang'd, whatever you were *fated* to, 'twould give you but small comfort.

BAYES. Never trouble your head with that, Mr. *Smith*, mind the business in hand.

> *Not so her young; their* Linsy-woolsy *line,*
> *Was Hero's make, half humane, half Divine.*

SMI. Certainly these *Hero's, half Humane, half Divine*, have very little of the *Mouse* their *Mother.*

BAYES. Gadsokers! Mr. *Johnson*, does your Friend think I mean nothing but a *Mouse*, by all this? I tell thee, Man, I mean a *Church*, and these young Gentlemen her Sons, signifie *Priests*, *Martyrs* and *Confessors*, that were hang'd in *Oat's Plot*. There 's an excellent *Latin* Sentence, which I had a mind to bring in, *Sanguis Martyrum semen Ecclesiæ*, and I think I have not wrong'd it in the Translation.

> *Of these a slaughter'd Army lay in Blood,*
> *Whose sanguine Seed encreas'd the sacred* Brood;
> *She multipli'd by these, now rang'd alone,*
> *And wander'd in the Kingdoms once her own.*

SMI. Was She *alone* when *the sacred Brood was encreased?*

BAYES. Why thy Head 's running on the *Mouse* again. . . .

(b)

BAYES.

> *Quickned with Fire below, these Monsters breed*
> *In Fenny* Holland, *and in Fruitful* Tweed.

Now to write something new and out of the way, to elevate and surprize, and all that, I fetch, you see this *Quickning Fire* from the Bottom of *Boggs* and *Rivers*.

JOHNS. Why, Faith, that 's as ingenious a Contrivance as the *Virtuoso's* making a Burning-Glass of Ice.

BAYES. Why was there ever any such thing? Let me perish if ever I heard of it. The Fancy was sheer new to me; and I thought no Man had reconcil'd those Elements but my self. Well Gentlemen! Thus far I have followed Antiquity, and as *Homer* has numbred his Ships, so I have rang'd my Beasts. Here is my *Boar* and my *Bear*, and my *Fox*, and my *Wolf*, and the rest of 'em all against my poor *Mouse*. Now what do you think I do with all these?

SMI. Faith I do'nt know, I suppose you make 'em fight.

BAYES. Fight! I'gad I'd as soon make 'em Dance. No, I do no earthly thing with 'em, nothing at all, I'gad: I think they have play'd their Parts sufficiently already; I have walk'd 'em out, show'd 'em to the Company, and rais'd your Expectation. And now whilst you hope to see 'em bated, and are dreaming of Blood and Battels, they sculk off, and you hear no more of 'em.

SMI. Why, Faith, Mr. *Bayes*, now you have been at such expence in setting forth their Characters, it had been too much to have gone through with 'em.

BAYES. I'gad so it had: And then I'le tell you another thing, 'tis not every one that reads a Poem through. And therefore I fill the first part with Flowers, Figures, fine Language, and all that; and then I'gad sink by degrees, till at last I write but little better than other People. And whereas most Authors *creep servilely* after the Old Fellows, and strive to grow upon their Readers; I take another Course, I bring in all my Characters together, and let 'em see I could go on with 'em; but I'gad, I wo'nt.

JOHNS. Could go on with 'em Mr. *Bayes*! there 's no Body doubts that; You have a most particular *Genius* that way. . . .

(*c*)

BAYES. . . . But now, Gentlemen, the Plot thickens, here comes my t'other Mouse, the City Mouse.

> A *spotted* Mouse, the prettiest next the White,
> Ah! were her Spots wash'd out, as pretty quite,

With *Phylacteries* on her Forehead spred,
Crozier in Hand, and *Miter* on her Head.
Three Steeples Argent on her Sable Shield,
Liv'd in the *City*, and disdain'd the *Field*.[1]

JOHNS. This is a glorious *Mouse* indeed! but, as you have dress'd her, we do'nt know whether she be *Jew, Papist* or *Protestant*.

BAYES. Let me embrace you, Mr. *Johnson*, for that; you take it right. She is a meer *Babel* of *Religions*, and therefore she 's a *spotted Mouse* here, and will be a *Mule* presently. But to go on.

This Princess—

SMI. What *Princess*, Mr. *Bayes*?

BAYES. Why this *Mouse*, for I forgot to tell you, an *Old Lyon* made a *left Hand Marriage*[2] with her Mother, and begot *on her Body Elizabeth Schism*, who was married to *Timothy Sacriledg*, and had Issue *Graceless Heresy*. Who all give the same Coat with their Mother, *Three Steeples Argent*, as I told you before.

This Princess tho *estrang'd* from what was *best,*
Was least Deform'd, because Reform'd the least.

There 's *De* and *Re* as good I'gad as ever was.

She in a Masquerade of Mirth and Love,
Mistook the Bliss of Heaven for Bacchinals above,
And grub'd the Thorns beneath our tender Feet,
To make the Paths of Paradise more sweet.[3]

There 's a Jolly Mouse for you, let me see any Body else that can shew you such another. Here now have I one damnable severe reflecting Line, but I want a Rhime to it, can you help me Mr. *Johnson*. . . .

(d)

SMI. . . . I have heard you quote *Reynard the Fox*.

BAYES. Why there 's it now; take it from me, Mr. *Smith*, there is as good *Morality*, and as sound *Precepts*, in the *delectable History of Reynard the Fox*, as in any Book I know, except *Seneca*. Pray tell me where in any other Author could I have found so pretty a Name for a Wolf

---

[1] Parodying *The Hind and the Panther*, i. 327–9, 395, 399, and iii. 193–4.
[2] *The Hind*, i. 351–6.
[3] *Ibid.* i. 408–9, i. 382–7.

as *Isgrim*? But prithee, Mr. *Smith*, give me no more trouble, and let me go on with my *Mouse*.

> *One Evening*, when she went away from Court,
> *Levee's and Couchee's past without resort.*[1]

There 's Court Language for you; nothing gives a Verse so fine a turn as an Air of good Breeding.

SMI. But methinks the *Levee's and Couchee's* of a *Mouse* are too great, especially when she is walking from Court to the cooler Shades.

BAYES. I'gad now have you forgot what I told you that she was a *Princess*. But pray mind; here the two Mice meet.

> She met the Country Mouse, whose *fearful Face*
> *Beheld from far the common watering Place,*
> *Nor durst approach—*

SMI. Methinks, Mr. *Bayes*, this Mouse is strangely alter'd, since she *fear'd no Danger*.

BAYES. Godsokers! Why no more she does not yet fear either Man or Beast: But, poor Creature, she 's afraid of the Water, for she could not swim, as you see by this.

> *Nor durst approach, till with an awful Roar*
> *The Soveraign Lyon bad her fear no more.*

But besides, 'tis above thirty Pages off that I told you she *fear'd no Danger*; and I'gad if you will have no variation of the Character, you must have the same thing over and over again; 'tis the Beauty of Writing to strike you still with something new. Well, but to proceed.

> *But when she had this sweetest Mouse in view,*
> *Good Lord, how she admir'd her Heavenly Hiew!*

Here now to show you I am Master of all Stiles, I let my self down from the *Majesty* of *Virgil*, to the *Sweetness* of *Ovid*.

> *Good Lord, how she admir'd her Heavenly Hiew!*

What more easy and familiar! I writ this Line for the *Ladies*: the little Rogues will be so fond of me to find I can yet be so tender. I hate such a rough unhewen Fellow as *Milton*, that a Man must sweat to read Him; I'gad you may run over this and be almost asleep.

---

[1] For the passages parodied in this extract, see *The Hind*, i. 511, 516, 528–30, 542–3, 549; ii. 410; i. 570; Preface; i. 572.

Th' Immortal Mouse who saw the *Viceroy* come
So far to see Her, did invite her Home.

There 's a pretty Name now for the *Spotted Mouse*, the *Viceroy*!
SMI. But pray why d'e call her so?
BAYES. Why! Because it sounds prettily: I'le call her the *Crown-General*
presently if I've a mind to it. Well.

—did invite her Home
To smoak a Pipe, and o're a sober Pot
Discourse of *Oates* and *Bedloe*, and the *Plot*.
She made a Court'sy, like a Civil Dame,
And, being *much a Gentlewoman*, came.

Well, Gentlemen, here 's my first part finish'd, and I think I have kept
my Word with you, and given it the *Majestick turn of Heroick Poesy*.
The rest *being matter of Dispute, I had not such frequent occasion for the
magnificence of Verse*, tho I'gad they speak very well. And I have heard
Men, and *considerable Men* too, talk the very same things, a great deal
worse.
JOHNS. Nay, without doubt, Mr. *Bayes*, they have received no small
advantage from the smoothness of your numbers.
BAYES. Ay, ay, I can do't, if I list: though you must not think I have
been so dull as to' mind these things my self, but 'tis the advantage of
our *Coffee-house*, that from their talk one may write a very good
polemical discourse, without ever troubling ones head with the Books
of *Controversie*. For I can take the slightest of their Arguments, and
clap 'em pertly into four Verses, which shall stare any *London Divine*
in the face. Indeed your knotty Reasonings with a long train of *Majors*
and *Minors*, and the Devil and all, are too barbarous for my stile; but
i' gad I can flourish better with one of these twinkling Arguments,
than the best of 'em can fight with t' other. But we return to our
Mouse, and now I've brought 'em together, let 'em 'en speak for
themselves, which they will do extreamly well, or I'm mistaken: and
pray observe, Gentlemen, if in one you don't find all the delicacy of a
luxurious City-Mouse, and in the other all the plain simplicity of a
sober serious Matron. . . .

37. Gentle George reads
The Hind and the Panther

1687, 1689

Extracts from letters of Sir George Etherege (c. 1634–91), James II's ambassador at Ratisbon, (a) to Lord Middleton on 23 June 1687, (b) to Mr. Guy on 4 August 1687, and (c) to the Duke of Buckingham on 21 October (?) 1689. Dryden and Etherege were old friends. Dryden wrote an Epilogue for *The Man of Mode* (1676), and sent a jocular verse epistle to Etherege in 1686. For the full texts of these letters, see *The Letterbook of Sir George Etherege* (1928), ed. Sybil Rosenfeld, pp. 227, 224, 421.

(a) 'Mr. Wynne has sent me the *Hind and Panther*, by which I find John Dryden has a noble ambition to restore poetry to its ancient dignity in wrapping up the mysteries of religion in verse. What a shame it is to me to see him a saint and remain still the same devil. . . . Dryden finds his *Mackflecknoe* does no good;[1] I wish better success with his Hind and Panther.'

(b) 'You have a war in England between the Hind and the Panther. General Dryden is an expert captain, but I always thought him fitter for execution than for council. . . .'

(c) 'They tell me my old Acquaintance Mr. Dryden has left off the Theatre, and wholly applies him self to the Study of the Controversies between the two Churches. Pray Heaven! this strange alteration in him portends nothing disastrous to the State; but I have all along observed, That Poets do Religion as little Service by drawing their Pens for it, as the Divines do Poetry by pretending to Versification.'

---

[1] I.e. has not made Shadwell less dull?

38. Clifford's poison pen

1687

Notes upon Mr. Dryden's Poems in Four Letters by Martin Clifford
(*d.* 1677), who became Master of the Charterhouse in 1671 and is
said to have been associated with Buckingham in writing *The
Rehearsal* (*supra*, No. 10).

The First Letter

SIR,

I had pass'd by the gross Scurrility of your last Prologue with the
same Contempt that I have always had for the rest of your Scribling,
had not some of my Acquaintance suggested to me, that it was unfit
to suffer you any longer to go on without Reproof. I will now therefore take you as much into my consideration as so trifling a subject does
deserve: Not at all doubting but to kill this Tetter[1] of yours with the
ordinary Remedy of a little Ink. The Method I purpose to use, shall
be, First to expose your Faults, (I do not mean all) for that were as
Diego[2] said of the Poor of his Parish, All the Parish. No—you are too
abundant and plentifull a Fop for any man to misemploy so much time
upon, but enough to satisfie any man of Judgment with the Abilities
of our *Poet Laureat.*

And next I will detect your Thefts, letting the World know how
great a Plagiary you are; and that for all your pretences to Wit and
Judicious Censure, you do live in as much Ignorance and Darkness
as you did in the Womb: That your Writings are like a Jack of all
Trades Shop, they have Variety, but nothing of value. And that if
thou art not the dullest Plant-Animal that ever the Earth produced,
all that I have convers'd with are strangely mistaken in thee.

---

[1] A pustular skin disease.
[2] Unidentified.

So dull thou art, as if thou'dst largely quaft
All sleepy Juyces for thy mornings draught;
Henbane and Hemlock, which mans Soul benight,
Mandrake and Poppy, &c.

For this time farewel: Within two or three days you shall hear further from me.

The Second Letter

I have written to you within the Time to which I was by my promise engaged, and you may perceive by this Letter with what care I have read over your Conquest of *Granada*, a dull heavy task, which few but my self, except *some Choice Female Spirits, and Peculiar Friends of yours at Court* (as your Brother *Bayes* has it in the *Rehearsal*) would have undertaken. You have therefore, to use one of your own Compliments, *the more grand obligement* to me, for going through with a Work of that difficulty. I must confess I did not make an end of it without twenty Stops, sorry Oaths, and at least an hundred and fifty Resolutions at every Page to give it over, and truly

—I did dare
To be so impudent as to despair—[1]

that I should ever finish it. In this vexation of mind I frequently threw the paltry Book to the ground, I scratch'd my Head, I rubb'd my Forehead, put up my Black Lead Pen, and exprest all the postures that men use, when they are troubled with an Impertinent. Yet after all this, with much strugling *Opus exegi,*[2] and send you the Fruits of my Labour, to whom of right they are most due; *being beforehand assured that you will not be concern'd for any thing I say, since the common Opinion (how unjust soever) has been to your advantage; and having swept the stakes, you can be content to sit quietly, to hear your Fortune curs'd by some, and your Faults arraigned by others.*[3]

The plain and natural construction of which words as they lie before us, is, that having received your Money from the Door-keepers, having pick'd the Pockets of your Auditors, you care not a Rush with what Contempt and Nauseousness the Judicious speak of your Bauble; yet you grant that *a severe Critick is the greatest help to a*

---

[1] *Alman.* Page 33 [Clifford].
[2] I elucidated the work.
[3] Preface to *Almanzor* [i.e. *The Conquest of Granada*; Clifford].

good Wit. He does the Office of a Friend, whilst he designs that of an Enemy; and his malice keeps a Pœt within those Bounds which the Luxuriancy of his Wit and Fancy would tempt him to over-leap.[1] How luxuriant your Wit and Fancy is, will presently appear without any need of great severity in the Critick, who has omitted at least a hundred good thumping substantial Faults, for one he has taken notice of.

To begin with your Character of *Almanzor, which you avow to have taken from the Achilles in Homer*; pray hear what *Famianus Strada* says of such Takers as Mr. *Dryden, Ridere soleo cum video homines ab Homeri virtutibus strenuè declinantes, si quid vero irrepsit vitii, id avidè arripientes.*[2] But I might have spared this Quotation, and you your avowing: For this Character might as well have been borrowed from some of the Stalls in *Bedlam*, or any of your own hair-brain'd Coxcombs, which you call *Heroes*, and Persons of Honour. I remember just such another fuming *Achilles* in *Shakespear*, one Ancient *Pistol, whom he avows to be a man of so fiery a temper, and so impatient of an injury, even from Sir John Falstaff his Captain, and a Knight, that he not onely disobeyed his Commands about carrying a Letter to Mrs. Page, but return'd him an answer* as full of contumely, and in as opprobrious terms as he could imagine.[3]

> Let Vultures gripe thy guts, for gourd and Fullam holds,
> And high and low beguiles the rich and poor.
> Tester I'll have in pouch, when thou shall lack,
> Base Phrygian Turk, &c.

Let's see e'er an *Abencerrago*[4] fly at a higher pitch. Take him at another turn quarrelling with Corporal *Nym*, an old *Zegri*:[4] The difference arose about mine Hostess, *Quickly* (for I would not give a Rush for a man unless he be particular in matters of this moment); they both aimed at her body, but *Abencerrago Pistol* defies his Rival in these words:

> Fetch from the Powdring-Tub of Infamy
> That Lazar-Kite of Cressids kind,
> Doll Tearsheet, she by name, and her espouse: I have and I will hold
> The quondam Quickly for the onely she.
> And pauca—[5]

[1] Preface [Clifford].
[2] Famiano Strada (1572–1649), humanist and historian: 'I am accustomed to laugh when I see men actively turning away from the virtues of Homer and greedily laying hold of any real sort of vice that has crawled in.'
[3] *Merry Wives of Windsor* [Clifford; I. iii. 92].
[4] Moorish factions in *The Conquest of Granada*.
[5] *Henry V*, II. i. 79–82.

There 's enough. Does not Quotation sound as well as

'Οινοβαρὴς κυνὸς ὄμματ' ἔχων, κραδίην τ' ἐλαφεῖο
Δημοβόρος Βασιλεύς.[1]

But the Four Sons of *Ammon*, the Three bold *Beachams*, the Four *London* Prentices, *Tamerlain* the *Scythian* Shepherd, *Muleasses*, *Amurath*, and *Bajazet*, or any raging Turk at the *Red Bull* and *Fortune*,[2] might as well have been urged by you as a Pattern of your *Almanzor*, as the *Achilles* in *Homer*, but then our Laureat had not pass'd for so Learned a man as he desires his unlearned Admirers should esteem him.

But I am strangely mistaken if I have not seen this very *Almanzor* of yours in some disguise about this Town, and passing under another Name. Prethee tell me true, was not this Huff-cap once the Indian Emperour, and at another time did not he call himself *Maximine*? Was not *Lyndaraxa* once called *Almeria*, I mean under *Montezuma* the Indian Emperour? I protest and vow they are either the same, or so alike, that I can't for my heart distinguish one from the other. You are therefore a strange unconscionable Thief, that art not content to steal from others, but do'st rob thy poor wretched Self too.

I have thus far made bold with you out of meer Charity; for *you say that observing your Errors is a great step to the correcting them.*[3]

But pray give me leave without any offence, to ask you why it was a Fault in *Shakespear*, that *his Plays were grounded upon Impossibilities, and so meanly written, that the Comedy neither caused your Mirth, nor the serious part your Concernment?* This you say in your Postscript, and in your Preface, you tell us, *that a Poet was not tied to a bare Representation of what is possible, but might let himself loose: For he has only his Fancy for his Guide, which sees farther in its own Empire, and produces more satisfactory notions.*

I understand not well your meaning, but my dear Friend, thou may'st remember *Aristotle* was of another opinion.

Δράμματα καλεῖσθαι φάσι τίνες οἷον μιμοῦνται τοὺς ποιοῦντας καὶ Δρῶντας.[4]

---

[1] Homer, *Iliad* i. 225 and 231: 'You, heavy with wine, with the face of a dog and the heart of a deer . . . folk-devouring king!'

[2] Brawlers and Turks in popular farces and in the older drama (Amurath, the name of Sultans in Shakespeare, *2 Henry IV*, V. ii; Tamerlain and Bajazet in Marlowe's play). The Fortune Theatre was burnt down in 1621. The Red Bull, one of the last of the open-air theatres, was playing a Shakespeare and Beaumont and Fletcher repertoire after the Restoration.

[3] Preface [Clifford].

[4] A corrupt version of Aristotle's statement that according to some, plays are called *dramas* because they present people as doing things (*Poetics*, iii. 4).

I was about six years since a little acquainted with a Name-sake and Countreyman of yours, who pilfer'd out of Monsieur *Hedelin*, *Menardière*, and *Corneille*,[1] an Essay of Dramatick Poetry, wherein he tells us another tale, and says, *a Play ought to be a just and lively Image of Humane Nature, Representing its Passions and Humours*, &c.

—*Si sic*
omnia dixisset.[2]

You shall hear further from me e're it be long.

The Third Letter

When you have wiped off all former stains from your Reputation, I shall think you worthy to be called to another manner of Account, but till then I will content my self to proceed in this mild way of Correcting your Insolence which I have begun, submitting it to the Judgment of all Men, which of us two deserve best the Honourable Title of a Railer.

And now if you were not too peevish to endure a Question, I would make bold to ask you the meaning of this Simile:

> *The Brave* Almanzor
> *Who like a Tempest that out-rides the Wind.*
> *Almanz.* Act. 2. *pag.* 13

The sense of it to my weak and shallow Understanding, is, a Tempest that out-rides it self: And if it be so, pray resolve me **whether you be not cozen'd with the sound, and never took the pains to examine the sense of your own Verses*, which is a Fault you object to others in your modest Preface.

Another of the same.

> *Great Souls discern not when the leap 's too wide,*
> *Because they onely view the farther side.*
> Act. 4

Turn that into Prose, and then this is the Nonsense of it; They do not discern the distance, because they only view the distance. And if that be the best Construction it can bear, then answer me, *Whether you†*
who have undertaken to write Verse without being form'd by Art or Nature

---

* Preface.
† Preface to *Almanz.* [Clifford].
[1] For the sources of the *Essay*, see the notes in J. T. Boulton's edition, 1964.
[2] If only he'd said everything like that.

for it, whether you who have written one of the worst in it, could have written worse without it?

I think this Instance I am going to give you, would have done every jot as well in Prose, as in Heroick Verse.

LYNDARAXA

This is my Will, and this I will have done.
Or this:
None could be seen whilst Almahid *was by,*
Because she was to be her Majesty.

Therefore to reprehend you in your own lofty Stile, by applying an ingenious Couplet.

Either confess your Fault, or hold your Tongue;
For I am sure I am not now i' th' wrong.

Mr. *Dryden,*
There is one of your Virtues which I cannot forbear to animadvert upon, which is your excess of Modesty; When you tell us in your Postscript to *Granada,* That *Shakespear is below the Dullest Writer of Our, or any precedent Age.* In which by your Favour, you Recede as much from your own Right, as you disparage *Almanzor,* because he is yours, in preferring *Ben. Johnson's Cethegus* before him; saying in your Preface, that his Rodomontadoes are neither so irrational as the others, nor so impossible to be put in execution. I'll give you so many instances to the contrary, as shall convince you, and bring you over to my side.

I'll face this storm that thickens in the Wind;
And with bent forehead full against it go,
Till I have found the last and utmost Foe.

Act. 2

If Fate weaves a common Thred, he'll change the doom,
And with new Purple spread a Nobler Loom.

Act. 3

But here 's a dreadfull one:

—My word is past,
I'll take his heart by th' Roots and hold it fast.

If the proudest hard-hearted *Cethegus* of 'em all heard this terrible menace, I believe

—The busie thing
His Soul would straight pack up, and be on Wing;
Like parting Swallows when they seek the Spring.
He 'd shuder up with cold:

Almanz. Act. 4, p. 123

as you elegantly express it in your *Maiden Queen*, pag. 60.

I'll hector Kings to grant my wild Demands.

Act. 3

Fate after him below with pain did move,
And Victory could scarce keep pace above.

Part I, Act. 2

Cætera de genere hoc adeo sunt multa, &c.[1]

We follow Fate which does too fast pursue.
'Tis just that Flames shou'd be condemn'd to Fire.

You must not take it ill, Mr. *Dryden*, if I suspect both those Verses to have a strong Tincture of Nonsense, but if you'l defend 'em, of all loves I beg of thee that thou would'st construe them, and put them into sense: for to me, as Parson *Hugh* says in *Shakespear*,[2] they seemed Lunacies, it is mad as a mad Dog, it is affectatious.

I once thought to have ended this Letter here with a Distich of your own:

Let us at length so many faults forget,
And lose the tale, and take 'em by the great.

But if I had so concluded, I should have omitted a memorable conceit or two; the one is in a Speech of *Almanzor* to his Mothers Ghost.

I'll rush into the Covert of thy Night,
And pull thee backward by thy Shroud to Light.
Or else I'll squeeze thee like a Bladder there,
And make thee groan thy self away to air.

The second is a Speech of *Porphyrius* to *Maximine*, in thy *Tyrannick Love*.

Where'er thou stand'st, I'll level at thy face,
My gushing blood, and spout it at that place.

---

[1] I.e. there are so many other examples.
[2] *Merry Wives*, I. i. 152.

181

The Fourth Letter

Charter-House,
July, 1. 1672.

Since I cannot draw you to make a reply to me, assure your self that after this Letter you shall hear no further from me.

> *An horrid Silence shall invade your Ear,*
> *But in that Silence a fierce Tempest fear.*
> *On the Kings Restoration.*

I intended to have made no more Animadversions upon the viciousness of your Style, till in reviewing the several Pamphlets you have published, I found so much good new matter of that kind, that I could not forbear to return once more to the same subject, and reserve the other heads for the Press.

My first observation shall be of the admirable facility of your Muse in Similes, which allude to nothing. This your Brother *Bayes* has before taken notice of in the *Rehearsal.* But I think it not amiss to insist a little longer on that point; referring it wholly to the Judgment of those fair Ladys, who have hitherto been the best strength of your party, hoping there will be no need of further pains than just transcribing, and laying them before them.

The first I light upon is an excellent Illustration of Grief.

> *Then setting free a sigh from her fair Eyes*
> *She wip'd two Pearles the remnant of Wild Showers,*
> *And hung like drops upon the Bells of Flowers.*
> *Maiden Queen, p. 49*

Another

> *My Soul lies hid in shades of grief,*
> *When like the Bird of Night with half shut Eyes,*
> *She peeps and sickens at the sight of day.*
> *Riv. Lad., p. 32*

A melting Simile upon the like Occasion

> *As some fair Tulip by a storm opprest*
> *Shrinks up, and folds its silken Armes to rest,*
> *And bending to the blast, all pale and dead,*
> *Hears from within the Wind sing round its Head,*
> *So shrouded up that beauty disappears.*
> *Alm[anzor] p. 61*

Upon Anger

> *Why will you in your breast your passion crowd*
> *Like unborn Thunder rowling in a Cloud?*
>
> *Alm.* p. 101

Upon Famine

> *As callow Birds whose Mother's kill'd in seeking of the prey*
> *Cry in their Nests, and think her long away,*
> *And at each leaf that stirs each blast of Wind*
> *Gape for the food which they must never find,*
> *So cry the People in their Misery.*
>
> *Ind. Emp.*

> *Pensive like Kings in their declining State.*
>
> *Riv. Lad.*

Pray, why not like States in their declining State? Where by the way, Mr. *Dryden*, if you had reserv'd this *Davenantism* till the opportunity, you might have given the *Hollanders* a frump, and very honestly have got a Clinch into the Bargain.

> *I shall keep the fasts of Seraphims*
> *And wake for Joy, like Nightingals in May.*
>
> *Maiden Queen*

Bless me! What stuff is this? prethee speak impartially, does not this worthless Collection now seem to you a confused Mass of thoughts tumbling o're one another, in the *Dark?* as you wittily say to my Lord of *Orrery* in the Dedication of the *Rival Ladies?*

Now I'll make bold to have a fling at that kind of thy Writing, which thou, thy Comerades, and thy Admirers, call great and noble thoughts.

> *Now Chance assert thy own inconstancy*
> *And fortune fight, that thou may'st fortune be.*
>
> *Alm.* p. 106

> —*Birds ne'er impose*
> *A Rich plum'd Mistriss, on their feather'd Sons,*
> *But leave their loves more open yet and free*
> *Than all the Fields of Air, their spacious Birth-right.*
>
> *Riv. Lad.,* p. 28

> *Harsh words from her, like blows from angry Kings*
> *Though they are meant affronts, are construed favours.*
>
> *Idem*

Seas are the Fields of Combat for the Winds:
But when they sweep along some flowry Coast
Their Wings move mildly, and their rage is lost.
Move swiftly Sun; and fly a Lovers pace,
Leave Weeks and Months behind thee in thy race.

Al., p. 158

The Sun, honest Mr. *Dryden*, would have done so though *Almanzor* had not commanded him, and if you doubt of it, I refer you to *Gadbury*, *Sanders*, *Lilly*, *Rider*, Poor *Robin*, or any of those learned Men,[1] for your satisfaction.

Zulema. *Dare you what sense and reason prove deny?*
Alm. *When she's in question, sense and reason lye.*

Al., p. 138

Thou hast within thee, without thee, and about thee a most inexhaustible store of such Trumpery; that I must quit this and pass to another head, which is thy dull *Quarlism*, or *Witherism*,[2] to save my own labour and my Readers (if any be so idle as to read this.)

Quis leget hæc?—nemo Hercule nemo,
Vel duo, vel nemo.

Persius[3]

For Example

Whatever Izabella shall command,
Shall always be a Law to Ferdinand.

Alm., part 2, p. 13

To what e'er service you ordain my hand
Name your request, and call it your Command.
Imagine what must needs be brought to pass,
My heart's not made of Marble, or of Brass.

p. 89

Orbella. *Your Father wonders much at your delay.*
Cydaria. *So great a wonder for so small a stay?*

Ind. Emp., p. 13

---

[1] Seventeenth-century astrologers and almanac-makers.
[2] Francis Quarles (1592–1644), and George Wither (1588–1667); at this time representative bad poets.
[3] *Sat.* i. 1–2, in Dryden's version: 'Friend. ... None will read thy Satyrs. *Persius.* This to Me? *Friend.* None; or what's next to none; but two or three.'

Without delay th' unlucky Gift restore,
Or from this Minute never see me more.

Al., p. 104

Grant that she loves me not, at least I see
She loves not others, if she loves not me.

p. 89

Canst thou after this have the Confidence to say thy Plays are written with more Flame than Art? I vow to thee, I cannot perceive either Art, Flame, or the least Spark of fire in thy Poetry. I must acknowledge it has all the qualities of another Element, I mean the Earth, 'tis cold, dry, and so heavy, that at the hearing of it, the judicious part of thy company fall asleep, and one would have thought, thou had'st done so too, at the writing. I foresee that this is labour ill bestow'd upon you, for when thou art reprehended for producing a Chymerical Ninny upon the Stage, thy defence runs thus.

Who told my over-wise Censors I intended him a perfect Character, or, indeed, what necessity was there that he should be so?—or when we quarrel at some other fault, you straight slap us in the Mouth, and tell us, you design'd it so on purpose to make your Play go off more smartly. Which Apology how it differs from what *Bayes* the *Laureat* says, Ile make you your self Judge.

Some will say, this sense is not much to the purpose. Why I grant it, I meant it so, but then 'tis as full of Wit and Drollery as ever it can hold, 'tis like an Orange stuck with Cloves.*

I thought to have rebuked thee for thy scattering of Nonsense under another distinct and peculiar head, but if I had enter'd upon that Theme, I should never have made an end. Therefore I'll conclude with a word, or two, only of advice, for the discharge of my Conscience, as a friend, and one that wishes you well; though I know before hand, you are so prejudiced against me, that you'l be deaf to all I can say; yet not withstanding your aversion I will take the liberty of Counselling you to give over this way of mistaken Poetry, and apply your self to some honest Calling, wherein you may, (and [I] truly hope will) thrive better, than at this damn'd Trade of a Play-wright. And for your *Almanzor*, *Porphyrius*, *Maximin*, with the old *Roman* Legions the *Abencerrages* and *Zegrys*, and the rest of your invincible *Heroes*, which you have already rais'd, since you have now no furthur use of their service, to ease your self of the charge of continuing them in

* Rehearsal.

pay, faith, e'en do a deed of Charity, let 'em not lie upon your hands, but lend any one of 'em to the *Dutch* against the K. of *France*. Who knows what an *Almanzor* may do? he if any Man may save the Country. As for your Ladies, *Orbella, Lyndaraxa, Almeria, Cydaria,* &c.—You know they have already those that will take care of and provide for them.—*Longum formose vale, vale.*[1]

Martin Clifford

39. Reflections on
The Hind and the Panther

1687

The opening and closing passages of the *Reflections* written by Tom Brown (1663–1704), schoolmaster and wit, 'In a Letter to a Friend'; published with Clifford's *Notes* (*supra*, No. 38). The main part of the *Reflections* is a criticism of Dryden's theology.

SIR,

The Present you have made me of the *Hind and Panther*, is variously talked of here in the Countrey. Some wonder what kind of Champion the Roman Catholicks have now gotten: for they have had divers ways of *representing* themselves; but this of *Rhiming* us to death, is altogether new, and unheard of, before Mr. *Bayes* set about it. And indeed he hath done it in the *Sparkishest* Poem that ever was seen: 'Tis true, he hath written a great *many fine things*; but he never had such *pure Swiftness* of Thought, as in this Composition, nor such *fiery Flights* of Fancy. Such hath always been his *Dramatical* and *Scenical* way of Scribling, that there was no Post nor Pillar in the Town exempt from the pasting up of the Titles of his Plays; Insomuch that the *Foot-boys*,

[1] 'Farewell, farewell, my fair one' (Virgil, *Ecl.* iii. 79).

for want of skill in Reading, do now (as we hear) often bring away by mistake, the Title of a new Book against the *Church of England*, instead of taking down the *Play* for the Afternoon: yet if he did it *well or handsomly*, he might deserve some Pardon; but alas! how ridiculously doth he appear in Print for any Religion, who hath made it his business to laugh at all! How can he stand up for any mode of Worship, who hath been accustomed to bite, and spit his Venom against the very Name thereof?

Wherefore I cannot but with our Adversaries Joy in their New-converted *Hero*, Mr. *Bayes*; whose Principle it is to fight single *with whole Armies*; and this one quality he prefers before all the *moral Vertues* put together: The Roman Catholicks may talk what they will, of their *Bellarmin* and *Perrone*, their *Hector* and *Achilles*, and I know not who; but I desire them all, to shew one such Champion for the Cause, as this *Drawcansir*:[1] For he is the Man, that kills whole Nations at once; who, as he never wrote any thing, that any one can imagin has ever been the practise of the World, so in his late endeavours to pen Controversie, you shall hardly find one word to the purpose: He is that accomplished Person, who loves *Reasoning so much in Verse*, and hath got a knack of writing it smoothly. The Subject (he treats of in this Poem) did in his Opinion, require more than ordinary *Spirit and Flame*; therefore he supposed it to be too great *for Prose*; for he is too proud, to creep servilly after sense; so that in his *Verse*, he soares high above the reach of it; to do this, there is no need of Brain; 'tis but scanning right; the labour is in the *Finger*, not in the *Head*.

However, if Mr. *Bayes* would be pleased to abate a little of the exuberancy of his Fancy and Wit; to dispense with his Ornaments and Superfluencies of *Invention and Satyr*, a Man might consider, whether he should submit to his Argument; but take away the *Railing*, and *no Argument remains*; so that one may beat the Bush a whole day, and after so much labour, only spring a *Butterfly*, or start an *Hedg-hog*.

For all this, is it not great pity to see a Man in the flower of his *Romantick* Conceptions, in the full vigour of his Studies on *Love* and *Honour*, to fall into such a distraction, as to walk through the *Thorns and Briars* of Controversie, unless his *Confessor* hath commanded it, as a *Penance* for some past sins: that a Man, who hath read *Don Quixot* for the greatest part of his Life, should pretend to interpret the *Bible*, or trace the Footsteps of *Tradition*, even in the darkest Ages?

But hold, we have a *Battel* just coming in; and now Mr. *Bayes* speaks

[1] *Supra*, p. 50.

as big, as if Ten Thousand Men were really engaged; at the same time he sings in his Verse, and puts himself into a Warlike posture; so that our Ears are at once entertained with *Musick and good Language*, and our Eye is also surprised with the *Garb* and *Accoutrements* of a Controversial War: Notwithstanding, methinks this *blustring Wight* is hardly strong and wise enough to demonstrate two such untoward Points, as *Transubstantiation* and *Infallibility*; I fancy, he is as able *to Square the Circle*. His Brains indeed, have been a long time used to *Chimera's, the Raptures and Visions of Poetry, gaudy Scenes, unaccountable flights of Non-sense, and big Absurdities*: consequently, he may have a good head for the believing of *Legends*.

But let us see how he proves his several Positions; which for brevity and distinction sake, I must denominate. . . .

It hath been an odious Task to me all along to pick out the *most noxious pieces* of his Satyr; therefore I shall leave many passages unsearcht, nor read any farther upon his *Swallows* and *Pigeons*, where Mr. *Bayes* makes the *bravest Work that ever Man saw*; and This is the *Bane* of all such kind of Writers; the Vulgar never understand them, and if they did, they would *not be one jot the better*: No *Romance* can furnish us with *such pleasant and worshipful Tales*; they want nothing of perfection, but that they do not begin with *once upon a time*; which Mr. *Bayes, according to his Accuracy,* if he had thought on 't, would never have omitted: And more than this, by changing some Lines, and bringing in a few People talking in the way of Dialogue, this very *Poem may serve for a Play*, as *smiling* and *frowning* are performed in the Face with the *same Muscles* very little altered. But still I cannot imagin the reason, why He should make use of these *tedious and impertinent Allegories*, unless he thought, that what was *solid* and *argumentative*, being imp'd with something more *light* and *airy*, might carry further and pierce deeper: Unless in this time of Heat and Anger the *Roman Catholicks* may think fit to employ him, as being a *spightful Creature*, or the *good Fathers* may divert themselves awhile with an *Animal*, that is *unlucky, mimical,* and *gamesom*.

Yet let me tell you, Mr. *Bayes*, your best Friends declare you a more competent Judge of some sort of Wit and Delight, than of Religion, or any Controversie about it; they say, you manage *Rhythmes well*; and that you have a good Art in making *high Idea's* of Honour, and in *speaking noble things*: In this Debate, it had been more edifying, if you had wrote *in Prose*; it would have rendred your Speech more natural, and you would never have made so much Contention, as you have done, between the *Rhythme* and the *Sense*. But I see, he is not in a condition of taking Counsel, or of correcting his Vices; therefore he will continue in defiance of all the means, that can be used to the contrary, *an endless Scribler, an empty Politician, an insolent Poet, and an idle Pretender to Controversie*; so that he is resolved to Rave against us as so many *vile Hereticks*; just as the *Italians, French,* and *Spaniards,* have had the Vanity to boast, that all Wit is to be sought for, no where, but amongst themselves; it is their establish'd Rule, that good Sense has always kept near the warm Sun, and scarce ever yet dared to come farther, *than the forty ninth degree Northward*; This is a very unaccountable Fancy; but they have the same Opinion of Religion too, as if all *Orthodoxy* could not go *out of the Bounds*, which they have set it.

So Mr. *Bayes* his Controversial Writings, are *unanswerable*, just as some places are *impregnable*, by reason of the *Dirt* that lies about them; and to maintain a conflict any longer with his Reasons, were to renew the old way of fighting with *Sand-bags*, the true *Emblem of his unjoynted, incoherent* Stuff; For if he goes on thus in making Volumes of Controversie, his best Confuters, will be the *Grocers* and *Haberdashers of Small Wares*, who will bind up their *rotten Raisons*, and *Mundungus*[1] in his Papers; and his *Book-sellers* will dwell at the *South-side* of *Paul's*, where his Works shall be bound up, as his *Forefather William Prynnes*[2] were, in Trunks, Hat-cases, and Bandboxes. I am

Yours, &c.

[1] Offal, refuse.
[2] (1600–69); Puritan pamphleteer who battled against (in turn) Laud, the Independents, and the Cromwellian government.

40. Dryden's rhyming poetry

1690

Extract from the anonymous Preface to the second part of Edmund
Waller's *Poems* (1690; *Works*, 1744, ed. E. Fenton, pp. 290–1).

Among other improvements, we may reckon that of [Mr. *Waller's*]
Rhymes: which are always good, and very often the better for being
new. ... My Lord *Roscommon* was more impartial: no man ever
rhym'd truer and evener than he: yet, he is so just as to confess, that
'tis but a trifle; and to wish the tyrant dethron'd, and Blank Verse
set up in its room. There is a third person,* the living glory of our
English Poetry, who has disclaim'd the use of it upon the Stage: tho'
no man ever employ'd it there so happily as he. 'Twas the strength
of his Genius that first brought it into credit in Plays; and 'tis the force
of his example that has thrown it out again. In other kinds of writing
it continues still; and will do so, 'till some excellent spirit arises, that
has leisure enough, and resolution to break the Charm, and free us
from the troublesome bondage of rhyming, as Mr. *Milton* very well
calls it; and has prov'd it as well, by what he has wrote in another way.

* *Mr.* Dryden.

41. Objections to *Don Sebastian*

1689–90

Extracts from Dryden's Preface (paras. 1 and 6) to *Don Sebastian, King of Portugal: A Tragedy* (1690; first performed 4 December 1689).

(*a*) 'Whether it happen'd through a long disuse of Writing, that I forgot the usual compass of a Play; or that by crowding it, with Characters and Incidents, I put a necessity upon my self of lengthning the main Action, I know not; but the first day's Audience sufficiently convinc'd me of my error; and that the Poem was insupportably too long. 'Tis an ill ambition of us Poets, to please an Audience with more than they can bear: And, supposing that we wrote as well, as vainly we imagin our selves to write; yet we ought to consider, that no man can bear to be long tickled. There is a nauseousness in a City feast when we are to sit four hours after we are cloy'd. I am, therefore, in the first place, to acknowledg with all manner of gratitude, their civility; who were pleas'd to endure it with so much patience, to be weary with so much good nature and silence, and not to explode an entertainment, which was design'd to please them; or discourage an Author, whose misfortunes have once more brought him against his will, upon the Stage. While I continue in these bad circumstances,[1] (and truly I see very little probability of coming out:) I must be oblig'd to write. . . . Having been longer acquainted with the Stage, than any Poet now living, and having observ'd how difficult it was to please; that the humours of Comedy were almost spent, that Love and Honour (the mistaken Topicks of Tragedy) were quite worn out; that the Theaters cou'd not support their charges, that the Audience forsook them, that young men without Learning set up for Judges,

[1] Dryden lost his poet-laureateship to Shadwell on the advent of William and Mary, and as a Roman Catholic incurred double taxation. His last play before *Don Sebastian* had been the opera *Albion and Albanius* (1685).

and that they talk'd loudest, who understood the least: all these discouragements had not only wean'd me from the Stage, but had also
given me a loathing of it. But enough of this: the difficulties continue;
they increase, and I am still condemn'd to dig in those exhausted
Mines. Whatever fault I next commit, rest assur'd it shall not be that
of too much length: Above twelve hunder'd lines have been cut off
from this Tragedy, since it was first deliver'd to the Actors. They were
indeed so judiciously lopt by Mr. *Betterton*,[1] to whose care and excellent
action, I am equally oblig'd, that the connexion of the story was not
lost. . . .'

(b) 'I have been listning what objections have been made, against the
conduct of the Play, but found them all so trivial, that if I shou'd
name them, a true critick wou'd imagin that I play'd booty,[2] and only
rais'd up fantoms for my self to conquer. Some are pleas'd to say the
Writing is dull; but *ætatem habet de se loquatur*.[3] Others that the double
poyson is unnatural; let the common received opinion, and *Ausonius*
his famous Epigram[4] answer that. Lastly a more ignorant sort of
Creatures than either of the former, maintain that the Character of
Dorax, is not only unnatural, but inconsistent with it self; let them
read the Play and think again, and if yet they are not satisfied, cast
their eyes on that Chapter of the Wise *Montaigne*, which is intituled
de l'Inconstance des actions humaines.[5] A longer reply, is what those
Cavillers deserve not; but I will give them and their fellows to understand, that the Earl of *Dorset*,[6] was pleas'd to read the Tragedy twice
over before it was Acted; and did me the favour to send me word,
that I had written beyond any of my former Plays; and that he was
displeas'd any thing shou'd be cut away. If I have not reason to prefer
his single judgment to a whole Faction, let the World be Judge; for
the opposition is the same with that of *Lucan*'s Heroe against an Army;
concurrere bellum, atque virum.[7] I think I may modestly conclude that
whatever errors there may be, either in the design, or writing of this

---

[1] Thomas Betterton (1635?–1710), who played Dorax.

[2] Lost deliberately in order to stimulate heavy betting.

[3] John ix. 21 (Vulgate).

[4] Decim. Magnus Ausonius (4th cent.), epigram iii; a wife gives her husband two
poisons which cancel one another out.

[5] Montaigne, *Essais*, ii. 1.

[6] Charles Sackville (1638–1706), sixth Earl of Dorset, Dryden's friend and patron since
the 1660s.

[7] *Pharsalia*, vi. 191–2, [Fortune sees a new pair of combatants,] a man against an army.

Play, they are not those which have been objected to it. I think also, that I am not yet arriv'd to the Age of doating; and that I have given so much application to this Poem, that I cou'd not probably let it run into many gross absurdities; which may caution my Enemies from too rash a censure. . . .'

42. Two actors in 1690

1739

Extracts from *An Apology for the Life of Colley Cibber* (1740), ch. 5, 'The Theatrical Characters of the Principal Actors, in the Year 1690'. Cibber (1671–1757) was educated at Grantham, took arms in the Revolution of 1688, and became an actor in 1690. He eventually shared the management of Drury Lane, and in 1730 was appointed poet laureate. The actors he recalls here were Edward Kynaston, who began acting after the Restoration and made a reputation in women's parts ('the loveliest lady that ever I saw in my Life'; Pepys, *Diary*, 18 August 1660); and Mrs Mountford, 'mistress of more variety of humour,' (says Cibber), 'than I ever knew in any one woman actress.'

(a) 'Kynaston . . . had a piercing eye, and in characters of heroick life, a quick imperious vivacity, in his tone of voice, that painted the tyrant truly terrible. There were two plays of Dryden in which he shone, with uncommon lustre; in *Aurenge-Zebe* he play'd Morat, and in *Don Sebastian*, Muley Moloch; in both these parts, he had a fierce, lion-like majesty in his port and utterance that gave the spectator a kind of trembling admiration!

Here I cannot help observing upon a modest mistake, which I thought the late Mr. Booth committed in his acting the part of Morat. There are in this fierce character so many sentiments of avow'd barbarity, insolence, and vain-glory, that they blaze even to a ludicrous lustre, and doubtless the poet intended those to make his spectators laugh, while they admir'd them; but Booth thought it depreciated the dignity of tragedy to raise a smile, in any part of it, and therefore cover'd these kind of sentiments with a scrupulous coldness, and unmov'd delivery, as if he had fear'd the audience might take too familiar a notice of them. ... Now whether Dryden in his Morat, *feliciter Audet*,[1]—or may be allow'd the happiness of having hit his mark, seems not necessary to be determin'd by the actor; whose business, sure, is to make the best of his author's intention, as in this part Kynaston did, doubtless not without Dryden's approbation. For these reasons then, I thought my good friend, Mr. Booth (who certainly had many excellencies) carried his reverence for the buskin too far, in not allowing the bold flights of the author with that wantonness of spirit which the nature of those sentiments demanded. For example: Morat having a criminal passion for Indamora, promises, at her request, for one day, to spare the life of her lover Aurenge-Zebe: but not chusing to make known the real motive of his mercy, when Nourmahal says to him,

> *'Twill not be safe to let him live an hour!*

Morat silences her with this heroical rhodomontade,

> *I'll do 't, to shew my arbitrary power.*

Risum teneatis?[2] It was impossible not to laugh, and reasonably too, when this line came out of the mouth of Kynaston with the stern and haughty look that attended it. But above this tyrannical, tumid superiority of character, there is a grave and rational majesty in Shakespear's Harry the Fourth, which tho' not so glaring to the vulgar eye, requires thrice the skill and grace to become and support. Of this real majesty Kynaston was entirely master. ...'

(*b*) 'What found most employment for [Mrs. Monfort's] whole various excellence at once, was the part of Melantha, in *Marriage-Alamode*. Melantha is as finish'd an impertinent as ever flutter'd in a drawing-room, and seems to contain the most complete system of female foppery that could possibly be crowded into the tortured form of a fine lady. Her language, dress, motion, manners, soul, and body, are in a continual hurry to be something more than is necessary or

---

[1] Dares successfully.
[2] Would you suppress your laughter?

commendable. And though I doubt it will be a vain labour, to offer you a just likeness of Mrs. Monfort's action, yet the fantastick impression is still so strong in my memory, that I cannot help saying something, tho' fantastically, about it. The first ridiculous airs that break from her are upon a gallant, never seen before, who delivers her a letter from her father, recommending him to her good graces as an honourable lover. Here now, one would think she might naturally shew a little of the sex's decent reserve, tho' never so slightly cover'd! No, sir; not a tittle of it; modesty is the virtue of a poor-soul'd country gentlewoman; she is too much a court lady, to be under so vulgar a confusion; she reads the letter, therefore, with a careless, dropping lip, and an erected brow, humming it hastily over, as if she were impatient to outgo her father's commands, by making a compleat conquest of him at once; and that the letter might not embarrass her attack, crack! she crumbles it at once into her palm, and pours upon him her whole artillery of airs, eyes, and motion; down goes her dainty, diving body, to the ground, as if she were sinking under the conscious load of her own attractions; then launches into a flood of fine language, and compliment, still playing her chest forward in fifty falls and risings, like a swan upon waving water; and, to complete her impatience, she is so rapidly fond of her own wit, that she will not give her lover leave to praise it. Silent assenting bows, and vain endeavours to speak, are all the share of the conversation he is admitted to, which, at last, he is relieved from by her engagement to half a score visits, which she *swims* from him to make, with a promise to return in a twinkling. If this sketch has colour enough to give you any near conception of her, I then need only tell you, that throughout the whole character, her variety of humour was every way proportionable; as, indeed, in most parts that she thought worth her care.'

43. Milbourne blows hot and cold

1690, 1698

Extracts from (a) a letter from a clerical poet, Luke Milbourne (1649–1720), to Dryden's bookseller Tonson (Malone, *Prose Works of Dryden*, 1800, I. i. 315–17); and (b) Milbourne's *Notes on Dryden's Virgil. In a Letter to a Friend* (1698; Johnson's *Lives of the English Poets* (1903), ed. G. B. Hill, i. 450–1). In 1688 Milbourne had published a version of *Aeneid* i, '*with a design to go through the poem.* It was the misfortune of that first attempt to appear just about the time of the late Revolution, when few had leisure to mind such books' (*Gentleman's Journal*, August 1692). His outrages against Dryden's translation of Virgil (1697) 'seem to be the ebullitions of a mind agitated by stronger resentment than bad poetry can excite, and previously resolved not to be pleased' (Johnson). A little of Milbourne is more than enough.

Yarmouth, Novemb. 24. —90.

(*a*) Mr. TONSON,

You'l wonder perhaps at this from a stranger; but ye reason of it may perhaps abate somewhat of ye miracle, and it's this. On Thursday the twentyth instant, I receiv'd Mr. Drydens AMPHITRYO: I leave out the Greeke termination, as not so proper in my opinion, in English. But to passe that; I liked the play, and read it over with as much of criticisme and ill nature as ye time (being about one in ye morning, and in bed,) would permit. Going to sleep very well pleasd, I could not leave my bed in ye morning without this sacrifice to the authours genius: it was too sudden to be correct, but it was very honestly meant, and is submitted to yours and Mr. D.^s disposall.

Haill, Prince of Witts! thy fumbling Age is past,
Thy youth and witt and art's renew'd at last.
So on some rock the Joviall bird assays

Her re-grown beake, that marke of age, to rayse;
That done, through yield'ing air she cutts her way,
And strongly stoops againe, and breaks the trembling prey.
What though prodigious thunder stripp'd thy brows
Of envy'd bays, and the dull world allows
Shadwell should wear them,[1]—wee'll applaud the change;
Where nations feel it, who can thinke it strange!

$\qquad\cdot\qquad\cdot\qquad\cdot\qquad\cdot\qquad\cdot$

Hang 't! give the fop ingratefull world its will;
He wears the laurell,—thou deservs't it still.
Still smooth, as when, adorn'd with youthful pride,
For thy dear sake the blushing virgins dyed;
When the kind gods of witt and love combined,
And with large gifts thy yielding soul refined.

$\qquad\cdot\qquad\cdot\qquad\cdot\qquad\cdot\qquad\cdot$

Yet briske and airy too, thou fill'st the stage,
Unbroke by fortune, undecayed by age.
French wordy witt by thine was long surpast;
Now Rome 's thy captive, and by thee wee taste
Of their rich dayntyes; but so finely drest,
Theirs was a country meal, thine a triumphant feast.
If this to thy necessityes wee ow,
O, may they greater still and greater grow!
Nor blame the wish; Plautus could write in chaines,
Wee'll blesse thy wants, while wee enjoy thy pains.
Wealth makes the poet lazy, nor can fame,
That gay attendant of a spritely flame,
A Dorset or a Wycherly invite,
Because they feel no pinching wants, to write.

$\qquad\cdot\qquad\cdot\qquad\cdot\qquad\cdot\qquad\cdot$

Nor would we have thee live on empty praise
The while, for, though we cann't restore the bays,
While thou writ'st thus,—to pay thy merites due,
Wee'll give the claret and the pension too.

By this you may guesse I'm none of the author's enemyes; and, to
prove that the better, I desire you'ld supply me with his Essay on
Dramatick Poetry, Wild Gallant, Rival Lady, Sir Martin Marall,
Evening Love, Conquest of Granada, both parts, Amboyna, Annus

[1] He replaced Dryden as poet-laureate after the Revolution of 1688.

Mirabilis, Poeme on the returne of Charles the 2d, On his Coronation, To Ld. Ch. Hide, On the death of Charles the 2d. The rest I have allready. . . .

(b) [*Georgics*, I.]

> Ver. 1. What makes a plenteous harvest, when to turn
> The fruitful soil, and when to sow the corn.

It 's unlucky, they say, 'to stumble at the threshold,' but what has a 'plenteous harvest' to do here? Virgil would not pretend to prescribe *rules* for *that* which depends not on the *husbandman's* care, but the *disposition of Heaven* altogether. Indeed, the *plenteous crop* depends somewhat on the *good method of tillage*, and where the *land 's* ill manur'd the *corn* without a miracle can be but *indifferent*; but the *harvest* may be *good*, which is its *properest* epithet, tho' the *husbandman's skill* were never so *indifferent*. The next *sentence* is *too literal*, and *when to plough* had been Virgil's meaning, and intelligible to every body; 'and when to sow the corn' is a needless *addition*. . . .

> Ver. 5. The birth and genius of the frugal bee
> I sing, Mæcenas, and I sing to thee.—

But where did *experientia* ever signify *birth and genius*? or what ground was there for such a *figure* in this place? How much more manly is Mr. Ogylby's version![1]

> Ver. 23, 24. Inventor Pallas, of the fattening oil,
> Thou founder of the plough, and ploughman's toil!

Written as if *these* had been *Pallas's invention*. The *ploughman's toil 's* impertinent.

> Ver. 25. —The shroud-like cypress—

Why 'shroud-like?' Is a *cypress* pulled up by the *roots*, which the *sculpture* in the *last Eclogue* fills *Silvanus's* hand with, so very like a *shroud*? Or did not Mr. D. think of that kind of *cypress* us'd often for *scarves and hatbands* at funerals formerly, or for *widow's vails*, &c.? if so, 'twas a *deep good thought*.

> Ver. 26.   . . . that wear
> The [rural] honours, and increase the year.

---

[1] 1654; a version despised and used by Dryden.

What's meant by *increasing the year*? Did the *gods* or *goddesses* add more *months*, or *days*, or *hours* to it?[1] Or how can '*arva tueri*' signify to 'wear rural honours'? Is this to *translate*, or *abuse* an *author*? The next *couplet* are borrow'd from Ogylby I suppose, because *less to the purpose* than ordinary.

Ver. 33. The patron of the world, and Rome's peculiar guard.

Idle, and none of Virgil's, no more than the sense of the *precedent couplet*; so again, he *interpolates* Virgil with that

> And the round circle [circuit] of the year to guide;
> Powerful of blessings, which thou strew'st around.

A ridiculous *Latinism*, and an *impertinent addition*; indeed the whole *period* is but one piece of *absurdity* and *nonsense*, as those who lay it with the *original* must find. . . .

[1] Milbourne misses Dryden's latinism: *annus*, produce of the year.

44. Langbaine's observations and remarks

1691

Gerard Langbaine (1656–92) was a son of the Provost of Queen's College, Oxford, and compiler of *A New Catalogue of English Plays* (1688). The *Catalogue* first appeared in November 1687 with a spurious title-page, *Momus Triumphans: or, The Plagiaries of the English Stage*, mocking Langbaine's obsession with plagiarism. 'My friends', he said in an advertisement in the second issue with the correct title, 'may think me Lunatick.' He blamed Dryden for the hoax, and took his revenge in *An Acccunt of The English Dramatick Poets. Or, Some Observations and Remarks on the Lives and Writings of all those that have Published either Comedies, Tragedies . . . in the English Tongue* (1691). See J. M. Osborn, *John Dryden: Some Biographical Facts and Problems*, revd. edn. (1965), pp. 234–40. The long entry on Dryden is substantially an arraignment for plagiarism, and of no serious critical interest. The opening paragraphs (pp. 130–4) are reprinted here for the historical record.

John DRYDEN, *Esq.*;

A Person whose Writings have made him remarkable to all sorts of Men, as being for a long time much read, and in great Vogue. It is no wonder that the Characters given of him, by such as are, or would be thought, Wits, are various; since even those, who are generally allow'd to be such, are not yet agreed in their Verdicts. And as their Judgments are different, as to his Writings; so are their Censures no less repugnant to the Managery of his Life, some excusing what these condemn, and some exploding what those commend: So that we can scarce find them agreed in any One thing, save this, That he was Poet Laureat and Historiographer to His late Majesty. For this, and other Reasons, I shall wave all Particularities of his Life; and let pass the Historiographer, that I may keep the closer to the Poet, toward whom

I shall use my accustom'd Freedome; and having spoken my Sentiments of his Predecessors Writings, shall venture without partiality, to exercise my slender Judgment in giving a Censure of his Works.

Mr. *Dryden* is the most Voluminous Dramatick Writer of our Age, he having already extant above Twenty Plays of his own writing, as the Title-page of each would perswade the World; tho' some people have been so bold as to call the Truth of this in question, and to propogate in the world another Opinion.

His Genius seems to me to incline to Tragedy and Satyr, rather than Comedy: and methinks he writes much better in *Heroicks*, than in *blank Verse*. His very Enemies must grant that *there* his Numbers are sweet, and flowing; that he has with success practic'd the new way of Versifying introduc'd by his Predecessor Mr. *Waller*, and follow'd since with success, by Sr. *John Denham*, and others. But for Comedy, he is for the most part beholding to French Romances and Plays, not only for his Plots, but even a great part of his Language: tho' at the same time, he has the confidence to prevaricate, if not flatly deny the Accusation, and equivocally to vindicate himself; as in the Preface to the *Mock Astrologer*: where he mentions *Thomas Corneille*'s *le Feint Astrologue* because 'twas translated, and the Theft prov'd upon him; but never says One word of *Molière*'s *Dépit amoreux*, from whence the greatest part of *Wild-blood* and *Jacinta*, (which he owns are the chiefest parts of the Play) are stollen. I cannot pass by his Vanity in saying, 'That those who have called *Virgil*, *Terence* and *Tasso*, Plagiaries (tho' they much injur'd them) had yet a better Colour for their Accusation': nor his Confidence in sheltring himself under the protection of their great Names, by affirming, 'That he is able to say the same for his Play, that he urges for their Poems; *viz.* That the Body of his Play is his own, and so are all the Ornaments of Language, and Elocution in them'. I appeal only to those who are vers'd in the French Tongue, and will take the pains to compare this Comedy with the French Plays above-mention'd; if this be not somewhat more than Mental Reservation, or to use one of his own Expressions, **A Sophisticated Truth, with an allay of Lye in 't.*

Nor are his Characters less borrow'd in his Tragedies, and the serious parts of his Tragi-Comedies; as I shall observe in the sequel. It shall suffice me at present, to shew how Magisterially he huffs at, and domineers over, the French in his Preface to the *Conquest of Granada* .... Now the Reader is desir'd to observe that all the Characters

* *Love in a Nunnery*, p. 59.

of that Play are stollen from the French: so that Mr. *Dryden* took a secure way to Conquest, for having robb'd them of their Weapons, he might safely challenge them and beat them too, especially having gotten *Ponce de Leon*★ on his side, in disguise, and under the Title of *Almanzor*: and should *Monsieur de Voiture* presume to lay claim to his own Song *L' Amour sous sa Loy* &c.† which Mr. *Dryden* has robb'd him of, and plac'd in the Play of Sr. *Martin Marr-all*, (being that Song which begins *Blind Love to this Hour* &c.) our Poet would go nigh to beat him with a Staff of his own Rimes, with as much ease, as Sr. *Martin* defeated the Bailiffs in rescue of his Rival.

But had he only extended his Conquests over the *French* Poets, I had not medled in this Affair, and he might have taken part with *Achilles*, and *Rinaldo*, against *Cyrus*, and *Oroondates*, without my engaging in this Forreign War: but when I found him flusht with his Victory over the great *Scudéry*, and with *Almanzor's* assistance triumphing over the noble Kingdome of *Granada*; and not content with Conquests abroad, like another *Julius Cæsar*, turning his Arms upon his own Country; and as if the proscription of his Contemporaries Reputation, were not sufficient to satiate his implacable thirst after Fame, endeavouring to demolish the Statues and Monuments of his Ancestors, the Works of those his Illustrious Predecessors, *Shakespear*, *Fletcher*, and *Johnson*: I was resolv'd to endeavour the rescue and preservation of those excellent Trophies of Wit, by raising the *Posse-comitatus* upon this Poetick *Almanzor*, to put a stop to his Spoils upon his own Country-men. Therefore I present my self a Champion in the Dead Poets Cause, to vindicate their Fame, with the same Courage, tho' I hope different Integrity than *Almanzor* engag'd in defence of Queen *Almahide*, when he bravely Swore like a *Hero*, that his Cause was right, and She was innocent; tho' just before the Combat, when alone, he own'd he knew her false

[quotation, *The Conquest of Granada*, Pt. II., V. i, 'I have out-fac'd my self', &c.]

But to wave this digression, and proceed to the Vindication of the Ancients . . . I shall set down the Heads of his Depositions against our ancient English Poets, and then endeavour the Defence of those great Men, who certainly deserv'd much better of Posterity, than to be so disrespectively treated as he has used them.

★ The Chief *Hero* in a Romance call'd *Almatride*.
† *Poésies de M. de Voiture*, p. 457.

45. Dryden and Congreve

1693

Lines from (a) Thomas Southerne's 'To Mr. *Congreve*' and (b) Bevil Higgons's 'To Mr. *Congreve* on ... *The Old Batchelor*', prefixed to the 1693 edition of the play. Southerne engaged Dryden in favour of *The Old Batchelour*: he 'sayd he never saw such a first play in his life ... the stuff was rich indeed, it wanted only the fashionable cutt of the town. To help that Mr Dryden, Mr Arthur Manwayring, and Mr Southerne red it with great care, Mr Dryden putt it in the order it was playd' (see Congreve, *Complete Plays* (1967), ed. Herbert Davis, pp. 24–5). For Congreve's repayment of his debt to Dryden, see No. 66.

(*a*)   Nature so coy, so hardly to be Woo'd
Flies, like a Mistress, but to be pursu'd.
O *CONGREVE*! boldly follow on the Chase;
She looks behind, and wants thy strong Embrace:
She yields, she yields, surrenders all her Charms,
Do you but force her gently to your Arms:
Such Nerves, such Graces, in your Lines appear,
As you were made to be her Ravisher.
DRYDEN has long extended his Command,
By Right-Divine, quite through the Muses Land,
Absolute Lord; and holding now from none,
But great *Apollo*, his undoubted Crown:
(That Empire settled, and grown old in Pow'r)
Can wish for nothing, but a Successor:
Not to enlarge his Limits, but maintain
Those Provinces, which he alone could gain.
His eldest *Wicherly*, in wise Retreat,
Thought it not worth his quiet to be great.
Loose, wandring, *Etherege*, in wild Pleasures tost,

And foreign Int'rests, to his hopes long lost:
Poor *Lee* and *Otway* dead![1] *CONGREVE* appears,
The Darling, and last Comfort of his Years:
May'st thou live long in thy great Masters smiles,
And growing under him, adorn these Isles:
But when—when part of him (be that but late)
His body yielding must submit to Fate,
Leaving his deathless Works, and thee behind,
(The natural Successor of his Mind)
Then may'st thou finish what he has begun:
Heir to his Merit, be in Fame his Son. . . .

(*b*)   How wilt thou shine at thy Meridian height?
Who, at thy rising, give so vast a Light.
When *DRYDEN* dying, shall the World deceive,
Whom we Immortal, as his Works, believe;
Thou shalt succeed, the Glory of the Stage,
Adorn and entertain the coming Age.

---

[1] Wycherley's first play was published in 1672, his last in 1677; Etherege's third and last play was published in 1676; Nathaniel Lee died in 1692, and Thomas Otway in 1685.

46. Congreve to Mr Dryden, on his translation of *Persius*

1693

Verses by the dramatist William Congreve (1670–1729) prefixed to Dryden's *Satires of Aulus Persius Flaccus*, published with *The Satires of Decimus Junius Juvenalis. Translated into English Verse. By Mr. Dryden, and Several other Eminent Hands* (1793).

As when of Old Heroique Story tells
Of Knights Imprison'd long by Magick Spells;
Till future Time, the destin'd Hero send,
By whom, the dire Enchantment is to end:
Such seems this Work, and so reserv'd for thee,
Thou great Revealer of dark Poesie.[1]
    Those sullen Clouds, which have for Ages past,
O're *Persius*'s too-long-suff'ring Muse been cast,
Disperse, and flie before thy Sacred Pen,
And, in their room, bright tracks of light are seen.
Sure *Phœbus* self, thy swelling Breast inspires,
The God of Musick, and Poetique Fires:
Else, whence proceeds this great Surprise of Light!
How dawns this day, forth from the Womb of Night!
    Our Wonder, now, does our past Folly show,
Vainly Contemning what we did not know:
So, Unbelievers impiously despise
The Sacred Oracles, in Mysteries.

---

[1] *Cf.* Dryden's Dedication (p. xxx): Persius is 'obscure: Whether he affected not to be understood, but with difficulty; or whether the fear of his safety under *Nero*, compell'd him to this darkness in some places; or that it was occasion'd by his close way of thinking, and the brevity of his Style, and crowding of his Figures; or lastly, whether after so long a time, many of his Words have been corrupted, and many Customs, and Stories relating to them, lost to us. . . .'

Persius, before, in small Esteem was had,
Unless, what to Antiquity is paid;
But like Apocrypha, with Scruple read,
(So far, our Ignorance, our Faith misled)
Till you, *Apollo*'s darling Priest thought fit
To place it, in the Poet's Sacred Writ.

   As Coin, which bears some awful Monarchs Face,
For more than its Intrinsick Worth will pass:
So your bright Image, which we here behold,
Adds Worth to Worth, and dignifies the Gold.
To you, we, all this following Treasure owe,
This *Hippocrene*,[1] which from a Rock did flow.

   Old *Stoick* Virtue, clad in rugged lines,
Polish'd by you, in Modern Brillant shines:
And as before, for *Persius* our Esteem,
To his Antiquity was paid, not him:
So now, whatever Praise, from us is due,
Belongs not to Old *Persius*, but the New.
For still Obscure, to us no Light he gives;
Dead in himself, in you alone he lives.

   So, stubborn Flints, their inward heat conceal,
'Till Art and Force, th' unwilling Sparks reveal;
But through your Skill, from those small Seeds of Fire,
Bright Flames arise, which never can Expire.

Will. Congreve.

---

[1] The 'horse's fountain' near Mount Helicon, struck from the ground by the feet of Pegasus and sacred to the Muses.

47. Higgons on *Persius*

1693

From *Examen Poeticum: Being the Third Part of Miscellany Poems. . . . By the Most Eminent Hands* (1693), pp. 250–2. Bevil Higgons (1670–1735), historian, was a cousin of Dryden's friend George Granville, Lord Lansdowne.

To Mr. Dryden on his Translation of Persius.
By Mr. B. Higgons.

As Mariners at Sea, far off descry
Some unknown Land, and pass regardless by,
Their Charts some eminent Cape, or Mountain tell,
And all the rest but Blanks and Cyphers fill;
So we at distance gloomy *Persius* view'd,
But none approach'd, and his rough Tracts pursu'd,
Till mighty *Dryden* ventur'd first on Shoar,
And the dark unknown Region did explore:
Drest by thy artful Hand, he does appear
Bright and perspicuous, as he is severe:
With this rich Present you oblige our Isle,
And in his Urn make *Persius* Ashes smile;
By thee preserv'd from the ignoble Grave,
Whose Reputation will his Credit save.
If with another's Arms so keen you fight,
How will your own well-pointed Satire bite?
Our Vices, as old *Rome's*, are not so few,
And we do wait to be chastis'd by you;
To see unchain'd thy Generous Muse's Rage,
At once t' oblige, and lash an Impious Age:
What don't the wondring World expect from thee?
Thou hast more cause, a greater *Persius* we.

Nor is thy Talent to our Art confin'd,
But Universal as thy boundless Mind:
Thy knowing Muse all sorts of Men does teach,
Philosophers instructs to live, Divines to preach,
States-men to govern, Generals to fight,
At once Mankind you profit and delight.
Virtue so lovely drest by thee, doth shine,
So bright appears in each instructing Line:
Vast the Ideas which from thee we take,
While the dull Pulpits no impression make.

But where to Love thy softer thoughts unbend,
There all the Graces on thy Muse attend.
Thy charming Numbers do our Souls inthrall,
The Rigid melt, and we turn Lovers all;
The *Cupids* dance in ev'ry Ladies eye,
Who reading Love as they were acting, die.

48. Dryden on *Examen Poeticum*

1693

Extracts from Dryden's Dedication, to Lord Radcliffe, of *Examen Poeticum: Being the Third Part of Miscellany Poems* (1693; *Poems*, 1958, ed. Kinsley, ii. 795 and 799).

(*a*) 'Your Lady and You have done me the favour to hear me Read my Translations of *Ovid*: And you both seem'd not to be displeas'd with them. Whether it be the partiality of an Old Man to his Youngest Child, I know not: But they appear to me the best of all my Endeavours in this kind. Perhaps this Poet, is more easie to be Translated, than some others, whom I have lately attempted: Perhaps too, he was more according to my Genius. He is certainly more palatable to the Reader, than any of the *Roman* Wits, though some of them are more lofty, some more Instructive, and others more Correct.'

(*b*) 'This *Miscellany*, is without dispute one of the best of the kind, which has hitherto been extant in our Tongue. At least, as Sir *Samuel Tuke* has said before me,[1] a Modest Man may praise what 's not his own. My Fellows have no need of any Protection, but I humbly recommend my part of it, as much as it deserves, to your Patronage and Acceptance, and all the rest to your Forgiveness.'

49. Dennis on *Oedipus*

1693

Extract from John Dennis, *The Impartial Critick* (1693), Dialogue II. Beaumont and Freeman are discussing the tragic hero. Dennis (1657–1734) was a minor poet and dramatist, but one of the most considerable and independent critics of his time. *The Impartial Critick* was a rejoinder to Rymer's *Short View of Tragedy* (1692).

BEAUM. What sort of Person must be made choice of then?
FREEM. Why one who is neither vertuous in a sovereign degree, nor excessively vicious; but who keeping the middle between these extreams, is afflicted with some terrible calamity, for some involuntary fault.
BEAUM. Well, and just such a Man is Mr. *Dryden*'s *Oedipus*, who cannot be said to be perfectly vertuous, when he is both Parricide and Incestuous: nor yet on the other side excessively vicious, when neither his Parricide nor Incest are voluntary, but caused by a fatal ignorance.

[1] In the Prologue to *The Adventures of Five Hours* (1663).

FREEM. Aye, but says *Dacier*,[1] to punish a Man for Crimes, that are caused by invincible ignorance, is in some measure unjust, especially if that Man has other ways extraordinary Vertues. Now Mr. *Dryden* makes his *Oedipus* just, generous, sincere, and brave; and indeed a Heroe, without any Vices, but the foremention'd two, which were unavoidable both. Now *Sophocles* represents *Oedipus* after another manner; the distinguishing Qualities which he gives him, are only Courage, Wit, and Success, Qualities which make a Man neither good, nor vitious. The extraordinary things that he pretends to have done in *Sophocles*, are only to have kill'd four Men in his Rage, and to have explain'd the Riddle of *Sphinx*, which the worst Man in the World that had Wit, might have done as well as *Oedipus*.

BEAUM. Well, but does not *Sophocles* punish *Oedipus* for the very same Crimes that Mr. *Dryden* does, *vid.* for his Incest and Parricide? If not, for what involuntary faults, does the *Sophoclean Oedipus* suffer?

FREEM. *Aristotle* by those Offences, which his Interpreter *Dacier* calls involuntary, does not mean only such faults as are caus'd by invincible ignorance, but such to which we are strongly inclin'd, either by the bent of our Constitutions, or by the force of prevailing Passions. The faults for which *Oedipus* suffers in *Sophocles*, are his vain Curiosity, in consulting the Oracle about his Birth, his Pride in refusing to yield the way, in his return from that Oracle, and his Fury and Violence in attacking four Men on the Road, the very day after he had been fore-warn'd by the Oracle, that he should kill his Father.

BEAUM. But, pray, how were those involuntary Faults?

FREEM. *Dacier* means here by involuntary faults, faults that have more of human frailty in them, than any thing of design, or of black malice. The Curiosity of *Oedipus* proceeded from a Vanity, from which no Man is wholly exempt; and his Pride, and the Slaughter that it caused him to commit on the Road, were partly caused by his Constitution, and an unhappy and violent Temper. These are faults that both *Aristotle* and *Dacier* suppose, that he might have prevented, if he would have used all his diligence; but being guilty of them thro' his neglect, they afterwards plunged him in those horrible Crimes, which were follow'd by his final Ruine. Thus you see the Character of the *Athenean Oedipus*, is according to these Rules of *Aristotle*, the fittest that can be imagin'd to give Compassion and Terrour to an Audience: For how can an Audience choose but tremble, when it sees a Man involv'd in the most deplorable Miseries, only for indulging those Passions and

---

[1] *Poétique d'Aristote* (1692); the basis of the first part of this discussion.

Frailties, which they are but too conscious that they neglect in them-selves? And how can they choose but melt with compassion, when they see a Man afflicted by the avenging Gods with utmost severity, for Faults that were without malice, and which being in some measure to be found in themselves, may make them apprehensive of like Catastrophes? For all our Passions, as *Dacier* observes, are grounded upon the Love of ourselves, and that Pity which seems to espouse our Neighbor's Interest, is founded still on our own.

BEAUM. Why, will you perswade me, that because an Audience finds in itself the same vain Curiosity, and the same ungovern'd Passions, that drew *Oedipus* to Murder and Incest, that therefore each Spectator should be afraid of killing his Father, and committing Incest with his Mother?

FREEM. No, you cannot mistake me so far; but they may very well be afraid of being drawn in by the like neglected Passions to deplorable Crimes and horrid Mischiefs, which they never design'd.

BEAUM. Well then, now I begin to see the reason, why, according to the Sence of *Aristotle*, the Character of Mr. *Dryden*'s *Oedipus* is alter'd for the worse: For he, you 'll say, being represented by Mr. *Dryden* Soveraignly Vertuous, and guilty of Parricide only by a fatal invincible Ignorance, must by the severity of his Sufferings, instead of compassion create horrour in us, and a murmuring, as it were, at Providence. Nor can those Sufferings raise terrour in us, for his Crimes of fatal invincible Ignorance, not being prepar'd, as they are in *Sophocles*, by some less faults, which led him to those Crimes, as it were, by so many degrees. I do not conceive how we can be concern'd at this; for Terrour, you say, arises from the Sufferings of others, upon the account of Faults which are common to us with them. Now what Man can be afraid, because he sees *Oedipus* come down at two Leaps from the height of Vertue to Parricide, and to Incest, that therefore this may happen to him? For a Man who is himself in Security, cannot be terrified with the Sufferings of others, if he is not conscious to himself of the Faults that caus'd them: but every Man who is disturb'd by unruly Passions, when he sees, how the giving way to the same Passions, drew *Sophocles*'s *Oedipus* into Tragical Crimes, which were never design'd, must by reflection necessarily be struck with Terrour, and the apprehension of dire Calamities. This, I suppose, is your Sence.

FREEM. Exactly.

BEAUM. Well, but the Authority of Aristotle avails little with me, against irrefutable Experience. I have seen our *English Oedipus* several times, and have constantly found, that it hath caus'd both Terrour and Pity in me.

FREEM. I will not tell you, that possibly you may have mistaken Horrour for Terrour and Pity: for perhaps it is not absolutely true, that the Sufferings of those, who are Sovereignly Vertuous, cannot excite Compassion. But this is indubitable, that they cannot so effectually do it, as the Misfortunes of those, who having some Faults, do the more resemble ourselves: And I think, that I may venture to affirm two things: First, That if any one but so great a Master as Mr. *Dryden*, had had the management of that Character, and had made the same mistake with it, his Play would have been hiss'd off the Stage. And Secondly—

BEAUM. I must beg leave to interrupt you: Why should you believe that another Man's Play upon the same Subject, would have miscarried upon that mistake, when I never heard it yet taken Notice of?

FREEM. It would have miscarried, tho' the mistake had ne're been found out: For a common Author proceeding upon such wrong Principles, could never have touch'd the Passions truly. But Mr. *Dryden* having done it by his extraordinary Address, the Minds of his Audience have been still troubled, and so the less able to find his Error.

BEAUM. But what was that second thing, which you were going to observe?

FREEM. It was this: That if Mr. *Dryden* had not alter'd the Character of *Sophocles*, the Terrour and Compassion had been yet much stronger.

BEAUM. But how could so great a Man as Mr. *Dryden*, make such a mistake in his own Art?

FREEM. How did *Corneille* do it before him, who was certainly a great Man too? And if you 'll believe *Dacier*, *C'etoit le plus grand genie pour le Theatre qu'on avoit Jamais veu*:[1] Great Men have their Errors, or else they would not be Men. Nay, they are mistaken in several things, in which Men of a lower Order may be in the right. This has been wisely order'd by Providence, that they may not be exalted too much; for if it were not for this, they would look down upon the rest of Mankind, as upon Creatures of a lower Species.

BEAUM. Do you believe then, that *Aristotle*, if he could rise again, would condemn our *English Oedipus*?

FREEM. He would condemn it, or he would be forc'd to recede from his own Principles; but at the same time that he passed Sentence on it,

---

[1] He was the greatest dramatic genius ever seen.

he would find it so beautiful, that he could not choose but love the Criminal; and he would certainly crown the Poet, before he would damn the Play.

BEAUM. But 'tis high time to return to Mr. *Rymer's* Book. ...

50. Tribute from Addison

1693

From *Examen Poeticum: Being the Third Part of Miscellany Poems*. ...
By the Most Eminent Hands (1693), pp. 247–9. Addison (1672–1719)
graduated M.A. at Oxford in this year, and became a crony of
Dryden's.

To Mr. Dryden. By Mr. Jo. Addison.

How long, Great Poet, shall thy Sacred Lays,
Provoke our Wonder, and transcend our Praise?
Can neither Injuries of Time, or Age,
Damp thy Poetick Heat, and quench thy Rage?
Not so thy *Ovid* in his Exile wrote,
Grief chill'd his *Breast*, and checkt his *rising Thought*;
Pensive and sad, his drooping Muse betrays
The *Roman* Genius in its last Decays.
    Prevailing Warmth has still thy Mind possest,
And second Youth is kindled in thy *Breast*.
Thou mak'st the *Beauties* of the *Romans* known,
And *England* boasts of Riches not her own;
Thy Lines have heighten'd *Virgil's* Majesty,
And *Horace* wonders at himself in Thee.[1]

[1] Dryden included versions of Virgil and Horace in the first and second parts of *Miscellany Poems* (1684, 1685).

Thou teachest *Persius* to inform our Isle
In smoother Numbers, and a clearer Stile;
And *Juvenal* instructed in thy Page,
Edges his Satire, and improves his Rage.
Thy Copy casts a fairer Light on all,
And still out-shines the bright Original.

   Now *Ovid* boasts th' advantage of thy Song,[1]
And tells his Story in the *Brittish* Tongue;
Thy charming Verse, and fair Translations show
How thy own Lawrel first began to grow;
How wild *Lycaon* chang'd by angry Gods,
And frighted at himself, ran howling through the Woods.

   O may'st thou still the Noble Tale prolong,
Nor Age, nor Sickness interrupt thy Song:
Then may we wondring read how Human Limbs,
Have water'd Kingdoms, and dissolv'd in Streams;
Of those rich Fruits that on the Fertile Mould
Turn'd yellow by degrees, and ripen'd into Gold:
How some in Feathers, or a ragged Hide
Have liv'd a second Life, and different Natures try'd.
Then will thy *Ovid*, thus transform'd, reveal
A Nobler Change than he himself can tell.
                         Mag. Coll. *Oxon.*,
                         June 2. 1693.

---

[1] Versions of *Metamorphoses* i and parts of ix and xiii by Dryden appeared in *Examen Poeticum.*

51. Dryden on *The Satires of Juvenalis*

1693

Extract from 'A Discourse concerning ... Satire' prefixed to the collaborative translation of Juvenal's satires (1693; *Poems*, 1958, ed. Kinsley, ii. 669–70).

This must be said for our Translation, that if we give not the whole Sense of *Juvenal*, yet we give the most considerable Part of it: We give it, in General, so clearly, that few Notes are sufficient to make us Intelligible: We make our Authour at least appear in a Poetique Dress. We have actually made him more Sounding, and more Elegant, than he was before in *English*: And have endeavour'd to make him speak that kind of *English*, which he wou'd have spoken had he liv'd in *England*, and had Written to this Age. If sometimes any of us (and 'tis but seldome) make him express the Customs and Manners of our Native Country, rather than of *Rome*; 'tis, either when there was some kind of Analogy, betwixt their Customes and ours; or when, to make him more easy to Vulgar Understandings, we gave him those Manners which are familiar to us. But I defend not this Innovation, 'tis enough if I can excuse it. . . .

52. Dryden on *Love Triumphant*

1694

From the Dedication of *Love Triumphant; or, Nature will Prevail.
A Tragi-Comedy* (1694) to the Earl of Salisbury (Dryden's *Comedies,
Tragedies, and Operas* (1701), ii. 513–14).

A Man may be just to himself, though he ought not to be partial.
And I dare affirm, that the several Manners which I have given to the
Persons of this *Drama*, are truly drawn from Nature; all perfectly
distinguish'd from each other. That the Fable is not injudiciously
contriv'd; that the turns of Fortune are not manag'd unartfully; and
that the last Revolution is happily enough invented. *Aristotle*, I acknowledge, has declar'd, that the Catastrophe which is made from the
change of Will is not of the first Order for Beauty: But it may reasonably be alledg'd, in defence of this Play, as well as of the *Cinna* (which
I take to be the very best of *Corneille's*) that the Philosopher who made
the Rule, copy'd all the Laws, which he gave for the *Theatre*, from the
Authorities and Examples of the *Greek* Poets, which he had read: And
from their Poverty of Invention he cou'd get nothing but mean
Conclusions of Wretched Tales: where the mind of the chief Actor
was for the most part chang'd without Art or Preparation; only because the Poet could not otherwise end his Play. Had it been possible
for *Aristotle* to have seen the *Cinna*, I am confident he would have
alter'd his Opinion. . . . As for the Mechanick Unities, that of Time
is much within the compass of an Astrological Day, which begins at
Twelve, and ends at the same hour the Day following. That of Place
is not observ'd so justly by me, as by the Ancients. . . . I have follow'd
the Example of *Corneille*, and stretch'd the Latitude to a Street and
Palace, not far distant from each other in the same City. They who will
not allow this Liberty to a Poet, make it a very ridiculous thing, for an
Audience to suppose themselves, sometimes to be in a Field, sometimes
in a Garden, and at other times in a Chamber. There are not indeed

so many Absurdities in their Supposition, as in ours; but 'tis an Original Absurdity, for the Audience to suppose themselves to be in any other place, than in the very *Theatre*, in which they sit; which is neither Chamber, nor Garden, nor yet a Publick Place of any Business, but that of the Representation. For my Action, 'tis evidently double; and in that I have most of the Ancients for my Examples. Yet I dare not defend this way by Reason, much less by their Authority: For their Actions, though double, were of the same Species; that is to say, in their *Comedies* two Amours: And their Persons were better link'd in Interests than mine. Yet even this is a fault which I should often practise, if I were to write again; because 'tis agreeable to the *English Genius*. We love variety more than any other Nation; and so long as the Audience will not be pleas'd without it, the Poet is oblig'd to humour them. On condition they were cur'd of this publick Vice, I cou'd be contented to change my Method, and gladly give them a more reasonable Pleasure. . . .

53. Verses on *Virgil*

1697

Verses by an anonymous poet—perhaps Edward Howard, the dramatist (d. *c.* 1700)—and Henry Grahame, Henry St John (1678–1751; later Lord Bolingbroke), James Wright (1643–1713; historian of the theatre), and George Granville (1667–1735; Baron Lansdowne 1711, and the friend of Pope); prefixed to Dryden's *Works of Virgil . . . Translated into English Verse* (1697).

To Mr. Dryden, *on his Excellent Translation of* VIRGIL.

When e're Great *VIRGIL*'s lofty Verse I see,
The Pompous Scene Charms my admiring Eye:
There different Beauties in perfection meet;

The Thoughts as proper, as the Numbers sweet:
And when wild Fancy mounts a daring height,
Judgment steps in, and moderates her flight.
Wisely he manages his Wealthy Store,
Still says enough, and yet implies still more:
For tho' the weighty Sense be closely wrought,
The Reader 's left t' improve the pleasing thought.

Hence we despair'd to see an English dress
Should e're his Nervous Energy express;
For who could that in fetter'd Rhyme inclose,
Which without loss can scarce be told in Prose?

But you, Great Sir, his Manly Genius raise;
And make your Copy share an equal praise.
O how I see thee in soft Scenes of Love,
Renew those Passions he alone could move!
Here *Cupid*'s Charms are with new Art exprest,
And pale *Eliza*[1] leaves her peaceful rest:
Leaves her *Elisium*, as if glad to live,
To Love, and Wish, to Sigh, Despair and Grieve, }
And Die again for him that would again deceive. }
Nor does the Mighty *Trojan* less appear
Than *Mars* himself amidst the storms of War.
Now his fierce Eyes with double fury glow,
And a new dread attends th' impending blow:
The *Daunian* Chiefs their eager rage abate,
And tho' unwounded, seem to feel their Fate.

Long the rude fury of an ignorant Age,
With barbarous spight prophan'd his Sacred Page.
The heavy *Dutchmen* with laborious toil,
Wrested his Sense, and cramp'd his vigorous Style:
No time, no pains the drudging Pedants spare;
But still his Shoulders must the burthen bear.
While thro' the Mazes of their Comments led,
We learn not what he writes, but what they read.
Yet thro' these Shades of undistinguish'd Night
Appear'd some glimmering intervals of Light;
'Till mangled by a vile Translating Sect,

[1] Elissa, Dido.

Like Babes by Witches in Effigie rackt:
'Till *Ogleby*,[1] mature in dulness, rose,
And *Holbourn* Dogrel, and low chiming Prose, ⎫
His Strength and Beauty did at once depose. ⎭
But now the Magick Spell is at an end,
Since even the Dead in you have found a Friend.
You free the Bard from rude Oppressor's Power,
And grace his Verse with Charms unknown before:
He, doubly thus oblig'd, must doubting stand,
Which chiefly should his Gratitude command;
Whether should claim the Tribute of his Heart,
The Patron's Bounty, or the Poet's Art.

Alike with wonder and delight we view'd
The *Roman* Genius in thy Verse renew'd:
We saw thee raise soft *Ovid*'s Amorous Fire,
And fit the tuneful *Horace* to thy Lyre:
We saw new gall imbitter *Juvenal*'s Pen,
And crabbed *Persius* made politely plain:
Virgil alone was thought too great a task;
What you could scarce perform, or we durst ask:
A Task! which *Waller*'s Muse could ne're engage;
A Task! too hard for *Denham*'s stronger rage:
Sure of Success they some slight Sallies try'd,[2]
But the fenc'd Coast their bold Attempts defy'd:
With fear their o're-match'd Forces back they drew,
Quitted the Province Fate reserv'd for you.
In vain thus *Philip* did the *Persians* storm;
A Work his Son[3] was destin'd to perform.

O had *Roscommon*[4] liv'd to hail the day,
And Sing loud Pœans thro' the crowded way;
When you in Roman *Majesty* appear,

---

[1] John Ogilby (1600–76), Scottish cartographer, printer, founder of the Dublin theatre, and translator of Virgil (1649) and Homer (1665). Dryden unjustly derides his translations in *Mac Flecknoe* and elsewhere.

[2] Sir John Denham (1615–69) translated 'The Destruction of Troy' and 'The Passion of Dido for Aeneas', which Dryden found useful; Edmund Waller (1608–87) translated part of *Aeneid* IV.

[3] Alexander the Great.

[4] Wentworth Dillon, 4th Earl of Roscommon (1633?–85), *An Essay on Translated Verse* (1684). Dryden contributed commendatory lines.

Which none know better, and none come so near:
The happy Author would with wonder see,
His Rules were only Prophecies of thee:
And were he now to give Translators light,
He 'd bid them only read thy Work, and write.

For this great Task our loud applause is due;
We own old Favours, but must press for new.
Th' expecting World demands one Labour more;
And thy lov'd *Homer* does thy aid implore,
To right his injur'd Works, and set them free
From the lewd Rhymes of groveling *Ogleby*.[1]
Then shall his Verse in graceful Pomp appear,
Nor will his Birth renew the ancient jar;
On those *Greek* Cities we shall look with scorn,
And in our *Britain* think the Poet Born.

To Mr. Dryden *on his Translation of* VIRGIL.

We read, how Dreams and Visions heretofore,
  The Prophet, and the Poet cou'd inspire;
And make 'em in unusual Rapture soar,
  With Rage Divine, and with Poetick Fire.

2.

O could I find it now!—Wou'd *Virgil*'s Shade
  But for a while vouchsafe to bear the Light;
To grace my Numbers, and that Muse to aid,
  Who sings the Poet, that has done him right.

3.

It long has been this Sacred Author's Fate,
  To lye at ev'ry dull Translator's Will;
Long, long his Muse has groan'd beneath the weight
  Of mangling *Ogleby*'s presumptuous Quill.

4.

Dryden, at last, in his Defence arose;
  The Father now is righted by the Son:

[1] Dryden tried his hand at Homer in 'The Last Parting of *Hector* and *Andromache*' (*Examen Poeticum*, 1693) and a version of *Iliad* I in *Fables* (1700).

And while his Muse endeavours to disclose
    The Poet's Beauties, she declares her own.

5.

In your smooth, pompous Numbers drest, each Line,
    Each Thought, betrays such a Majestick Touch;
He cou'd not, had he finish'd his Design,
    Have wisht it better, or have done so much.

6.

You, like his Heroe, though your self were free,
    And disentangl'd from the War of Wit;
You, who secure might others danger see,
    And safe from all malicious Censure sit:

7.

Yet because Sacred *Virgil*'s Noble Muse,
    O'relay'd by Fools, was ready to expire:
To risque your Fame again, you boldly chuse,
    Or to redeem, or perish with your Sire.

8.

Ev'n first and last, we owe him half to you,
    For that his *Aeneids* miss'd their threatned Fate,[1]
Was—that his Friends by some Prediction knew,
    Hereafter who correcting should translate.

9.

But hold my Muse, thy needless Flight restrain,
    Unless like him thou cou'dst a Verse indite:
To think his Fancy to describe, is vain,
    Since nothing can discover Light, but Light.

10.

'Tis want of Genius that does more deny;
    'Tis Fear my Praise shou'd make your Glory less.
And therefore, like the modest Painter, I
    Must draw the Vail, where I cannot express.

Henry Grahme.

---

[1] In his will Virgil directed that the unfinished *Aeneid* should be burnt.

To Mr. *DRYDEN*.

No undisputed Monarch Govern'd yet
With Universal Sway the Realms of Wit:
Nature cou'd never such Expence afford,
Each several Province own'd a several Lord.
A Poet then had his Poetick Wife,
One Muse embrac'd, and Married for his Life.
By the stale thing his appetite was cloy'd,
His Fancy lessned, and his Fire destroy'd.
But Nature grown extravagantly kind,
With all her Treasures did adorn your Mind.
The different Powers were then united found,
And you Wit's Universal Monarch Crown'd.
Your Mighty Sway your great Desert secures,
And ev'ry Muse and ev'ry Grace is yours.
To none confin'd, by turns you all enjoy,
Sated with this, you to another flye.
So *Sultan*-like in your *Seraglio* stand,
While wishing Muses wait for your Command.
Thus no decay, no want of vigour find,
Sublime your Fancy, boundless is your Mind.
Not all the blasts of time can do you wrong,
Young spight of Age, in spight of Weakness strong.
Time like *Alcides*, strikes you to the ground,
You like *Antæus* from each fall rebound.

H. St. John.

To Mr. *Dryden* on his *VIRGIL*.

'Tis said that *Phidias* gave such living Grace
To the carv'd Image of a beauteous Face,
That the cold Marble might ev'n seem to be
The Life, and the true Life, the Imag'ry.

You pass that Artist, Sir, and all his Powers,
Making the best of *Roman* Poets ours;
With such Effect, we know not which to call
The Imitation, which th' Original.

What *Virgil* lent, you pay in equal Weight,
  The charming Beauty of the Coin no less;
  And such the Majesty of your Impress,
You seem the very Author you translate.

'Tis certain, were he now alive with us,
  And did revolving Destiny constrain,
  To dress his Thoughts in *English* o're again,
Himself cou'd write no otherwise than thus.

His old Encomium never did appear
  So true as now; Romans *and* Greeks *submit*,
  Something of late is in our Language writ,
More nobly great than the fam'd Iliads *were.*

Ja. Wright.

To Mr. *Dryden* on his Translations.

As Flow'rs transplanted from a *Southern* Sky,
But hardly bear, or in the raising dye,
Missing their Native Sun, at best retain
But a faint Odour, and but live with Pain:
So *Roman* Poetry by Moderns taught,
Wanting the Warmth with which its Author wrote,
Is a dead Image, and a worthless Draught.
While we transfuse, the nimble Spirit flies,
Escapes unseen, evaporates, and dyes.

Who then attempt to shew the Ancients Wit,
Must copy with the Genius that they writ.
Whence we conclude from thy translated Song,
So just, so warm, so smooth, and yet so strong,
Thou Heav'nly Charmer! Soul of Harmony!
That all their Geniusses reviv'd in thee.

Thy Trumpet sounds, the dead are rais'd to Light,
New-born they rise, and take to Heav'n their Flight;
Deckt in thy Verse, as clad with Rayes, they shine
All Glorify'd, Immortal and Divine.

As *Britain*, in rich Soil abounding wide,
Furnish'd for Use, for Luxury, and Pride,

Yet spreads her wanton Sails on ev'ry Shore,
For Foreign Wealth, insatiate still of more;
To her own Wooll, the Silks of *Asia* joins,
And to her plenteous Harvests, *Indian* Mines:
So *Dryden*, not contented with the Fame
Of his own Works, tho' an immortal Name,
To Lands remote he sends his learned Muse,
The Noblest Seeds of Foreign Wit to chuse.
Feasting our Sense so many various Ways,
Say, Is 't thy Bounty, or thy Thirst of Praise?
That by comparing others, all might see,
Who most excell'd, are yet excell'd by thee.

George Granville.

54. Dryden on his *Virgil*

1697

Extracts from Dryden's Dedication of and Postscript to *Virgil's Æneis* (*The Works of Virgil*, 1697; *Poems*, 1958, ed. Kinsley, iii. 1051–9, 1062, 1424). The Dedication was addressed to the Earl of Mulgrave.

(*a*) 'What I have said, though it has the face of arrogance, yet is intended for the honour of my Country; and therefore I will boldly own, that this *English* Translation has more of *Virgil's* Spirit in it, than either the *French*, or the *Italian*. . . . I thought fit to steer betwixt the two Extreams, of Paraphrase, and literal Translation . . . I have endeavour'd to make *Virgil* speak such *English*, as he wou'd himself have spoken, if he had been born in *England*, and in this present Age. . . . I have not succeeded in this attempt, according to my desire: yet I shall not be wholly without praise, if in some sort I may be allow'd to have copied the Clearness, the Purity, the Easiness and the Magnificence of his Stile. . . .

Lay by *Virgil*, I beseech your Lordship, and all my better sort of Judges, when you take up my Version, and it will appear a passable Beauty, when the Original Muse is absent: But like *Spencer*'s false *Florimel* made of Snow,[1] it melts and vanishes, when the true one comes in sight. I will not excuse but justifie my self for one pretended Crime, with which I am liable to be charg'd by false Criticks, not only in this Translation, but in many of my Original Poems; that I latinize too much. 'Tis true, that when I find an *English* word, significant and sounding, I neither borrow from the *Latin* or any other Language: But when I want at home, I must seek abroad.'

(*b*) 'I have done great Wrong to *Virgil* in the whole Translation: Want of Time, the Inferiority of our Language, the Inconvenience of Rhyme, and all the other Excuses I have made, may alleviate my Fault, but cannot justifie the boldness of my Undertaking. What avails it me to acknowledge freely, that I have not been able to do him right in any line? For even my own Confession makes against me; and it will always be return'd upon me, Why then did you attempt it? To which, no other Answer can be made, than that I have done him less Injury than any of his former Libellers.'

(*c*) 'What *Virgil* wrote in the vigour of his Age, in Plenty and at Ease, I have undertaken to *Translate* in my Declining Years: strugling with Wants, oppress'd with Sickness, curb'd in my Genius, lyable to be misconstrued in all I write; and my Judges, if they are not very equitable, already prejudic'd against me, by the *Lying Character* which has been given them of my Morals. . . . In the first place therefore, I thankfully acknowledge to the Almighty Power, the Assistance he has given me in the beginning, the Prosecution, and *Conclusion* of my present Studies, which are more happily perform'd than I could have promis'd to my self, when I labour'd under such Discouragements. For, what I have done, Imperfect as it is, for want of Health and leisure to Correct it, will be judg'd in after Ages, and possibly in the present, to be no dishonour to my Native Country; whose Language and Poetry wou'd be more esteem'd abroad, if they were better understood. Somewhat (give me leave to say) I have added to both of them in the choice of *Words*, and Harmony of Numbers which were wanting,

[1] *The Faerie Queene*, V. iii. 22–4.

especially the last, in all our Poets, even in those who being endu'd with Genius, yet have not Cultivated their Mother-Tongue with sufficient Care; or relying on the Beauty of their Thoughts, have judg'd the Ornament of Words, and sweetness of Sound unnecessary.'

55. *Alexander's Feast*

1697

From Dryden's letter to Tonson, December 1697 (British Museum Egerton MS. 2869, f. 34). *Alexander's Feast; or The Power of Musique. An Ode* was performed on 22 November 1697.

I am glad to heare from all Hands, that my Ode is esteemd the best of all my poetry, by all the Town: I thought so my self when I writ it but being old, I mistrusted my own Judgment. I hope it has done you service, and will do more. You told me not, but the Town says, you are printing Ovid de Arte Amandi;[1] I know my Translation is very uncorrect: but at the same time I know no body else can do it better, with all their pains.

[1] Tonson published *Ovid's Art of Love*, translated by Dryden and others, in 1709.

56. Immorality and profaneness

1698

Extracts from Jeremy Collier (1650–1726), *A Short View of the Immorality and Profaneness of the English Stage: Together with The Sense of Antiquity upon this Argument* (1698). 'I have been wrongfully accus'd', says Dryden in the Preface to *Fables Ancient and Modern* (1700), 'and my Sense wire-drawn into Blasphemy or Bawdry, as it has often been by a Religious Lawyer [Collier], in a late Pleading against the Stage; in which he mixes Truth with Falshood, and has not forgotten the old Rule, of calumniating strongly, that something may remain' (*Poems*, 1958, ed. Kinsley, iv. 1447 and note). Text from the fourth edition (1699).

(*a*) 'The Business of *Plays* is to recommend Virtue, and discountenance Vice; To shew the Uncertainty of Humane Greatness, the suddain Turns of Fate, and the Unhappy Conclusions of Violence and Injustice: 'Tis to expose the Singularities of Pride and Fancy, to make Folly and False-hood contemptible, and to bring every Thing that is Ill under Infamy, and Neglect. This Design has been odly pursued by the *English-Stage*. Our *Poets* write with a different View, and are gone into another Interest. 'Tis true, were their Intentions fair, they might be *Serviceable* to this *Purpose*. They have in a great measure the Springs of Thought and Inclination in their Power. *Show*, *Musick*, *Action*, and *Rhetorick*, are moving Entertainments; and, rightly employ'd, would be very significant. But Force and Motion are Things indifferent, and the Use lies chiefly in the Application. These Advantages are now in the Enemie's Hand, and under a very dangerous Management. Like Cannon seiz'd, they are pointed the wrong way; and by the Strength of the Defence, the Mischief is made the greater. That this Complaint is not unreasonable, I shall endeavour to prove by shewing the Misbehaviour of the *Stage*, with respect to *Morality*, and *Religion*. Their *Liberties* in the following Particulars are intolerable, *viz.* Their *Smuttiness*

227

of *Expression*; Their *Swearing, Prophaneness,* and *Lewd Application
of Scripture*; Their *Abuse* of the *Clergy*; Their *making* their *top Characters Libertines,* and giving them *Success* in their *Debauchery.* This Charge,
with some other Irregularities, I shall make good against the *Stage,*
and shew both the *Novelty* and *Scandal* of the *Practice*' (pp. 1–2,
Introduction).

[In Chap. 1 Collier goes on to illustrate 'The Immodesty of the Stage'.]

(*b*) 'Another Instance of the Disorders of the *Stage,* is their Profaneness; This Charge may come under these two Particulars.

> 1st.   *Their Cursing and Swearing.*
> 2dly.   *Their Abuse of Religion, and Holy Scripture.* . . .

In the First *Act* [of *Dryden's Mock Astrologer*], the *Scene* is a *Chappel*'
and that the Use of such Consecrated places may be the better understood, the time is taken up in Courtship, Raillery, and Ridiculing
Devotion. *Jacinta* takes her turn among the rest. She interrupts
Theodosia, and cries out: *Why Sister, Sister—will you pray? What injury
have I ever done you that you shou'd pray in my Company?* *Wildblood*
swears by *Mahomet,* rallies smuttily upon the other World, and gives
the preference to the Turkish Paradise. This Gentleman, to encourage
Jacinta to a Compliance in Debauchery, tells her, *Heaven is all Eyes
and no Tongue.* That is, it sees Wickedness but conceals it. He Courts
much at the same rate a little before. *When a Man comes to a great
Lady, he is fain to approach her with Fear, and Reverence, methinks there's
something of Godliness in 't.* Here you have the Scripture burlesqu'd,
and the Pulpit-Admonition apply'd to Whoring. Afterwards *Jacinta*
out of her great Breeding and Christianity, swears by *Alla,* and
Mahomet, and makes a Jest upon Hell. *Wildblood* tells his Man that
such undesigning Rogues as he, make a Drudge of poor Providence. And
Maskall, to shew his proficiency under his Masters, replies to *Bellamy,*
who would have had him told a Lie, *Sir, upon the Faith of a Sinner, you
have had my last Lie already, I have not one more to do me Credit, as I
hope to be saved, Sir.*

In the close of the *Play,* they make sport with Apparitions and
Fiends. One of the Devils sneezes, upon this they give him the Blessing
of the Occasion, and conclude *he has got cold by being too long out of
the Fire.* . . .

Let us now take a view of *Don Sebastian.* And here the *Reader* can't
be long unfurnish'd. *Dorax* shall speak first.

> *Shall I trust Heaven—*
> *With my Revenge? then where? my Satisfaction?*
> *No, it must be my own, I scorn a Proxy.*

But *Dorax* was a Renegado, what then? He had renounc'd Christianity, but not Providence. Besides, such hideous Sentences ought not to be put in the Mouth of the Devil. For that which is not fit to be heard, is not fit to be spoken. But to some People an Atheistical Rant is as good as a Flourish of Trumpets. To proceed; *Antonio*, tho' a profess'd Christian, mends the matter very little. He is looking on a Lot which he had drawn for his Life: This proving unlucky, after the preamble of a Curse or two, he calls it,

> *As black as Hell; another lucky saying!*
> *I think the Devil's in me:—good again,*
> *I cannot speak one Syllable but tends*
> *To Death or to Damnation.*

Thus the Poet prepares his Bullies for the other World! Hell and Damnation are strange entertaining Words upon the *Stage*! Were it otherwise, the Sense in these Lines, would be almost as bad as the Conscience. The Poem warms and rises in the working; and the next Flight is extremely remarkable.

> *Not the Last Sounding could surprize me more,*
> *That summons drowsy Mortals to their Doom,*
> *When call'd in hast they fumble for their Limbs.*

Very Solemnly and Religiously express'd! *Lucian* and *Celsus*[1] could not have ridiculed the Resurrection better! Certainly the Poet never expects to be there. Such a light Turn would have agreed much better to a Man who was in the Dark, and was feeling for his Stockings. But let those who talk of *Fumbling* for their Limbs, take care they don't find them too fast. ... The same Author in his Dedication of *Juvenal* and *Persius*, has these Words: *My Lord, I am come to the Last Petition of Abraham; If there be ten Righteous Lines in this vast Preface, spare it for their sake; and also spare the next City, because it is but a little one.*[2] Here the Poet stands for *Abraham*, and the Patron for God Almighty: And where lies the Wit of all this? In the Decency of the Comparison? I doubt not. And for the *next City* he would have spared, he is out in the Allusion. 'Tis no *Zoar*, but much rather *Sodom* and

---

[1] A pagan satirist and an anti-Christian philosopher of the second century.
[2] Gen. xix, Luke xvi. 19–31.

Gomorrah; Let them take care the Fire and Brimstone does not follow: And that those who are so bold with *Abraham*'s Petition, are not forced to that of *Dives*. To beg Protection for a Lewd Book in *Scripture-Phrase*, is very extraordinary! ... *Juvenal* has a very untoward way with him in some of his Satyrs. His Pen has such a Libertine stroak, that 'tis a Question whether the Practice, or the Reproof, the Age, or the Author were the more Licentious. He teaches those Vices he would correct, and writes more like a Pimp than a *Poet*. And truly I think there is but little of Lewdness lost in the *Translation*. ... To do Right to such an Author is to burn him. I hope Modesty is much better than Resemblance. The Imitation of an ill Thing is the worse for being exact: And sometimes to report a Fault is to repeat it.

To return to [*Dryden's*] *Plays*. In *Love Triumphant*, *Garcia* makes *Veramond* this Compliment:

> May Heaven and your brave Son, and above all,
> Your own prevailing Genius guard your Age.

What is meant by his Genius, in this place, is not easy to Discover, only that 'tis something which is a better Guard than Heaven. But 'tis no Matter for the Sense, as long as the Profaneness is clear. In this *Act*, Colonel *Sancho* lets *Carlos* know the old Jew is dead, which he calls good news.

Carl. *What Jew?*
Sanch. *Why the rich Jew my Father, he is gone to the Bosom of* Abraham *his Father, and I his Christian Son am left sole Heir.*

A very mannerly Story! But why does the Poet acquaint us with *Sancho*'s Religion? The case is pretty plain: 'Tis to give a lustre to his Profaneness, and make him burlesque St. *Luke* with the better Grace. *Alphonso* complains to *Victoria* that *Nature dotes with Age*. His reason is, because Brother and Sister can't Marry as they did at first: 'Tis very well! We know what *Nature* means in the Language of Christianity, and especially under the Notion of a Law-giver. *Alphonso* goes on, and compares the Possession of Incestuous Love to Heaven. Yes, *'tis Eternity in Little*. ...' (pp. 56, 60–1, 64–6, 69–72).

(c) 'What a fine time Lewd People have on the *English-Stage*. No Censure, no mark of Infamy, no Mortification must touch them. They keep their Honour untarnish'd, and carry off the Advantage of their Character. They are set up for the Standard of Behaviour, and

the Masters of Ceremony and Sense. And at last that the Example
may work the better, they generally make them Rich, and Happy,
and reward them with their own Desires.

Mr. *Dryden* in the *Preface* to his *Mock-Astrologer*, confesses himself
blamed for this Practice. *For making debauch'd Persons his Protagonists,
or chief Persons of the Drama; And for making them happy in the Conclusion
of the Play, against the Law of Comedy, which is to reward Virtue, and
punish Vice.* To this Objection He makes a lame Defence. And answers

1*st*. *That he knows no such Law constantly observ'd in Comedy by the
Ancient or Modern Poets.* What then? *Poets* are not always exactly in
Rule. It may be a good Law tho' 'tis not constantly observ'd; some
Laws are constantly broken, and yet ne're the worse for all that. He
goes on, and pleads the Authorities of *Plautus*, and *Terence*. I grant
there are Instances of Favour to vicious young People in those Authors,
but to this I reply

1*st*. That those *Poets* had a greater compass of Liberty in their
Religion. Debauchery did not lie under those Discouragements of
Scandal, and Penalty, with them as it does with us. Unless therefore
He can prove *Heathenism*, and *Christianity* the same, his *Precedents* will
do him little service.

2*ly*. *Horace* who was as good a Judge of the *Stage*, as either of those
Comedians, seems to be of another Opinion. He condemns the
Obscenities of *Plautus*, and tells you, Men of Fortune and Quality in
his time, would not endure immodest Satyr. . . .*

Lastly, Horace having expresly mentioned the beginning and progress
of *Comedy*, discovers himself more fully: He advises a *Poet* to form his
Work upon the Precepts of *Socrates* and *Plato*, and the Models of
Moral Philosophy. This was the way to preserve Decency, and to
assign a proper Fate and Behaviour to every *Character*. Now if *Horace*
would have his *Poet* govern'd by the Maxims of Morality, he must
oblige him to Sobriety of Conduct, and a just Distribution of Rewards,
and Punishments.

Mr. *Dryden* makes Homewards, and endeavours to fortifie himself
in Modern Authority. He lets us know that *Ben Johnson after whom he
may be proud to Err, gives him more than one Example of this Conduct;
That in the* Alchimist *is notorious*, where neither *Face* nor his *Master*
are corrected according to their Demerits. But how Proud soever
Mr. *Dryden* may be of an Errour, he has not so much of *Ben Johnson's*

---

* *De Art. Poet.*

company as he pretends. His Instance of *Face, &c.* in the *Alchimist* is rather *notorious* against his Purpose than for it.

For *Face* did not Counsel his Master *Lovewit* to debauch the Widow; neither is it clear that the Matter went thus far. He might gain her consent upon Terms of Honour for ought appears to the contrary. . . . *But Face continued in the Cousenage till the last without Repentance.* Under Favour I conceive this is a Mistake. For does not *Face* make an *Apology* before he leaves the *Stage?* Does he not set himself at the *Bar*, arraign his own Practice, and cast the Cause upon the Clemency of the Company? And are not all these Signs of the Dislike of what he had done? Thus careful the *Poet* is to prevent the Ill Impressions of his *Play*! He brings both Man and Master to Confession. He dismisses them like Malefactors; And moves for their Pardon before he gives them their Discharge. But the *Mock-Astrologer* has a gentler Hand: *Wild-Blood* and *Jacinta* are more generously used: There is no Acknowledgment exacted; no Hardship put upon them: They are permitted to talk on in their Libertine way to the Last: and take Leave without the least Appearance of Reformation. . . .

Ben Johnson's Fox is clearly against Mr. *Dryden.* And here I have his own Confession for Proof. He declares the *Poet's End in this Play was the Punishment of Vice, and the Reward of Virtue.* . . . I shall take a Testimony or two from *Shakespear* . . . I could give some Instances of this kind out of *Beaumont* and *Fletcher,* But there 's no need of any farther Quotation; For Mr. *Dryden* is not satisfied with his Apology from Authority: He does as good as own that this may be construed no better than defending one ill Practice by another. . . .

However, now we know the Reason of the Profaneness, and Obscenity of the Stage. . . . 'Tis all to Satisfie the Company, and make People Laugh! . . . *Delight* is the *Chief End of Comedy. Delight!* He should have said *Debauchery*: That 's the *English* of the Word, and the Consequence of the Practice. But the Original Design of *Comedy* was otherwise: And granting 'twas not so, what then? If the *Ends* of Things are naught, they must be mended. . . . To conclude. If *Delight* without Restraint, or Distinction, without Conscience or Shame, is the Supream Law of *Comedy*, 'twere well if we had less on 't. Arbitrary Pleasure, is more dangerous than Arbitrary Power. Nothing is more Brutal than to be abandon'd to Appetite; And nothing more wretched than to serve in such a Design. The *Mock-Astrologer*, to clear himself of this Imputation, is glad to give up his Principle at Last. *Lest any Man should think* (says he) *that I write this to make Libertinism amiable, or that I cared not to debase the End, and Institution of* Comedy (It seems then *Delight* is not the Chief End.) *I must farther declare that we make not Vicious Persons Happy, but only as Heaven makes Sinners so,* &c. If this will hold, all 's well. But *Heaven* does not forgive without Repentance. Let us see then what Satisfaction he requires from his *Wild-Blood,* and what Discipline he puts him under. Why, He helps him to his Mistress, he Marries him to a Lady of Birth and Fortune. And now do you think He has not made him an Example, and punish'd him to some Purpose! These are frightful Severities! Who would be vicious when such Terrors hang over his Head? And does *Heaven make Sinners happy* upon these Conditions? Sure some People have a good Opinion of Vice, or a very ill one of Marriage, otherwise they would have charged the Penance a little more. But I have nothing farther with the *Mock-Astrologer.* . . .

Don-Sebastian . . . after all the Violence of his Repentance, his grasping at self Murther, and Resolutions for the *Cell,* is strangely pleased with the Remembrance of his *Incest,* and wishes the Repetition of it: And *Almeida* out of her Princely Modesty, and singular Compunction, is of the same Mind. This is somewhat surprising! *Oedipus* and *Jocasta* in *Sophocles* don't Repent at this rate. No: The horror of the first Discovery continues upon their Spirits: They never relapse into any fits of Intemperance, nor entertain themselves with a lewd Memory. This sort of Behaviour is not only more Instructive but more Natural too. . . .

If we step to the *Spanish Fryar* He will afford us a Flight worth the observing. 'Tis part of the Addresses of *Torrismond* to *Leonora.*

> *You are so Beautiful,*
> *So wondrous Fair, you justifie Rebellion;*
> *As if that faultless Face could make no Sin,*
> *But Heaven by looking on it must forgive.*[1]

These are strange Complements! *Torrismond* calls his Queen Rebel to her Head, when he was both her General and her Lover. This is powerful Rhetorick to Court a Queen with! Enough one would think to have made the Affair desperate. But he has a Remedy at Hand. The *Poet's Nostrum* of Profaneness cures all. He does as good as tell Her, she may Sin as much as she has a Mind to. Her Face is a Protection to her Conscience. For Heaven is under a necessity to forgive a Handsom Woman. To say all this ought to be pass'd over in *Torrismond* on the

[1] III. iii.

score of his Passion, is to make the Excuse more scandalous than the Fault, if possible. Such Raptures are fit only for *Bedlam*, or a place which I shan't Name. *Love Triumphant* will furnish another Rant not altogether inconsiderable. Here *Celadea* a Maiden Lady, when she was afraid her Spark would be married to another, calls out presently for a *Chaos*. She is for pulling the World about her Ears, tumbling all the Elements together, and Expostulates with Heaven for making Humane Nature otherwise than it should have been.

> *Great Nature break thy chain that links together*
> *The Fabrick of this Globe, and make a Chaos,*
> *Like that within my Soul.*—[1]

Now to my fancy, if she had call'd for a *Chair* instead of a *Chaos*, trip'd off, and kept her folly to her self, the Woman had been much wiser. And since we have shown our Skill in vaulting on the High-Ropes, a little *Tumbling* on the *Stage*, may not do amiss for variety.

Now then for a jest or two. *Don Gomez* shall begin: And here he'll give us a Gingle upon the double meaning of a Word.

I think, says *Dominick* the Fryar, *it was my good Angel that sent me hither so opportunely.* *Gomez* suspects him brib'd for no creditable Business, and Answers.

> Gom. *Ay, whose good Angels sent you hither, that you know best, Father.*[2]

These *Spaniards* will entertain us with more of this Fine Raillery. Colonel *Sancho* in *Love Triumphant* has a great stroak at it. He says his Bride *Dalinda* is no more *Dalinda*, but *Dalilah* the *Philistine*. This Colonel as great a Soldier as he is, is quite puzzled at a *Herald*. *He thinks they call him* Herod, *or some such Jewish Name.*[3] Here you have a good Officer spoil'd for a miserable jest. . . .' (pp. 148–9, 151–3, 162–5, 166–9).

(*d*) 'I shall now give the *Reader* a few Instances of the Courtship of the *Stage*, and how decently they treat the Women, and *Quality* of both *Sexes*. The *Women* who are secured from Affronts by Custom, and have a Privilege for Respect, are sometimes but roughly saluted by these Men of Address. . . . Enter *Raymond* a Noble-man in the *Spanish Fryar.*[4]

[1] IV. i.
[2] IV. i.
[3] V. i, IV. i.
[4] IV. ii.

O Virtue! Virtue! What art thou become?
That men should leave thee for that Toy a woman,
Made from the Dross and Refuse of a Man;
Heaven took him sleeping when he made her too,
Had Man been waking he had ne'er consented.

I did not know before that a Man's Dross lay in his *Ribs*; I believe sometimes it lies higher. But the Philosophy, the Religion, and the Ceremony of these Lines, are too tender to to be touched ...' (pp 170–1).

(e) In *Amphitryon* 'Mr. *Dryden* represents *Jupiter* with the Attributes of the supreme Being: He furnishes him with Omnipotence, makes him the Creator of Nature, and the Arbiter of Fate; puts all the Functions of Providence in his Hand, and describes him with the Majesty of the true God. And when he has put Him in this glorious Equipage, he brings him out for Diversion. He makes him express himself in the most intemperate Raptures: He is willing to *Renounce* his *Heaven* for his Brutality, and employ a whole *Eternity* in Lewdness. He draws his Debauch at its full Length, with all the Art, and Heightnings, and Foulness of Idea imaginable. ... The truth is, Our *Stage-Poets* seem to sence against Censure by the excess of Lewdness; And to make the overgrown size of a Crime, a Ground for Impunity. As if a Malefactor should project his Escape by appearing too scandalous for Publick Tryal. However, This is their Armour of Proof, this is the Strength they retreat to. They are fortified in Smut, and almost impregnable in Stench, so that where they deserve most, there's no coming at them. To proceed. I desire to know what Authority Mr. *Dryden* has for this extraordinary Representation? His Original *Plautus*, is no Precedent. Indeed *Plautus* is the only bold Heathen that ever made *Jupiter* tread the *Stage*. But then he stops far short of the Liberties of the *English Amphytrion*. ... Why must the beaten Road be left? He tells us, *That the difference of our* Stage *from the* Roman *and the* French *did so require it.* That is, our *Stage* must be much more Licentious. For you are to observe that Mr. *Dryden*, and his Fraternity, have help'd to debauch the *Town*, and Poyson their Pleasures to an unusual Degree: And therefore the Diet must be dress'd to the Palate of the *Company*. And since they are made *Scepticks* they must be entertain'd as such. That the *English Amphytrion* was contriv'd with this View is too plain to be better interpreted. To what purpose else does *Jupiter* appear in the shape of *Jehovah*? ... Nothing but Mr. *Dryden*'s *Absalom and Achitophel* out-do This. Here I confess the Motion of his Pen is bolder, and the Strokes more Black'd. Here we have Blasphemy on the top of the Letter, without any trouble of Inference, or Construction. This Poem runs all upon Scripture Names, upon Supposition of the true Religion, and the right Object of Worship. Here Profaneness is shut out from Defence, and lies open without Colour or Evasion. Here are no Pagan Divinities in the Scheme, so that all the Atheistick Raillery must point upon the true God. In the Beginning we are told that *Absalom*, was *David*'s Natural Son: So then there 's a Blot in his *Scutcheon*, and a blemish upon his Birth. The *Poet* will make admirable use of this Remark presently! This *Absalom* it seems was very extraordinary in his Person and Performances. Mr. *Dryden* does not certainly know how this came about, and therefore enquires of himself in the first place

> *Whether, inspired with a diviner Lust,*
> *His Father got him—*

This is down right Defiance of the Living God? Here you have the very Essence and Spirit of Blasphemy, and the Holy Ghost brought in upon the most hideous Occasion. I question whether the Torments and Despair of the Damn'd, dare venture at such Flights as these. They are beyond Description, I Pray God they may not be beyond Pardon too. . . .

To use *Mercury* thus ill, and make the God of Eloquence speak so unlike himself, is somewhat strange! But tho' the *Ancients* knew nothing of it, there are Considerations above those of *Decency*. And when this happens, *A Rule must rather be trespass'd on, than a Beauty left out.* 'Tis Mr. *Dryden*'s Opinion in his *Cleomenes*, where he breaks the *Unity of Time*, to describe the *Beauty* of a Famine. Now Beauty is an arbitrary Advantage, and depends upon Custom and Fancy. With some People the Blackest Complexions are the handsomest. 'Tis to these *African* Criticks that Mr. *Dryden* seems to make his Appeal. And without doubt he bespeaks their Favour, and strikes their Imagination luckily enough. For to lodge Divinity and Scandal together; To make the Gods throw *Stars*, like *Snow-balls* at one another, but especially to Court in Smut, and rally in Blasphemy, is most admirably entertaining! This is much better than all the Niceties of *Decorum*. 'Tis handsomly contriv'd, to slur the Notion of a Superiour Nature, to disarm the Terrors of Religion, and make the Court above as Romantick as that of the *Fairies*. . . .

I shall pass on to *King Arthur* for a Word or two. Now here is a

strange Jumble and Hotch-potch of Matters, if you mind it. Here we
have *Genii*, and *Angels*, *Cupids*, *Syrens*, and *Devils*; *Venus* and St.
George, *Pan* and the *Parson*, the Hell of Heathenism, and the Hell of
Revelation; A fit of Smut, and then a Jest about Original Sin. And why
are Truth and Fiction, Heathenism and Christianity, the most Serious
and the most Trifling Things blended together, and thrown into one
Form of Diversion? Why is all this done unless it be to ridicule the
whole, and make one as incredible, as the other? His *Airy* and *Earthy*
Spirits discourse of the first state of Devils, of their *Chief*, of their
Revolt, their Punishment, and Impostures. This Mr. *Dryden* very
Religiously calls a *Fairy way of Writing, which depends only on the Force*
of Imagination.* What then, is the Fall of the Angels a Romance?
Has it no basis of Truth, nothing to support it, but strength of Fancy,
and Poetick Invention? After He had mention'd Hell, Devils, &c.
and given us a sort of *Bible*-description of these formidable Things;
I say after he had formed his Poem in this manner, I am surprized to
hear him call it a *Fairy kind of Writing*. Is the History of *Tophet* no
better prov'd than that of *Styx*? Is the Lake of *Brimstone* and that of
Phlegeton alike dreadful? And have we as much Reason to believe the
Torments of *Titius* and *Prometheus*, as those of the Devils and Damn'd?
These are lamentable Consequences! And yet I can't well see how the
Poet can avoid them. But setting aside this miserable Gloss in the
Dedication, the Representation it self is scandalously irreligious. To droll
upon the Vengeance of Heaven, and the Miseries of the Damn'd, is a
sad Instance of Christianity! Those that bring Devils upon the *Stage*,
can hardly believe them any where else. Besides the Effects of such an
Entertainment must needs be admirable! To see Hell thus play'd with
is a mighty Refreshment to a lewd Conscience, and a byass'd Understanding. It heartens the Young Libertine, and confirms the Well-
wishers to Atheism, and makes Vice bold, and enterprizing. Such
Diversions serve to dispel the Gloom, and guild the Horrors of the
Shades below, and are a sort of Ensurance against Damnation. One
would think these *Poets* went upon absolute Certainty, and could
demonstrate a Scheme of Infidelity. If they could, they had much
better keep the Secret. The divulging it tends only to debauch Mankind, and shake the Securities of Civil Life. ... Is any Man so vain as
to pretend to know the Extent of Nature, and the Stretch of Possibility, and the Force of the Powers Invisible? So that notwithstanding

---

* *Ep. Ded.*

the Boldness of this *Opera*, there may be such a Place as Hell; And if so, a Discourse about Devils, will be no *Fairy Way of Writing*. For a *Fairy Way of Writing*, is nothing but a *History of Fiction*; A Subject of Imaginary Beings; such as never had any existence in Time, or Nature. And if as Monsieur *Rapin* observes, *Poetry* requires a mixture of *Truth* and *Fable*; Mr. *Dryden* may make his Advantage, for his *Play* is much better founded on Reality than He was aware of.

It may not be improper to consider in a Word or Two, what a frightful Idea the *Holy Scriptures* give us of Hell. . . .

Let us now see how Mr. *Dryden* represents these unhappy Spirits, and their Place of Abode. Why, very entertainingly! Those that have a true Tast for Atheism, were never better regaled. One would think by this *Play* the Devils were meer Mormo's[1] and Bugbears, fit only to fright Children and Fools. They rally upon Hell and Damnation, with a great deal of Air and Pleasantry; and appear like *Robin Goodfellow*, only to make the Company Laugh. *Philidel* is call'd a *Puling Sprite*. And why so? For this pious Reason, because

> *He trembles at the yawning Gulph of Hell,*
> *Nor dares approach the Flames lest he should Singe*
> *His gaudy silken Wings.*
> *He sighs when he should plunge a Soul in Sulphur,*
> *As with Compassion touch'd of Foolish Man.*

The answer is, *What a half Devil's he?*[2]

You see how admirably it runs all upon the Christian Scheme! Sometimes they are *Half-Devils*, and sometimes *Hopeful-Devils*, and what you please to make sport with. *Grimbald* is afraid of being *whooped through Hell at his return*,[3] for miscarrying in his Business. It seems there is great Leisure for Diversion! There 's *Whooping* in Hell, instead of *Weeping* and *Wailing*. One would fancy Mr. *Dryden* had Daylight and Company, when these lines were written. I know his Courage is extraordinary; but sure such Thoughts could never bear up against Solitude and a Candle!

And now since he has diverted himself with the *Terrors* of *Christianity*, I don't wonder he should treat those that Preach them with so much Civility! Enter *Poet* in the Habit of a *Peasant*.

---

[1] Monsters, hobgoblins.
[2] I. ii.
[3] IV. i.

We ha' Cheated the Parson we'll Cheat him again,
For why should a Blockhead have one in ten?
For prating so long like a Booklearned Sot,
Till Pudding and Dumpling burn to Pot.[1]

These are fine comprehensive Stroaks! Here you have the *Iliads* in a Nutshel! Two or three courtly Words take in the whole Clergy: And what is wanting in Wit, is made up in abuse, and that 's as well. This is an admirable *Harvest-Catch,* and the poor Tith-stealers stand highly indebted. They might have been tired with Cheating in *Prose,* had they not been thus seasonably reliev'd in Doggrel: But now there is Musick in playing the Knave. A Country-man now may fill his Barn, and humour his ill Manners, and sing his Conscience asleep, and all under one. I don't question but these *four Lines* steal many a Pound in the Year. Whether the *Muse* stands indictable or not, the Law must determine. But after all, I must say the Design is notably laid. For Place and Person, for Relish and Convenience, nothing could have been better. The Method is Short, Clear, and Practicable. 'Tis a fine portable Infection, and costs no more Carriage than the Plague.

Well! The Clergy must be contented: It might possibly have been worse for them if they had been in his Favour: For he has sometimes a very unlucky way of shewing his Kindness. He commends the Earl of *Leicester, for considering the Friend, more than the Cause;*[*] that is, for his Partiality; The Marquess of *Halifax,* for *quitting the Helm, at the approach of a Storm;*[†] As if Pilots were made only for fair Weather. 'Tis Presum'd these Noble Persons are unconcern'd in this Character. However the *Poet* has shewn his Skill in Panegyrick, and 'tis only for that I mention it. He commends *Atticus* for his Trimming, and *Tully* for his Cowardise, and speaks meanly of the Bravery of *Cato.*[‡] Afterwards he professes his Zeal for the Publick Welfare, and is pleas'd to *see the Nation so well secur'd from Foreign Attempts,* &c. However he is in some pain about the coming of the *Gauls:* 'Tis possible for fear they should invade the *Muses,* and carry the *Opera's* into Captivity, and deprive us of the *Ornaments of Peace.*

And now he has serv'd his Friends, he comes in the last place like a modest Man, to commend Himself. He tells us there were a great many *Beauties* in the Original Draught of this *Play.* But it seems Time

[*] *Ep. Ded. Don. Sebast.*
[†] *Ded. King Arthur.*
[‡] *Sebast. King Arthur.*
[1] V. i.

has since tarnish'd their Complexion; And he gives *Heroick* Reasons for their not appearing. To speak Truth, (all Politicks apart), there are strange Flights of Honour, and Consistencies of Pretention in this Dedication! But I shall forbear the Blazon of the *Atchievement*, for fear I should commend as unluckily as Himself' (pp. 177–8, 179, 182–4, 186–7, 188–91, 192–5).

57. *Fables Ancient and Modern*

1700

From Dryden's letters to Mrs Steward, (a) 12 March 1699/1700, (b) 11 April 1700. His *Fables* were published in the first week of March. Mrs Steward was the daughter of Dryden's cousin Elizabeth Creed. (*Letters of John Dryden*, 1942, ed. C. E. Ward, nos. 74 and 75.)

(a) '... my new Poems ... are a debt to you I must Confess, and I am glad, because they are so Unworthy to be made a Present. Your Sisters I hope, will be so kind to have them convey'd to you; that my writeings may have the honour of waiting on you, which is denyd to me. The Town encourages them with more Applause than any thing of mine deserves; And particularly My Cousin Driden[1] accepted One from me so so very Indulgently, that it makes me more and more in Love with him.'

(b) 'The Ladies of the Town have infected you at a distance: they are all of your opinion; and like my last Book of Poems, better than any thing they have formerly seen of mine. I always thought my Verses

---

[1] John Dryden of Chesterton (1635–1708), Dryden's cousin and M.P. for Huntingdon. Dryden's eulogy of him was published in *Fables*.

to my Cousin Driden were the best of the whole; and to my comfort the Town thinks them so; and He, which pleases me most is of the same Judgment....'

58. On a portrait of Dryden

1700

From J. E. [John Elsum], *Epigrams on the Paintings of the Most Eminent Masters* (1700); Malone, *The ... Prose Works of John Dryden*, 1800, I. i. 437, note.

The Effigies of Mr. DRYDEN, by Closterman.
Epig. CLXIV.

A sleepy eye he shews, and no sweet feature,
Yet was indeed a favourite of nature:
Endow'd and graced with an exalted mind,
With store of wit; and that, of every kind.
Juvenal's tartness, Horace's sweet air,
With Virgil's force, in him concenter'd were.
But though the painter's art can never shew it,
That his exemplar was so great a poet,
Yet are the lines and tints so subtly wrought,
You may perceive he was a man of thought.
Closterman, 'tis confess'd, has drawn him well,
But short of ABSALOM AND ACHITOPHEL.

59. Farce and heroicks

1700

Extract from a letter by the dramatist George Farquhar (1677–1707) on Dryden's burial in Westminster Abbey on 13 May 1700. 'No Ambassador from the greatest Emperor in all the Universe,' said *The London Spy* (1700; II. vi), 'sent over with a Welcome Embassy to the Throne of *England*, ever made his Publick Entry to the Court, with half that Honour, as the Corps of the Great *Dryden* did its last *Exit* to the Grave'. Farquhar saw more deeply into the event. Text from Dryden's *Prose Works* (1800), ed. E. Malone, I. i. 363.

I come now from Mr. Dryden's funeral, where we had an Ode in Horace sung,[1] instead of David's Psalms; whence you may find, that we don't think a poet worth Christian burial. The pomp of the ceremony was a kind of rhapsody, and fitter, I think, for Hudibras, than him; because the cavalcade was mostly burlesque: but he was an extraordinary man, and buried after an extraordinary fashion; for I do believe there was never such another burial seen. The oration[2] indeed, was great and ingenious, worthy the subject, and like the author; whose prescriptions can restore the living, and his pen embalm the dead.—And so much for Mr. Dryden; whose burial was the same as his life, variety and not of a piece:—the quality and mob, farce and heroicks; the sublime and ridicule mix'd in a piece;—great Cleopatra in a hackney coach.

---

[1] *Od.* III. xxx.
[2] In Latin; delivered by Garth (see *infra*, No. 65).

60. Dryden's unnatural flights

1701

Extract from George Granville, Lord Lansdowne (1667–1735), *An Essay upon Unnatural Flights in Poetry* (ll. 77–104 and note), published in *A New Miscellany of Original Poems on Several Occasions* (1701), pp. 311–22; based on Bouhours's *La Manière de bien penser dans les Ouvrages d' Esprit* (1687).

> Our King return'd, and banisht Peace restor'd,
> The Muse ran Mad to see her exil'd Lord;
> On the crackt Stage the Bedlam Heroes roar'd,
> And scarce cou'd speak one reasonable word;
> *Dryden* himself,* to please a frantick Age,

* Mr. *Dryden* in some Prologue has these two Lines:

> *He 's bound to please, not to write well; And knows*
> *There is a mode in Plays as well as Cloaths.*[1]

Let the Censurers of Mr. *Dryden* therefore be satisfied that where he has expos'd himself to be criticiz'd, it has been only when he has endeavour'd to follow the fashion, To humour others, and not to please himself. It may likewise be observ'd that at the time when those Characters were form'd, Bullying was altogether the Mode, off the Stage as well as upon it: And tho' that humour is since much abated in the Conversation of the World, yet there remains so far a relish for it that to this day an Audience is never so well pleas'd as when an Actor foams with some extravagant rant: neither can we ever expect a thorow reformation of this Sacrifice to the People, till the writer has some more certain encouragement than the bare profits of a third day; For those who write to live will be always under a necessity to comply in some measure with the Generality by whose approbation they subsist.

Mr. *Dryden*, for further Satisfaction, in his Epistle Dedicatory to the *Spanish-Fryar* thus censures himself: I remember some Verses of my own *Maximin* and *Almanzor* which cry vengeance upon me for their extravagance, &c. . . .[2]

This may serve for a standing Apology for Mr. *Dryden* against all his Criticks; and likewise for an unquestionable Authority to confirm those principles which the Authour of the foregoing Poem has pretended to lay down, &c.

[1] Prologue to *The Rival Ladies*.
[2] See *supra*, p. 41.

Was forc'd to let his judgment stoop to Rage;
To a wild Audience he conform'd his Voice,
Comply'd to Custom, but not err'd thro' Choice.
Deem then the Peoples, not the Writer's Sin,
Almanzor's Rage, and Rants of *Maximin*;
That Fury spent, in each elaborate Peice
He vies for Fame with ancient *Rome* and *Greece*.

   Roscommon first, Then *Mulgrave* rose,[1] Like light,
To clear our Darkness, and to guide our flight;
With steady Judgment, and in lofty Sounds,
They gave us patterns, and they set us bounds.
The *Stagyrite*[2] and *Horace* laid aside,
Inform'd by Them, we need no foreign Guide.

   Who seek from Poetry a lasting Name,
May in their Lessons learn the road to Fame;
But let the bold Adventurer be sure
That every line the test of Truth endure;
On this Foundation may the Fabrick rise,
Firm and unshaken, till it touch the Skies.

   From Pulpits banisht, from the Court, from Love,
Abandon'd Truth seeks shelter in the Grove;
Cherish, ye Muses, the forsaken Fair,
And take into Your Train this Wanderer.

---

[1] Roscommon's *Essay on Translated Verse* (1684; circulated earlier in manuscript); Mulgrave's *Essay upon Poetry* (1682).
[2] Aristotle.

61. Swift on Dryden

1704, 1710, 1735

Jonathan Swift (1667–1745), satirist, poet, and political pamphleteer, was distantly related to Dryden. He 'began early to think,
or to hope, that he was a poet, and wrote Pindarick Odes. . . .
I have been told that Dryden, having perused these verses, said,
"Cousin Swift, you will never be a poet"; and that this denuncia-
tion was the motive of Swift's perpetual malevolence to Dryden'
(Johnson, *Lives of the English Poets*, 1905, ed. G. B. Hill, iii. 7–8).

(*a*) 'I profess to *Your Highness*, in the Integrity of my Heart, that what
I am going to say is literally true this Minute I am writing: What
Revolutions may happen before it shall be ready for your Perusal,
I can by no means warrant: However I beg You, to accept it as a
Specimen of our Learning, our Politeness and our Wit. I do therefore
affirm upon the Word of a sincere Man, that there is now actually in
being, a certain Poet called *John Dryden*, whose Translation of *Virgil*
was lately printed in a large Folio, well bound, and if diligent search
were made, for ought I know, is yet to be seen.' (*A Tale of a Tub*,
1704, Epistle Dedicatory; ed. D. Nichol Smith, 1958, p. 36.)

(*b*) '*The Hind and Panther*. This is the Master-piece of a famous Writer
*now living, intended for a compleat Abstract of sixteen thousand
Schoolmen from *Scotus* to *Bellarmin*.' (*A Tale of a Tub*, Introduction;
ed. *cit.*, p. 69.)

(*c*) 'I do utterly disapprove and declare against that pernicious Custom,
of making the Preface a Bill of Fare to the Book. For I have always
lookt upon it as a high Point of Indiscretion in *Monster-Mongers* and
other *Retailers of strange Sights*; to hang out a fair large Picture over the

---

* Viz. *in the Year* 1698.

Door, drawn after the Life, with a most eloquent Description underneath: This hath saved me many a Threepence, for my Curiosity was
fully satisfied, and I never offered to go in. ... Such is exactly the
Fate, at this Time, of *Prefaces*, *Epistles*, *Advertisements*, *Introductions*,
Prolegomena's, *Apparatus's*, *To-the-Reader's*. This Expedient was admirable at first; Our Great *Dryden* has long carried it as far as it would go,
and with incredible Success. He has often said to me in Confidence,
that the World would have never suspected him to be so great a
Poet, if he had not assured them so frequently in his Prefaces, that it
was impossible they could either doubt or forget it. Perhaps it may be
so; However, I much fear, his Instructions have edify'd out of their
Place, and taught Men to grow Wiser in certain Points, where he
never intended they should; For it is lamentable to behold, with what
a lazy scorn, many of the yawning Readers in our Age, do now a-days
twirl over forty or fifty Pages of *Preface* and *Dedication*, (which is the
usual *Modern* Stint[1]) as if it were so much *Latin*. Tho' it must be also
allowed on the other Hand that a very considerable Number is known
to proceed *Criticks* and *Wits*, by reading nothing else.'[2] (*A Tale of a
Tub*, 'A Digression in the Modern Kind'; ed. *cit.*, pp. 130–1.)

(d) '... about this time, there was a strange Confusion of Place among
all the *Books* in the Library; for which several Reasons were assigned.
Some ... maintained, that by walking much in the dark about the
Library, [the *Keeper*] had quite lost the Situation of it out of his Head;
And therefore, in replacing his *Books*, he was apt to mistake, and clap
Des-Cartes next to *Aristotle*; Poor *Plato* had got between *Hobbes* and
the *Seven Wise Masters*, and *Virgil* was hemm'd in with *Dryden* on one
side, and *Withers*[3] on the other.' (*The Battel of the Books*; with *A Tale
of a Tub*, ed. *cit.*, pp. 225–6.)

(e) 'On the left Wing of the Horse, *Virgil* appeared in shining Armour
compleatly fitted to his Body; He was mounted on a dapple grey

---

[1] E.g. Dryden's dedications of his *Juvenal* and *Æneis*.
[2] Nichol Smith compares Swift, *On Poetry* (1733), ll. 249–54:

> Judicious *Rymer* oft review:
> Wise *Dennis*, and profound *Bossu*.
> Read all the *Prefaces* of *Dryden*,
> For these our Criticks much confide in,
> (Tho' meerly writ at first for filling
> To raise the Volume's Price, a Shilling.)

[3] George Wither (1588–1667), used by Dryden and Pope to typify the bad poet.

Steed, the slowness of whose Pace, was an Effect of the highest Mettle and Vigour. He cast his Eye on the adverse Wing, with a desire to find an Object worthy of his Valour, when behold, upon a sorrel Gelding of a monstrous Size, appear'd a Foe, issuing from among the thickest of the Enemy's Squadrons; But his Speed was less than his Noise; for his Horse, old and lean, spent the Dregs of his Strength in a high Trot, which tho' it made slow advances, yet caused a loud Clashing of his Armor, terrible to hear. The two Cavaliers had now approached within the Throw of a Lance, when the Stranger desired a Parley, and lifting up the Vizard of his Helmet, a Face hardly appeared from within, which after a pause, was known for that of the renowned *Dryden*. The brave *Antient* suddenly started, as one possess'd with Surprize and Disappointment together: For, the Helmet was nine times too large for the Head, which appeared Situate far in the hinder Part, even like the Lady[1] in a Lobster, or like a Mouse under a Canopy of State, or like a shrivled Beau from within the Penthouse of a modern Perewig: And the voice was suited to the Visage, sounding weak and remote. *Dryden* in a long Harangue[2] soothed up the good *Antient*, called him *Father*, and by a large deduction of Genealogies, made it plainly appear, that they were nearly related. Then he humbly proposed an Exchange of Armor, as a lasting Mark of Hospitality between them. *Virgil* consented (for the Goddess *Diffidence* came unseen, and cast a Mist before his Eyes) tho' his was of Gold,* and cost a hundred Beeves, the others but of rusty Iron. However, this glittering Armor became the *Modern* yet worse than his own. Then, they agreed to exchange Horses; but when it came to the Trial, *Dryden* was afraid, and utterly unable to mount.' (*Ibid.*, pp. 246–7.)

(*f*) Extract from Swift's letter to Thomas Beach, 12 April 1735: the verse triplet 'was a vicious way of rhyming, wherewith Dryden abounded, and was imitated by all the bad versifiers in Charles the Second's reign. Dryden, though my near relation, is one I have often blamed as well as pitied. He was poor, and in great haste to finish his plays, because by them he chiefly supported his family, and this made him so very uncorrect; he likewise brought in the Alexandrine verse at the end of the triplets. I was so angry at these corruptions, that above twenty-four years ago I banished them all by one triplet, with the

---

* Vid. Homer [*Iliad*, vi. 234–6].
[1] Part of the stomach.
[2] The Dedication of the *Æneis*.

Alexandrine, upon a very ridiculous subject.[1] I absolutely did prevail with Mr. Pope, and Gay, and Dr. Young, and one or two more, to reject them.' (*Correspondence*, 1965, ed. Harold Williams, iv. 320–1.)

62. Hughes: Verses on Dryden's *Fables*

1706

Verses Occasion'd by Reading Mr. Dryden's Fables, by Jabez Hughes (1720); text from Dryden's *Works*, 1808, ed. Walter Scott, xviii. 227–33. Hughes (1685?–1731) was a civil servant and translator. The *Verses* were reprinted in his *Miscellanies* (1737).

Musaeum ante omnes, medium nam plurima turba
Hunc habet, atque humeris extantem suspicit altis.
—Virg.[2]

To the Reader

1720–1, *March*.

It is now almost fourteen years since these lines were first written; and as I had no thought of making them public, I laid them aside among other papers; where they had still continued private, if it had not, in a manner, become my duty to print them, by the noble regard which is paid to Mr Dryden's memory, by his grace the Duke of Buckingham. . . . I have had the happiness to see one part of these verses abundantly disproved by Mr Pope, and accordingly I retract it with pleasure; for that admirable author, who evidently inherits the bright invention, and the harmonious versification of Mr Dryden, has increased the reputation his other ingenious writings had obtained him, by the

---

[1] The conclusion of *A Description of a City Shower*.
[2] *Aen.* vi. 667–8: 'Musaeus before the others; for he stood central in the crowd that gazed up at him, and towered head and shoulders over them.'

permanent fame of having finished a translation of the *Iliad* of Homer, with surprising genius and merit.

Upon reading Mr Dryden's *Fables*

Our great forefathers, in poetic song,
Were rude in diction, though their sense was strong;
Well-measured verse they knew not how to frame,
Their words ungraceful, and the cadence lame.
Too far they wildly ranged to start the prey,
And did too much of Fairy-land display;
And in their rugged dissonance of lines,
True manly thought debased with trifles shines.
Each gaudy flower that wantons on the mead,
Must not appear within the curious bed;
But nature's chosen birth should flourish there,
And with their beauties crown the sweet parterre.

Such was the scene, when Dryden came to found
More perfect lays, with harmony of sound:
What lively colours glow on every draught!
How bright his images, how raised his thought!
The parts proportioned to their proper place,
With strength supported, and adorned with grace.

With what perfection did his artful hand
The various kinds of poesy command!
And the whole choir of Muses at his call,
In his rich song, which was inspired of all,
Spoke from the chords of his enchanting lyre,
And gave his breast the fulness of their fire.
As while the sun displays his lordly light,
The host of stars are humbly veiled from sight,
Till when he falls, they kindle all on high,
And smartly sparkle in the nightly sky:
His fellow bards suspended thus their ray,
Drowned in the strong effulgence of his day;
But glowing to their rise, at his decline,
Each cast his beams, and each began to shine.
As years advance, the abated soul, in most,
Sinks to low ebb, in second childhood lost;

And spoiling age, dishonouring our kind,
Robs all the treasures of the wasted mind;
With hovering clouds obscures the muffled sight,
And dim suffusion of enduring night:
But the rich fervour of his rising rage,
Prevailed o'er all the infirmities of age;
And, unimpaired by injuries of time,
Enjoyed the bloom of a perpetual prime.
His fire not less, he more correctly writ,
With ripened judgment, and digested wit;
When the luxuriant ardour of his youth,
Succeeding years had tamed to better growth,
And seemed to break the body's crust away,
To give the expanded mind more room to play;
Which, in its evening, opened on the sight,
Surprising beams of full meridian light;
As thrifty of its splendour it had been,
And all its lustre had reserved till then.

So the descending sun, which hid his ray
In mists before, diminishing the day,
Breaks radiant out upon the dazzled eye,
And in a blaze of glory leaves the sky.

Revolving time had injured Chaucer's name,
And dimmed the brilliant lustre of his fame;
Deformed his language, and his wit depressed,
His serious sense oft sinking to a jest;
Almost a stranger even to British eyes,
We scarcely knew him in the rude disguise:
But, clothed by thee, the burnished bard appears
In all his glory, and new honours wears.
Thus Ennius was by Virgil changed of old;
He found him rubbish, and he left him gold.

Who but thyself could Homer's weight sustain,
And match the voice of his majestic strain;
When Phœbus' wrath the sovereign poet sings,
And the big passion of contending kings!
No tender pinions of a gentle muse,
Who little points in epigram pursues,

And, with a short excursion, meekly plays
Its fluttering wings in mean enervate lays,
Could make a flight like this; to reach the skies,
An eagle's vigour can alone suffice.

In every part the courtly Ovid's style,
Thy various versions beautifully foil.
Here smoothly turned melodious measures move,
And feed the flame, and multiply the love:
So sweet they flow, so touch the heaving heart,
They teach the doctor* in his boasted art.
But when the theme demands a manly tone,
Sublime he speaks in accents not his own.
The bristly boar, and the tremendous rage
When the fell Centaurs in the fight engage;
The cruel storm where Ceyx lost his life,
And the deep sorrows of his widowed wife;
The covered cavern, and the still abode
Of empty visions, and the Sleepy God;
The powers of nature, in her wonderous reign,
Old forms subverting, to produce again,
And mould the mass anew, the important[1] verse
Does with such dignity of words rehearse,
That Virgil, proud of unexampled fame,
Looks with concern, and fears a rival name.
What vaunting Grecians, of their knowledge vain,
In lying legends insolently feign
Of magic verses, whose persuasive charm
Appeased the soul with glowing passion warm;
Then discomposed the calm, and changed the scene,
And with the height of madness vexed again,—
Thou hast accomplished in thy wondrous song,†
With utmost energy of numbers strong.
A flow of rage comes hurrying on amain,
And now the refluent tide ebbs out again;
A quiet pause succeeds; when unconfined
It rushes back, and swells upon the mind.

---

* *Ego sum Preceptor Amoris* [I am the teacher of love]. Art. Am. Lib.
† His Ode on St Cecilia's Day, entitled, Alexander's Feast, or the Power of Music.
[1] Grand, grave.

The inimitable lay, through all the maze ⎫
Of harmony's sweet labyrinth, displays ⎬
The power of music, and Cecilia's praise. ⎭

   At first it lifts the flattered monarch high,
With boasted lineage, to his kindred sky;
Then to the pleasures of the flowing bowl,
And mellow mirth, unbends his easy soul;
And humbles now, and saddens all the feast,
With sense of human miseries expressed;
Relenting pity in each face appears,
And heavy sorrow ripens into tears.
Grief is forbid: and see! in every eye
The gaiety of love, and wanton joy!
Soft smiles and airs, which tenderly inspire
Delightful hope, and languishing desire.
But lo! the pealing verse provokes around
The frown of rage, and kindles with the sound;
Behold the low'ring storm at once arise,
And ardent vengeance sparkling in their eyes;
Fury boils high, and zeal of fell debate,
Demanding ruin, and denouncing fate.

   Ye British beauties, in whose finished face
Smile the gay honours of each bloomy grace;
Whose forms, inimitably fair, invite
The sighing heart, and cheer the ravished sight,
Say, what sweet transports, and complacent joy,
Rise in your bosoms, and your soul employ,
When royal Emily, the tuneful bard
Paints in his song, and makes the rich reward
Of knightly arms, in costly lists arrayed,
The world at once contending for the maid.
How nobly great does Sigismonda shine,
With constant faith, and courage masculine!
No menaces could bend her mind to fear,
But for her love she dies without a tear.
There Iphigenia, with her radiant eyes,
As the bright sun, illuminates the skies;
In clouded Cymon chearful day began,
Awaked the sleeping soul, and charmed him into man.

The pleasing legends, to your honour, prove
The power of beauty, and the force of love.

Who, after him, can equally rehearse
Such various subjects, in such various verse?
And with the raptures of his strain controul,
At will, each passion, and command the soul?
Not ancient Orpheus, whose surprising lyre
Did beasts, and rocks, and rooted woods, inspire,
More sweetly sung, nor with superior art
Soothed the sad shades, and softened Pluto's heart.
All owned, at distance, his distinguished name,
Nor vainly vied to share his awful fame;
Unrivalled, living, he enlarged his praise,
And, dying, left without an heir his bays.
So Philip's son his universal reign
Extended amply over earth and main;
Through conquered climes with ready triumph rode,
And ruled the nations with his powerful nod;
But when fate called the mighty chief away, ⎫
None could succeed to his imperial sway, ⎬
And his wide empire languished to decay. ⎭

63. *The Spectator*

1711, 1712

(*a*) Extract from No. 40, 16 April 1711 (Addison): 'I shall here add a
Remark, which I am afraid our Tragick Writers may make an ill use
of. As our Heroes are generally Lovers, their Swelling and Blustring
upon the Stage very much recommends them to the fair Part of their
Audience. The Ladies are wonderfully pleased to see a Man insulting
Kings, or affronting the Gods, in one Scene, and throwing himself at
the Feet of his Mistress in another. Let him behave himself insolently

towards the Men, and abjectly towards the Fair One, and it is ten to one but he proves a Favourite of the Boxes. *Dryden* and *Lee*, in several of their Tragedies, have practised this Secret with good Success.

But to shew how a *Rant* pleases beyond the most just and natural Thought that is not pronounced with Vehemence, I would desire the Reader, when he sees the Tragedy of *Oedipus*, to observe how quietly the Hero is dismissed at the End of the third Act, after having pronounced the following Lines, in which the Thought is very natural, and apt to move Compassion:

> To you, good Gods, I make my last Appeal,
> Or clear my Virtues, or my Crimes reveal.
> If in the Maze of Fate I blindly run,
> And backward trod those Paths I sought to shun;
> Impute my Errors to your own Decree:
> My Hands are guilty, but my Heart is free.

Let us then observe with what Thunder-claps of Applause he leaves the Stage, after the Impieties and Execrations at the End of the fourth Act;[1] and you will wonder to see an Audience so cursed and so pleased at the same time.

> O that as oft I have at Athens seen,
>   [Where, by the way, there was no Stage till many
>   Years after Oedipus.]
> The Stage arise, and the big Clouds descend;
> So now, in very deed, I might behold
> This pond'rous Globe, and all yon marble Roof,
> Meet, like the Hands of Jove, and crush Mankind.
> For all the Elements, &c.'

(*b*) Extract from No. 71, 22 May 1711 (Steele), on 'refining our Passions to a greater Elegance, than we receive them from Nature': 'When the Passion is Love, this Work is performed in innocent, tho' rude and uncultivated Minds, by the mere Force and Dignity of the Object. There are Forms which naturally create Respect in the Beholders, and at once inflame and chastise the Imagination. Such an Impression as this gives an immediate Ambition to deserve, in order to please. This Cause and Effect are beautifully described by Mr. *Dryden* in the Fable of *Cymon* and *Iphigenia*.[2] After he has represented *Cymon* so stupid, that

> He whistled as he went, for want of Thought,

---

[1] Act III is Dryden's, Act IV Lee's.
[2] In *Fables*, 1700.

he makes him fall into the following Scene, and shews its influence upon him so excellently, that it appears as Natural as Wonderful.'

(Ll. 79–116.)

(c) Extract from No. 297, 9 February 1712 (Addison), on Milton's fondness for 'Technical Words, or Terms of Art': 'It is one of the greatest Beauties of Poetry, to make hard Things intelligible, and to deliver what is abstruse of it self in such easy Language as may be understood by ordinary Readers: Besides that the Knowledge of a Poet should rather seem born with him, or inspired, than drawn from Books and Systems. I have often wondered how Mr. *Dryden* could translate a Passage out of *Virgil* after the following manner.

> *Tack to the Larboard, and stand off to Sea,*
> *Veer Star-board Sea and Land.'*
> (*Aeneis*, iii. 526–7.)

(d) Extract from No. 341, 1 April 1712 (Budgell), replying to criticism of an epilogue spoken after Ambrose Philips's *Distressed Mother* by Mrs. Oldfield, who played Andromache: 'The Moment the Play ends, Mrs. *Oldfield* is no more *Andromache*, but Mrs. *Oldfield*; and tho' the Poet had left *Andromache stone-dead upon the Stage*, as your ingenious Correspondent phrases it, Mrs. *Oldfield* might still have spoke a merry Epilogue. We have an Instance of this in a Tragedy [Dryden's *Tyrannick Love*] where there is not only a Death but a Martyrdom. St. *Catherine* was there personated by *Nell Gwin*; she lies *stone-dead upon the Stage*, but upon those Gentlemen's offering to remove her Body, whose Business it is to carry off the Slain in our *English* Tragedies, she breaks out into that abrupt Beginning, of what was a very ludicrous, but at the same Time thought a very good Epilogue.

> *Hold, are you mad? you damn'd confounded Dog,*
> *I am to rise and speak the Epilogue.*

This diverting Manner was always practised by Mr. *Dryden*, who, if he was not the best Writer of Tragedies in his Time, was allowed by every one to have the happiest Turn for a Prologue or an Epilogue. The Epilogues to *Cleomenes, Don Sebastian, The Duke of Guise, Aureng-zebe*, and *Love Triumphant*, are all Precedents of this Nature.'

(e) Extract from No. 400, 9 June 1712 (Steele): the 'prevailing gentle

Art' of Sir Charles Sedley, 'a Wit of the last Age', 'was made up of Complaisance, Courtship, and artful Conformity to the Modesty of a Woman's Manners. Rusticity, broad Expression, and forward Obtrusion, offend those of Education, and make the Transgressors odious to all who have Merit enough to attract Regard. It is in this Taste that the Scenary is so beautifully ordered in the Description which *Antony* makes, in the Dialogue between him and *Dolabella*, of *Cleopatra* in her Barge [*All for Love*, III].

> Her Galley down the Silver Cydnos row'd. . . .

Here the Imagination is warmed with all the Objects presented, and yet there is nothing that is luscious, or what raises any Idea more loose than that of a beautiful Woman set off to Advantage.'

(*f*) Extract from No. 512, 17 October 1712 (Addison): 'This natural Pride and Ambition of the Soul is very much gratified in the reading of a Fable; for in Writings of this Kind, the Reader comes in for half of the Performance; Every Thing appears to him like a Discovery of his own; he is busied all the While in applying Characters and Circumstances, and is in this Respect both a Reader and a Composer. It is no Wonder therefore that on such Occasions, when the Mind is thus pleased with it self, and amused with its own Discoveries, that it is highly delighted with the Writing which is the Occasion of it. For this Reason the *Absalon* and *Achitophel* was one of the most popular Poems that ever appeared in *English*. The Poetry is indeed very fine, but had it been much finer it would not have so much pleased, without a Plan which gave the Reader an Opportunity of exerting his own Talents.'

64. Dennis on Dryden

1711, 1715, 1717, 1720, 1728

(a) Extract from *Reflections Critical and Satyrical, upon ... An Essay upon Criticism*, 1711:

'And such as Chaucer *is shall* Dryden *be. ...*[1]

Whether the Language of Mr. *Dryden* will ever be as obsolete as is at present that of *Chaucer*, is what neither this Author nor any one else can tell. For ev'ry Language hath its particular period of Time to bring it to Perfection, I mean to all the Perfection of which that Language is capable. And they who are alive cannot possibly tell whether that period hath happen'd or not ... yet this is certain, that Mr. *Dryden* had one Quality in his Language, which *Chaucer* had not, and which must always remain. For having acquir'd some Justness of Numbers, and some Truth of Harmony and of Versification, to which *Chaucer* thro' the Rudeness of the Language, or want of Ear, or want of Experience, or rather perhaps a mixture of all, could not possibly attain, that Justness of Numbers, and Truth of Harmony and of Versification can never be destroy'd by any alteration of Language; and therefore Mr. *Dryden*, whatever alteration happens to the Language, can never be like to *Chaucer.*' (Cf. Dennis, *Critical Works*, 1939 and 1943, ed. E. N. Hooker, i. 410–11.)

(b) Dennis's letter of 4 June 1715 '*To Mr.* Jac[ob] Ton[son] Sen. *On the Conspiracy against the Reputation of Mr.* Dryden': 'When I had the good Fortune to meet you in the City, it was with Concern that I heard from you of the Attempt to lessen the Reputation of Mr. *Dryden*;[2] and 'tis with Indignation that I have since learnt that that Attempt has chiefly been carried on by small Poets, who ungratefully strive to eclipse the Glory of a Great Man, from whom alone they derive their own faint Lustre. But that Eclipse will be as Momentary as

---

[1] Pope, *An Essay on Criticism*, 1711, l. 483.
[2] Nothing is known of this.

that of the Sun was lately. The Reputation of Mr. *Dryden* will soon break out again in its full Splendor, and theirs will disappear. It was upon hearing of this Attempt that I reflected with some Amazement, that I should have got the Reputation of an ill-natur'd Man, by exposing the Absurdities of living Authors; and Authors for the most part of great Mediocrity, tho' I have always done it openly and fairly, and upon just and personal Provocations; and that these should basely arraign the Reputation of a great Man deceas'd, who now can make no Answer for himself, and upon whom they fawn'd while living, and should yet escape uncensur'd. But when I heard that that Attempt was in favour of little *Pope*, that diminutive of Parnassus and of humanity, 'tis impossible to express to what a height my Indignation and Disdain were rais'd. Good God! was there ever any Nation in which (I will not say a false Taste, for we never had a true one, but in which) a wrong Sense and a fatal Delusion so generally prevail'd! For have not too many of us lately appear'd to contemn every thing that is great and glorious, and to praise and exalt every thing that is base and infamous? Have not too many of us shewn to all the World, by a manifest execrable Choice, that they prefer Weakness to Power, Folly to Wisdom, Poverty to Wealth, Fury and Madness to Moderation, Infamy to Glory, Submission to Victory, Slavery to Liberty, Idolatry to Religion, the Duke of O[rmond] to the D. of M[arlborough], the empty Pretender to the Royal *George* our only rightful King, and the little Mr. *Pope* to the illustrious Mr. *Dryden*? If I appear a little too warm, I hope you will excuse my Affection for the Memory, and my Zeal for the Reputation of my departed Friend, whom I infinitely esteem'd when living for the Solidity of his Thought, for the Spring, the Warmth, and the beautiful Turn of it; for the Power, and Variety, and Fulness of his Harmony; for the Purity, the Perspicuity, the Energy of his Expression; and (whenever the following great Qualities are requir'd) for the Pomp and Solemnity and Majesty of his Style. But Pope is the very reverse of all this: he scarce ever thought once solidly, but is an empty eternall babbler: and as his thoughts almost always are false or trifling, his expression is too often obscure, ambiguous, and uncleanly. He has indeed a smooth verse and a rhyming jingle, but he has noe power or variety of harmony; but always the same dull cadence, and a continuall bagpipe drone. Mr. Dryden's expressions are always worthy of his thoughts: but Pope never speaks nor thinks at all; or, which is all one, his language is frequently as barbarous, as his thoughts are false.

This I have ventured to say, in spight of popular errour. But popular errour can be of noe significancy either to you or me, who have seen Mr. Settle in higher reputation than Mr. Pope is at present. And they who live thirty years hence, will find Mr. Pope in the same classe in which Mr. Settle is now; unlesse the former makes strange improvements. Good sense is the sole foundation of good writing; and noe authour who wants solidity, can ever long endure. This I have ventur'd to say in spight of popular errour; and this is in my power, when ever I please, to prove to all the world.

You may now see, Sir, by this Letter, how little most Men know one another, who converse daily together. How many were there in Mr. *Dryden's* Life-time, who endeavour'd to make him believe, that I should be the foremost, if I surviv'd him, of all his Acquaintance to arraign his Memory; whereas I am he of all his Acquaintance, who, tho' I flatter'd him least while living, having been contented to do him Justice both behind his Back and before his Enemies Face, am now the foremost to assert his Merit, and to vindicate his Glory.

If Mr. *Dryden* has Faults, (as where is the Mortal who has none?) I by searching for them perhaps could find them. But whatever the mistaken World may think, I am always willing to be pleas'd, nay, am always greedy of Pleasure as any *Epicurean* living; and whenever I am naturally touch'd, I give my self up to the first Impression, and never look for Faults. But whenever a cried-up Author, upon the first reading him, does not make a pleasing Impression on me; I am apt to seek for the Reason of it, that I may know if the Fault is in him or in me. Whenever Genius runs thro' a Work, I forgive its Faults, and wherever that is wanting no Beauties can touch me. Being struck by Mr. *Dryden's* Genius, I have no Eyes for his Errors; and I have no Eyes for his Enemies Beauties, because I am not struck by their Genius.' (*Critical Works*, ii. 399–401; the text of Dennis's *Original Letters* (1721) supplemented from Malone.)

(c) Extract from *Remarks upon Mr. Pope's Translation of Homer*, 1717, 'Observations': 'Mr. DRYDEN, who had so many great Qualities, who refin'd the Language of our Rhyming Poetry, and improv'd its Harmony, who thought often, so finely, so justly, so greatly, so nobly, who had the Art of Reasoning very strongly in very elegant Verse; and who of all our Rhyming Poets wrote beyond comparison with most Force, and with most Elevation; was often sacrific'd to his worthless Contemporaries; could never receive Encouragement enough to set him entirely at Ease, died without leaving behind him enough to inter him, and left behind him a destitute and deplorable Family.' (1717 edition; cf. Hooker, *op. cit.*, ii. 121.)

(*d*) Extract from Dennis's third Letter to Sir John Edgar, 1720: 'We have ... had Libels which have pass'd for Satires, as *Absalom* and *Achitophel*, the *Medal*, *Mac Fleckno*, and the *Dispensary*.[1] They are indeed, if you please, beautiful Libels, but they are every where full of Flattery or Slander, and a just Satire admits of neither. In the two first, how many were abus'd only for being true to the Religion and Liberties of their Country? And on the other side, some were extoll'd only for being false to both. The attempt to lessen *Shadwell* in *Mackflecno*, is every whit as unworthy of Satire. For *Shadwell* pretended to no Species of Poetry but the Comick, in which he was certainly very much superiour to *Dryden*; as the latter acknowledges by a very fair implication in his *Preface* to the *State of Innocence*, which was writ before the Quarrel between them began. The business of Sir *Samuel Garth* in his *Dispensary* was to expose much better Physicians than himself, for no other reason but because they were not of his Opinion in the affair of the *Dispensary*. Now tho' these were Libels, and very injurious, yet the Authors justly thought it more creditable to suffer them to be publish'd without any Name, rather than to make use of false ones.' (*The Characters and Conduct of Sir John Edgar*, 1720; cf. Hooker, *op. cit.*, ii. 201.)

(*e*) Extract from a letter to the *Daily Journal*, 11 May 1728, on Alexander Pope: 'In the *Ode* which the same *Pantomimical* Creature wrote upon St. *Cæcilia*'s Day, an Ode which was vainly and foolishly writ in Emulation of Mr. *Dryden*'s *Feast of Alexander*, he has not the least Shadow of any of Mr. *Dryden*'s great Qualities, neither of his Art, his Variety, his Passion, his Enthusiasm, or his Harmony. The very Numbers in Mr. *Dryden*'s incomparable Ode, are themselves incomparable, and are always adapted and adjusted by that great Poet to his Passion and his Enthusiasm.' (Cf. Hooker, *op. cit.*, ii. 416–7; not certainly by Dennis.)

---

[1] By Garth; see No. 65.

65. Garth's Memorial to Dryden

1717

The close of Garth's Preface to *Ovid's Metamorphoses in Fifteen Books. Translated by the most Eminent Hands* (1717). The translations are by Dryden, Addison, Congreve, Gay, Tate, Garth, and others. Sir Samuel Garth (1661–1719), author of *The Dispensary* (1699) and a Fellow of the Royal College of Physicians, delivered a Latin oration before Dryden's body, after lying in state at the College for nearly two weeks, was carried to Westminster Abbey on 13 May 1700.

I cannot pass by that Admirable *English* Poet, without endeavouring to make his Country sensible of the Obligations they have to his Muse. Whether they consider the flowing Grace of his Versification; the vigorous Sallies of his Fancy; or the peculiar Delicacy of his Periods; they 'll discover Excellencies never to be enough admir'd. If they trace him from the first Productions of his Youth, to the last Performances of his Age, they 'll find, that as the Tyranny of Rhyme never impos'd on the Perspicuity of the Sense; so a languid Sense never wanted to be set off by the Harmony of Rhyme. And as his earlier Works wanted no Maturity; so his latter wanted no Force, or Spirit. The falling off of his Hair, had no other Consequence, than to make his Lawrels be seen the more.

As a Translator he was just; as an Inventer he was rich. His Versions of some parts of *Lucretius*, *Horace*, *Homer*, and *Virgil* throughout, gave him a just pretence to that Compliment which was made to *Monsieur d'Ablancourt*, a celebrated *French* Translater; *It is uncertain who have the greatest Obligations to Him, the Dead or the Living.*

With all these wondrous Talents, He was Libell'd in his Life-time by the very Men, who had no other Excellencies, but as they were his Imitators. Where he was allow'd to have Sentiments superior to all others, they charged him with Theft: But how did he Steal? no

261

otherwise, than like those, that steal Beggars Children, only to cloath them the better.

'Tis to be lamented, that Gentlemen still continue this unfair Behaviour, and treat one another every Day with most injurious Libels. The Muses should be Ladies of a chaste and fair Behaviour: when they are otherwise, they are Furies. ... The only Talents in Esteem at present are those of *Exchange-Ally*; one Tally is worth a Grove of Bays; and 'tis of much more Consequence to be well read in the Tables of Interest, and the Rise and Fall of Stocks, than in the Revolution of Empires.

Mr. *Dryden* is still a sad, and shameful Instance of this Truth: The Man, that cou'd make Kings immortal, and raise triumphant Arches to Heroes, now wants a poor square Foot of Stone, to show where the Ashes of one of the greatest Poets, that ever was upon Earth, are deposited.

66. Congreve's memoir

1717

Extract from the Epistle Dedicatory addressed to the Duke of Newcastle by Congreve in *The Dramatick Works of John Dryden, Esq: in Six Volumes*, 1717, i. William Congreve (1670–1729) met Dryden when he came to London from Trinity College, Dublin, after the Revolution of 1688. His commendatory lines introduced Dryden's *Persius* in 1693; he was one of the 'Eminent Hands' who helped Dryden in the collaborative translation of Juvenal (published with *Persius*) and of Ovid's *Art of Love* (published in 1709). Cf. *supra*, No. 45.

MY LORD,

It is the Fortune of this Edition of the Dramatick Works of the late Mr. *Dryden*, to come into the World at a Time, when Your Grace has just given Order for Erecting, at Your own Expence, a Noble Monument to his Memory. . . .[1]

. . . as I had the Happiness to be very Conversant, and as intimately acquainted, with Mr. *Dryden*, as the great Disproportion in our Years could allow me to be; I hope it will not be thought too assuming in me, if in Love to his Memory, and in Gratitude for the many friendly Offices, and favourable Instructions, which in my early Youth I received from him, I take upon me to make this publick Acknowledgement to Your Grace, for so publick a Testimony as You are pleas'd to give the World of that high Esteem in which You hold the Performances of that eminent Man.

I can in some Degree justify my self for so doing, by a Citation of a kind of Right to it, bequeath'd to me by him. And it is indeed, upon that Pretension that I presume even to make a Dedication of these his Works to You.

---

[1] It was, however, John Sheffield, Duke of Buckingham, who arranged for a monument in Westminster Abbey in 1720.

In some very Elegant, tho' very partial Verses which he did me the Honour to write to me, he recommended it to me to *be kind to his Remains*.[1] I was then, and have been ever since most sensibly touched with that Expression: and the more so, because I could not find in my self the Means of satisfying the Passion which I felt in me, to do something answerable to an Injunction laid upon me in so Pathetick and so Amicable a Manner. You, my Lord, have furnish'd me with ample means of acquitting my self, both of my Duty and Obligation to my *departed Friend*. . . .

Whoever shall Censure me, I dare be confident, You, my Lord, will Excuse me, for any thing that I shall say with due Regard to a Gentleman, for whose Person I had as just an Affection as I have an Admiration of his Writings. And indeed Mr. *Dryden* had Personal Qualities to challenge both Love and Esteem from All who were truly acquainted with him.

He was of a Nature exceedingly Humane and Compassionate; easily forgiving Injuries, and capable of a prompt and sincere Reconciliation with them who had offended him.

Such a Temperament is the only solid Foundation of all moral Virtues, and sociable Endowments. His Friendship, where he profess'd it, went much beyond his Professions; and I have been told of strong and generous Instances of it, by the Persons themselves who received them: Tho' his Hereditary Income was little more than a bare Competency.

As his Reading had been very extensive, so was he very happy in a Memory tenacious of every thing that he had read. He was not more possess'd of Knowledge than he was Communicative of it. But then his Communication of it was by no means pedantick, or impos'd upon the Conversation; but just such, and went so far as by the natural Turns of the Discourse in which he was engag'd it was necessarily promoted or required. He was extream ready and gentle in his Correction of the Errors of any Writer, who thought fit to consult him; and full as ready and patient to admit of the Reprehension of others in respect of his own Oversight or Mistakes. He was of very easy, I may say of very pleasing Access: But something slow, and as it were diffident in his Advances to others. He had something in his Nature that abhorr'd Intrusion into any Society whatsoever. Indeed it is to be

---

[1] In the fine compliment *To my Dear Friend Mr. Congreve, On His Comedy, call'd The Double-Dealer* (1694).

regretted, that he was rather blameable in the other Extream: For by that means, he was Personally less known, and consequently his Character might become liable both to Misapprehensions and Mis-representations.

To the best of my Knowledge and Observation, he was, of all the Men that ever I knew, one of the most Modest, and the most Easily to be discountenanced, in his Approaches, either to his Superiors, or his Equals.

I have given Your Grace this slight Sketch of his personal Character, as well to vindicate his Memory, as to justify my self for the Love which I bore to his Person; and I have the rather done it, because I hope it may be acceptable to You to know that he was worthy of the Distinction You have shewn him, as a Man, as well as an Author.

As to his Writings, I shall not take upon me to speak of them; for, to say little of them, would not be to do them right: And to say all that I ought to say, would be, to be very Voluminous. But, I may venture to say in general Terms, that no Man hath written in our Language so much, and so various Matter, and in so various Manners, so well. Another thing I may say very peculiar to him; which is, that his Parts did not decline with his Years: But that he was an improving Writer to his last, even to near seventy Years of Age; improving even in Fire and Imagination, as well as in Judgement: Witness his Ode on St. *Cecelia*'s Day, and his Fables, his latest Performances.

He was equally excellent in Verse, and in Prose. His Prose had all the Clearness imaginable, together with all the Nobleness of Expression; all the Graces and Ornaments proper and peculiar to it, without deviating into the Language or Diction of Poetry. I make this Observa-tion, only to distinguish his Stile from that of many Poetical Writers, who meaning to write harmoniously in Prose, do in truth often write meer Blank Verse.

I have heard him frequently own with Pleasure, that if he had any Talent for *English* Prose, it was owing to his having often read the Writings of the great Archbishop *Tillotson*.[1]

His Versification and his Numbers he could learn of no Body: For he first possess'd those Talents in Perfection in our Tongue. And they who have best succeeded in them since his Time, have been indebted

---

[1] John Tillotson (1630–94), Dean of St Paul's (1689) and (1691) Archbishop of Canter-bury; praised at his funeral by Bishop Burnet as always saying 'what was just necessary to give clear Ideas of things, and no more. . . . His Sentences were short and clear; and the whole Thread was of a piece, plain and distinct.'

to his Example; and the more they have been able to imitate him, the better they have succeeded.

As his Stile in Prose is always specifically different from his Stile in Poetry; so, on the other hand, in his Poems, his Diction is, wherever his Subject requires it, so Sublimely, and so truly Poetical, that its Essence, like that of pure Gold, cannot be destroy'd. Take his Verses, and divest them of their Rhimes, disjoint them in their Numbers, transpose their Expressions, make what Arrangement and Disposition you please of his Words, yet shall there Eternally be Poetry, and something which will be found incapable of being resolv'd into absolute Prose: An incontestable Characteristick of a truly Poetical Genius.

I will say but one Word more in general of his Writings, which is, that what he has done in any one Species, or distinct Kind, would have been sufficient to have acquir'd him a great Name. If he had written nothing but his Prefaces, or nothing but his Songs, or his Prologues, each of them would have intituled him to the Preference and Distinction of excelling in his Kind. . . .

67. Dennis on *All for Love*

1719

Extract from a letter from John Dennis (see p. 209, *supra*) to Sir Richard Steele, patentee of the Drury Lane theatre, 26 March 1719. Published in Dennis's *Original Letters*, 1721 (*Critical Works* (1939 and 1943), ed. E. N. Hooker, ii. 162–5).

It was upon the 27th of *February*, 171$\frac{7}{8}$, that I receiv'd a Letter from Mr. *Booth*[1] by your Direction, and the Direction of the Managers under you, desiring me to dine at your House on the 28th, and after

---

[1] Barton Booth, the actor.

Dinner to read the Tragedy of *Coriolanus* to you, which I had alter'd from *Shakespear*. You cannot but remember, Sir, that upon reading it, the Play with the Alterations was approv'd of, nay and warmly approv'd of, by your self, Mr. *Cibber*,[1] and Mr. *Booth*, (the other Manager was not there) and that Resolutions were taken for the acting it in the beginning of this Winter. . . .

Well, Sir! when the Winter came on, what was done by your Deputies? Why, instead of keeping their Word with me, they spent above two Months of the Season in getting up *All for Love, or the World well lost*, a Play which has indeed a noble first Act, an Act which ends with a Scene becoming of the Dignity of the Tragick Stage. But if *Horace* had been now alive, and been either a Reader or Spectator of that Entertainment, he would have passed his old Sentence upon the Author.

Infelix operis summa quia ponere totum Nesciet.[2]

For was ever any thing so pernicious, so immoral, so criminal, as the Design of that Play? I have mention'd the Title of it, give me leave to set before you the two last Lines:

And Fame to late Posterity shall tell,
No Lovers liv'd so great, or dy'd so well.

And this Encomium of the Conduct and the Death of *Anthony* and *Cleopatra*, a Conduct so immoral, and a Self-murder so criminal, is, to give it more Force, put into the Mouth of the High-Priest of *Isis*; tho' that Priest could not but know, that what he thus commended, would cause immediately the utter Destruction of his Country, and make it become a Conquer'd and a *Roman* Province. Certainly never could the Design of an Author square more exactly with the Design of *White-Hall*, at the time when it was written, which was by debauching the People absolutely to enslave them.

For, pray Sir, what do the Title and the two last Lines of this Play amount to in plain *English*? Why to this, that if any Person of Quality or other shall turn away his Wife, his young, affectionate, virtuous, charming Wife (for all these *Octavia* was) to take to his Bed a loose abandon'd Prostitute, and shall in her Arms exhaust his Patrimony, destroy his Health, emasculate his Mind, and lose his Reputation and

---

[1] Colley Cibber (1671–1757), actor and dramatist.
[2] *Ars Poetica*, ll. 34–5: 'failing in his work as a whole because he does not know how to represent its totality.'

all his Friends, why all this is well and greatly done, his Ruine is his Commendation. And if afterwards in Despair, he either hangs or drowns himself, or goes out of the World like a Rat, with a Dose of Arsenick or Sublimate, why 'tis a great and an envied Fate, he dies nobly and heroically. It is, Sir, with extream Reluctance that I have said all this. For I would not be thought to affront the Memory of Mr. *Dryden*, for whose extraordinary Qualities no Man has a greater Veneration than my self. But that all Considerations ought to give Place to the Publick Good, is a Truth of which you, of all Men, I am sure, can never doubt.

And can you believe then, after having recommended Virtue and Publick Spirit for so many Years to the World, that you can give your Subalterns Authority to preach up Adultery to a Town, which stands so little in need of their Doctrine? Is not the Chastity of the Marriage Bed one of the chief Incendiaries of Publick Spirit, and the Frequency of Adulteries one of the chief Extinguishers of it; according to that of *Horace* [*Odes*, III. vi. 17-20]. For when Adultery's become so frequent, especially among Persons of Condition, upon whose Sentiments all Publick Spirit chiefly depends, that a great many Husbands begin to believe, or perhaps but to suspect, that they who are called their Children are not their own; I appeal to you, Sir, if that Belief or that Suspicion must not exceedingly cool their Zeal for the Welfare of those Children, and consequently for the Welfare of Posterity.

As I had infinitely the Advantage of *All for Love* in the Moral of *Coriolanus*, I had it by Consequence in the whole Tragedy; for the *Coriolanus*, as I have alter'd it, having a just Moral, and by Consequence at the Bottom a general and allegorical Action, and universal and allegorical Characters, and for that very reason a Fable, is therefore a true Tragedy, if it be not a just and a regular one; but 'tis as just and as regular as I could make it, upon so irregular a Plan as *Shakespear*'s: Whereas *All for Love* having no Moral, and consequently no general and allegorical Action, nor general and allegorical Characters, can for that Reason have no Fable, and therefore can be no Tragedy. 'Tis indeed only a particular Account of what happen'd formerly to *Anthony* and *Cleopatra*, and a most pernicious Amusement. . . .

68. Alexander Pope on Dryden

1730–43

The prose passages here are from the *Observations, Anecdotes, and Characters of Books and Men* collected from conversation by the Oxford professor Joseph Spence and first published in 1820 (ed. J. M. Osborn, 2 vols., 1966). The numbering is Dr Osborn's.

(*a*) 'In versification there's a sensible difference between softness and sweetness that I could distinguish from a boy. Thus, on the same points, Dryden will be found to be softer and Waller sweeter. 'Tis the same with Ovid and Virgil, and Virgil's Eclogues in particular are the sweetest poems in the world.' (403; Pope, May 1730).

(*b*) 'Hard to name anyone for our best tragedy. *All for Love* has been reckoned the most complete.' (486; Pope, 1733 or 1734.)

(*c*) ' 'Tis easy to mark out the general course of our poetry. Chaucer, Spenser, Milton, and Dryden are the great land-marks for it.' (410; Pope, 1736.)

(*d*) 'I don't think Dryden so bad a dramatic writer as you seem to do. There are as many things finely said in his plays as almost by anybody. Beside his three best (*All for Love*, *Don Sebastian*, and the *Spanish Friar*) there are others that are good, as *Cleomenes*, *Sir Martin Mar-all*, *Limberham*,[1] and the *Conquest of Mexico*. His *Wild Gallant* was written while he was a boy, and is very bad.' (64; Pope, 1736.)

(*e*) 'I learned versification wholly from Dryden's works, who had improved it much beyond any of our former poets, and would probably have brought it to its perfection, had not he been unhappily obliged to write so often in haste.' (55; Pope, March 1743.)

[1] *The Kind Keeper.*

(*f*) 'Dryden always uses proper language: lively, natural, and fitted to the subject. 'Tis scarce ever too high or too low—never perhaps, except in his plays.' (56; Pope, March 1743.)

(*g*) Extracts from *Imitations of Horace*, Ep. II. i (1737); ll. 263–9 and 276–81:

> 'We conquer'd France, but felt our captive's charms;
> Her Arts victorious triumph'd o'er our Arms:
> Britain to soft refinements less a foe,
> Wit grew polite, and Numbers learn'd to flow.
> Waller was smooth; but Dryden taught to join
> The varying verse, the full resounding line,
> The long majestic march, and energy divine.[1]

> Not but the Tragic spirit was our own,
> And full in Shakespear, fair in Otway shone:
> But Otway fail'd to polish or refine,
> And fluent Shakespear scarce effac'd a line.
> Ev'n copious Dryden, wanted, or forgot,
> The last and greatest Art, the Art to blot.'

69. Thomas Gray on Dryden

1742, 1754, 1765

(*a*) Extract from letter, 8 April 1742, to West: 'As to matter of stile, I have this to say: The language of the age is never the language of poetry; except among the French, whose verse, where the thought or image does not support it, differs in nothing from prose. Our poetry, on the contrary, has a language peculiar to itself; to which almost

---

[1] *Cf.* Pope, letter to Caryll, 25 June 1711: 'I keep the pictures of Dryden, Milton, Shakespear, &c., in my chamber, round about me, that the constant remembrance of 'em may keep me always humble.'

every one, that has written, has added something by enriching it with foreign idioms and derivatives: Nay sometimes words of their own composition or invention. Shakespear and Milton have been great creators this way; and no one more licentious than Pope or Dryden, who perpetually borrow expressions from the former. Let me give you some instances from Dryden, whom every body reckons a great master of our poetical tongue.—Full of *museful mopeings*—unlike the *trim* of love—a pleasant *beverage*—a *roundelay* of love—stood silent in his *mood*—with knots and *knares* deformed—his *ireful mood*—in proud *array*—his *boon* was granted—and *disarray* and shameful rout—*wayward* but wise—*furbished* for the field—the *foiled dodderd* oaks—*disherited*—*smouldring* flames—*retchless* of laws—*crones* old and ugly—the *beldam* at his side—the *grandam-hag*—*villanize* his Father's fame.[1]—But they are infinite: And our language not being a settled thing (like the French) has an undoubted right to words of an hundred years old, provided antiquity have not rendered them unintelligible' (publ. 1775; *Correspondence of Thomas Gray* (1935), ed. Paget Toynbee and Leonard Whibley, i. 192–3.)

(*b*) Extract from *The Progress of Poesy*, ll. 95–111 (written in 1752–54; *Complete Poems* (1966), ed. H. W. Starr and J. R. Hendrickson, pp. 16–17):

III. 2.

Nor second He,[2] that rode sublime
Upon the seraph-wings of Extasy,
The secrets of th' Abyss to spy.
He pass'd the flaming bounds of Place and Time:[3]
The living Throne, the saphire-blaze,[4]
Where Angels tremble, while they gaze,
He saw; but blasted with excess of light,
Closed his eyes in endless night.[5]
Behold, where Dryden's less presumptuous car,
Wide o'er the fields of Glory bear

---

[1] Gray reached for his copy of Dryden's *Fables*. His illustrations come from 'Palamon and Arcite', i. 540, 541; ii. 15, 78, 328, 536, 582; iii. 61, 187, 304, 385, 446, 905, 968, 980, 1074; and from the later tale of the Wife of Bath, ll. 126, 261, 312, 405.
[2] Milton.
[3] Lucretius, *De Rerum Natura*, i. 74 (Gray).
[4] Ezekiel i. 20–8.
[5] Homer, *Odyssey*, viii. 64 (Gray).

Two Coursers of ethereal race,[1]
With necks in thunder cloath'd,[2] and long-resounding
pace.

III. 3.

Hark, his hands the lyre explore!
Bright-eyed Fancy hovering o'er
Scatters from her pictur'd urn
Thoughts, that breathe, and words, that burn.[3]
But ah! 'tis heard no more—[4]

(c) Postscript to letter, 2 October 1765, to James Beattie, Professor of
Moral Philosophy at Aberdeen: 'Remember Dryden, and be blind to
all his faults.' (*Correspondence*, ii. 896.)[5]

---

[1] 'Meant to express the stately march and sounding energy of Dryden's rhimes' (Gray).
[2] Job xxxix. 19.
[3] Echoing Cowley's *Mistress*, 'The Prophet', l. 20.
[4] 'We have had in our language no other odes of the sublime kind, than that of Dryden on St. Cecilia's day: for Cowley (who had his merit) yet wanted judgment, style, and harmony, for such a task. That of Pope is not worthy of so great a man. . . .' (Gray).

[5] According to William Mason, Gray's literary executor and editor, 'Mr Beattie, it seems, in their late interview [at Glamis], had expressed himself with less admiration of Dryden than Mr Gray thought his due. He told him in reply, that if there was any excellence in his own numbers, he had learned it wholly from that great Poet; and pressed him with great earnestness to study him, as his choice of words and versification were singularly happy and harmonious.'

70. Instant criticism

1744

The Adventures of David Simple, a novel by Henry Fielding's sister
Sarah (1710–68), was published in May 1744 and—with corrections
and improvements by Henry—again later in the year. This extract
is part of a platitudinous performance by a tavern-critic, who can
'run through most of the famous Authors, without committing
any Error ... yet ... like a *School-boy* saying his Lesson' (II. iii;
ed. Malcolm Kelsall, Oxford English Novels (1969), p. 89).

'The Smoothness of *Waller*'s Verse resembles a *gentle cooling Stream*,
which gives Pleasure, and yet keeps the Mind in Calmness and
Serenity; while *Dryden*'s Genius is like a rapid River, ready to over-leap
its Bounds; which we view with Admiration, and find, while we are
reading him, our Fancy heighten'd to rove thro' all the various
Labyrinths of the *human Mind*. It is a thousand pities he should ever have
been *forced to write for Money*; for who that has read his *Guiscarda* and
Sigismonda,[1] could ever have thought he could have pen'd some other
Things that go in his Name? *Prior*'s Excellence lay in telling of Stories:
And *Cowley* had a great deal of *Wit*. . . .

---

[1] The title, misread, of one of the *Fables*.

273

71. Joseph Warton on Dryden

1756, 1782

Dr Joseph Warton (1722–1800), brother of Thomas, the Oxford literary historian and poet laureate, was headmaster of Winchester, 1766–93. The first part of his *Essay on Pope* appeared in 1756, arguing that Pope's 'species of poetry is not the most excellent one of the art'. The second volume was delayed until 1782, when the critical climate was under change. Extracts from *An Essay of the Genius and Writings of Pope*, 'The Fifth Edition, Corrected', 1806.

(*a*) Pope's *Pastorals* are 'the first specimen of that harmony in English verse, which is now become indispensably necessary, and which has so forcibly and universally influenced the public ear, as to have rendered every moderate rhymer melodious. Pope lengthened the abruptness of Waller, and at the same time contracted the exuberance of Dryden.' (*Essay*, i. 9–10.)

(*b*) Pope 'used to declare, that if Dryden had finished a translation of the *Iliad*, he would not have attempted one after so great a maste : he might have said with more propriety, I will not write a music-ode after *Alexander's Feast*, which the variety and harmony of its numbers, and the beauty and force of its images, have conspired to place at the head of modern lyric compositions. . . . [The effects of Pope's] animating song that Orpheus sung[1] . . . do not equal the force and spirit of what Dryden ascribes to the song of his Grecian artist: for when Timotheus cries out REVENGE, raises the furies, and calls up to Alexander's view a troop of Grecian ghosts, that were slain, and left unburied, inglorious and forgotten . . . he instantly started from his throne,

> —Seiz'd a flambeau with zeal to destroy;*

* 'These anapests, for such they are, have a fine effect' (Warton).
[1] *Ode for Musick. On St. Cecilia's Day*, ll. 36 ff.

while Thais, and the attendant princes, rushed out with him to set fire to the city. The whole train of imagery in this stanza of Dryden is alive, sublime, and animated to an unparalleled degree: the poet had so strongly possessed himself of the action described, that he places it fully before the eyes of the reader. ... No poem, indeed, affords so much various matter for a composer to work upon, as Dryden has here introduced and expressed all the greater passions, and as the transitions from one to the other are sudden and impetuous; of which we feel the effects in the pathetic description of the fall of Darius, that immediately succeeds the joyous praises of Bacchus. The symphony, and air particularly, that accompanies the four words, 'fallen, fallen, fallen, fallen,' is strangely moving, and consists of a few simple and touching notes.[1] ...' (ibid., i. 50–3, 61.)

(c) On Dryden's *Song for St. Cecilia's Day*, 1687, ll. 16–24: 'This is so complete and engaging a history-piece, that I knew a person of taste who was resolved to have it executed on one side of his saloon: "In which case, (said he,) the painter has nothing to do, but to substitute colours for words, the design being finished to his hands." The reader doubtless observes the fine effect of the repetition of the last line; as well as the stroke of nature, in making these rude hearers imagine some god lay concealed in this first musician's instrument.' (ibid., i. 51–2, footnote.)

(d) 'Du Bos fixes the period of time at which, generally speaking, the poets and painters have arrived at as high a pitch of perfection as their geniuses will permit. ... Raphäel was about thirty years old when he displayed the beauty and sublimity of his genius in the Vatican.... When Shakespeare wrote his *Lear*, Milton his *Paradise Lost*, Spenser his *Fairy Queen*, and Dryden his *Music Ode*, they all had exceeded the middle age of man.' (ibid., i. 100–1.)

(e) On the alexandrine: 'Dryden was the first who introduced the frequent use of this measure into our English heroic; for we do not ever find it even in the longer works of Sandys, nor in Waller. Dryden has often used it very happily, and it gives a complete harmony to many of his triplets. By scrupulously avoiding it, Pope has fallen into an unpleasing and tiresome monotony in his *Iliad*.' (ibid., i. 143.)

[1] In Handel's setting.

(*f*) Pope's '*Prologue* to *Addison's Tragedy of Cato*, is superior to any prologue of Dryden; who, notwithstanding, is so justly celebrated for this species of writing. The prologues of Dryden are satirical and facetious; this of Pope is solemn and sublime, as the subject required. Those of Dryden contain general topics of criticism and wit, and may precede any play whatsoever, even tragedy or comedy.[1] This of Pope is particular. ... With respect to sprightly turns, and poignancy of wit, the prologues of Dryden have not been equalled.' (*ibid.*, i. 253–5.)

(*g*) Dryden's prefaces 'are very pleasing, notwithstanding the opposite opinions they contain, because his prose is the most numerous and sweet, the most *mellow* and *generous*,[2] of any our language has yet produced. His digressions and ramblings, which he himself says he learned of honest Montaigne, are interesting and amusing.' (*ibid.*, ii. 8.)

(*h*) Chaucer's *Wife of Bath's Tale* 'has been versified by Dryden; and is supposed to have been of Chaucer's own contrivance: as is also the elegant *Vision* of *The Flower and the Leaf*,[3] which has received new graces from the spirited and harmonious Dryden. It is to his *Fables*, though wrote in his old age,* that Dryden will owe his immortality; and among them, particularly, to *Palamon and Arcite, Sigismunda and Guiscardo, Theodore and Honoria*; and, above all, to his exquisite music ode. The warmth and melody of these pieces has never been excelled in our language; I mean in rhyme. As general and unexemplified criticism is always useless and absurd, I must beg leave to select a few passages from these three poems. ... The picture of Arcite, in the absence of Emilia, is highly expressive of the deepest distress, and a complete image of anguish

[quotation, i. 522–9]

The image of the Suicide is equally picturesque and pathetic

[quotation, ii. 576–9]

[approving quotation of *Palamon and Arcite*, i. 445–9, 464–7, 'passages ... chiefly of the pathetic sort'; ii. 530–5 and 546–55, a 'scene of terror'; ii. 643–5.]

* 'The falling off of his hair, said a man of wit, had no other consequence, than to make his laurels to be seen the more' (Warton). Cf. *supra*. p. 261.
[1] A grotesque generalization.
[2] Rich and strong.
[3] At this time still ascribed to Chaucer.

But, above all, the whole description of the entering the lists, and of the ensuing combat, which is told at length, in the middle of the third book, is marvellously spirited; and so lively, as to make us spectators of that interesting and magnificent tournament. Even the absurdity of feigning ancient heroes, such as Theseus and Lycurgus, present at the lists and a modern combat, is overwhelmed and obliterated amidst the blaze, the pomp, and the profusion, of such animated poetry. Frigid and phlegmatic must be the critic, who could have leisure dully and soberly to attend to the anachronism on so striking an occasion. The mind is whirled away by a torrent of rapid imagery, and propriety is forgot.

The tale of Sigismunda and Guiscardo is heightened with many new and affecting touches by Dryden. I shall select only the following picture of Sigismunda, as it has the same attitude in which she appears in a famous piece of Correggio.

[quotation, ll. 685–90]

There is an incomparable wildness in the vision of Theodore and Honoria, that represents the furious spectre of 'the horseman ghost that came thundering for his prey'; and of the gaunt mastiffs that tore the sides of the shrieking damsel he pursued; which is a subject worthy the pencil of Spagnoletti,[1] as it partakes of that savageness which is so striking to the imagination.[2] I shall confine myself to point out only two passages, which relate the two appearances of this formidable figure; and I place them last, as I think them the most lofty of any part of Dryden's works [ll. 88–94, 272–3, 264–6].' (ibid., ii. 11–18.)

(i) 'I know a person, whose name would be an ornament to these papers, if I was suffered to insert it, who, after reading a book of the

---

[1] Jusepe Ribera, 'Spagnoletto' (1588–1656), Spanish painter in Naples.
[2] Cf. Byron, Don Juan, iii (1821), sts. 105–6:

> Sweet hour of twilight!—in the solitude
>   Of the pine forest, and the silent shore
> Which bounds Ravenna's immemorial wood,
>   Rooted where once the Adrian wave flow'd o'er,
> To where the last Caesarean fortress stood,
>   Evergreen forest! which Boccaccio's lore
> And Dryden's lay made haunted ground to me,
> How have I loved the twilight hour and thee!
> ... The spectre huntsman of Onesti's line,
> His hell-dogs, and their chase, and the fair throng
> Which learn'd from this example not to fly
> From a true lover,—shadow'd my mind's eye.

Dunciad, always *sooths* himself, as he calls it, by turning to a canto in the *Faery Queen*. This is not the case in that very delightful and beautiful poem, *Mac Flecnoe*, from which Pope has borrowed so many hints, and images, and ideas. But Dryden's poem was the offspring of *contempt*, and Pope's of *indignation*: one is full of mirth, and the other of *malignity*. A vein of pleasantry is uniformly preserved through the whole of *Mac Flecnoe*, and the piece begins and ends in the *same key*. It is natural and obvious to borrow a metaphor from music, when we are speaking of a poem whose versification is particularly and exquisitely sweet and harmonious. The numbers of the *Dunciad*, by being much laboured, and encumbered with epithets, have something in them of stiffness and harshness.' (*ibid.*, ii. 377, footnote.)

72. Applauding hands and dry eyes

1759

Dr Edward Young (1683–1765), lawyer, divine, tragedian and author of the once celebrated *Night Thoughts on Life, Death and Immortality* (1742–5), published his *Conjectures on Original Composition* as a tribute to Addison. The essay takes the form of a letter to the novelist Samuel Richardson. After discussing Shakespeare and Ben Jonson, Young turns to Dryden the dramatist. (*English Critical Essays* (1922), ed. E. D. Jones, World's Classics, pp. 350–52.)

Dryden, destitute of Shakespeare's genius, had almost as much learning as Jonson, and, for the buskin, quite as little taste. He was a stranger to the pathos, and, by numbers, expression, sentiment, and every other dramatic cheat, strove to make amends for it; as if a saint could make amends for the want of conscience; a soldier, for the want of valour; or a vestal, of modesty. The noble nature of tragedy disclaims an

(*w*) Extract from Johnson's Life of Pope: 'Dryden never desired to apply all the judgement that he had. He wrote, and professed to write, merely for the people; and when he pleased others, he contented himself. He spent no time in struggles to rouse latent powers; he never attempted to make that better which was already good, nor often to mend what he must have known to be faulty. . . . Pope was not content to satisfy; he desired to excel. . . .

In acquired knowledge the superiority must be allowed to Dryden, whose education was more scholastick, and who before he became author had been allowed more time for study. . . . His mind has a larger range, and he collects his images and illustrations from a more extensive circumference of science. Dryden knew more of man in his general nature, and Pope in his local manners. The notions of Dryden were formed by comprehensive speculation, and those of Pope by minute attention. There is more dignity in the knowledge of Dryden, and more certainty in that of Pope.

Poetry was not the sole praise of either, for both excelled likewise in prose; but Pope did not borrow his prose from his predecessor. The style of Dryden is capricious and varied, that of Pope is cautious and uniform; Dryden obeys the motions of his own mind, Pope constrains his mind to his own rules of composition. Dryden is sometimes vehement and rapid; Pope is always smooth, uniform, and gentle. Dryden's page is a natural field, rising into inequalities, and diversified by the varied exuberance of abundant vegetation; Pope's is a velvet lawn, shaven by the scythe, and levelled by the roller.

Of genius, that power which constitutes a poet; that quality without which judgement is cold and knowledge is inert; that energy which collects, combines, amplifies, and animates—the superiority must, with some hesitation, be allowed to Dryden. It is not to be inferred that of this poetical vigour Pope had only a little, because Dryden had more, for every other writer since Milton must give place to Pope; and even of Dryden it must be said that if he has brighter paragraphs, he has not better poems. Dryden's performances were always hasty, either excited by some external occasion, or extorted by domestick necessity; he composed without consideration, and published without correction. What his mind could supply at call, or gather in one excursion, was all that he sought, and all that he gave. The dilatory caution of Pope enabled him to condense his sentiments, to multiply his images, and to accumulate all that study might produce, or chance might supply. If the flights of Dryden therefore are higher,

Pope continues longer on the wing. If of Dryden's fire the blaze is brighter, of Pope's the heat is more regular and constant. Dryden often surpasses expectation, and Pope never falls below it. Dryden is read with frequent astonishment, and Pope with perpetual delight.

This parallel will, I hope, when it is well considered, be found just; and if the reader should suspect me, as I suspect myself, of some partial fondness for the memory of Dryden, let him not too hastily condemn me; for meditation and enquiry may, perhaps, shew him the reasonableness of my determination.' (*ibid.*, iii. 220–1, 222–3.)

(*x*) Extract from *The Rambler*, No. 31, 3 July 1750: 'DRYDEN, whose warmth of fancy, and haste of composition, very frequently hurried him into inaccuracies, heard himself sometimes exposed to ridicule for having said in one of his tragedies,

I follow fate, which does too fast pursue.[1]

That no man could at once follow and be followed was, it may be thought, too plain to be long disputed; and the truth is, that DRYDEN was apparently betrayed into the blunder by the double meaning of the word FATE, to which in the former part of the verse he had annexed the idea of FORTUNE, and in the latter that of DEATH; so that the sense only was, *though pursued by* DEATH, *I will not resign myself to despair, but will follow* FORTUNE, *and do and suffer what is appointed*. This, however, was not completely expressed, and DRYDEN, being determined not to give way to his critics, never confessed that he had been surprised by an ambiguity; but finding luckily in *Virgil* an account of a man moving in a circle, with this expression, *Et se sequiturque fugitque*, "Here," says he, "is the passage in imitation of which I wrote the line that my critics were pleased to condemn as nonsense; not but I may sometimes write nonsense, though they have not the fortune to find it."[2]

Every one sees the folly of such mean doublings to escape the pursuit of criticism; nor is there a single reader of this poet, who would not have paid him greater veneration, had he shewn con-

---

[1] *The Indian Emperour* (1667), IV. iii.

[2] Johnson's haste of composition has hurried him into inaccuracy. In the Preface to *Tyrannick Love* (1672 edn.) Dryden replies to 'some fool' who had charged him with nonsense in *The Indian Emperour*, saying that his line was borrowed from Virgil's *Aeneid*, xi. 695, *eludit gyro interior, sequitur sequentem:* 'she eludes him ... and pursues the pursuer.' 'I quote not these to prove that I never writ nonsense, but only to shew that they are so unfortunate as not to have found it.'

sciousness enough of his own superiority to set such cavils at defiance, and owned that he sometimes slipped into errors by the tumult of his imagination, and the multitude of his ideas.'

77. Comments by Cowper

1780, 1782, 1784

The poet William Cowper (1731–1800) had surprisingly little to say on Dryden; his preoccupations were with Milton and Pope. But then 'poetry, English poetry', he said, 'I never touch, being pretty much addicted to the writing of it, and knowing that much intercourse with those gentlemen betrays us unavoidably into a habit of imitation, which I hate and despise most cordially' (letter of 23 November 1783; *Life and Works* (1836–7), ed. Robert Southey, xv. 137. Extracts from this edition).

(*a*) From letter to Unwin, 11 July 1780: 'I have often wondered that Dryden's illustrious epigram on Milton (in my mind the second best that ever was made) has never been translated into Latin, for the admiration of the learned in other countries. I have at last presumed to venture upon the task myself.'

(*b*) From letter to Unwin, 5 January 1782: 'In the last Review, I mean in the last but one, I saw Johnson's critique upon Prior and Pope. I am bound to acquiesce in his opinion of the latter, because it has always been my own. I could never agree with those who preferred him to Dryden. ... He was certainly a mechanical maker of verses, and in every line he ever wrote, we see indubitable marks of the most indefatigable industry and labour. ... With the unwearied application of a plodding Flemish painter, who draws a shrimp with the most minute exactness, he had all the genius of one of the first

313

masters. Never, I believe, were such talents and such drudgery united. But I admire Dryden most, who has succeeded by mere dint of genius, and in spite of a laziness and carelessness almost peculiar to himself. His faults are numberless, but so are his beauties. His faults are those of a great man, and his beauties are such, (at least sometimes,) as Pope, with all his touching and retouching, could never equal.'

(c) From letter to Unwin, 21 March 1784: 'Last night I made an end of reading Johnson's Prefaces. . . . After all, it is a melancholy observation, which it is impossible not to make, after having run through this series of poetical lives, that where there were such shining talents, there should be so little virtue. . . . What vanity, what petulance in Pope! . . . To what mean artifices could Addison stoop. . . . What a sycophant to the public taste was Dryden; sinning against his feelings, lewd in his writings, though chaste in his conversation.'

78. A professorial view

1783

Dr Hugh Blair (1718–1800) was minister of the High Kirk, *elegantiae arbiter* in the city, and Professor of Rhetoric and Belles Lettres in the University of Edinburgh. He presumed to declare Macpherson's *Ossian* authentic, and to instruct Burns in the art of poetry. Extracts from his *Lectures on Rhetoric and Belles Lettres*, 2 vols. (1783), for too long a standard text-book.

(a) 'The restoration of King Charles II. seems to be the æra of the formation of our present style. Lord Clarendon was one of the first who laid aside those frequent inversions which prevailed among writers of the former age. After him, Sir William Temple, polished the Language still more. But the author, who, by the number and

reputation of his works, formed it more than any one, into its present
state, is Dryden. Dryden began to write at the Restoration, and continued long an author both in poetry and prose. He had made the
language his study; and though he wrote hastily, and often incorrectly,
and his style is not free from faults, yet there is a richness in his diction,
a copiousness, ease, and variety in his expression, which has not been
surpassed by any who have come after him. Since his time, considerable attention has been paid to Purity and Elegance of Style: But it is
Elegance, rather than Strength, that forms the distinguishing quality
of most of the good English writers.' (*Lectures*, i. 378–9.)

(*b*) 'The present form of our English heroic rhyme in couplets, is a
modern species of Versification. The measure generally used in the
days of Queen Elizabeth, King James, and King Charles I. was the
stanza of eight lines, such as Spencer employs, borrowed from the
Italian; a measure very constrained and artificial. Waller was the first
who brought couplets into vogue; and Dryden afterwards established
the usage. Waller first smoothed our Verse; Dryden perfected it. Mr.
Pope's Versification has a peculiar character. It is flowing and smooth,
in the highest degree; far more laboured and correct than that of any
who went before him. He introduced one considerable change into
Heroic Verse, by totally throwing aside the triplets, or three lines
rhyming together, in which Mr. Dryden abounded. Dryden's Versification, however, has very great merit; and, like all his productions,
has much spirit, mixed with carelessness. If not so smooth and correct
as Pope's, it is however more varied and easy. He subjects himself
less to the rule of closing the sense with the couplet; and frequently
takes the liberty of making his couplets run into one another, with
somewhat of the freedom of Blank Verse.' (*ibid.*, ii. 333–4.)

(*c*) 'Dryden was the first considerable Dramatic Writer after the
Restoration; in whose Comedies, as in all his works, there are found
many strokes of genius, mixed with great carelessness, and visible
marks of hasty composition. As he sought to please only, he went
along with the manners of the times; and has carried through all his
Comedies that vein of dissolute licentiousness, which was then fashionable. In some of them, the indecency was so gross as to occasion, even
in that age, a prohibition of being brought upon the Stage.' (*ibid.*, ii.
544.)

79. Burns reads Dryden's *Virgil*

1788

Robert Burns (1759–96) early became familiar with Dryden's original poems; the *Virgil* was lent to him by his friend Mrs Dunlop in April 1788, together with Pope's *Homer* and Hoole's *Tasso*, as a kind of crash course in epic poetry (*Robert Burns and Mrs Dunlop* (1898), ed. W. Wallace, p. 52). Extracts from Burns's letters to Mrs Dunlop, (*a*) 28 April and (*b*) 4 May 1788; *Works*, ed. Currie (2nd. edn., 1801), ii. 134 and 143–4.

(*a*) 'Your books have delighted me: *Virgil*, *Dryden*, and *Tasso*, were all equally strangers to me. . . .'

(*b*) 'Dryden's *Virgil* has delighted me. I do not know whether the critics will agree with me, but the *Georgics* are to me by far the best of Virgil. It is indeed a species of writing entirely new to me; and has filled my head with a thousand fancies of emulation: but alas! when I read the *Georgics*, and then survey my own powers, 'tis like the idea of a Shetland poney, drawn up by the side of a thorough-bred hunter, to start for the plate. I own I am disappointed in the *Æneid*. Faultless correctness may please, and does highly please the lettered critic: but to that aweful character I have not the most distant pretensions. I do not know whether I do not hazard my pretensions to be a critic of any kind, when I say that I think Virgil in many instances, a *servile* copier of Homer. If I had the *Odyssey* by me,[1] I could parallel many passages where Virgil has evidently copied, but by no means improved, Homer. Nor can I think there is any thing of this owing to the translators; for, from every thing I have seen of Dryden, I think him in genius, and fluency of language, Pope's master. . . .'

[1] Either Mrs Dunlop did not send the *Homer* she promised, or she sent the *Iliad* only (Burns having the *Odyssey*)?

80. Malone on Dryden

1800

Extracts from the 'Account of the Life and Writings of the Author' in Malone's *Critical and Miscellaneous Prose Works of John Dryden, now first Collected* (1800). Edmond Malone (1741–1812) was an Irish antiquary and Shakespearean scholar. For his general service to the study of Dryden, see J. M. Osborn's essay in *John Dryden: Some Biographical Facts and Problems* (revd. edn., 1965). He was 'the first person to call the attention of the literary public to the body of Dryden's prose'; and he allows himself an occasional critical comment. But his main business was

to delineate the *man* rather than the *poet*, by collecting from every quarter, and from sources hitherto unexplored, whatever might contribute to throw new light upon his character, and illustrate the history of his works. . . . A critical examination of the merits and defects of his various productions formed no part of the present undertaking; and indeed may be well dispensed with, after Dr. Johnson's elaborate and admirable disquisition . . . ; than which a more beautiful and judicious piece of criticism perhaps has not appeared since the days of Aristotle. (I. i. 548–9)

Extracts are all from Vol. I, Part 1.

(a) 'The great author of the following works has long had the honour of being ranked in the first class of English Poets; for to the names of Shakespeare, Spencer, and Milton, we have now for near a century been in the habit of annexing those of DRYDEN, and his scholar, Pope. The present publication will shew, that he is equally entitled to our admiration as a writer of Prose; and that among his various merits, that of having cultivated, refined, and improved our language, is not the least. . . .

The PROSE of Dryden has been so long and so justly admired for its copiousness, harmony, richness, and variety, that to adduce any

testimony in its favour seems unnecessary. ... I may however add
the authority of the late Mr. Burke,[1] who had very diligently read
all his miscellaneous Essays, which he held in high estimation, not
only for the instruction which they contain, but on account of the
rich and numerous prose in which that instruction is conveyed. On
the language of Dryden, on which perhaps his own style was originally in some measure formed, I have often heard him expatiate with
great admiration; and if the works of Burke be examined with this
view, he will, I believe, be found more nearly to resemble this great
author than any other English writer.

Dr. Johnson has said, that "whoever wishes to attain an English
style, familiar but not coarse, and elegant but not ostentatious, must
give his days and nights to the volumes of Addison."[2] He who has
this object in view, may surely, with equal propriety, be counselled
to study the pages of Dryden; for in them, with the ease, simplicity,
and familiar language of Addison, will be found conjoined more
fervour, more strength, and more variety. The great characteristick
of Addison is his frequent use of vernacular idiom; of which Dryden
was so fond, that having on one occasion employed the Anglo-Latin
word, *diction*, he makes a kind of apology, by translating it:[3] in this
respect, therefore, he is entitled to the encomium given to the ancient
bard whose TALES he has so happily modernized, and may with equal
truth be called—"the well of English undefiled".'[4] (pp. i, vi–viii,
Advertisement.)

(*b*) In 1663 'he prefixed to his friend Dr. Charleton's Account of
Stonehenge some elegant lines, in which we find more vigour than in
[*To his Sacred Majesty* or *To my Lord Chancellor*], and much of that
copiousness, animation, and harmony, for which his poetical compositions were afterwards distinguished.' (pp. 47–9.)

(*c*) 'His elegant ESSAY OF DRAMATICK POESY ... he ... published in
the latter end of the year 1667. Though the Art of Criticism at this
period had not been so diligently cultivated in England, as it has been
in the present century, some essays had been made to ascertain and
teach its principles, and a few strictures on English versification had

[1] Edmund Burke (*c.* 1729–97), the politician.
[2] *Lives of the English Poets* (1905), ed. G. B. Hill, ii. 150.
[3] In the Preface to *Fables; Poems* (1958), ed. James Kinsley, iv. 1448.
[4] Spenser on Chaucer, *The Faerie Queene*, IV. ii. 32.

appeared. Gascoigne, before 1575, ... Sir Philip Sydney ... Webbe
a few years afterwards [1586] ... Puttenham, in 1589 ... Thomas
Campion, in 1602 ... Daniel, the poet, in the following year ...
Ben Jonson's DISCOVERIES ... written about the year 1630 ...—
Still, however, no regular treatise had clearly and methodically
delivered the elements of criticism, or established those great principles
on which a true judgment concerning the various works addressed
to the imagination, might be formed; nor had scenick exhibitions
engaged much of the attention of any of the writers who have been
mentioned, except Sydney and Jonson: whilst in France, Hedelin and
Corneille had furnished their countrymen with express disquisitions
on the principal laws of the drama. Our author's ESSAY OF DRAMATICK
POESY therefore, beside its other merits, had also in some measure
the attraction of novelty. The colloquial form which he adopted, has
been always acknowledged to be attended with some inconvenience;
which, however, he had so happily overcome, that none of his critical
works have been more generally read and admired than this Essay,
for it passed through three editions in his life-time, and has since his
death been frequently reprinted. Nor has its success been dispro-
portioned to its value; for perhaps our language does not furnish us
with any discursive treatise more nearly resembling the excellent
models which the ancients have left us, in this difficult species of
composition: the introduction, particularly, need not shun a comparison with the best proems of Plato's or Cicero's dialogues.

In this piece, written, as the author has modestly said, "when he
was but in the rudiments of his poetry, without name or reputation
in the world, having rather the ambition of a writer than the skill,"
his great object was, "to vindicate the honour of the English Poets
from the censures of those who unjustly preferred the French before
them:" an object which he has completely attained. Nor should it
be forgotten, that he was the first who, in this dialogue, had the
hardihood to displace Jonson from the eminence to which by the
unanimous voice of Dryden's contemporaries he had most unjustly
been elevated, and to set Shakspeare far above him, in that admirable
character, which, as his last great biographer[1] has truly observed,
"may stand as a perpetual model of encomiastick criticism ...".'
(pp. 58–62.)

(d) Dr Johnson's charge of 'the meanness and servility of hyperbolical

[1] Johnson; *supra*, p. 289.

adulation'[1] 'has been stated far more unfavourably for Dryden, than the history of the period during which he wrote will justify. The encomiastick language which is sometimes found in his Dedications, was the vice of the time, not of the man. The Dedication of almost every other author of the last age was equally loaded with flattery, and sometimes far surpassed any of Dryden's in extravagance of praise: nor was any kind of disgrace annexed to this exercise of men's talents; the contest among the whole tribe of writers of every description, however humble or however eminent, being, who should go furthest in panegyrick, in the most graceful way, and with the happiest turns of expression. Butler, as the late Mr. Burke several years ago observed to me, has well illustrated the principle on which they went, where he compares their endeavours to those of the archer, who *draws his arrow to the head*, whether his object be a swan, or a goose.[2] The addresses prefixed to the various pieces issued from the press from the Restoration to the end of the reign of Queen Anne, fully support this remark. Though very few of them are written with the spirit and elegance that are found in our author's Dedications, they by no means fall short of them in hyperbolical adulation.' (pp. 243–5.)

(e) 'In the review of the old English poets, which, in conformity to the advice of Sir George Mackenzie,[3] he had made soon after he obtained the laurel, I doubt whether he went so high[4] as Chaucer; but however that may have been, it is certain that he had at no period very deeply studied our ancient language; and that when he resolved to give rejuvenescence to the venerable father of English poetry, he brought to his task only such a knowledge of his author, as would enable him to clothe Chaucer's meaning with the rich trappings of his own mellifluous verse. In this neglect of archaiologick lore he was by no means singular; for to the great mass of English readers at that time there is good reason for believing that this ancient bard was nearly as difficult to be understood, as if his works had been written in a foreign language. Even a certain portion of ridicule was then, and for forty years afterwards, attached to all antiquarian researches;

---

[1] *Supra*, p. 287.

[2] Samuel Butler, *Hudibras*, II (1663), i. 621–34.

[3] 'That Noble Wit of *Scotland*' (1636–91), with whom Dryden had a conversation about poetry in the 1670s (*Poems*, ed. James Kinsley, ii. 665–6).

[4] 'Far ... into antiquity' (Johnson).

and he who expended any part of his time in investigating the customs and manners of preceding ages, was generally considered extremely whimsical, if not slightly deranged in his understanding.' (pp. 318–19.)

(*f*) 'Though his morals were aspersed, and his writings censured and ridiculed, in innumerable libels, he seldom condescended to mention his opponents: trusting, that the blameless tenour of his life would sufficiently confute his calumniators; and that when *partiality and prejudice should be forgotten, posterity would be more favourable to him,* and rightly appreciate his works. Of their great excellence he could not be ignorant; but it is no inconsiderable proof of both his genius and his candour, that he was not insensible to their defects. Whatever praises of his performances may have occasionally fallen from him, which were in some measure extorted by the ungenerous attempts of his adversaries to depreciate him, he has himself told us, that he *was rarely pleased with his own endeavours.* His mind had too large a grasp, to permit him to be entirely satisfied with his compositions, "*which seldom reached to those ideas that he had within him*:"[1] and hence probably it was, that he submitted many of his pieces in manuscript to his friends, and read his works aloud to them for their judgment: and he was extremely patient of their observations and corrections. Like some other of our English poets, he read so ill, that his productions suffered greatly by his delivery. ... "When Dryden, our first great master of verse and harmony, brought his play of AMPHITRYON to the Stage, I heard him (says Cibber,) give it his first reading to the Actors; in which, though it is true he delivered the plain sense of every period, yet the whole was in so cold, so flat, and unaffecting a manner, that I am afraid of not being believed, when I affirm it." '[2] (pp. 513–16.)

(*g*) 'Since the death of Dryden, nearly a century has elapsed; during the latter part of which period his reputation has greatly increased, in common with that of our other most famous poets; who for the last fifty years have been more read, and are now much better understood, than they were by our ancestors. Some of the most distinguished wits of Queen Anne's time, however, seem to have thought themselves obscured by the shade of his laurels; and for a few years, endeavoured

---

[1] Opening of the Dedication of *The Spanish Fryar* (1681); Preface to *Sylvae* (1685; *Poems* (1958), ed. James Kinsley, i. 396).
[2] Cibber's *Life* (1740), p. 95. Malone also cites Theobald in the *Censor* (1717), no. 9.

to depreciate him. Old Jacob Tonson[1] informed Mr. Spence, that
Addison was so eager to be the first name in modern literature, that,
with Steele to assist him, he used to decry Dryden, as far as he could,
while Pope and Congreve defended him;[2] and in this unworthy
attempt, as we learn from Dennis,[3] Addison and his followers were
joined by a numerous band. It is painful to observe, in all times, how
much men's judgments are warped by the violence of party....
These petty assaults, however, in no degree diminished the reputation of Dryden, which is now elevated beyond the reach of envy,
ridicule, or satire; and posterity, to whose judgment with great
calmness and magnanimity he appealed from his contemporary
adversaries, has done him ample justice, by allotting to him that
distinguished place in the Temple of Fame, to which no one now
presumes to controvert his title.' (pp. 540–2, 547–8.)

(h) 'I shall ... no longer detain the reader from the perusal of the
ensuing volumes [of Dryden's prose]; which contain such a variety
of excellence, that,—so long as justness of thought and vigour of
expression, fertility of mind and copiousness of illustration, shall have
the power of enchaining the attention and commanding the admiration of mankind,—to all who seek to amuse the fancy and to inform
the judgment, they must continue to prove an abundant source of
instruction and delight.' (p. 549.)

[1] Dryden's bookseller (c. 1656–1736).
[2] Joseph Spence, *Observations, Anecdotes, and Characters* (1966), ed. J. M. Osborn, i.
no. 814.
[3] See *supra*, pp. 257–9.

81. No great favourite of Wordsworth's

1805

Extract from Wordsworth's letter of 7 November 1805 to Sir Walter Scott (see, No. 83). The Scotts had toured the Lakes with Wordsworth earlier in the year. Wordsworth's autograph is in the National Library of Scotland. For the full text, see *The Letters of William and Dorothy Wordsworth* (1967), ed. E. de Selincourt and revd. C. L. Shaver, i. 640–4.

Patterdale, November 7th, 1805.

My dear Scott,

... Your Letter was very welcome; I am not apt to haunt myself with fears of accident from flood and field, &c., it was nevertheless pleasant to hear that you had got home well. ...

I was much pleased to hear of your engagement with Dryden: not that he is, as a *Poet*, any great favourite of mine: I admire his talents and Genius greatly, but his is not a poetical Genius: the only qualities I can find in Dryden that are *essentially* poetical are a certain ardour and impetuosity of mind with an excellent ear: it may seem strange that I do not add to this, great command of language: *that* he certainly has and of such language also as it is most desirable that a Poet should possess, or rather should not be without; but it is not language that is in the high sense of the word poetical, being neither of the imagination or the passions; I mean of the amiable, the ennobling or intense passions; I do not mean to say that there is nothing of this in Dryden, but as little, I think, as is possible, considering how much he has written. You will easily understand my meaning when I refer to his versification of Palamon and Arcite as contrasted with the language of Chaucer. Dryden had neither a tender heart nor a lofty sense of moral dignity: where his language is poetically impassioned it is mostly upon unpleasing subjects; such as the follies, vice, and crimes of classes of men or of individuals. That his cannot be the language of the imagination must have necessarily followed from this, that there is not a single image from Nature in the whole body of his works; and in his translation from Vergil whenever Vergil can be fairly said to have had his *eye* upon his object, Dryden always spoils the passage.

But too much of this; I am glad that you are to be his editor: his political and satirical Poems may be greatly benefited by illustration, and even absolutely require it. ... I wish it were in my power to do any service to your Book: I have read Dryden's Works (all but his plays) with great attention, but my observations refer entirely to matters of taste; and things of this kind appear better any where than when tagged to a Poet's works where they are absolute impertinences. ...

A correct text is the first object of an editor: then such notes as explain difficult or unintelligible passages or throw light upon them; and lastly, which is of much less importance, notes pointing out passages or authors to which the Poet has been indebted, not in the piddling way of [a] phrase here and phrase there (which is detestable as a general practice) but where the Poet has really had essential obligations either as to matter or manner.

Let me hear from you as soon as convenient; if I can be of any use do not fail to apply to me. One thing I may take the liberty to suggest which is, when you come to the Fables might it not be advisable to print the whole of the tales of Boccace in a small type in the original language? If this should look too much like swelling a Book; I should certainly make such extracts as would shew when Dryden had most strikingly improved upon or fallen below his original. I think his translations from Boccace are the best at least the most poetical of his Poems. It is many years since I saw Boccace, but I remember that Sigismonda is not married by him to Guiscard (the names are different in Boccace I believe in both tales certainly in Theodore, &c.).[1] I think Dryden has much injured the story by the marriage, and degraded Sigismonda's character by it. He has also to the best of my remembrance degraded her character still more by making her love absolute sensuality and appetite, (Dryden had no other notion of the passion). With all these defects, and some other very gross ones it is a noble Poem. Guiscard's answer when first reproached by Tancred is noble

---

[1] 'Sigismonda and Guiscardo' and 'Theodore and Honoria' in *Fables Ancient and Modern*. In Boccaccio's *Decameron* the characters are named Ghismonda and Guiscardo (iv. 1), and Nastagio and merely 'la giovane' (v. 8).

in Boccace, nothing but this. Amor può molto più che ne voi ne Io possiamo. This, Dryden has spoiled; he says first very well, 'The faults of love by love are justified,' and then come four lines of miserable rant, quite à la Maximin. . . .[1]

82. Scott's *Dryden*: Cause for alarm

1805, 1806

Extracts from correspondence in late 1805 and 1806 between Walter Scott and the antiquary George Ellis over Scott's proposed edition of Dryden (see *infra*, No. 83). Text from J. G. Lockhart's *Life of Sir Walter Scott* (1837–9; 1914 edn.), i. 429–33, 449.

(*a*) Ellis: 'The late Dr. Warton, you may have heard, had a project of editing Dryden *à la* Hurd; that is to say, upon the same principle as the castrated edition of Cowley.[2] His reason was, that Dryden, having written for bread, became of necessity a most voluminous author, and poured forth more nonsense of indecency, particularly in his theatrical compositions, than almost any scribbler in that scribbling age. Hence, although his transcendent genius frequently breaks out, and marks the hand of the master, his comedies seem, by a tacit but general consent, to have been condemned to oblivion; and his tragedies, being printed in such bad company, have shared the same fate. But Dr. W. conceived that, by a judicious selection of these, together with his fables and prose works, it would be possible to exhibit him in a much more advantageous light than by a republication

---

[1] Slightly misquoting Boccaccio's 'Love is more potent than either you or I'; Dryden's ll. 281–5, recalling the extravagances of Maximin in *Tyrannick Love*.

[2] For Joseph Warton see *supra*, No. 71. A selection from Cowley was edited in 2 vols. by the pious (and later episcopal) Richard Hurd in 1772.

of the whole mass of his writings. Whether the Doctor (who, by the way, was by no means scrupulously chaste and delicate, as you will be aware from his edition of Pope)[1] had taken a just view of the subject, you know better than I; but I must own that the announcement of a *general* edition of Dryden gave me some little alarm. . . .'

(*b*) Scott: 'I will not castrate John Dryden. I would as soon castrate my own father, as I believe Jupiter did of yore. What would you say to any man who would castrate Shakespeare, or Massinger, or Beaumont and Fletcher? I don't say but that it may be very proper to select correct passages for the use of boarding schools and colleges, being sensible no improper ideas can be suggested in these seminaries, unless they are intruded or smuggled under the beards and ruffs of our old dramatists. But in making an edition of a man of genius's works for libraries and collections, and such I conceive a complete edition of Dryden to be, I must give my author as I find him, and will not tear out the page, even to get rid of the blot, little as I like it. Are not the pages of Swift, and even of Pope, larded with indecency, and often of the most disgusting kind, and do we not see them upon all shelves and dressing-tables, and in all boudoirs? Is not Prior the most indecent of tale-tellers, not even excepting La Fontaine, and how often do we see his works in female hands? In fact, it is not passages of ludicrous indelicacy that corrupt the manners of a people —it is the sonnets which a prurient genius like Master Little sings *virginibus puerisque*[2]—it is the sentimental slang, half lewd, half methodistic, that debauches the understanding, inflames the sleeping passions, and prepares the reader to give way as soon as a tempter appears. At the same time, I am not at all happy when I peruse some of Dryden's comedies: they are very stupid, as well as indelicate; sometimes, however, there is a considerable vein of liveliness and humour, and all of them present extraordinary pictures of the age in which he lived. . . .'

(*c*) Ellis: 'I will not disturb you by contesting any part of your ingenious apology for your intended *complete* edition of Dryden, whose genius I venerate as much as you do, and whose negligences, as he was not rich enough to doom them to oblivion in his own life-

---

[1] 1797.
[2] Apparently Thomas Moore (1779–1852), whose first volume of original verse was entitled *The Poetical Works of the late Thomas Little, Esq.* (1801).

time, it is perhaps incumbent on his editor to transmit to the latest posterity. Most certainly I am not so squeamish as to quarrel with him for his immodesty on any moral pretence. Licentiousness in writing, when accompanied by wit, as in the case of Prior, La Fontaine, etc., is never likely to excite any *passion*, because every passion is serious; and the grave epistle of Eloisa is more likely to do moral mischief and convey infection to lovesick damsels, than five hundred stories of Hans Carvel and Paulo Purgante;[1] but whatever is in point of expression vulgar—whatever disgusts the taste—whatever might have been written by any fool, and is therefore unworthy of Dryden —whatever might have been suppressed, without exciting a moment's regret in the mind of any of his admirers—*ought*, in my opinion, to be suppressed by any editor who should be disposed to make an appeal to the public taste upon the subject; because a man, who was perhaps the best poet and best prose writer in the language—but it is foolish to say so much, after promising to say nothing. Indeed I own *myself* guilty of possessing all his works in a very indifferent edition, and I shall certainly purchase a better one whenever you put it in my power. . . .'

(*d*) Scott: 'My principal companion in this solitude is John Dryden. After all, there are some passages in his translations from Ovid and Juvenal that will hardly bear reprinting, unless I would have the Bishop of London and the whole corps of Methodists about my ears. I wish you would look at the passages I mean. One is from the fourth book of Lucretius; the other from Ovid's Instructions to his Mistress. They are not only double-entendres, but good plain single-entendres —not only broad, but long, and as coarse as the mainsail of a first-rate.[2] What to make of them I know not; but I fear that, without absolutely gelding the bard, it will be indispensable to circumcise him a little by leaving out some of the most obnoxious lines.[3] Do, pray, look at the poems and decide for me. . . .'

---

[1] Pope's *Eloisa to Abelard*; the story of Hans Carvel transmitted from Poggio through Rabelais and La Fontaine to Prior (1700).

[2] First-class warship.

[3] But the pieces were printed *in toto* in Scott's twelfth volume.

83. Walter Scott: The great appraisal

1808

Extracts from *The Works of John Dryden, now first Collected in Eighteen Volumes. Illustrated with Notes, Historical, Critical, and Explanatory, and a Life of the Author, by Walter Scott, Esq.* (1808): A, from the Life; and B, from the Commentary. 'This was the bold speculation of William Miller of Albemarle Street, London; and the editor's fee, at forty guineas the volume, was £756' (Lockhart). See Introduction, pp. 17–23; and J. M. Osborn's discussion in *John Dryden: Some Biographical Facts and Problems* (revd. edn., 1965).

A

(*a*) 'After the lapse of more than a century since the author's death, the Works of Dryden are now, for the first time, presented to the public in a complete and uniform edition. In collecting the pieces of one of our most eminent English classics,—one who may claim at least the third place in that honoured list, and who has given proofs of greater versatility of talent than either Shakespeare or Milton, though justly placed inferior to them in their peculiar provinces,— the Editor did not feel himself entitled to reject any part of his writings; even of those which reflect little honour on the age, by whose taste they were dictated. Had a selection been permitted, he would have excluded several of the Comedies, and some part of the Translations: but this is a liberty which has not lately been indulged to editors of classical poetry. Literary history is an important step in that of man himself; and the unseductive coarseness of Dryden is rather a beacon than a temptation. . . . The general critical view of Dryden's works being sketched by Johnson with unequalled felicity, and the incidents of his life accurately discussed and ascertained by Malone,[1] something seemed to remain for him who should consider these literary productions in their succession, as actuated by, and operating

[1] *Supra*, Nos. 76 and 80.

upon, the taste of an age, where they had so predominant influence; and who might, at the same time, connect the life of Dryden with the history of his publications, without losing sight of the fate and character of the individual.' (i, Advertisement.)

(*b*) 'The Life of Dryden may be said to comprehend a history of the literature of England, and its changes, during nearly half a century. While his great contemporary Milton was in silence and secrecy laying the foundation of that immortal fame, which no poet has so highly deserved, Dryden's labours were ever in the eye of the public: and he maintained, from the time of the Restoration till his death, in 1700, a decided and acknowledged superiority over all the poets of his age. As he wrote from necessity, he was obliged to pay a certain deference to the public opinion; for he, whose bread depends upon the success of his volume, is compelled to study popularity: but, on the other hand, his better judgment was often directed to improve that of his readers; so that he alternately influenced and stooped to the national taste of the day. If, therefore, we would know the gradual changes which took place in our poetry during the above period, we have only to consult the writings of an author, who produced yearly some new performance, allowed to be most excellent in the particular style which was fashionable for the time. It is the object of this memoir to connect, with the account of Dryden's life and publications, such a general view of the literature of the time, as may enable the reader to estimate how far the age was indebted to the poet, and how far the poet was influenced by the taste and manners of the age.' (i. 3–4.)

(*c*) 'The elegy on Lord Hastings, the lines prefixed to "Sion and Parnassus," and some complimentary stanzas which occur in a letter to his cousin Honor Driden, would have been enough to assure us, even without his own testimony, that Cowley was the darling of his youth; and that he imitated his points of wit, and quirks of epigram, with a similar contempt for the propriety of their application. From these poems, we learn enough to be grateful, that Dryden was born at a later period in his century; for had not the road to fame been altered in consequence of the Restoration, his extensive information and acute ingenuity would probably have betrayed the author of the "Ode to St Cecilia," and the father of English poetical harmony, into rivalling the metaphysical pindarics of Donne and Cowley. The verses, to which we allude, display their subtlety of thought, their puerile extravagance of conceit, and that structure of verse, which, as the poet himself says of Holyday's translations, has nothing of verse in it except the worst part of it—the rhime, and that far from being unexceptionable.' (i. 32.)

(*d*) 'The elegy on Cromwell, although doubtless sufficiently faulty, contained symptoms of a regenerating taste; and, politically considered, although a panegyric on an usurper, the topics of praise are selected with attention to truth, and are, generally speaking, such as Cromwell's worst enemies could not have denied to him. Neither had Dryden made the errors, or misfortunes, of the royal family, and their followers, the subject of censure or of contrast. With respect to them, it was hardly possible that a eulogy on such a theme could have less offence in it. This was perhaps a fortunate circumstance for Dryden at the Restoration; and it must be noticed to his honour, that as he spared the exiled monarch in his panegyric on the usurper, so, after the Restoration, in his numerous writings on the side of royalty, there is no instance of his recalling his former praise of Cromwell.' (i. 41–2.)

(*e*) Dryden 'added to those which hailed the coronation, in 1661, the verses entitled, "A Panegyric to his Sacred Majesty". These pieces testify, that the author had already made some progress in harmonizing his versification. But they also contain many of those points of wit, and turns of epigram, which he condemned in his more advanced judgment. The same description applies, in a yet stronger degree, to the verses addressed to Lord Chancellor Hyde (Lord Clarendon) on the new-year's-day of 1662, in which Dryden has more closely imitated the metaphysical poetry than in any poem, except the juvenile elegy on Lord Hastings. I cannot but think, that the poet consulted the taste of his patron, rather than his own, in adopting this peculiar style. Clarendon was educated in the court of Charles I., and Dryden may have thought it necessary, in addressing him, to imitate the "strong verses," which were then admired.' (i. 50–1.)

(*f*) 'Science, as well as poetry, began to revive after the iron dominion of military fanaticism was ended; and Dryden, who through life was attached to experimental philosophy, speedily associated himself with those who took interest in its progress. He was chosen a member of the newly instituted Royal Society, 26th November, 1662; an honour which cemented his connection with the most learned men of the time, and is an evidence of the respect in which he was already held. Most of these, and the discoveries by which they had distinguished themselves, Dryden took occasion to celebrate in his "Epistle to Dr Walter Charleton'. ... In these elegant verses, the author divests himself of all the flippant extravagance of point and quibble, in which, complying with his age, he had hitherto indulged, though of late in a limited degree.' (i. 55–6.)

(*g*) 'The victory gained by the Duke of York over the Dutch fleet on the 3d of June, 1665, and his Duchess's subsequent journey into the north, furnished Dryden with the subject of a few occasional verses; in which the style of Waller (who came forth with a poem on the same subject) is successfully imitated. In addressing her grace, the poet suppresses all the horrors of the battle, and turns her eyes upon the splendour of a victory. ... In these verses, not the least vestige of metaphysical wit can be traced; and they were accordingly censured, as wanting height of fancy, and dignity of words. This criticism Dryden refuted, by alleging, that he had succeeded in what he did attempt, in the softness of expression and smoothness of the measure, (the appropriate ornaments of an address to a lady,) and that he was accused of that only thing which he could well defend. It seems, however, very possible, that these remarks impelled him to undertake a task, in which vigour of fancy and expression might, with propriety, be exercised. Accordingly, his next poem was of greater length and importance ... *Annus Mirabilis*. ... The poem being in the elegiac stanza, Dryden relapsed into an imitation of "Gondibert", from which he had departed ever since the "Elegy on Cromwell". From this it appears, that the author's admiration of Davenant had not decreased. Indeed, he, long afterwards, bore testimony to that author's quick and piercing imagination; which at once produced thoughts remote, new, and surprising, such as could not easily enter into any other fancy.[1] Dryden at least equalled Davenant in this quality; and certainly excelled him in the powers of composition, which are to embody the conceptions of the imagination; and in the extent of acquired knowledge, by which they were to be enforced and illustrated. In his preface, he has vindicated the choice of his stanza, by a reference to the opinion of Davenant, which he

[1] Preface to *The Tempest* (1670).

sanctions by affirming, that he had always, himself, thought quatrains, or stanzas of verse in alternate rhyme, more noble, and of greater dignity, both for sound and number, than any other verse in use among us. By this attention to sound and rhythm, he improved upon the school of metaphysical poets, which disclaimed attention to either; but in the thought and expression itself, the style of Davenant more nearly resembled Cowley's, than that of Denham and Waller. The same ardour for what Dryden calls "wit-writing", the same unceasing exercise of the memory, in search of wonderful thoughts and allusions, and the same contempt for the subject, except as the medium of displaying the author's learning and ingenuity, marks the style of Davenant, though in a less degree, than that of the metaphysical poets, and though chequered with many examples of a simpler and chaster character. Some part of this deviation was, perhaps, owing to the nature of the stanza; for the structure of the quatrain prohibited the bard, who used it, from rambling into those digressive similes, which, in the pindaric strophe, might be pursued through endless ramifications. If the former started an extravagant thought, or a quaint image, he was compelled to bring it to a point within his four-lined stanza. The snake was thus scotched, though not killed; and conciseness being rendered indispensible, a great step was gained towards concentration of thought, which is necessary to the simple and to the sublime. The manner of Davenant, therefore, though short-lived, and ungraced by public applause, was an advance towards true taste, from the unnatural and frantic indulgence of unrestrained fancy; and, did it claim no other merit, it possesses that of having been twice sanctioned by the practice of Dryden, upon occasions of uncommon solemnity.

The *Annus Mirabilis* evinces a considerable portion of labour and attention; the lines and versification are highly polished, and the expression was probably carefully corrected. Dryden, as Johnson remarks, already exercised the superiority of his genius, by recommending his own performance, as written upon the plan of Virgil; and as no unsuccessful effort at producing those well-wrought images and descriptions, which create admiration, the proper object of heroic poetry. The *Annus Mirabilis* may indeed be regarded as one of Dryden's most elaborate pieces; although it is not written in his later, better, and most peculiar style of poetry. . . .

The *Annus Mirabilis* being the last poetical work of any importance produced by our author, until *Absalom and Achitophel*, the reader may here pause, and consider, in the progressive improvement of Dryden, the gradual renovation of public taste. The irregular pindaric ode was now abandoned to Arwaker, Behn, Durfey, and a few inferior authors; who, either from its tempting facility of execution, or from an affected admiration of old times and fashions, still pestered the public with imitations of Cowley. The rough measure of Donne (if it had any pretension to be called a measure) was no longer tolerated, and it was expected, even of those who wrote satires, lampoons, and occasional verses, that their rhimes should be rhimes, both to the ear and eye; and that they should neither adore their mistresses, nor abuse their neighbours, in lines which differed only from prose in the fashion of printing. Thus the measure used by Rochester, Buckingham, Sheffield, Sedley, and other satirists, if not polished or harmonized, approaches more nearly to modern verse, than that of Hall or Donne. In the "Elegy on Cromwell," and the *Annus Mirabilis*, Dryden followed Davenant, who abridged, if he did not explode, the quaint-nesses of his predecessors. In *Astræa Redux*, and his occasional verses, to Dr Charlton, the Duchess of York, and others, the poet proposed a separate and simpler model, more dignified than that of Suckling or Waller; more harmonious in measure, and chaste in expression, than those of Cowley and Crashaw. Much, there doubt-less remained, of ancient subtlety, and ingenious quibbling; but when Dryden declares, that he proposes Virgil, in preference to Ovid, to be his model in the *Annus Mirabilis*, it sufficiently implies, that the main defect of the poetry of the last age had been discovered, and was in the way of being amended by gradual, and almost imper-ceptible, degrees. In establishing, or refining, the latter style of writing, in couplet verse, our author found great assistance from his dramatic practice.' (i. 57–64.)

(*h*) *The Wild Gallant* (acted 1663) 'contained too many of those prize-fights of wit, as Buckingham called them, in which the plot stood absolutely still, while two of the characters were shewing the audience their dexterity at repartee. ... The *Indian Emperor* was probably the first of Dryden's performances which drew upon him, in an eminent degree, the attention of the public. It was dedicated to Anne, Duchess of Monmouth ... [who] probably liked ... not only the beauty of the numbers, and the frequently exquisite turn of the description, but also the introduction of incantations and apparitions, of which romantic style of writing she was a professed admirer. The *Indian Emperor* had the most ample success. . . . The tragic scenes of the *Maiden Queen* were deservedly censured, as falling beneath the *Indian Emperor*. They have neither the stately march of the heroic dialogue, nor, what we would be more pleased to have found in them, the truth of passion, and natural colouring, which characterized the old English drama. But the credit of the piece was redeemed by the comic part, which is a more light and airy representation of the fashionable and licentious manners of the time than Dryden could afterwards attain, excepting in *Marriage à-la-Mode*. The king, whose judgment on this subject was unquestionable, graced the *Maiden Queen* with the title of *his play*. . . .

The *Maiden Queen* was followed by the *Tempest*, an alteration of Shakespeare's play. . . . It seems probable that Dryden furnished the language, and D'Avenant the plan of the new characters introduced. They do but little honour to his invention, although Dryden has highly extolled it in his preface. The idea of a counter-part to Shakespeare's plot, by introducing a man who had never seen a woman, as a contrast to a woman who had never seen a man, and by furnishing Caliban with a sister monster, seems hardly worthy of the delight with which Dryden says he filled up the characters so sketched. In mixing his tints, Dryden did not omit that peculiar colouring, in which his age delighted. Miranda's simplicity is converted into indelicacy, and Dorinda talks the language of prostitution before she has ever seen a man. . . . The *Evening's Love, or the Mock Astrologer* [has] that lively bustle, intricacy of plot, and surprising situation, which the taste of the time required, and [is] enlivened by the characters of Wildblood and Jacinta. . . . In the preface . . . Dryden anxiously justifies himself from the charge of encouraging libertinism, by crowning his rake and coquette with success. But after he has arrayed all the authority of the ancient and modern poets, and has pleaded that these licentious characters are only made happy after being reclaimed in the last scene, we may be permitted to think, that more proper heroes may be selected than those, who, to merit the reward assigned them, must announce a violent and sudden change from the character they have sustained during five acts; and the attempt to shroud himself under authority of others, is seldom resorted to by Dryden, when a cause is otherwise tenable. . . .

The *Royal Martyr* . . . is, in every respect, a proper heroic tragedy, and had a large share of the applause with which those pieces were then received. It abounds in bombast, but is not deficient in specimens of the sublime and of the tender.' (i. 80–1, 85, 104, 105–6, 109–10.)

(*i*) 'The rage for imitating the French stage, joined to the successful efforts of our author, had now carried the heroic or rhyming tragedy to its highest pitch of popularity. The principal requisites of such a drama are summed up by Dryden in the two first lines of the *Orlando Furioso*,

> *Le Donne, i cavalier, l'arme, gli amori*
> *Le cortesie, l'audaci imprese.*—[1]

The story thus partaking of the nature of a romance of chivalry, the whole interest of the play necessarily turned upon love and honour, those supreme idols of the days of knight-errantry. The love introduced was not of that ordinary sort, which exists between persons of common mould; it was the love of Amadis and Oriana, of Oroondates and Statira;[2] that love which required a sacrifice of every wish, hope, and feeling unconnected with itself, and which was expressed in the language of prayer and of adoration. It was that love which was neither to be chilled by absence, nor wasted by time, nor quenched by infidelity. No caprice in the object beloved entitled her slave to emancipate himself from her fetters; no command, however unreasonable, was to be disobeyed; if required by the fair mistress of his affections, the hero was not only to sacrifice his interest, but his friend, his honour, his word, his country, even the gratification of his love itself, to maintain the character of a submissive and faithful adorer. Much of this mystery is summed up in the following speech of Almahide to Almanzor, and his answer, from which it appears, that a lover of the true heroic vein never thought himself so happy, as when he had an opportunity of thus shewing the purity and disinterestedness of his passion. Almanzor is commanded by his mistress to stay to assist his rival, the king, her husband. The lover very naturally asks,

> *Almanz.* What recompence attends me, if I stay?
> *Almah.* You know I am from recompence debarred,
> But I will grant you merit a reward;
> Your flame 's too noble to deserve a cheat,
> And I too plain to practise a deceit,
> I no return of love can ever make,
> But what I ask is for my husband's sake;

---

[1] In Harington's version:
> Of dames, of knights, or arms, of love's delight,
> Of courtesies, of high attempts I speak.

[2] In the fifteenth-century Spanish romance, *Amadis of Gaul*.

He, I confess, has been ungrateful too,
But he and I are ruined if you go:
Your virtue to the hardest proof I bring;—
Unbribed, preserve a mistress and a king.
Almanz. I'll stop at nothing that appears so brave:
I'll do 't, and now I no reward will have.
You've given my honour such an ample field,
That I may die, but that shall never yield.[1]

The king, however, not perhaps understanding this nice point of honour, grows jealous, and wishes to dismiss the disinterested ally, whom his spouse's beauty had enlisted in his service. But this did not depend on him; for Almanzor exclaims,

Almanz. I wonnot go; I'll not be forced away:
I came not for thy sake; nor do I stay.
It was the queen who for my aid did send;
And 'tis I only can the queen defend:
I, for her sake, thy sceptre will maintain;
And thou, by me, in spite of thee, shalt reign.

The most applauded scenes in these plays turned upon nice discussions of metaphysical passion, such as in the days of yore were wont to be agitated in the courts or parliaments of love. Some puzzling dilemma, or metaphysical abstraction, is argued between the personages on the stage, whose dialogue, instead of presenting a scene of natural passion, exhibits a sort of pleading, or combat of logic, in which each endeavours to defend his own opinion by catching up the idea expressed by the former speaker, and returning him his illustration, or simile, at the rebound; and where the lover hopes every thing from his ingenuity, and trusts nothing to his passion. Thus, in the following scene between Almanzor and Almahide, the solicitations of the lover, and the denials of the queen, are expressed in the very carte and tierce of poetical argumentation:

Almah. My light will sure discover those who talk.—
Who dares to interrupt my private walk?
Almanz. He, who dares love, and for that love must die,
And, knowing this, dares yet love on, am I.
Almah. That love which you can hope, and I can pay,
May be received and given in open day:
My praise and my esteem you had before;
And you have bound yourself to ask no more.

[1] *The Conquest of Granada*, Second Part, II. iii.

> *Almanz.* Yes, I have bound myself; but will you take
> The forfeit of that bond, which force did make?
> *Almah.* You know you are from recompence debarred;
> But purest love can live without reward. . . .[1]

This kind of Amabæan dialogue was early ridiculed by the ingenious author of *Hudibras*.[2] It partakes more of the Spanish than of the French tragedy, although it does not demand that the parody shall be so very strict, as to re-echo noun for noun, or verb for verb. . . . The English heroic poet did enough if he displayed sufficient point in the dialogue, and alertness in adopting and retorting the image presented by the preceding speech; though, if he could twist the speaker's own words into an answer to his argument, it seems to have been held the more ingenious mode of confutation.

While the hero of a rhyming tragedy was thus unboundedly submissive in love, and dexterous in applying the metaphysical logic of amorous jurisprudence, it was essential to his character that he should possess all the irresistible courage and fortune of a *preux chevalier*.[3] Numbers, however unequal, were to be as chaff before the whirlwind of his valour; and nothing was to be so impossible, that, at the command of his mistress, he could not with ease achieve. When, in the various changes of fortune which such tragedies demand, he quarrelled with those whom he had before assisted to conquer,

> Then to the vanquished part his fate he led,
> The vanquished triumphed, and the victor fled.

The language of such a personage, unless when engaged in argumentative dialogue with his mistress, was, in all respects, as magnificent and inflated as might beseem his irresistible prowess. Witness the famous speech of Almanzor:

> *Almanz.* To live!
> If from thy hands alone my death can be,
> I am immortal, and a god to thee.
> If I would kill thee now, thy fate 's so low,
> That I must stoop ere I can give the blow:
> But mine is fixed so far above thy crown,
> That all thy men,

---

[1] *Ibid.*, IV. iii.
[2] Butler, 'Repartees between Cat and Puss at a caterwauling, in the modern heroic way.'
[3] Valiant knight.

337

Piled on thy back, can never pull it down:
But, at my ease, thy destiny I send,
By ceasing from this hour to be thy friend.

   .   .   .   .

I'll whistle thy tame fortune after me;
And whirl fate with me whereso'er I fly,
As winds drive storms before them in the sky.[1]

It was expected by the audience, that the pomp of scenery, and bustle of action, in which such tremendous heroes were engaged, should in some degree correspond with their lofty sentiments and super-human valour. Hence solemn feasts, processions, and battles by sea and land, filled the theatre. Hence, also, the sudden and violent changes of fortune, by which the hero and his antagonists are agitated through the whole piece. Fortune has been often compared to the sea; but in a heroic play, her course resembled an absolute Bay of Biscay, or Race of Portland, disturbed by an hundred contending currents, and eddies, and never continuing a moment in one steady flow. . . .

Lastly, the action of the heroic drama was to be laid, not merely in the higher, but in the very highest walk of life. No one could with decorum aspire to share the sublimities which it annexed to character, except those made of the "porcelain clay of the earth", dukes, princes, kings, and kaisars. The matters agitated must be of moment, proportioned to their characters and elevated station, the fate of cities and the fall of kingdoms. . . .

When we consider these various essentials of a rhyming play, we may perhaps, without impropriety, define it to be a metrical romance of chivalry in form of a drama. The hero is a perfect knight-errant, invincible in battle, and devoted to his dulcinea by a love, subtle, metaphysical, and abstracted from all the usual qualities of the instinctive passion; his adventures diversified by splendid descriptions of bull-feasts, battles, and tournaments; his fortune undergoing the strangest, most causeless, and most unexpected varieties; his history chequered by the marvellous interference of ghosts, spectres, and hell itself; his actions effecting the change of empires, and his co-agents being all lords, and dukes, and noble princes, in order that their rank might, in some slight degree, correspond to the native exaltation of the champion's character.

The reader may smile at this description, and feel some surprise,

[1] *The Conquest of Granada*, First Part, III. i.

how compositions, involving such gross absurdities, were tolerated
by an audience having pretence to taste and civilization. But something may be said for the heroic drama.

Although the manners were preposterous, and the changes of
fortune rapid and improbable, yet the former often attained a sublime,
though forced elevation of sentiment; and the latter, by rapidity of
transition and of contrast, served in no slight degree to interest as
well as to surprise the audience. If the spectators were occasionally
stunned with bombast, or hurried and confused by the accumulation
of action and intrigue, they escaped the languor of a creeping dialogue,
and the tædium of a barren plot, of which the termination is descried
full three acts before it can be attained. Besides, if these dramas were
sometimes extravagant, beautiful passages often occurred to atone for
these sallies of fury. In others, ingenuity makes some amends for the
absence of natural feeling, and the reader's fancy is pleased at the
expence of his taste. In representation, the beauty of the verse, assisted
by the enunciation of such actors as Betterton and Mohun, gilded
over the defects of the sense, and afforded a separate gratification. The
splendour of scenery also, in which these plays claimed a peculiar
excellence, afforded a different but certain road to popular favour;
and thus this drama, with all its faults, was very far from wanting
the usual requisites for success. But another reason for its general
popularity may be sought in a certain correspondence with the
manners of the time.

Although in Charles the Second's reign the age of chivalry was
totally at an end, yet the sentiments, which had ceased to be motives
of action, were not so obsolete as to sound totally strange to the public
ear. The French romances of the lower class, such as *Cassandra*,
Cleopatra, &c. were the favourite pastime of the ladies, and retained
all the extravagancies of chivalrous sentiment, with a double portion
of tedious form and metaphysical subtlety. There were occasionally
individuals romantic enough to manage their correspondence and
amours on this exploded system. The admired Mrs Philips[1] carried
on an extensive correspondence with ingenious persons of both sexes,
in which she called herself *Orinda*, and her husband, Mr Wogan, by
the title of *Antenor*. Shadwell, an acute observer of nature, in one of
his comedies,[2] describes a formal coxcomb of this class, who courts

[1] Katherine Philips, 'the matchless Orinda' (1631–64); her *Poems* were published in
1664, her *Letters* in 1705.
[2] *Bury-Fair* (1689).

his mistress out of the *Grand Cyrus*, and rejoices in an opportunity of shewing, that his passion could subsist in despite of her scorn. It is probable he had met with such an original in the course of his observation. The *Précieuses* of Molière, who affected a strange mixture of the romantic heroine and modern fine lady, belong to the same class of oddities, and had their prototypes under the observation of the satirist. But even those who were above such foppery had been early taught to read and admire the conceits of Donne, and the metaphysical love-poems of Cowley. They could not object to the quaint and argumentative dialogues which we have described; for the course of their studies had formed their taste upon a model equally artificial and fantastic: and thus, what between real excellence, and false brilliancy, the age had been accustomed not only to admit, but to admire heroic plays.

Perhaps even these favourable circumstances, of taste and opportunity, would hardly have elevated the rhyming drama so high in the public opinion, had it been supported by less powers than those of Dryden, or even by equal talents less happily adapted to that style of composition. His versification flowed so easily, as to lessen the bad effects of rhyme in dialogue; and, at the same time, abounded with such splendid and sonorous passages, as, in the mouth of a Betterton, awed into silence even those critics, who could distinguish that the tumid and unnatural was sometimes substituted for the heroic and sublime. The felicity of his language, the richness of his illustrations, and the depth of his reflections, often supplied what the scene wanted in natural passion; and, while enjoying the beauty of his declamation, it was only on cool reflection, that the hearer discovered it had passed upon him for the expression of genuine feeling. Even then, the pleasure which he actually received from the representation, was accepted as an apology for the more legitimate delight, which the rules of criticism entitled him to have expected. To these considerations, the high rank and consequent influence, which Dryden already held in the fashionable and literary circles of the time, must unquestionably be added. Nor did he fail to avail himself of his access to the great, whose applause was often cheaply secured by a perusal of the piece, previous to its being presented to the public; and thus it afterwards came forth with all the support of a party eminent for rank and literature, already prepossessed in its favour.

For all these reasons the heroic drama appears to have gradually risen in reputation, from the return of Charles till about the year

Paradise Lost of Milton into a dramatic poem, called the *State of Innocence, or the Fall of Man.* . . . Dryden at this period engaged in a research recommended to him by "a noble wit of Scotland", as he terms Sir George Mackenzie, the issue of which, in his apprehension, pointed out farther room for improving upon the epic of Milton. This was an enquiry into the "turn of words and thoughts" requisite in heroic poetry. These "turns", according to the definition and examples which Dryden has given us, differ from the points of wit, and quirks of epigram, common in the metaphysical poets, and consist in a happy, and at the same time a natural recurrence of the same form of expression, melodiously varied. Having failed in his search after these beauties in Cowley, the darling of his youth, "I consulted," says Dryden, "a greater genius, (without offence to the manes of that noble author,) I mean—Milton. . . . I found in him a true sublimity . . . but I found not there neither that for which I looked." . . .[1] Dryden, holding [his judgment] for just, conceived, doubtless, that in his *State of Innocence*, he might exert his skill success-fully, by supplying the supposed deficiency, and for relieving those "flats of thought" which he complains of, where Milton, for a hundred lines together, runs on in a "track of scripture". . . . The graces, also, which Dryden ventured to interweave with the lofty theme of Milton, were rather those of Ovid than of Virgil, rather turns of verbal expression than of thought. Such is that conceit which met with censure at the time:

> Seraph and cherub, careless of their charge,
> And wanton, in full ease now live at large;
> Unguarded leave the passes of the sky,
> And all dissolved in hallelujahs lie.

"I have heard," said a petulant critic, "of anchovies dissolved in sauce; but never of an angel dissolved in hallelujahs." But this raillery Dryden rebuffs with a quotation from Virgil:

> Invadunt urbem, somno vinoque sepultam.[2]

It might have been replied, that Virgil's analogy was familiar and simple, and that of Dryden was far-fetched, and startling by its novelty.

The majesty of Milton's verse is strangely degraded in the following

---

[1] 'Discourse concerning Satire'; *Poems* (1958), ed. James Kinsley, ii. 610.
[2] *Aeneid*, ii. 265, 'They rushed upon the city, lying buried in sleep and wine.'

speeches, which precede the rising of Pandæmonium. Some of the couplets are utterly flat and bald, and, in others, the balance of point and antithesis is substituted for the simple sublimity of the original:

> *Moloch.* Changed as we are, we're yet from homage free;
> We have, by hell, at least gained liberty:
> That 's worth our fall; thus low though we are driven,
> Better to rule in hell, than serve in heaven.
> *Lucifer.* There spoke the better half of Lucifer!
> *Asmoday.* 'Tis fit in frequent senate we confer, . . .
> *Lucif.* A golden palace let be raised on high;
> To imitate? No, to outshine the sky!
> All mines are ours, and gold above the rest:
> Let this be done; and quick as 'twas exprest.

I fancy the reader is now nearly satisfied with Dryden's improvements on Milton. Yet some of his alterations have such peculiar reference to the taste and manners of his age, that I cannot avoid pointing them out. Eve is somewhat of a coquette even in the state of innocence. She exclaims,—

> —from each tree
> The feathered kind press down to look on me;
> The beasts, with up-cast eyes, forsake their shade,
> And gaze, as if I were to be obeyed.
> Sure, I am somewhat which they wish to be,
> And cannot,—I myself am proud of me.

Upon receiving Adam's addresses, she expresses, rather unreasonably in the circumstances, some apprehensions of his infidelity; and, upon the whole, she is considerably too knowing for the primitive state. The same may be said of Adam, whose knowledge in school divinity, and use of syllogistic argument, Dryden, though he found it in the original, was under no necessity to have retained. . . .' (i. 163–4, 165, 170–5.)

(*l*) '*Aureng-Zebe* was his first performance after the failure of the *Assignation*. It was acted in 1675 with general applause. *Aureng-Zebe* is a heroic, or rhyming play, but not cast in a mould quite so romantic as the *Conquest of Granada*. There is a grave and moral turn in many of the speeches, which brings it nearer the style of a French tragedy. It is true, the character of Morat borders upon extravagance; but a certain license has been always given to theatrical tyrants, and we excuse bombast in him more readily than in Almanzor. There is perhaps some reason for this indulgence. The possession of unlimited power, vested in active and mercurial characters, naturally drives them to an extravagant indulgence of passion, bordering upon insanity; and it follows, that their language must outstrip the modesty of nature. Propriety of diction in the drama is relative, and to be referred more to individual character than to general rules: to make a tyrant sober-minded, is to make a madman rational. But this discretion must be used with great caution by the writer, lest he should confound the terrible with the burlesque. Two great actors, Kynaston and Booth, differed in their style of playing Morat.[1] The former, who was the original performer, and doubtless had his instructions from the author, gave full force to the sentiments of avowed and barbarous vain-glory, which mark the character. When he is determind to spare Aureng-Zebe, and Nourmahal pleads,

> Twill not be safe to let him live an hour,

Kynaston gave all the stern and haughty insolence of despotism to his answer,

> I'll do 't to shew my arbitrary power.

But Booth, with modest caution, avoided marking and pressing upon the audience a sentiment hovering between the comic and terrible, however consonant to the character by whom it was delivered. . . .

Aureng-Zebe was followed, in 1678, by *All for Love*, the only play Dryden ever wrote for himself; the rest, he says, were given to the people. The habitual study of Shakespeare, which seems lately to have occasioned, at least greatly aided, the revolution in his taste, induced him, among a crowd of emulous shooters, to try his strength in this bow of Ulysses. . . . We must allow Dryden the praise of greater regularity of plot, and a happier combination of scene; but in sketching the character of Antony, he loses the majestic and heroic tone which Shakespeare has assigned him. There is too much of the lovelorn knight-errant, and too little of the Roman warrior, in Dryden's hero. The love of Antony, however overpowering and destructive in its effects, ought not to have resembled the love of a sighing swain of Arcadia. This error in the original conception of the character must doubtless be ascribed to Dryden's habit of romantic composition. Montezuma and Almanzor were, like the prophet's image, formed of a mixture of iron and clay; of stern and rigid demeanour to all the

---

[1] Scott is following Cibber's *Apology*.

universe, but unbounded devotion to the ladies of their affections. In Antony, the first class of attributes are discarded; he has none of that tumid and outrageous dignity which characterized the heroes of the rhyming plays, and in its stead is gifted with even more than an usual share of devoted attachment to his mistress. In the preface, Dryden piques himself upon venturing to introduce the quarrelling scene between Octavia and Cleopatra, which a French writer would have rejected, as contrary to the decorum of the theatre. But our author's idea of female character was at all times low; and the coarse, indecent violence, which he has thrown into the expressions of a queen and a Roman matron, is misplaced and disgusting, and contradicts the general and well-founded observation on the address and self-command, with which even women of ordinary dispositions can veil mutual dislike and hatred, and the extreme keenness with which they can arm their satire, while preserving all the external forms of civil demeanour. But Dryden more than redeemed this error in the scene between Antony and Ventidius, which he himself preferred to any that he ever wrote, and perhaps with justice, if we except that between Dorax and Sebastian: both are avowedly written in imitation of the quarrel between Brutus and Cassius. . . .

Dryden was now to do a new homage to Shakespeare, by refitting for the stage the play of *Troilus and Cressida*, which the author left in a state of strange imperfection, resembling more a chronicle, or legend, than a dramatic piece. Yet it may be disputed whether Dryden has greatly improved it even in the particulars which he censures in his original. His plot, though more artificial, is at the same time more trite than that of Shakespeare. The device by which Troilus is led to doubt the constancy of Cressida is much less natural than that she should have been actually inconstant; her vindication by suicide is a clumsy, as well as a hackneyed expedient; and there is too much drum and trumpet in the grand *finale*, where "Troilus and Diomede fight, and both parties engage at the same time. The Trojans make the Greeks retire. . . . Trumpets sound. Achilles enters with his Myrmidons. . . . Troilus, singling Diomede, gets him down, and kills him; and Achilles kills Troilus upon him. All the Trojans die upon the place, Troilus last." Such a *bellum internecinum* can never be waged to advantage upon the stage. . . .

The *Spanish Friar*, our author's must successful comedy, succeeded *Troilus and Cressida*. . . . In the tragic scenes [he] has attained that better strain of dramatic poetry, which he afterwards evinced in

Sebastian. In the comic part, the well-known character of Father Dominic, though the conception only embodies the abstract idea which the ignorant and prejudiced fanatics of the day formed to themselves of a Romish priest, is brought out and illustrated with peculiar spirit. The gluttony, avarice, debauchery, and meanness of Dominic, are qualified with the talent and wit necessary to save him from being utterly detestable; and, from the beginning to the end of the piece, these qualities are so happily tinged with insolence, hypocrisy, and irritability, that they cannot be mistaken for the avarice, debauchery, gluttony, and meanness of any other profession than that of a bad church-man. In the tragic plot, we principally admire the general management of the opening, and chiefly censure the cold-blooded barbarity and perfidy of the young queen, in instigating the murder of the deposed sovereign, and then attempting to turn the guilt on her accomplice. I fear Dryden here forgot his own general rule, that the tragic hero and heroine should have so much virtue as to entitle their distress to the tribute of compassion. Altogether, however, the *Spanish Friar*, in both its parts, is an interesting and almost a fascinating play; although the tendency, even of the tragic scenes, is not laudable, and the comedy, though more decent in language, is not less immoral in tendency than was usual in that loose age.

Dryden attached considerable importance to the art with which the comic and tragic scenes of the *Spanish Friar* are combined; and in doing so he has received the sanction of Dr Johnson. Indeed, as the ardour of his mind ever led him to prize that task most highly, on which he had most lately employed his energy, he has affirmed, in the dedication to the *Spanish Friar*, that there was an absolute necessity for combining two actions in tragedy, for the sake of variety. "The truth is," he adds, "the audience are grown weary of continued melancholy scenes; and I dare to prophecy, that few tragedies, except those in verse, shall succeed in this age, if they are not lightened with a course of mirth; for the feast is too dull and solemn without the fiddles." The necessity of the relief alluded to may be admitted, without allowing that we must substitute either the misplaced charms of versification, or a secondary comic plot, to relieve the solemn weight and monotony of tragedy. It is no doubt true, that a highly-buskined tragedy, in which all the personages maintain the funereal pomp usually required from the victims of Melpomene, is apt to be intolerably tiresome, after all the pains which a skilful and elegant poet can bestow upon finishing it. But it is chiefly tiresome, because it is unnatural; and, in respect of propriety, ought no more to be relieved by the introduction of a set of comic scenes, independent of those of a mournful complexion, than the *sombre* air of a funeral should be enlivened by a concert of fiddles. There appear to be two legitimate modes of interweaving tragedy with something like comedy. The first and most easy, which has often been resorted to, is to make the lower or less marked characters of the drama, like the porter in *Macbeth* or the fool in *King Lear*, speak the language appropriated to their station, even in the midst of the distresses of the piece; nay, they may be permitted to have some slight under-intrigue of their own. This, however, requires the exertion of much taste and discrimination; for if we are once seriously and deeply interested in the distress of the play, the intervention of any thing like buffoonery may unloosen the hold which the author has gained on the feelings of the audience. If such subordinate comic characters are of a rank to intermix in the tragic dialogue, their mirth ought to be chastened, till their language bears a relation to that of the higher persons. For example, nothing can be more absurd than in *Don Sebastian*, and some of Southerne's tragedies, to hear the comic character answer in prose, and with a would-be witticism, to the solemn, unrelaxed blank verse of his tragic companion. Mercutio is, I think, one of the best instances of such a comic person as may be reasonably and with propriety admitted into tragedy: from which, however, I do not exclude those lower characters, whose conversation appears absurd if much elevated above their rank. There is, however, another mode, yet more difficult to be used with address, but much more fortunate in effect when it has been successfully employed. This is, when the principal personages themselves do not always remain in the buckram of tragedy, but reserve, as in common life, lofty expressions for great occasions, and at other times evince themselves capable of feeling the lighter, as well as the more violent or more deep, affections of the mind. The shades of comic humour in Hamlet, in Hotspur, and in Falconbridge, are so far from injuring, that they greatly aid the effect of the tragic scenes, in which these same persons take a deep and tragical share. We grieve with them, when grieved, still more, because we have rejoiced with them when they rejoiced; and, on the whole, we acknowledge a deeper *frater feeling*,[1] as Burns has termed it, in men who are actuated by the usual changes of human

[1] *A Bard's Epitaph*, l. 11.

temperament, than in those who, contrary to the nature of humanity, are eternally actuated by an unvaried strain of tragic feeling. But whether the poet diversifies his melancholy scenes by the passing gaiety of subordinate characters; or whether he qualifies the tragic state of his heroes by occasionally assigning lighter tasks to them; or whether he chuses to employ both modes of relieving the weight of misery through five long acts; it is obviously unnecessary that he should distract the attention of his audience, and destroy the regularity of his play, by introducing a comic plot with personages and interest altogether distinct, and intrigue but slightly connected with that of tragedy. Dryden himself afterwards acknowledged, that though he was fond of the *Spanish Friar*, he could not defend it from the imputation of Gothic and unnatural irregularity; "for mirth and gravity destroy each other, and are no more allowed for decent, than a gay widow laughing in a mourning habit." ' (i. 209–10, 218–20, 223–4, 227–33.)

(*m*) The plan of *Absalom and Achitophel* 'was not new to the public. A catholic poet had, in 1679, paraphrased the scriptural story of Naboth's vineyard, and applied it to the condemnation of Lord Stafford, on account of the Popish Plot. . . . Neither was the obvious application of the story of Absalom and Achitophel to the persons of Monmouth and Shaftesbury first made by our poet. . . . But the vigour of the satire, the happy adaptation, not only of the incidents, but of the very names to the individuals characterised, gave Dryden's poem the full effect of novelty. It appeared a very short time after Shaftesbury had been committed to the Tower, and only a few days before the grand jury were to take under consideration the bill preferred against him for high treason. Its sale was rapid beyond example; and even those who were most severely characterised, were compelled to acknowledge the beauty, if not the justice, of the satire. The character of Monmouth, an easy and gentle temper, inflamed beyond its usual pitch by ambition, and seduced by the arts of a wily and interested associate, is touched with exquisite delicacy. The poet is as careful of the offending Absalom's fame, as the father in scripture of the life of his rebel son. The fairer side of his character is industriously presented, and a veil drawn over all that was worthy of blame. But Shaftesbury pays the lenity with which Monmouth is dismissed. The traits of praise, and the tribute paid to that statesman's talents, are so qualified and artfully blended with censure, that they seem to render his faults even more conspicuous, and more hateful. In this skilful mixture of applause and blame lies the nicest art of satire. There must be an appearance of candour on the part of the poet, and just so much merit allowed, even to the object of his censure, as to make his picture natural. It is a child alone who fears the aggravated terrors of a Saracen's head; the painter, who would move the awe of an enlightened spectator, must delineate his tyrant with human features. It seems likely, that Dryden considered the portrait of Shaftesbury, in the first edition of *Absalom and Achitophel*, as somewhat deficient in this respect; at least the second edition contains twelve additional lines, the principal tendency of which is to praise the ability and integrity with which Shaftesbury had discharged the office of lord high chancellor ... a tribute which [Dryden] seems to have judged it proper to pay to the merit even of an enemy. Others of the party of Monmouth, or rather of the opposition party ... were stigmatized with severity, only inferior to that applied to Achitophel. ... The account of the Tory chiefs ... included, of course, most of Dryden's personal protectors. ... The poet having thus arrayed and mustered the forces on each side, some account of the combat is naturally expected; and Johnson complains that, after all the interest excited, the story is but lamely winded up by a speech from the throne, which produces the instantaneous and even marvellous effect, of reconciling all parties, and subduing the whole phalanx of opposition. Even thus, says the critic, the walls, towers, and battlements of an enchanted castle disappear, when the destined knight winds his horn before it. Spence records in his *Anecdotes*,[1] that Charles himself imposed on Dryden the task of paraphrasing the speech to his Oxford parliament, at least the most striking passages, as a conclusion to his poem of *Absalom and Achitophel*.

But let us consider whether the nature of the poem admitted of a different management in the close. Incident was not to be attempted; for the poet had described living characters and existing factions, the issue of whose contention was yet in the womb of fate, and could not safely be anticipated in the satire. Besides, the dissolution of the Oxford parliament with that memorable speech, was a remarkable æra in the contention of the factions, after which the Whigs gradually declined, both in spirit, in power, and in popularity. Their boldest leaders were for a time appalled; and when they resumed their measures, they gradually approached rather revolution than reform,

[1] See *supra*, No. 68.

and thus alienated the more temperate of their own party, till at length their schemes terminated in the Rye-house Conspiracy. The speech having such an effect, was therefore not improperly adopted as a termination to the poem of *Absalom and Achitophel*.

The success of this wonderful satire was so great, that the court had again recourse to the assistance of its author. ... [In *The Medal*,] Shaftesbury's history; his frequent political apostacies; his licentious course of life, so contrary to the stern rigour of the fanatics, with whom he had associated; his arts in instigating the fury of the anti-monarchists; in fine, all the political and moral bearings of his character,—are sounded and exposed to contempt and reprobation, the beauty of the poetry adding grace to the severity of the satire. ...

[Scott gives an account of the Whig poets' counter-attacks on Dryden, and wrongly represents *Mac Flecknoe* (published in 1682 in a pirated text, but written in the later seventies) as a reply to Shadwell's lampoons (*supra*, Nos. 30 and 31).]

The body of [the Second Part of *Absalom and Achitophel*] was written by Nahum Tate, one of those second-rate bards, who, by dint of pleonasm and expletive, can find smooth lines if any one will supply them with ideas. ... But if the Second Part ... fell below the First in its general tone, the celebrated passage inserted by Dryden[1] possessed even a double portion of the original spirit. The victims whom he selected out of the partisans of Monmouth and Shaftesbury for his own particular severity, were Robert Ferguson, afterwards well known by the name of The Plotter; Forbes; Johnson, author of the parallel between James, Duke of York, and Julian the Apostate; but, above all, Settle and Shadwell, whom, under the names of Doeg and Og, he has depicted in the liveliest colours his poignant satire could afford. They who have patience to look into the lampoons which these worthies had published against Dryden, will, in reading his retort, be reminded of the combats between the giants and knights of romance. His antagonists came on with infinite zeal and fury, discharged their ill-aimed blows on every side, and exhausted their strength in violent and ineffectual rage. But the keen and trenchant blade of Dryden never makes a thrust in vain, and never strikes but at a vulnerable point ...; it is difficult for one assailed on a single ludicrous foible to make good his respectability, though possessed of a thousand valuable qualities; as it was impossible for Achilles,

[1] Lines 310–509.

invulnerable every where else, to survive the wound which a dexterous archer had aimed at his heel. With regard to Settle, there is a contempt in Dryden's satire which approaches almost to good-humour, and plainly shews how far our poet was now from entertaining those apprehensions of rivalship, which certainly dictated his portion of the *Remarks on the Empress of Morocco*. Settle had now found his level, and Dryden no longer regarded him with a mixture of rage and apprehension, but with more appropriate feelings of utter contempt. ... As Dryden was probably more apprehensive of Shadwell, who, though a worse poet than Settle, has excelled even Dryden in the lower walks of comedy, he had treated him with sterner severity. ...

As the publication [of these poems] gave to Dryden, hitherto chiefly known as a dramatist, the formidable character of an inimitable satirist, we may here pause to consider their effect upon English poetry. The witty Bishop Hall had first introduced into our literature that species of poetry; which, though its legitimate use be to check vice and expose folly, is so often applied by spleen or by faction to destroy domestic happiness, by assailing private character. Hall possessed a good ear for harmony; and, living in the reign of Elizabeth, might have studied it in Spenser, Fairfax, and other models. But from system, rather than in ignorance or inability, he chose to be "hard of conceit, and harsh of style", in order that his poetry might correspond with the sharp, sour, and crabbed nature of his theme. Donne, his successor, was still more rugged in his versification, as well as more obscure in his conceptions and allusions. The satires of Cleveland ... are, if possible, still harsher and more strained in expression than those of Donne. Butler can hardly be quoted as an example of the sort of satire we are treating of. *Hudibras* is a burlesque tale, in which the measure is intentionally and studiously rendered as ludicrous as the characters and incidents. Oldham, who flourished in Dryden's time, and enjoyed his friendship, wrote his satires in the crabbed tone of Cleveland and Donne. Dryden, in the copy of verses dedicated to his memory, alludes to this deficiency, and seems to admit the subject as an apology:

> O early ripe! to thy abundant store
> What could advancing age have added more!
> It might (what nature never gives the young)
> Have taught the numbers of thy native tongue.
> But satire needs not those, and wit will shine
> Through the harsh cadence of a rugged line.

Yet the apology which he admitted for Oldham, Dryden disdained to make use of himself. He did not, as has been said of Horace, wilfully untune his harp when he commenced satirist. Aware that a wound may be given more deeply with a burnished than with a rusty blade, he bestowed upon the versification of his satires the same pains which he had given to his rhyming plays and serious poems. He did not indeed, for that would have been pains misapplied, attempt to smooth his verses into the harmony of those in which he occasionally celebrates female beauty; but he gave them varied tone, correct rhyme, and masculine energy, all which had hitherto been strangers to the English satire. Thus, while Dryden's style resembled that of Juvenal rather than Horace, he may claim a superiority, for uniform and undeviating dignity, over the Roman satirist. The age, whose appetite for scandal had been profusely fed by lampoons and libels, now learned, that there was a more elevated kind of satire, in which poignancy might be united with elegance, and energy of thought with harmony of versification. The example seems to have produced a strong effect. No poet, not even Settle, (for even the worst artist will improve from beholding a masterpiece,) afterwards conceived he had sufficiently accomplished his task by presenting to the public, thoughts, however witty or caustic he might deem them, clothed in the hobbling measure of Donne or Cleveland; and expression and harmony began to be consulted, in satire, as well as sarcastic humour or powerful illustration.

Mac-Flecknoe, in some degree, differs from the other satires which Dryden published at this time. It is not confined to the description of character, but exhibits an imaginary course of incidents, in which the principal personage takes a ludicrous share. In this it resembles *Hudibras*; and both are quoted by Dryden himself as examples of the Varronian satire.[1] But there was this pointed difference, that Butler's poem is burlesque, and Dryden's mock-heroic. *Mac-Flecknoe* is, I rather believe, the first poem in the English language, in which the dignity of a harmonized and lofty style is employed, not only to excite pleasure in itself, but to increase, by contrast, the comic effect of the scenes which it narrates; the subject being ludicrous, while the verse is noble. The models of satire afforded by Dryden, as they have never been equalled by any succeeding poet, were in a tone of excellence superior far to all that had preceded them.

These reflections on the nature of Dryden's satires, have, in some

[1] See *supra*, p. 16.

degree, interrupted our account of his political controversies. . . .'
(i. 244–9, 250–1, 268–70, 275–9.)

(*n*) '*Albion and Albanius* was a sort of introductory masque, in which,
under a very thin veil of allegory, first, the restoration of the Stuarts
to the throne, and, secondly, their recent conquest over their Whig
opponents, were successively represented. . . . Its death-blow was the
news of the Duke of Monmouth's invasion, which reached London
on Saturday, 13th June, 1685, while *Albion and Albanius* was perform-
ing for the sixth time: the audience broke up in consternation, and
the piece was never again repeated. This opera was prejudicial to the
company, who were involved by the expence in a considerable debt,
and never recovered half the money laid out. Neither was it of service
to our poet's reputation, who had, on this occasion, to undergo the
gibes of angry musicians, as well as the reproaches of disappointed
actors and hostile poets. One went so far as to suggest, with some
humour, that probably the laureat and Grabut had mistaken their
trade; the former writing the music, and the latter the verse.' (i.
300–3.)

[Scott passes on to an account of Dryden's conversion to Roman
Catholicism, of the movement from *Religio Laici* to *The Hind and
the Panther*, which remains the most judicious and understanding
view.]

(*o*) 'In [1699], *Amphitryon*, in which Dryden displays his comic powers
to more advantage than anywhere, excepting in the *Spanish Friar*, was
acted with great applause. . . . The plot of [*Cleomenes*] is flat and unsatisfactory, involving no great event, and in truth being only the
question, whether Cleomenes should or should not depart upon an
expedition, which appears far more hazardous than remaining where
he was. The grave and stoical character of the hero is more suitable
to the French than the English stage; nor had the general conduct of
the play that interest, or perhaps bustle, which is necessary to fix the
attention of the promiscuous audience of London. In a theatre, where
every man may, if he will, express his dissatisfaction, in defiance of
beaux-esprits, *nobles*, or *mousquetaires*, that which is dull will seldom
be long fashionable: *Cleomenes* was accordingly coldly received. . . .
Love Triumphant, [Dryden's] last play, was acted in 1692 with very
bad success. Those who look over this piece, which is in truth one
of the worst our author ever wrote, can be at no loss to discover

sufficient reason for its condemnation. The comic part approaches to farce, and the tragic unites the wild and unnatural changes and counter-changes of the Spanish tragedy, with the involutions of un-natural and incestuous passion, which the British audience has been always averse to admit as a legitimate subject of dramatic pity or terror.' (i. 359, 363–4, 364–5.)

(*p*) 'The elegy on the Countess of Abingdon, entitled *Eleonora*. . . . The leading and most characteristic features of the lady's character were doubtless pointed out to our author as subjects for illustration; yet so difficult is it, even for the best poet, to feign a sorrow which he feels not, or to describe with appropriate and animated colouring a person whom he has never seen, that Dryden's poem resembles rather an abstract panegyric on an imaginary being, than an elegy on a real character.' (i. 376, 378.)

(*q*) Dryden, 'now retired from the stage, had bent his thoughts upon one great literary task, the translation of Virgil. This weighty and important undertaking was probably suggested by the experience of Tonson, the success of whose *Miscellanies* had taught him the value placed by the public on Dryden's translations from the classics. . . . The names of Virgil and of Dryden were talismans powerful to arrest the eyes of all that were literary in England, upon the progress of the work. . . .' (i. 382–3.)

(*r*) 'It is possible that Dryden may have completed, at one sitting, the whole Ode [*Alexander's Feast*], and yet have employed a fortnight, or much more, in correction.[1] There is strong internal evidence to shew, that the poem was, speaking with reference to its general structure, wrought off at once. A halt or pause, even of a day, would perhaps have injured that continuous flow of poetical language and description, which argues the whole scene to have arisen at once upon the author's imagination. It seems possible, more especially in lyrical poetry, to discover where the author has paused for any length of time; for the union of the parts is rarely so perfect as not to shew a different strain of thought and feeling. There may be something

---

[1] Referring to the story in Birch that Dryden 'was employed for almost a fortnight in composing and correcting' *Alexander's Feast*, and the apparently contradictory story of Bolingbroke that Dryden sat up all night at it, and 'could not leave it till I had *completed* it; here it is, *finished* at one sitting'.

fanciful, however, in this reasoning, which I therefore abandon to the reader's mercy; only begging him to observe, that we have no mode of estimating the exertions of a quality so capricious as a poetic imagination. ... Mr Malone has preserved a tradition, that the father of Lord Chief Justice Marlay, then a Templar, and frequenter of Will's coffee-house, took an opportunity to pay his court to Dryden, on the publication of *Alexander's Feast*; and, happening to sit next him, congratulated him on having produced the finest and noblest Ode that had ever been written in any language. "You are right, young gentleman, (replied Dryden,) a nobler Ode never *was* produced nor ever *will*!" This singularly strong expression cannot be placed to the score of vanity. It was an inward consciousness of merit, which burst forth, probably almost involuntarily, and I fear must be admitted as prophetic.' (i. 408–9, 411–12.)

(s) 'If Dryden received but a slender share of the gifts of fortune, it was amply made up to him in reputation. Even while a poet militant upon earth, he received no ordinary portion of that applause, which is too often reserved for the "dull cold ear of death". He combated, it is true, but he conquered; and, in despite of faction, civil and religious, of penury, and the contempt which follows it, of degrading patronage, and rejected solicitation, from 1666 to the year of his death the name of Dryden was first in English literature. Nor was his fame limited to Britain. Of the French literati, although Boileau, with unworthy affectation, when he heard of the honours paid to the poet's remains, pretended ignorance even of his name, yet Rapin, the famous critic, learned the English language on purpose to read the works of Dryden. Sir John Shadwell, the son of our author's ancient adversary, bore an honourable and manly testimony to the general regret among the men of letters at Paris for the death of Dryden. "The men of letters here lament the loss of Mr Dryden very much. The honours paid to him have done our countrymen no small service; for, next to having so considerable a man of our own growth, 'tis a reputation to have known how to value him; as patrons very often pass for wits, by esteeming those that are so." And from another authority we learn, that the engraved copies of Dryden's portrait were bought up with avidity on the Continent.

But it was in England where the loss of Dryden was chiefly to be felt. It is seldom the extent of such a deprivation is understood, till it has taken place; as the size of an object is best estimated, when we see the space void which it had long occupied. The men of literature, starting as it were from a dream, began to heap commemorations, panegyrics, and elegies: the great were as much astonished at their own neglect of such an object of bounty, as if the same had never been practised before; and expressed as much compunction, as it were never to occur again. The poets were not silent; but their strains only evinced their woeful degeneracy from him whom they mourned. . . .

In the school of reformed English poetry, of which Dryden must be acknowledged as the founder, there soon arose disciples not un-willing to be considered as the rivals of their master. Addison had his partizans, who were desirous to hold him up in this point of view; and he himself is said to have taken pleasure, with the assistance of Steele, to depreciate Dryden, whose fame was defended by Pope and Congreve.[1] No serious invasion of Dryden's pre-eminence can be said, however, to have taken place, till Pope himself, refining upon that structure of versification which our author had first introduced, and attending with sedulous diligence to improve every passage to the highest pitch of point and harmony, exhibited a new style of composition, and claimed at least to share with Dryden the sovereignty of Parnassus. I will not attempt to concentrate what Johnson has said upon this interesting comparison. . . .[2]

As the eighteenth century advanced, the difference between the styles of these celebrated authors became yet more manifest. It was then obvious, that though Pope's felicity of expression, his beautiful polish of sentiment, and the occasional brilliancy of his wit, were not easily imitated, yet many authors, by dint of a good ear, and a fluent expression, learned to command the unaltered sweetness of his melody, which, like a favourite tune, when descended to hawkers and ballad-singers, became disgusting as it became common. The admirers of poetry then reverted to the brave negligence of Dryden's versification, as, to use Johnson's simile, the eye, fatigued with the uniformity of a lawn, seeks variety in the uncultivated glade or swelling mountain. The preference for which Dennis, asserting the cause of Dryden, had raved and thundered in vain, began, by degrees, to be assigned to the elder bard; and many a poet sheltered his harsh verses and inequalities under an assertion that he belonged to the school of Dryden. Churchill—

[1] See *supra*, pp. 257–9.
[2] *Supra*, pp. 310–12.

Who, born for the universe, narrowed his mind,
And to party gave up what was meant for mankind,—[1]

Churchill was one of the first to seek in the *Mac-Flecknoe*, the *Absalom*, and the *Hind and the Panther*, authority for bitter and personal sarcasm, couched in masculine, though irregular versification, dashed from the pen without revision, and admitting occasional rude and flat passages, to afford the author a spring to comparative elevation. But imitation always approaches to caricature; and the powers of Churchill have been unable to protect him from the oblivion into which his poems are daily sinking, owing to the ephemeral interest of political subjects, and his indolent negligence of severe study and regularity. To imitate Dryden, it were well to study his merits, without venturing to adopt the negligencies and harshness, which the hurry of his composition, and the comparative rudeness of his age, rendered in him excusable. . . .

My present task is limited to deducing [Dryden's] poetic character from those works which he formed on his last and most approved model. The general tone of his genius, however, influenced the whole course of his publications; and upon that, however modified and varied by the improvement of his taste, a few preliminary notices may not be misplaced.

The distinguishing characteristic of Dryden's genius seems to have been, the power of reasoning, and of expressing the result in appropriate language. This may seem slender praise; yet these were the talents that led Bacon into the recesses of philosophy, and conducted Newton to the cabinet of nature. The prose works of Dryden bear repeated evidence to his philosophical powers. His philosophy was not indeed of a formed and systematic character; for he is often contented to leave the path of argument which must have conducted him to the fountain of truth, and to resort with indolence or indifference to the leaky cisterns which had been hewn out by former critics. But where his pride or his taste are interested, he shews evidently, that it was not want of the power of systematizing, but of the time and patience necessary to form a system, which occasions the discrepancy that we often notice in his critical and philological disquisitions. This power of ratiocination, of investigating, discovering, and appreciating that which is really excellent, if accompanied with the necessary command of fanciful illustration, and elegant expression, is the most interesting quality which can be possessed by a poet. It must

---

[1] Goldsmith's lines on Burke, in *Retaliation*.

indeed have a share in the composition of every thing that is truly estimable in the fine arts, as well as in philosophy. Nothing is so easily attained as the power of presenting the extrinsic qualities of fine painting, fine music, or fine poetry; the beauty of colour and outline, the combination of notes, the melody of versification, may be imitated by artists of mediocrity; and many will view, hear, or peruse their performances, without being able positively to discover why they should not, since composed according to all the rules, afford pleasure equal to those of Raphael, Handel, or Dryden. The deficiency lies in the vivifying spirit, which, like *alcohol*, may be reduced to the same principle in all, though it assumes such varied qualities from the mode in which it is exerted or combined. Of this power of intellect, Dryden seems to have possessed almost an exuberant share, combined, as usual, with the faculty of correcting his own conceptions, by observing human nature, the practical and experimental philosophy as well of poetry as of ethics or physics. The early habits of Dryden's education and poetical studies gave his researches somewhat too much of a metaphysical character; and it was a consequence of his mental acuteness, that his dramatic personages often philosophized or reasoned, when they ought only to have felt. The more lofty, the fiercer, the more ambitious feelings, seem also to have been his favourite studies. Perhaps the analytical mode in which he exercised his studies of human life, tended to confine his observation to the more energetic feelings of pride, anger, ambition, and other high-toned passions. He, that mixes in public life, must see enough of these stormy convulsions; but the finer and more imperceptible operations of love, in its sentimental modifications, if the heart of the author does not supply an example from its own feelings, cannot easily be studied at the expence of others. Dryden's bosom, it must be owned, seems to have afforded him no such means of information; the licence of his age, and perhaps the advanced period at which he commenced his literary career, had probably armed him against this more exalted strain of passion. The love of the senses he has in many places expressed, in as forceful and dignified colouring as the subject could admit; but of a mere moral and sentimental passion he seems to have had little idea, since he frequently substitutes in its place the absurd, unnatural, and fictitious refinements of romance. In short, his love is always in indecorous nakedness, or sheathed in the stiff panoply of chivalry. [The most pathetic verses which Dryden has composed, are unquestionably contained in the epistle to Congreve, where he recommends his laurels, in such moving terms, to the care of his surviving friend. The quarrel and reconciliation of Sebastian and Dorax, is also full of the noblest emotion. In both cases, however, the interest is excited by means of masculine and exalted passion, not of those which arise from the mere delicate sensibilities of our nature; and to use a Scottish phrase, "bearded men" weep at them, rather than Horace's audience of youths and maidens.][1] But if Dryden fails in expressing the milder and more tender passions, not only did the stronger feelings of the heart, in all its dark or violent workings, but the face of natural objects, and their operation upon the human mind, pass promptly in review at his command. External pictures, and their corresponding influence on the spectator, are equally ready at his summons; and though his poetry, from the nature of his subjects, is in general rather ethic and didactic, than narrative, yet no sooner does he adopt the latter style of composition, than his figures and his landscapes are presented to the mind with the same vivacity as the flow of his reasoning, or the acute metaphysical discrimination of his characters.

But the powers of observation and of deduction are not the only qualities essential to the poetical character. The philosopher may indeed prosecute his experimental researches into the *arcana* of nature, and announce them to the public through the medium of a friendly *redacteur*, as the legislator of Israel obtained permission to speak to the people by the voice of Aaron;[2] but the poet has no such privilege; nay, his doom is so far capricious, that, though he may be possessed of the primary quality of poetical conception to the highest possible extent, it is but like a lute without its strings, unless he has the subordinate, though equally essential, power of expressing what he feels and conceives, in appropriate and harmonious language. With this power Dryden's poetry was gifted in a degree, surpassing in modulated harmony that of all who had preceded him, and inferior to none that has since written English verse. He first shewed that the English language was capable of uniting smoothness and strength. The hobbling verses of his predecessors were abandoned even by the lowest versifiers; and by the force of his precept and example, the meanest lampooners of the year seventeen hundred wrote smoother lines than Donne and Cowley, the chief poets of the earlier half of the seventeenth century. What was said of Rome adorned by Augustus, has been, by Johnson, applied to English poetry improved by Dryden; that he found it of

---

[1] This passage was added by Scott in his second edition (1821).
[2] Lev. ix *et seq.*

brick, and left it of marble.[1] This reformation was not merely the effect of an excellent ear, and a superlative command of gratifying it by sounding language; it was, we have seen, the effect of close, accurate, and continued study of the power of the English tongue. Upon what principles he adopted and continued his system of versification, he long meditated to communicate in his projected prosody of English poetry. The work, however, might have been more curious than useful. . . . Strict attention might no doubt discover the principle of Dryden's versification; but it seems no more essential to the analysing his poetry, than the principles of mathematics to understanding music, although the art necessarily depends on them. . . .

Of the various kinds of poetry which Dryden occasionally practised, the drama was that which, until the last six years of his life, he chiefly relied on for support. His style of tragedy . . . varied with his improving taste, perhaps with the change of manners. Although the heroic drama . . . presented the strongest temptation to the exercise of argumentative poetry in sounding rhyme, Dryden was at length contented to abandon it for the more pure and chaste style of tragedy, which professes rather the representation of human beings, than the creation of ideal perfection, or fantastic and anomalous characters. The best of Dryden's performances in this latter style, are unquestionably *Don Sebastian*, and *All for Love*. Of these, the former is in the poet's very best manner; exhibiting dramatic persons, consisting of such bold and impetuous characters as he delighted to draw, well contrasted, forcibly marked, and engaged in an interesting succession of events. . . . Of *All for Love*, we may say, that it is successful in a softer style of painting; and that so far as sweet and beautiful versification, elegant language, and occasional tenderness, can make amends for Dryden's deficiencies in describing the delicacies of sentimental passion, they are to be found in abundance in that piece. But on these, and on the poet's other tragedies, we have enlarged in our preliminary notices prefixed to each piece.

Dryden's comedies, besides being stained with the license of the age, (a license which he seems to use as much from necessity as choice,) have, generally speaking, a certain heaviness of character. There are many flashes of wit; but the author has beaten his flint hard ere he struck them out. It is almost essential to the success of a jest, that it should at least seem to be extemporaneous. If we espy the joke at a distance, nay, if without seeing it we have the least reason to suspect

---

[1] *Supra*, p. 310.

we are travelling towards one, it is astonishing how the perverse obstinacy of our nature delights to refuse it currency. When, therefore, as is often the case in Dryden's comedies, two persons remain on the stage for no obvious purpose but to say good things, it is no wonder they receive but little thanks from an ungrateful audience. The incidents, therefore, and the characters, ought to be comic; but actual jests, or *bon mots*, should be rarely introduced, and then naturally, easily, without an appearance of premeditation, and bearing a strict conformity to the character of the person who utters them. Comic situation Dryden did not greatly study; indeed I hardly recollect any, unless in the closing scene of *The Spanish Friar*, which indicates any peculiar felicity of invention. For comic character, he is usually contented to paint a generic representative of a certain class of men or women; a Father Dominic, for example, or a Melantha, with all the attributes of their calling and manners, strongly and divertingly pourtrayed, but without any individuality of character. It is probable that, with these deficiencies, he felt the truth of his own acknowledgement, and that he was forced upon composing comedies to gratify the taste of the age, while the bent of his genius was otherwise directed.

In lyrical poetry, Dryden must be allowed to have no equal. *Alexander's Feast* is sufficient to shew his supremacy in that brilliant department. In this exquisite production, he flung from him all the trappings with which his contemporaries had embarrassed the ode. The language, lofty and striking as the ideas are, is equally simple and harmonious; without far-fetched allusions, or epithets, or metaphors, the story is told as intelligibly as if it had been in the most humble prose. The change of tone in the harp of Timotheus, regulates the measure and the melody, and the language of every stanza. The hearer, while he is led on by the successive changes, experiences almost the feelings of the Macedonian and his peers; nor is the splendid poem disgraced by one word or line unworthy of it, unless we join in the severe criticism of Dr Johnson, on the concluding stanzas.[1] It is true, that the praise of St Cecilia is rather abruptly introduced as a conclusion to the account of the Feast of Alexander; and it is also true, that the comparison,

> He raised a mortal to the sky,
> She drew an angel down,

is inaccurate, since the feat of Timotheus was metaphorical, and that

[1] *Supra*, p. 304.

of Cecilia literal. But, while we stoop to such criticism, we seek for blots in the sun.

Of Dryden's other pindarics, some, as the celebrated "Ode to the Memory of Mrs Killigrew", are mixed with the leaven of Cowley; others, like the "Threnodia Augustalis", are occasionally flat and heavy. All contain passages of brilliancy, and all are thrown into a versification, melodious amidst its irregularity. We listen for the completion of Dryden's stanza, as for the explication of a difficult passage in music; and wild and lost as the sound appears, the ear is proportionally gratified by the unexpected ease with which harmony is extracted from discord and confusion.

The satirical powers of Dryden were of the highest order. He draws his arrow to the head, and dismisses it straight upon his object of aim. In this walk he wrought almost as great a reformation as upon versification in general; as will plainly appear, if we consider, that the satire, before Dryden's time, bore the same reference to *Absalom and Achitophel*, which an ode of Cowley bears to *Alexander's Feast*. Butler, and his imitators, had adopted a metaphysical satire, as the poets in the earlier part of the century had created a metaphysical vein of serious poetry. Both required a store of learning to supply the perpetual expenditure of extraordinary and far-fetched illustration; the object of both was to combine and hunt down the strangest and most fanciful analogies; and both held the attention of the reader perpetually on the stretch, to keep up with the meaning of the author. There can be no doubt, that this metaphysical vein was much better fitted for the burlesque than the sublime. Yet the perpetual scintillation of Butler's wit is too dazzling to be delightful; and we can seldom read far in *Hudibras* without feeling more fatigue than pleasure. His fancy is employed with the profusion of a spendthrift, by whose eternal round of banquetting his guests are at length rather wearied out than regaled. Dryden was destined to correct this among other errors of his age; to shew the difference between burlesque and satire; and to teach his successors in that species of assault, rather to thrust than to flourish with their weapon. For this purpose he avoided the unvaried and unrelieved style of grotesque description and combination,[1] which had been fashionable since the satires of Cleveland and Butler. To render the objects of his satire hateful and contemptible, he thought it necessary to preserve the lighter shades of character, if not for the purpose of softening the portrait, at least for that of preserving the

[1] Connexions of ideas.

likeness. While Dryden seized, and dwelt upon, and aggravated, all the evil features of his subject, he carefully retained just as much of its laudable traits as preserved him from the charge of want of candour, and fixed down the resemblance upon the party. And thus, instead of unmeaning caricatures, he presents portraits which cannot be mistaken, however unfavourable ideas they may convey of the originals. The character of Shaftesbury, both as Achitophel, and as drawn in *The Medal*, bears peculiar witness to this assertion. While other court poets endeavoured to turn the obnoxious statesman into ridicule on account of his personal infirmities and extravagancies, Dryden boldly confers upon him all the praise for talent and for genius that his friends could have claimed, and trusts to the force of his satirical expression for working up even these admirable attributes with such a mixture of evil propensities and dangerous qualities, that the whole character shall appear dreadful, and even hateful, but not contemptible. But where a character of less note, a Shadwell or a Settle, crossed his path, the satirist did not lay himself under these restraints, but wrote in the language of bitter irony and unmeasurable contempt: even then, however, we are less called on to admire the wit of the author, than the force and energy of his poetical philippic. These are the verses which are made by indignation, and, no more than theatrical scenes of real passion, admit of refined and protracted turns of wit, or even the lighter sallies of humour. These last ornaments are proper in that Horatian satire, which rather ridicules the follies of the age, than stigmatizes the vices of individuals; but in this style Dryden has made few essays. He entered the field as champion of a political party, or as defender of his own reputation; discriminated his antagonists, and applied the scourge with all the vehemence of Juvenal. As he has himself said of that satirist, "his provocations were great, and he has revenged them tragically". This is the more worthy of notice, as, in the Essay on Satire,[1] Dryden gives a decided preference to those nicer and more delicate touches of satire, which consist in fine raillery. But whatever was the opinion of his cooler moments, the poet's practice was dictated by the furious party-spirit of the times, and the no less keen stimulative of personal resentment. It is perhaps to be regretted, that so much energy of thought, and so much force of expression, should have been wasted in anatomizing such criminals as Shadwell and Settle; yet we cannot account the amber less precious, because they are grubs and flies that are inclosed within it.

[1] In the *Juvenal* (1693); *Poems* (1958), ed. James Kinsley, ii. 654-5.

The *Fables* of Dryden are the best examples of his talents as a narrative poet; those powers of composition, description, and narration, which must have been called into exercise by the Epic Muse, had his fate allowed him to enlist among her votaries. The "Knight's Tale", the longest and most laboured of Chaucer's stories, possesses a degree of regularity which might satisfy the most severe critic. It is true, that the honour arising from thence must be assigned to the more ancient bard, who had himself drawn his subject from an Italian model; but the high and decided preference which Dryden has given to this story ... enables us to judge how much the poet held an accurate combination of parts, and coherence of narrative, essentials of epic poetry. .... Of the other tales, it can hardly be said that their texture is more ingenious or closely woven than that of ordinary novels or fables: but in each of them Dryden has displayed the superiority of his genius, in selecting for amplification and ornament those passages most susceptible of poetical description. The account of the procession of the Fairy Chivalry in the "Flower and the Leaf"; the splendid description of the champions who came to assist at the tournament in the "Knight's Tale"; the account of the battle itself, its alternations and issue,—if they cannot be called improvements on Chaucer, are nevertheless so spirited a transfusion of his ideas into modern verse, as almost to claim the merit of originality. Many passages might be shewn in which this praise may be carried still higher, and the merit of invention added to that of imitation. Such is the description of the commencement of the tourney, which is almost entirely original, and most of the ornaments in the translations from Boccaccio, whose prose fictions demanded more additions from the poet than the exuberant imagery of Chaucer. To select instances would be endless; but every reader of poetry has by heart the description of Iphigenia asleep, nor are the lines in "Theodore and Honoria", which describe the approach of the apparition, and its effects upon animated and inanimated nature, even before it becomes visible, less eminent for beauties of the terrific order:

> While listening to the murmuring leaves he stood,
> More than a mile immersed within the wood,
> At once the wind was laid; the whispering sound
> Was dumb; a rising earthquake rocked the ground;
> With deeper brown the grove was overspread,
> A sudden horror seized his giddy head,
> And his ears tingled, and his colour fled.

Nature was in alarm; some danger nigh
Seemed threatened, though unseen to mortal eye.

It may be doubted, however, whether the simplicity of Boccaccio's narrative has not sometimes suffered by the additional decorations of Dryden. The retort of Guiscard to Tancred's charge of ingratitude is more sublime in the Italian original,* than as diluted by the English poet into five hexameters. A worse fault occurs in the whole colouring of Sigismonda's passion, to which Dryden has given a coarse and indelicate character, which he did not derive from Boccaccio. In like manner, the pleas used by Palamon in his prayer to Venus,[1] is more nakedly expressed by Dryden than by Chaucer. The former, indeed, would probably have sheltered himself under the mantle of Lucretius; but he should have recollected, that Palamon speaks the language of chivalry, and ought not, to use an expression of Lord Herbert, to have spoken like a *paillard*,[2] but a *cavalier*. Indeed, we have before noticed it as the most obvious and most degrading imperfection of Dryden's poetical imagination, that he could not refine that passion, which, of all others, is susceptible either of the purest refinement, or of admitting the basest alloy. With Chaucer, Dryden's task was more easy than with Boccaccio. Barrenness was not the fault of the Father of English poetry; and amid the profusion of images which he presented, his imitator had only the task of rejecting or selecting. In the sublime description of the temple of Mars, painted around with all the misfortunes ascribed to the influence of his planet, it would be difficult to point out a single idea, which is not found in the older poem. But Dryden has judiciously omitted or softened some degrading and some disgusting circumstances; as the "cook scalded in spite of his long ladle", the "swine devouring the cradled infant", the "pickpurse", and other circumstances too grotesque or ludicrous, to harmonize with the dreadful group around them. Some points, also, of sublimity, have escaped the modern poet. Such is the appropriate and picturesque accompaniment of the statue of Mars:

A wolf stood before him at his feet,
With eyen red, and of a man he eat.

---

* '*Amor puo troppo piu, che ne voi ne io possiamo*'. This sentiment loses its dignity amid the 'levelling of mountains and raising plains,' with which Dryden has chosen to illustrate it. [Scott is incorporating a point made to him by Wordsworth; see *supra*, p. 325.—Ed.]

[1] *Palamon and Arcite*, iii. 129 ff.

[2] Bawdy person.

In the dialogue, or argumentative parts of the poem, Dryden has frequently improved on his original, while he falls something short of him in simple description, or in pathetic effect. Thus, the quarrel between Arcite and Palamon is wrought up with greater energy by Dryden than Chaucer, particularly by the addition of the following lines, describing the enmity of the captives against each other:

> Now friends no more, nor walking hand in hand,
> But when they met, they made a surly stand,
> And glared like angry lions as they passed,
> And wished that every look might be their last.

But the modern must yield the palm, despite the beauty of his versification, to the description of Emily by Chaucer; and may be justly accused of loading the dying speech of Arcite with conceits for which his original gave no authority.

When the story is of a light and ludicrous kind, as the "Fable of the Cock and Fox", and the "Wife of Bath's Tale", Dryden displays all the humorous expression of his satirical poetry, without its personality. There is indeed a quaint Cervantic gravity in his mode of expressing himself, that often glances forth, and enlivens what otherwise would be mere dry narrative. Thus, he details certain things which past,

> While Cymon was *endeavouring* to be wise;

the force of which single word contains both a ludicrous and appropriate picture of the revolution which the force of love was gradually creating in the mind of the poor clown. This tone of expression he perhaps borrowed from Ariosto, and other poets of Italian chivalry, who are wont, ever and anon, to raise the mask, and smile even at the romantic tale they are themselves telling.

Leaving these desultory reflections on Dryden's powers of narrative, I cannot but notice, that, from haste or negligence, he has sometimes mistaken the sense of his author. Into the hands of the champions in the "Flower and the Leaf", he has placed *bows* instead of *boughs*, because the word is in the original spelled *bowes*; and, having made the error, he immediately devises an explanation of the device which he had mistaken:

> For bows the strength of brawny arms imply,
> Emblems of valour, and of victory.[1]

[1] Ll. 542–5; in the original, l. 512.

He has, in like manner, accused Chaucer of introducing Gallicisms into the English language; not aware that French was the language of the court of England not long before Chaucer's time, and that, far from introducing French phrases into the English tongue, the ancient bard was successfully active in introducing the English as a fashionable dialect, instead of the French, which had, before his time, been the only language of polite literature in England. Other instances might be given of similar oversights, which, in the situation of Dryden, are sufficiently pardonable.

Upon the whole, in introducing these romances of Boccaccio and Chaucer to modern readers, Dryden has necessarily deprived them of some of the charms which they possess for those who have perused them in their original state. With a tale or poem, by which we have been sincerely interested, we connect many feelings independent of those arising from actual poetical merit. The delight, arising from the whole, sanctions, nay sanctifies, the faulty passages; and even actual improvements, like supplements to a mutilated statue of antiquity, injure our preconceived associations, and hurt, by their incongruity with our feelings, more than they give pleasure by their own excellence. But to antiquaries Dryden has sufficiently justified himself, by declaring his version made for the sake of modern readers, who understand sense and poetry as well as the old Saxon admirers of Chaucer, when that poetry and sense are put into words which they can understand. Let us also grant him, that, for the beauties which are lost, he has substituted many which the original did not afford; that, in passages of gorgeous description, he has added even to the chivalrous splendour of Chaucer, and has graced with poetical ornament the simplicity of Boccaccio; that, if he has failed in tenderness, he is never deficient in majesty; and that if the heart be sometimes untouched, the understanding and fancy are always exercised and delighted.

The philosophy of Dryden, we have already said, was that of original and penetrating genius; imperfect only, when, from want of time and of industry, he adopted the ideas of others, when he should have communed at leisure with his own mind. The proofs of his philosophical powers are not to be sought for in any particular poem or disquisition. Even the *Religio Laici*, written expressly as a philosophical poem, only shews how easily the most powerful mind may entangle itself in sophistical toils of its own weaving; for the train of argument there pursued was completed by Dryden's conversion to the Roman Catholic faith. It is therefore in the discussion of incidental subjects, in his mode of treating points of controversy, in the new lights which he seldom fails to throw upon a controversial subject, in his talent of argumentative discussion, that we are to look for the character of Dryden's moral powers. His opinions, doubtless, are often inconsistent, and sometimes absolutely contradictory; for, pressed by the necessity of discussing the object before him, he seldom looked back to what he said formerly, or forward to what he might be obliged to say in future. His sole subject of consideration was to maintain his present point; and that by authority, by declamation, by argument, by every means. But his philosophical powers are not the less to be estimated, because thus irregularly and unphilosophically employed. His arguments, even in the worst cause, bear witness to the energy of his mental conceptions; and the skill with which they are stated, elucidated, enforced, and exemplified, ever commands our admiration, though, in the result, our reason may reject their influence. It must be remembered also, to Dryden's honour, that he was the first to hail the dawn of experimental philosophy in physics; to gratulate his country on possessing Bacon, Harvey, and Boyle; and to exult over the downfal of the Aristotelian tyranny.[1] Had he lived to see a similar revolution commenced in ethics, there can be little doubt he would have welcomed it with the same delight; or had his leisure and situation permitted him to dedicate his time to investigating moral problems, he might himself have led the way to deliverance from error and uncertainty. But the dawn of reformation must ever be gradual, and the acquisitions even of those calculated to advance it must therefore frequently appear desultory and imperfect. The author of the *Novum Organum*[2] believed in charms and occult sympathy; and Dryden in the chimeras of judicial astrology,[3] and probably in the jargon of alchemy. When these subjects occur in his poetry, he dwells on them with a pleasure, which shows the command they maintained over his mind. Much of the astrological knowledge displayed in the Knight's Tale is introduced, or at least amplified, by Dryden; and while, in the fable of the Cock and the Fox, he ridicules the doctrine of prediction from dreams, the inherent qualities of the four complexions, and other abstruse doctrines of Paracelsus and his followers, we have good reason to suspect, that, like many

[1] Scott quotes *To Dr Charleton*, ll. 1–8, as a footnote.
[2] Francis Bacon.
[3] Star-divination, astrology in the modern sense, distinguished from 'natural astrology', or astronomy.

other scoffers, he believed in the efficacy and truth of the subject of his ridicule. However this shade of credulity may injure Dryden's character as a philosopher, we cannot regret its influence on his poetry. Collins has thus celebrated Fairfax:

> Prevailing poet, whose undoubting mind,
> Believed the magic wonders which he sung.[1]

Nor can there be a doubt, that, as every work of imagination is tinged with the author's passions and prejudices, it must be deep and energetic in proportion to the character of these impressions. ...

The occasional poetry of Dryden is marked strongly by masculine character. The Epistles vary with the subject; and are light, humorous, and satirical, or grave, argumentative, and philosophical, as the case required. In his Elegies, although they contain touches of true feeling, especially where the stronger passions are to be illustrated, the poet is often content to substitute reasoning for passion, and rather to shew us cause why we ought to grieve, than to set us the example by grieving himself. The inherent defect in Dryden's composition becomes here peculiarly conspicuous; yet we should consider, that, in composing elegies for the Countess of Abingdon, whom he never saw, and for Charles II., by whom he had been cruelly neglected, and doubtless on many similar occasions, Dryden could not even pretend to be interested in the mournful subject of his verse; but attended, with his poem, as much in the way of trade, as the under-taker, on the same occasion, came with his sables and his scutcheon. The poet may interest himself and his reader, even to tears, in the fate of a being altogether the creation of his own fancy, but hardly by a hired panegyric on a real subject, in whom his heart acknow-ledges no other interest than a fee can give him. Few of Dryden's elegiac effusions, therefore, seem prompted by sincere sorrow. That to Oldham may be an exception; but, even there, he rather strives to do honour to the talents of his departed friend, than to pour out lamentations for his loss. Some of the [Prologues and Epilogues] are coarsely satirical, and others grossly indelicate. Those spoken at Oxford are the most valuable, and contain much good criticism and beautiful poetry. But the worst of them was probably well worth the petty recompense which the poet received. The songs and smaller pieces of Dryden have smoothness, wit, and, when addressed to

[1] Collins, *Ode on the Popular Superstitions of the Highlands of Scotland* (1749); on Fairfax, translator of Tasso.

ladies, gallantry in profusion, but are deficient in tenderness. They seem to have been composed with great ease; thrown together hastily and occasionally; nor can we doubt, that many of them are now irrecoverably lost. . . .

The Translations of Dryden form a distinguished part of his poetical labours. No author, excepting Pope, has done so much to endenizen the eminent poets of antiquity. In this sphere, also, it was the fate of Dryden to become a leading example to future poets, and to abrogate laws which had been generally received, although they imposed such trammels on translation as to render it hardly intelligible. Before his distinguished success showed that the object of the translator should be to transfuse the spirit, not to copy servilely the very words of his original, it had been required, that line should be rendered for line, and, almost, word for word. It may easily be imagined, that, by the constraint and inversion which this cramping statute required, a poem was barely rendered *not Latin*, instead of being made English, and that, to the mere native reader, as the connoisseur complains in *The Critic*, the interpreter was sometimes "the harder to be understood of the two".[1] Those who seek examples, may find them in the jaw-breaking translations of Ben Jonson and Holyday. Cowley and Denham had indeed rebelled against this mode of translation, which conveys pretty much the same idea of an original, as an imitator would do of the gait of another, by studiously stepping after him into every trace which his feet had left upon the sand. But they assumed a license equally faulty, and claimed the privilege of writing what might be more properly termed imitations, than versions of the classics. It was reserved to Dryden manfully to claim and vindicate the freedom of a just translation; more limited than paraphrase, but free from the metaphrastic severity exacted from his predecessors.

With these free yet unlicentious principles, Dryden brought to the task of translation a competent knowledge of the language of the originals, with an unbounded command of his own.[2] The latter is however by far the most marked characteristic of his Translations. Dryden was not indeed deficient in Greek and Roman learning; but he paused not to weigh and sift those difficult and obscure passages, at which the most learned will doubt and hesitate for the correct meaning. The same rapidity, which marked his own poetry, seems to have

[1] Sheridan, *The Critic* (1779), I. i.
[2] Echoing Dryden's Preface to *Ovid's Epistles* (*Poems*, 1958, ed. J. Kinsley, i. 185, ll. 267–8).

attended his study of the classics. He seldom waited to analyze the sentence he was about to render, far less scrupulously to weigh the precise purport and value of every word it contained. If he caught the general spirit and meaning of the author, and could express it with equal force in English verse, he cared not if minute elegancies were lost, or the beauties of accurate proportion destroyed, or a dubious interpretation hastily adopted on the credit of a *scholium*. He used abundantly the licence he has claimed for a translator, to be deficient rather in the language out of which he renders, than of that into which he translates. If such be but master of the sense of his author, Dryden argues, he may express that sense with eloquence in his own tongue, though he understand not the nice turns of the original. "But without the latter quality he can never arrive at the useful and the delightful, without which reading is a penance and fatigue."* With the same spirit of haste, Dryden is often contented to present to the English reader some modern image, which he may at once fully comprehend, instead of rendering precisely a classic expression, which might require explanation or paraphrase. Thus the *pulchra Sicyonia*, or buskins of Sicyon, are rendered,

> Diamond-buckles sparkling in their shoes.[1]

By a yet more unfortunate adaptation of modern technical phraseology, the simple direction of Helenus,

> *Læva tibi tellus, et longo læva petantur*
> *Æquora circuitu: dextrum fuge littus et undas,*

is translated,

> Tack to the larboard, and stand off to sea,
> Veer starboard sea and land.—[2]

A counsel which, I shrewdly suspect, would have been unintelligible, not only to Palinurus, but to the best pilot in the British navy. In the same tone, but with more intelligibility, if not felicity, Dryden translates *palatia cœli* in Ovid, the *Louvre of the sky*;[3] and, in the version of the first book of Homer, talks of the court of Jupiter in the phrases used at that of Whitehall. These expressions, proper to

---

* Life of Lucian.
[1] *Lucretius The Fourth Book*, l. 100.
[2] *Aen*. iii. 412–13; Dryden, *Virgil's Æneis*, iii. 526–7.
[3] *Examen Poeticum*, 'The First Book of Ovid's Metamorphoses', l. 228.

modern manners, often produce an unfortunate confusion between the age in which the scene is laid, and the date of the translation. No judicious poet is willing to break the interest of a tale of ancient times, by allusions peculiar to his own period; but when the translator, instead of identifying himself as closely as possible with the original author, pretends to such liberty, he removes us a third step from the time of action, and so confounds the manners of no less than three distinct æras,—that in which the scene is laid, that in which the poem was written, and that, finally, in which the translation was executed. There are passages in Dryden's Æneid, which, in the revolution of a few pages, transport our ideas from the time of Troy's siege to that of the court of Augustus, and thence downward to the reign of William the Third of Britain.

It must be owned, at the same time, that when the translator places before you, not the exact words, but the image of the original, as the classic author would probably have himself expressed it in English, the licence, when moderately employed, has an infinite charm for those readers for whose use translations are properly written. Pope's Homer and Dryden's Virgil can never indeed give exquisite satisfaction to scholars, accustomed to study the Greek and Latin originals. The minds of such readers have acquired a classic tone; and not merely the ideas and poetical imagery, but the manners and habits of the actors have become intimately familiar to them. They will not, therefore, be satisfied with any translation in which these are violated, whether for the sake of indolence in the translator, or ease to the unlettered reader; and perhaps they will be more pleased that a favourite bard should move with less ease and spirit in his new habiliments, than that his garments should be cut upon the model of the country to which the stranger is introduced. In the former case, they will readily make allowance for the imperfection of modern language; in the latter, they will hardly pardon the sophistication of ancient manners. But the mere English reader, who finds rigid adherence to antique costume rather embarrassing than pleasing, who is prepared to make no sacrifices in order to preserve the true manners of antiquity, shocking perhaps to his feelings and prejudices, is satisfied that the Iliad and Æneid shall lose their antiquarian merit, provided they retain that vital spirit and energy, which is the soul of poetry in all languages, and countries, and ages whatsoever. He who sits down to Dryden's translation of Virgil, with the original text spread before him, will be at no loss to point out many passages that are faulty,

many indifferently understood, many imperfectly translated, some
in which dignity is lost, others in which bombast is substituted in its
stead. But the unabated vigour and spirit of the version more than
overbalances these and all its other deficiences. A sedulous scholar
might often approach more nearly to the dead letter of Virgil, and
give an exact, distinct, sober-minded idea of the meaning and scope
of particular passages. Trapp, Pitt, and others have done so. But the
essential spirit of poetry is so volatile, that it escapes during such an
operation, like the life of the poor criminal, whom the ancient
anatomist is said to have dissected alive, in order to ascertain the seat
of the soul. The carcase indeed is presented to the English reader, but
the animating vigour is no more. It is in this art, of communicating
the ancient poet's ideas with force and energy equal to his own, that
Dryden has so completely exceeded all who have gone before, and
all who have succeeded him. The beautiful and unequalled version
of the Tale of Myrrha in the *Metamorphoses*, the whole of the Sixth
Æneid, and many other parts of Dryden's translations, are sufficient,
had he never written one line of original poetry, to vindicate the well-
known panegyric of Churchill. . . .[1]

We are in this disquisition naturally tempted to inquire, whether
Dryden would have succeeded in his proposed design to translate
Homer, as happily as in his Virgil? And although he himself has
declared the genius of the Grecian to be more fiery, and therefore
better suited to his own than that of the Roman poet, there may be
room to question, whether in this case he rightly estimated his own
talents, or rather, whether, being fully conscious of their extent, he
was aware of labouring under certain deficiencies of taste, which
must have been more apparent in a version of the Iliad than of the
Æneid. If a translator has any characteristic and peculiar foible, it is
surely unfortunate to choose an original, who may give peculiar
facilities to exhibit them. Thus, even Dryden's repeated disclamation
of puns, points, and quibbles, and all the repentance of his more sober
hours, was unable, so soon as he began to translate Ovid, to prevent
his sliding back into the practice of that false wit with which his
earlier productions are imbued. Hence he has been seduced, by the
similarity of style, to add to the offences of his original, and introduce,
though it needed not, points of wit and antithetical prettinesses, for
which he cannot plead Ovid's authority. For example, he makes Ajax
say of Ulysses, when surrounded by the Trojans,

[1] *Supra*, No. 73(a).

No wonder if he roared that all might hear,
His elocution was increased by fear.

The Latin only bears, *conclamat socios*. A little lower,

Opposui molem clypei, texique jacentem,

is amplified by a similar witticism,

—My broad buckler hid him from the foe,
Even the shield trembled as he lay below.[1]

. . . In translating the most indelicate passage of Lucretius, Dryden
has rather enhanced than veiled its indecency. The story of Iphis in
the *Metamorphoses* is much more bluntly told by the English poet
than by Ovid. In short, where there was a latitude given for coarseness of description and expression, Dryden has always too readily laid
hold of it. The very specimen which he has given us of a version of
Homer, contains many passages in which the antique Grecian simplicity is vulgarly and inelegantly rendered. The Thunderer terms Juno

My household curse, my lawful plague, the spy
Of Jove's designs, his other squinting eye.

The ambrosial feast of Olympus concludes like a tavern revel:

Drunken at last, and drowsy, they depart
Each to his house, adorned with laboured art
Of the lame architect. The thundering God,
Even he, withdrew to rest, and had his load;
His swimming head to needful sleep applied,
And Juno lay unheeded by his side.

There is reason indeed to think, that, after the Revolution, Dryden's
taste was improved in this, as in some other respects. In his translation
of Juvenal, for example, the satire against women, coarse as it is, is
considerably refined and softened from the grossness of the Latin
poet; who has, however, been lately favoured by a still more elegant,
and (excepting perhaps one or two passages) an equally spirited translation, by Mr Gifford of London.[2] Yet, admitting this apology for
Dryden as fully as we dare, from the numerous specimens of indelicacy
even in his later translations, we are induced to judge it fortunate that

[1] *Fables*, 'The Speeches of Ajax and Ulysses', ll. 109–10 and 115–16.
[2] William Gifford, 1802.

Homer was reserved for a poet who had not known the age of
Charles II.;[1] and whose inaccuracies and injudicious decorations may
be pardoned, even by the scholar, when he considers the probability,
that Dryden might have slipped into the opposite extreme, by con-
verting rude simplicity into indecency or vulgarity. The Æneid, on
the other hand, if it restrained Dryden's poetry to a correct, steady,
and even flight, if it damped his energy by its regularity, and fettered
his excursive imagination by the sobriety of its decorum, had the
corresponding advantage of holding forth to the translator no temptation to license, and no apology for negligence. Where the fervency of
genius is required, Dryden has usually equalled his original; where
peculiar elegance and exact propriety is demanded, his version may
be sometimes found flat and inaccurate, but the mastering spirit of
Virgil prevails, and it is never disgusting or indelicate. Of all the
classical translations we can boast, none is so acceptable to the class
of readers, to whom the learned languages are a clasped book and a
sealed fountain. And surely it is no moderate praise to say, that a
work is universally pleasing to those for whose use it is principally
intended, and to whom only it is absolutely indispensable.

The prose of Dryden may rank with the best in the English language.
It is no less of his own formation than his versification, is equally
spirited, and equally harmonious. Without the lengthened and
pedantic sentences of Clarendon, it is dignified where dignity is becoming, and is lively without the accumulation of strained and
absurd allusions and metaphors, which were unfortunately mistaken
for wit by many of the author's contemporaries. Dryden has been
accused of unnecessarily larding his style with Gallicisms. It must be
owned, that, to comply probably with the humour of Charles, or
from an affectation of the fashionable court dialect, the poet-laureat
employed such words as *fougue*, *fraîcheur*, &c. instead of the corresponding expressions in English; an affectation which does not appear
in our author's later writings. But ... it will admit of question,
whether any single French word has been naturalized upon the sole
authority of Dryden.

Although Dryden's style has nothing obsolete, we can occasionally
trace a reluctance to abandon an old word or idiom; the consequence,
doubtless, of his latter studies in ancient poetry. In other respects,
nothing can be more elegant than the diction of the praises heaped
upon his patrons, for which he might himself plead the apology he

[1] Pope.

uses for Maimbourg, "who, having enemies, made himself friends by panegyrics". . . .

[quotation from Johnson on Dryden's prefaces; *supra*, pp. 291–2.]

The last paragraph is not to be understood too literally; for although Dryden never so far copied himself as to fall into what has been quaintly called *mannerism*; yet accurate observation may trace in his works, the repetition of some sentiments and illustrations from prose to verse, and back again to prose. In his preface to the Æneid, he has enlarged on the difficulty of varying phrases, when the same sense returned on the author; and surely we must allow full praise to his fluency and command of language, when, during so long a literary career, and in the course of such a variety of miscellaneous productions, we can detect in his style so few instances of repetition, or self-imitation.

The prose of Dryden, excepting his translations, and one or two controversial tracts, is entirely dedicated to criticism, either general and didactic, or defensive and exculpatory. There, as in other branches of polite learning, it was his lot to be a light to his people. About the time of the Restoration, the cultivation of letters was prosecuted in France with some energy. But the genius of that lively nation being more fitted for criticism than poetry; for drawing rules from what others have done, than for writing works which might be themselves standards; they were sooner able to produce an accurate table of laws for those intending to write epic poems and tragedies, according to the best Greek and Roman authorities, than to exhibit distinguished specimens of success in either department; just as they are said to possess the best possible rules for building ships of war, although not equally remarkable for their power of fighting them. . . . It is probable, that the tyranny of the French critics, fashionable as the literature of that country was with Charles and his courtiers, would have extended itself over England at the Restoration, had not a champion so powerful as Dryden placed himself in the gap. . . . In [his "Essay on Dramatic Poetry",] he was accused of entertaining private views, of defending some of his own pieces, at least of opening the door of the theatre wider, and rendering its access more easy, for his own selfish convenience. Allowing this to be true in whole, as it may be in part, we are as much obliged to Dryden for resisting the domination of Gallic criticism, as we are to the fanatics who repressed the despotism of the crown, although they buckled on their armour against white surplices, and the cross in baptism. The character which Dryden has drawn of our English dramatists in the Essay, and the various prefaces connected with it, have unequalled spirit and precision. The contrast of Ben Jonson with Shakespeare is peculiarly and strikingly felicitous. . . . While Dryden examined, discussed, admitted, or rejected the rules proposed by others, he forbore, from prudence, indolence, or a regard for the freedom of Parnassus, to erect himself into a legislator. His doctrines, which chiefly respect the intrinsic qualities necessary in poetry, are scattered, without system or pretence to it, over the numerous pages of prefatory and didactic essays, with which he enriched his publications. It is impossible to read far in any of them, without finding some maxim for doing or forbearing, which every student of poetry will do well to engrave upon the tablets of his memory. But the author's mode of instruction is neither harsh, nor dictatorial. When his opinion changed, as in the case of rhyming tragedies, he avows the change with candour, and we are enabled the more courageously to follow his guidance, when we perceive the readiness with which he retracts his path, if he strays into error. The gleams of philosophical spirit which so frequently illumine these pages of criticism; the lively and appropriate grace of illustration; the true and correct expression of the general propositions; the simple and unaffected passages, in which, when led to allude to his personal labours and situation, he mingles the feelings of the man with the instruction of the critic,—unite to render Dryden's Essays the most delightful prose in the English language.

The didactic criticism of Dryden is necessarily, at least naturally, mingled with that which he was obliged to pour forth in his own defence; and this may be one main cause of its irregular and miscellaneous form. What might otherwise have resembled the extended and elevated front of a regular palace, is deformed by barriers, ramparts, and bastions of defence; by cottages, mean additions, and offices necessary for personal accommodation. The poet, always most in earnest about his immediate task, used, without ceremony, those arguments which suited his present purpose, and thereby sometimes supplied his foes with weapons to assail another quarter. It also happens frequently, if the same allusion may be continued, that Dryden defends with obstinate despair, against the assaults of his foemen, a post which, in his cooler moments, he has condemned as untenable. However easily he may yield to internal conviction, and to the progress of his own improving taste, even those concessions, he sedulously informs us, are not wrung from him by the assault of his enemies; and he often goes out of his road to shew, that, though conscious he was in the wrong, he did not stand legally convicted by their arguments. To the chequered and inconsistent appearance which these circumstances have given to the criticism of Dryden, it is an additional objection, that through the same cause his studies were partial, temporary, and irregular. His mind was amply stored with acquired knowledge, much of it perhaps the fruits of early reading and application. But, while engaged in the hurry of composition, or overcome by the lassitude of continued literary labour, he seems frequently to have trusted to the tenacity of his memory, and so drawn upon this fund with injudicious liberality, without being sufficiently anxious as to accuracy of quotation, or even of assertion. If, on the other hand, he felt himself obliged to resort to more profound learning than his own, he was at little pains to arrange or digest it, or even to examine minutely the information he acquired, from hasty perusal of the books he consulted; and thus but too often poured it forth in the crude form in which he had himself received it, from the French critic, or Dutch schoolman. The scholarship, for example, displayed in the "Essay on Satire", has this raw and ill-arranged appearance; and stuck, as it awkwardly is, among some of Dryden's own beautiful and original writing, gives, like a borrowed and unbecoming garment, a mean and inconsistent appearance to the whole disquisition. But these occasional imperfections and inaccuracies are marks of the haste with which Dryden was compelled to give his productions to the world, and cannot deprive him of the praise due to the earliest and most entertaining of English critics.

I have thus detailed the life, and offered some remarks on the literary character, of JOHN DRYDEN: who, educated in a pedantic taste, and a fanatical religion, was destined, if not to give laws to the stage of England, at least to defend its liberties; to improve burlesque into satire; to free translation from the fetters of verbal metaphrase, and exclude it from the licence of paraphrase; to teach posterity the powerful and varied poetical harmony of which their language was capable; to give an example of the lyric ode of unapproached excellence; and to leave to English literature a name, second only to those of Milton and of Shakespeare.' (i. 470–534.)

B

(a) *The Conquest of Granada*. 'In the conduct of the story there is much brilliancy of event. The reader, or spectator, is never allowed to repose on the scene before him; and although the changes of fortune are too rapid to be either probable, or altogether pleasing, yet they arrest the attention by their splendour and importance, and interest us in spite of our more sober judgment. ... If ... the reader can abstract his mind from the qualities now deemed essential to a play, and consider the *Conquest of Granada* as a piece of romantic poetry, there are few compositions in the English language, which convey a more lively and favourable display of the magnificence of fable, of language, and of action, proper to that style of composition. Amid the splendid ornaments of the structure we lose sight of occasional disproportion and incongruity; and, at an early age particularly, there are few poems which make a more deep impression upon the imagination, than the *Conquest of Granada*.' (iv. 7–8.)

(b) 'The most proper introduction to *All for Love* may be a parallel betwixt it and Shakespeare's *Antony and Cleopatra*.

The first point of comparison is the general conduct, or plot, of the tragedy. And here Dryden, having, to use his own language, undertaken to shoot in the bow of Ulysses, imitates the wily Antinous in using art to eke out his strength, and suppling the weapon before he attempted to bend it.[1]

Shakespeare, with the license peculiar to his age and character, had diffused the action of his play over Italy, Greece, and Egypt; but Dryden, who was well aware of the advantage to be derived from a simplicity and concentration of plot, has laid every scene in the city of Alexandria. By this he guarded the audience from that vague and puzzling distraction which must necessarily attend a violent change of place. ... It may be true, that no spectator supposes that the stage before him is actually the court of Alexandria; yet, when he has once made up his mind to let it pass as such during the representation, it is a cruel tax, not merely on his imagination, but on his powers of comprehension, if the scene be suddenly transferred to a distant country. Time is lost before he can form new associations, and reconcile their bearings with those originally presented to him; and if he be a person of slow comprehension, or happens to lose any part of the

[1] Homer, *Odyssey* xxi.

dialogue, announcing the changes, the whole becomes unintelligible confusion. In this respect, and in discarding a number of uninteresting characters, the plan of Dryden's play must be unequivocally preferred to that of Shakespeare in point of coherence, unity, and simplicity. It is a natural consequence of this more artful arrangement of the story, that Dryden contents himself with the concluding scene of Antony's history, instead of introducing the incidents of the war with Cneius Pompey, the negociation with Lepidus, death of his first wife, and other circumstances, which, in Shakespeare, only tend to distract our attention from the main interest of the drama. The union of time . . . has, in like manner, been happily attained; and an interesting event is placed before the audience with no other change of place, and no greater lapse of time, than can be readily adapted to an ordinary imagination.

But, having given Dryden the praise of superior address in managing the story, I fear he must be pronounced in most other respects inferior to his grand prototype. Antony, the principal character in both plays, is incomparably grander in that of Shakespeare. The majesty and generosity of the military hero is happily expressed by both poets; but the awful ruin of grandeur, undermined by passion, and tottering to its fall, is far more striking in the Antony of Shakespeare. Love, it is true, is the predominant; but it is not the sole ingredient in his character. It has usurped possession of his mind, but is assailed by his original passions, ambition of power, and thirst for military fame. . . . But Dryden has taken a different view of Antony's character, and more closely approaching to his title of *All for Love.*—"He seems not now that awful Antony."—His whole thoughts and being are dedicated to his fatal passion; and though a spark of resentment is occasionally struck out by the reproaches of Ventidius, he instantly relapses into love-sick melancholy. The following beautiful speech exhibits the romance of despairing love, without the deep and mingled passion of a dishonoured soldier, and dethroned emperor:

> *Ant.* [*Throwing himself down*] Lie there, thou shadow of an
>   emperor;
> The place, thou pressest on thy mother earth,
> Is all thy empire now: Now, it contains thee;
> Some few days hence, and then 'twill be too large,
> When thou 'rt contracted in the narrow urn,
> Shrunk to a few cold ashes; then, Octavia,
> For Cleopatra will not live to see it,

Octavia then will have thee all her own,
And bear thee in her widowed hand to Cæsar;
Cæsar will weep, the crocodile will weep,
To see his rival of the universe
Lie still and peaceful there. I'll think no more on 't.
Give me some music; look that it be sad:

. . . . .

Stay, I fancy
I'm now turned wild, a commoner of nature;
Of all forsaken, and forsaking all. . . .

[I. i.]

Even when Antony is finally ruined, the power of jealousy is called upon to complete his despair, and he is less sensible to the idea of Cæsar's successful arms, than to the risque of Dolabella's rivalling him in the affections of Cleopatra. . . .

Having, however, adopted an idea of Antony's character, rather suitable to romance than to nature, or history, we must not deny Dryden the praise of having exquisitely brought out the picture he intended to draw. He has informed us, that this was the only play written to please himself; and he has certainly exerted in it the full force of his incomparable genius. Antony is throughout the piece what the author meant him to be; a victim to the omnipotence of love, or rather to the infatuation of one engrossing passion.

In the Cleopatra of Dryden, there is greatly less spirit and originality than in Shakespeare's. The preparation of the latter for death has a grandeur which puts to shame the same scene in Dryden. . . . No circumstance can more highly evince the power of Shakespeare's genius, in spite of his irregularities; since the conclusion in Dryden, where both lovers die in the same scene, and after a reconciliation, is infinitely more artful and better adapted to theatrical effect.

In the character of Ventidius, Dryden has filled up, with ability, the rude sketches, which Shakespeare has thrown off in those of Scæva and Eros. The rough old Roman soldier is painted with great truth; and the quarrel betwixt him and Antony, in the first act, is equal to any single scene that our author ever wrote, excepting, perhaps, that betwixt Sebastian and Dorax; an opinion in which the judgment of the critic coincides with that of the poet. . . . The inferior characters are better supported in Dryden than in Shakespeare. We have no low buffoonery in the former, such as disgraces Enobarbus, and is hardly redeemed by his affecting catastrophe. Even the Egyptian Alexas acquires some respectability, from his patriotic attachment to the interests of his country, and from his skill as a wily courtier. ... The Octavia of Dryden is a much more important personage than in ... Shakespeare. She is, however, more cold and unamiable; for, in the very short scenes in which the Octavia of Shakespeare appears, she is placed in rather an interesting point of view. But Dryden has himself informed us, that he was apprehensive the justice of a wife's claim upon her husband would draw the audience to her side, and lessen their interest in the lover and the mistress. He seems accordingly to have studiedly lowered the character of the injured Octavia, who, in her conduct towards her husband, shews much duty and little love; and plainly intimates, that her rectitude of conduct flows from a due regard to her own reputation, rather than from attachment to Antony's person, or sympathy with him in his misfortunes. ...

It would be too long a task to contrast the beauties of these two great poets in point of diction and style. But the reader will doubtless be pleased to compare the noted descriptions of the voyage of Cleopatra down the Cydnus. ... In judging betwixt these celebrated passages, we feel almost afraid to avow a preference for Dryden, founded partly upon the easy flow of the verse, which seems to soften with the subject, but chiefly upon the beauty of the language and imagery, which is flowery without diffusiveness, and rapturous without hyperbole. I fear Shakespeare cannot be exculpated from the latter fault; yet I am sensible, it is by sifting his beauties from his conceits that his imitator has been enabled to excel him.' (v. 287–93.)

(c) 'The Spanish Friar, or the Double Discovery, is one of the best and most popular of our poet's dramatic efforts. ... The felicity of Dryden's plot ... does not consist in the ingenuity of his original conception, but in the minutely artificial strokes, by which the reader is perpetually reminded of the dependence of the one part of the play on the other. These are so frequent, and appear so very natural, that the comic plot, instead of diverting our attention from the tragic business, recal[l]s it to our mind by constant and unaffected allusion. No great event happens in the higher region of the camp or court, that has not some indirect influence upon the intrigues of Lorenzo and Elvira; and the part which the gallant is called upon to act in the revolution that winds up the tragic interest, while it is highly in character, serves to bring the catastrophe of both parts of the

play under the eye of the spectator, at one and the same time. ....
But, although artfully conjoined, the different departments of this
tragi-comedy are separate subjects of critical remark.

The comic part of the *Spanish Friar*, as it gives the first title to the
play, seems to claim our first attention. Indeed, some precedence is
due to it in another point of view; for, though the tragic scenes may
be matched in *All for Love, Don Sebastian*, and else where, the *Spanish
Friar* contains by far the most happy of Dryden's comic effusions. It
has, comparatively speaking, this high claim to commendation, that,
although the intrigue is licentious, according to the invariable licence
of the age, the language is, in general, free from the extreme and
disgusting coarseness, which our author too frequently mistook for
wit, or was contented to substitute in its stead. The liveliness and even
brilliancy of the dialogue, shows that Dryden, from the stores of his
imagination, could, when he pleased, command that essential requisite
of comedy; and that, if he has seldom succeeded, it was only because
he mistook the road, or felt difficulty in travelling it. The character
of Dominic is of that broadly ludicrous nature, which was proper to
the old comedy. It would be difficult to show an ordinary conception
more fully brought out. He is, like Falstaff, a compound of sensuality
and talent, finely varied by the professional traits with which it suited
the author's purpose to adorn his character. Such an addition was, it
is true, more comic than liberal; but Dryden, whose constant dislike
to the clerical order glances out in many of his performances, was not
likely to be scrupulous, when called upon to pourtray one of their
members in his very worst colours. To counterbalance the Friar's
scandalous propensities of every sort, and to render him an object of
laughter, rather than abhorrence, the author has gifted this reprobate
churchman with a large portion of wit; by means of which, and by
a ready presence of mind, always indicative of energy, he preserves
an ascendence over the other characters, and escapes detection and
disgrace, until poetical justice, and the conclusion of the play, called
for his punishment. We have a natural indulgence for an amusing
libertine; and, I believe, that, as most readers commiserate the disgrace of Falstaff, a few may be found to wish that Dominic's penance
had been of a nature more decent and more theatrical than the poet
has assigned him. ....

The tragic part of the *Spanish Friar* has uncommon merit. The
opening of the Drama, and the picture of a besieged town in the last
extremity, is deeply impressive, while the description of the noise of

the night attack, and the gradual manner in which the intelligence
of its success is communicated, arrests the attention, and prepares
expectation for the appearance of the hero, with all the splendour
which ought to attend the principal character in tragedy. The subsequent progress of the plot is liable to a capital objection, from the
facility with which the queen, amiable and virtuous, as we are bound
to suppose her, consents to the murder of the old dethroned monarch.
We question if the operation of any motive, however powerful,
could have been pleaded with propriety, in apology for a breach of
theatrical decorum, so gross, and so unnatural. But, in fact, the queen
is only actuated by a sort of reflected ambition, a desire to secure to
her lover a crown, which she thought in danger; but which, according
to her own statement, she only valued on his account. This is surely
too remote and indirect a motive, to urge a female to so horrid a
crime. There is also something vilely cold-hearted, in her attempt to
turn the guilt and consequences of her own crime upon Bertran,
who, whatever faults he might have to others, was to the queen no
otherwise obnoxious, than because the victim of her own incon-
stancy. The gallant, virtuous, and enthusiastic character of Torrismond,
must be allowed, in some measure, to counterbalance that of his
mistress, however unhappily he has placed his affections. But the real
excellence of these scenes consists less in peculiarity of character, than
in the vivacity and power of the language, which, seldom sinking
into vulgarity, or rising into bombast, maintains the mixture of force
and dignity, best adapted to the expression of tragic passion. Upon
the whole, as the comic part of this play is our author's master-piece
in comedy, the tragic plot may be ranked with his very best efforts
of that kind, whether in *Don Sebastian*, or *All for Love*.' (vi. 367–8,
370–1.)

(*d*) *Don Sebastian*. 'The situation of Dryden, after the Revolution, was
so delicate as to require great caution and attention, both in his choice
of a subject, and his mode of treating it. His distressed circumstances
and lessened income compelled him to come before the public as an
author; while the odium attached to the proselyte of a hated religion,
and the partizan of a depressed faction, was likely, upon the slightest
pretext, to transfer itself from the person of the poet to the labours
on which his support depended. He was, therefore, not only obliged
to chuse a theme, which had no offence in it, and to treat it in a
manner which could not admit of misconstruction, but also so to

exert the full force of his talents, as, by the conspicuous pre-eminence of his genius, to bribe prejudice and silence calumny. An observing reader will accordingly discover, throughout the following tragedy, symptoms of minute finishing, and marks of accurate attention, which, in our author's better days, he deigned not to bestow upon productions, to which his name alone was then sufficient to give weight and privilege. . . .

The characters in *Don Sebastian* are contrasted with singular ability and judgment. Sebastian, high-spirited and fiery; the soul of royal and military honour; the soldier and the king; almost embodies the idea which the reader forms at the first mention of his name. Dorax, to whom he is so admirable a contrast, is one of those characters whom the strong hand of adversity has wrested from their natural bias; and perhaps no equally vivid picture can be found, of a subject so awfully interesting. Born with a strong tendency to all that was honourable and virtuous, the very excess of his virtues became vice, when his own ill fate, and Sebastian's injustice, had driven him into exile. By comparing, as Dryden has requested, the character of Dorax, in the fifth act, with that he maintains in the former part of the play, the difference may be traced betwixt his natural virtues, and the vices engrafted on them by headlong passion and embittering calamity. There is no inconsistence in the change which takes place after his scene with Sebastian; as was objected by those, whom the poet justly terms, "the more ignorant sort of creatures". It is the same picture in a new light; the same ocean in tempest and in calm; the same traveller, whom sunshine has induced to abandon his cloak, which the storm only forced him to wrap more closely around him. The principal failing of Dorax is the excess of pride, which renders each supposed wound to his honour more venomously acute; yet he is not devoid of gentler affections, though even in indulging these the hardness of his character is conspicuous. He loves Violante, but that is a far subordinate feeling to his affection for Sebastian. Indeed, his love appears so inferior to his loyal devotion to his king, that, unless to gratify the taste of the age, I see little reason for its being introduced at all. It is obvious he was much more jealous of the regard of his sovereign, than of his mistress; he never mentions Violante till the scene of explanation with Sebastian; and he appears hardly to have retained a more painful recollection of his disappointment in that particular, than of the general neglect and disgrace he had sustained at the court of Lisbon. The last stage of a virtuous heart, corroded

into evil by wounded pride, has been never more forcibly displayed
than in the character of Dorax. When once induced to take the fatal
step which degraded him in his own eyes, all his good affections seem
to be converted into poison. The religion, which displays itself in the
fifth act in his arguments against suicide, had, in his efforts to justify
his apostacy, or at least to render it a matter of no moment, been
exchanged for sentiments approaching, perhaps to atheism, certainly
to total scepticism. His passion for Violante is changed into contempt
and hatred for her sex, which he expresses in the coarsest terms. His
feelings of generosity, and even of humanity, are drowned in the
gloomy and stern misanthropy, which has its source in the self-
discontent that endeavours to wreak itself upon others. This may be
illustrated by his unfeeling behaviour, while Alvarez and Antonio,
well known to him in former days, approach, and draw the deadly
lot, which ratifies their fate. No yielding of compassion, no recollection of former friendship, has power to alter the cold and sardonic
sarcasm with which he sketches their characters, and marks their
deportment in that awful moment. Finally, the zealous attachment of
Alonzo for his king, which, in its original expression, partakes of
absolute devotion, is changed, by the circumstances of Dorax, into
an irritated and frantic jealousy, which he mistakes for hatred; and
which, in pursuing the destruction of its object, is almost more
inveterate than hatred itself. Nothing has survived of the original
Alonzo at the opening of the piece, except the gigantic passion which
has caused his ruin. This character is drawn on a large scale, and in a
heroic proportion; but it is so true to nature, that many readers must
have lamented, even within the circle of domestic acquaintance,
instances of feelings hardened, and virtues perverted, where a high
spirit has sustained severe and unjust neglect and disgrace. The whole
demeanour of this exquisite character suits the original sketch. From
"the long stride and sullen port", by which Benducar distinguishes
him at a distance, to the sullen stubbornness with which he obeys, or
the haughty contempt with which he resists, the commands of the
peremptory tyrant under whom he had taken service, all announce
the untamed pride which had robbed Dorax of virtue, and which
yet, when Benducar would seduce him into a conspiracy, and in his
conduct towards Sebastian, assumes the port and dignity of virtue
herself. In all his conduct and bearing, there is that mixed feeling
and impulse, which constitutes the real spring of human action. The
true motive of Alonzo in saving Sebastian, is not purely that of

honourable hatred, which he proposes to himself; for to himself every man endeavours to appear consistent, and readily finds arguments to prove to himself that he is so. Neither is his conduct to be ascribed altogether to the gentler feelings of loyal and friendly affection, relenting at the sight of his sovereign's ruin, and impending death. It is the result of a mixture of these opposite sensations, clashing against each other like two rivers at their conflux, yet urging their united course down the same channel. Actuated by a mixture of these feelings, Dorax meets Sebastian; and the art of the poet is displayed in that admirable scene, by suggesting a natural motive to justify to the injured subject himself the change of the course of his feelings. As his jealousy of Sebastian's favour, and resentment of his unjust neglect, was chiefly founded on the avowed preference which the king had given to Henriquez, the opportune mention of his rival's death, by removing the cause of that jealousy, gives the renegade an apology to his own pride, for throwing himself at the feet of that very sovereign, whom a moment before he was determined to force to combat. They are little acquainted with human passions, at least have only witnessed their operations among men of common minds, who doubt, that at the height of their very springtide, they are often most susceptible of sudden changes; revolutions, which seem to those who have not remarked how nearly the most opposite feelings are allied and united, the most extravagant and unaccountable. Muly Moloch is an admirable specimen of that very frequent theatrical character,—a stage tyrant. He is fierce and boisterous enough to be sufficiently terrible and odious, and that without much rant, considering he is an infidel Soldan, who, from the ancient deportment of Mahomed and Termagaunt, as they appeared in the old Mysteries, might claim a prescriptive right to tear a passion to tatters. Besides, the Moorish emperor has fine glances of savage generosity, and that free, unconstrained, and almost noble openness, the only good quality, perhaps, which a consciousness of unbounded power may encourage in a mind so firm as not to be totally depraved by it. .... It is enough to say of Benducar, that the cool, fawning, intriguing, and unprincipled statesman, is fully developed in his whole conduct; and of Alvarez, that the little he has to say and do, is so said and done, as not to disgrace his common-place character of the possessor of the secret on which the plot depends; for it may be casually observed, that the depositary of such a clew to the catastrophe, though of the last importance to the plot, is seldom himself of any interest whatever. The haughty and high-spirited Almeyda is designed by the author as the counterpart of Sebastian. She breaks out with the same violence, I had almost said fury, and frequently discovers a sort of kindred sentiment, intended to prepare the reader for the unfortunate discovery, that she is the sister of the Portuguese monarch.

Of the diction, Dr Johnson has said, with meagre commendation, that it has "some sentiments which leave a strong impression", and "others of excellence, universally acknowledged". This, even when the admiration of the scene betwixt Dorax and Sebastian has been sanctioned by that great critic, seems scanty applause for the *chef d'œuvre* of Dryden's dramatic works. The reader will be disposed to look for more unqualified praise, when such a poet was induced, by every pressing consideration, to combine, in one effort, the powers of his mighty genius, and the fruits of his long theatrical experience: Accordingly, Shakespeare laid aside, it will be perhaps difficult to point out a play containing more animatory incident, impassioned language, and beautiful description, than *Don Sebastian.* . . .

Don Sebastian has been weighed, with reference to its tragic merits, against *All for Love*; and one or other is universally allowed to be the first of Dryden's dramatic performances. To the youth of both sexes the latter presents the most pleasing subject of emotion; but to those whom age has rendered incredulous upon the romantic effects of love, and who do not fear to look into the recesses of the human heart, when agitated by darker and more stubborn passions, *Don Sebastian* offers a far superior source of gratification.' (vii. 274–7, 279.)

(*e*) *Annus Mirabilis.* 'Dryden has very seldom suffered his poem to languish. Every stanza presents us either with vivid description, or with some strong thought, which is seldom suffered to glide into tenuity. But this structure of verse has often laid him under an odd and rather unpleasing necessity, of filling up his stanza, by coupling a simile, or a moral, expressed in the two last lines, along with the fact, which had been announced in the two first. When these comments, or illustrations, however good in themselves, appear to be intruded upon the narrative or description, and not naturally to flow out of either, they must be considered as defects in composition . . .; in the passages which follow, there is produced a stiff and awkward kind of balance between the story and the poet's reflections and illustrations.

[stanzas 21, 23, 25 quoted]

... The love of conceit and point, that inveterate though decaying disease of the literature of the time, has not failed to infect the *Annus Mirabilis*. That monstrous verse, in which the extinction of the fire is described, cannot be too often quoted, both to expose the meanness of the image, and the confusion of the metaphor ...:

> An hollow crystal pyramid he takes,
> In firmamental waters dipt above;
> Of it a broad extinguisher he makes,
> And hoods the flames that to their quarry drove.

Passages also occur, in which, from the author's zealous desire to be technically minute, the style becomes low and vulgar. There is no doubt that, as Dryden has observed, the proper terms of art may be not only justly, but with the highest advantage, employed in poetry; but such technical phrases require to be selected with great judgment: they must bear relation to some striking and important object, or they are mean and trivial; and they must be at once generally intelligible, and more expressive in themselves than ordinary language, or they are unnecessarily obscure and pedantic. Dryden has failed in both these points, in his account of the repairs of the fleet. Stanza 148, in particular, combines the faults of meanness and unnecessary obscurity, from the affected use of the dialect of the dock-yard:

> Some the galled ropes with dawby marline bind,
> Or searcloth masts with strong tarpawling coats:
> To try new shrouds one mounts into the wind,
> And one below their ease or stiffness notes.

Other examples might be produced of the faults of this remarkable poem; but it is time to say, that they are much over-balanced by its beauties. ... [It] exhibits a far greater number of instances of happy and judicious illustration, beautiful description, and sublime morality. ... The 71st stanza will not lose, by being an hundred times quoted:

> In dreams they fearful precipices tread;
> Or, shipwrecked, labour to some distant shore;
> Or in dark churches walk among the dead;
> They wake with horror, and dare sleep no more.

... The description of the Loyal London partakes of the beauties and faults which are dispersed through the poem. Nothing can be more

majestic than her description, "firing the air with her sanguine
streamers", and "riding upon her shadow in floating gold". We
lament, that the weaver should have been so fascinated with his
labours as to commence seaman; and still more, that, after describing
her "roomy decks", and "depth of draught", she should furnish no
grander simile than that of

—a sea-wasp floating on the waves

[stanzas 151–5]. (ix. 83–7.)

(*f*) *Absalom and Achitophel.* "The more deeply we examine the plan
of the piece, the more reason we will find to applaud the exquisite
skill of the author. In the character of Absalom, particularly, he had
a delicate task to perform. He was to draw the misguided and offending son, but not the hardened reprobate; for Charles, notwithstanding
his just indignation, was to the end of his reign partial to this unfortunate prince, and anxious to detach him from his desperate
counsellors. Dryden has, accordingly, liberally transferred all the
fouler part of the accusation to the shoulders of Achitophel, while he
is tender of the fame of Absalom. . . . Even in drawing the character
of Achitophel, such a degree of justice is rendered to his acute talents,
and to his merits as a judge, that we are gained by the poet's apparent
candour to give him credit for the truth of the portrait in its harsher
features. . . .

It was not consistent with Dryden's subject to introduce much
imagery or description into *Absalom and Achitophel*; but, though Dr
Johnson has remarked this as a disadvantage to the poem, it was, I
think, amply compensated by the good effects which the restraint
produced on our author's style of composition. . . . A fiery horse is
taught his regular paces by the restraining discipline of the manege;
and, in the same way, the subject of *Absalom and Achitophel*, which
confined the poet to the expression of sentiment and character, and
left no room for excursions into the regions of metaphysical poetry,
probably had the effect of restraining his exertions within the bounds
of true taste, whose precincts he would be less likely to overleap,
even when again turned loose upon a more fanciful theme. It is
certain that *Absalom and Achitophel* is as remarkable for correctness of
taste, as for fire and spirit of composition; nor ought the reader,
amidst so many appropriate beauties, to regret those flights of imagination, which could not have been indulged without impropriety.

Another objection, stated to this poem, has been the abrupt and unsatisfactory nature of the conclusion. The factions, and their leaders, are described; and, when our expectation is at the highest, the danger is at once dispelled by a speech from the throne. "Who", says Johnson, "can forbear to think of an enchanted castle, with a wide moat, and lofty battlements, which vanishes at once into air, when the destined knight blows his horn before it." Yet, with great deference to such authority, it may be considered as somewhat hard to expect the merit of a well-conducted story in a poem merely intended as a designation of various living characters. He, who collects a gallery of portraits, disclaims, by the very act of doing so, any intention of presenting a series of historical events. Each separate style of poetry has its merits and disadvantages, but we should not expect a historical work to contain the poignancy of a satire, or a satire to exhibit the majestic and interesting story of an epic poem. Besides, there had actually been an important crisis, and highly favourable to the court, produced by the king's behaviour at Oxford. . . .' (ix. 200-1, 202-3.)

(g) 'The doctrine of the *Religio Laici* is admirably adapted to the subject: though treating of the most abstruse doctrines of Christianity, it is as clear and perspicuous as the most humble prose, while it has all the elegance and effect which argument is capable of receiving from poetry. . . . I cannot help remarking, that the style of the *Religio Laici* has been imitated successfully by the late Mr Cowper in some of his pieces. Yet he has not been always able to maintain the resemblance, but often crawls where Dryden would have walked. The natural dignity of our author may be discovered in the lamest lines of the poem, whereas his imitator is often harsh and embarrassed. Both are occasionally prosaic; but in such passages Dryden's verse resembles good prose, and Cowper's that which is feeble and involved.' (x. 7.)

(h) *The Hind and the Panther.* 'In composing this poem, it may be naturally presumed, that Dryden exerted his full powers. He was to justify, in the eyes of the world, a step which is always suspicious; and, by placing before the public the arguments by which he had been induced to change his religion, he was at once to exculpate himself, and induce others to follow his example. He chose, for the mode of conveying this instruction, that parabolical form of writing, which took its rise perhaps in the East, or rather which, in a greater or less degree, is common to all nations. . . . Dryden conceived the idea, of extending to religious communities the supposed resemblance between man and the lower animals. . . .

But Dryden's plan is far from coming within the limits of a fable or parable, strictly so called; for it is strongly objected, that the poet has been unable to avoid confounding the real churches themselves with the Hind and the Panther, under which they are represented. . . .

[Scott quotes Johnson and Prior; *supra*, pp. 300–2 and 167–73.]

This ridicule, and the criticism on which it is founded, seems, however, to be carried a little too far. If a fable, or parable, is to be entirely and exclusively limited to a detail which may suit the common actions and properties of the animals, or things introduced in it, we strike out from the class some which have always been held the most beautiful examples of that style of fiction. It is surely as easy to conceive a Hind and Panther discussing points of religion, as that the trees of the forest should assemble together to chuse a king, invite different trees to accept of that dignity, and, finally, make choice of a bramble. Yet no one ever hesitates to pronounce Jotham's "Parable of the Trees" one of the finest which ever was written.[1] Or what shall we say of one of the most common among Æsop's apologues, which informs us in the outset, that the lion, the ox, the sheep, and the ass went a hunting together, on condition of dividing equally whatever should be caught? Yet this and many other fables, in which the animals introduced act together contrary to their nature, are permitted to rank without censure in the class which they assume. Nay, it may be questioned whether the most proper fables are not those in which the animals are introduced as acting upon the principles of mankind. For instance, if an author be compared to a daw, it is no fable, but a simile; but if a tale be told of a daw who dressed himself in borrowed feathers, a thing naturally impossible, the simile becomes a proper fable. Perhaps, therefore, it is sufficient for the fabulist, if he can point out certain original and leading features of resemblance betwixt his emblems, and that which they are intended to represent, and he may be permitted to take considerable latitude in their farther approximation. It may be farther urged in Dryden's behalf, that the older poets whom he professed to imitate, Spenser, for example, in "Mother Hubbart's Tale", which he has actually quoted, and Chaucer, in that of the Nun's Priest . . ., have stepped beyond the simplicity of the

[1] Judges ix.

ancient fable, and introduced a species of mixed composition, between that and downright satire. . . . Dryden seems to have proposed as his model this looser kind of parable; giving his personages, indeed, the names of the Hind and Panther, but reserving to himself the privilege of making the supposed animals use the language and arguments of the communities they were intended to represent. I must own, however, that this licence appears less pardonable in the First Part, where he professes to use the majestic turn of heroic poetry, than in those which are dedicated to argument and satire. . . .

[Dryden's] plan . . . necessarily limited the interest of the poem to that crisis of politics when it was published. A work, which the author announces as calculated to attract the favour of friends, and to animate the malevolence of enemies, is now read with cold indifference. He launched forth into a tide of controversy, which, however furious at the time, has long subsided, leaving his poem a disregarded wreck, stranded upon the shores which the surges once occupied.

Setting aside this original defect, the First and Last Parts of the poem, in particular, abound with passages of excellent poetry. In the former, it is worthy attention, with what ease and command of his language and subject Dryden passes from his sublime description of the immortal Hind, to brand and stigmatise the sectaries by whom she was hated and persecuted; a rare union of dignity preserved in satire, and of satire engrafted upon heroic poetry. The reader cannot, at the same time, fail to observe the felicity with which the poet has assigned prototypes to the dissenting churches, agreeing in character with that which he meant to fix upon their several congregations. . . . The whole of this First Part of the poem abounds with excellent poetry, rising above the tone of ordinary satire, and yet possessing all its poignancy. The difference, to those against whom it is directed, is like that of being blasted by a thunder-bolt, instead of being branded with a red-hot iron. . . .

The verse in which these doctrines, polemical and political, are delivered, is among the finest specimens of the English heroic stanza. The introductory verses, in particular, are lofty and dignified in the highest degree; as are those, in which the splendour and majesty of the Church of Rome are set forth, in all the glowing colours of rich imagery and magnificent language. But the same praise extends to the versification of the whole poem. It never falls, never becomes rugged; rises with the dignified strain of the poetry; sinks into quaint familiarity, where sarcasm and humour are employed; and winds through all the mazes of theological argument, without becoming either obscure or prosaic. The arguments are in general advanced with an air of conviction and candour, which, in those days, must have required the protestant reader to be on his guard in the perusal, and which seems completely to ascertain the sincerity of the author in his new religious creed.' (x. 89, 91–5, 97–8, 100–1.)

(*i*) *Prologues and Epilogues*. 'With the revival of dramatic entertainments, after the Restoration, these addresses were revived also; and a degree of consequence seems to have been attached to them in that witty age, which they did not possess before, and which has not since been given to them. They were not only used to propitiate the audience; to apologize for the players, or poet; or to satirize the follies of the day, which is now their chief purpose; but they became, during the collision of contending factions, vehicles of political tenets and political sarcasm, which could, at no time, be insinuated with more success, than when clothed in nervous verse, and delivered with all the advantages of elocution to an audience, whose numbers rendered the impression of poetry and eloquence more contagious.

It is not surprising that Dryden soon obtained a complete and absolute superiority in this style of composition over all who pretended to compete with him. While the harmony of his verse gave that advantage to the speaker, which was wanting in the harsh, coarse, broken measure of his contemporaries, his powers of reasoning and of satire left them as far behind in sense as in sound. . . .

The collection of these pieces . . . is far from being the least valuable part of our author's labours. The variety and richness of fancy which they indicate, is one of Dryden's most remarkable poetical attributes. Whether the theme be, the youth and inexperience, or the age and past services, of the author; the plainness or magnificence of a new theatre; the superiority of ancient authors, or the exaltation of the moderns; the censure of political faction, or of fashionable follies; the praise of the monarch, or the ridicule of the administration; the poet never fails to treat it with the liveliness appropriate to verses intended to be spoken, and spoken before a numerous assembly. The manner which Dryden assumes, varies also with the nature of his audience. The prologues and epilogues, intended for the London stage, are written in a tone of superiority, as if the poet, conscious of the justice of his own laws of criticism, rather imposed them upon the public as absolute and undeniable, than as standing in need of their ratification.

And if he sometimes condescends to solicit, in a more humble style, the approbation of the audience, and to state circumstances of apology, and pleas of favour, it is only in the case of other poets; for, in the prologues of his own plays, he always rather demands than begs their applause; and if he acknowledges any defects in the piece, he takes care to intimate, that they are introduced in compliance with the evil taste of the age; and that the audience must take the blame to themselves, instead of throwing it upon the writer. This bold style of address, although it occasionally drew upon our author the charge of presumption, was, nevertheless, so well supported by his perception of what was just in criticism, and his powers of defending even what was actually wrong, that a miscellaneous audience was, in general, fain to submit to a domination, as successfully supported as boldly claimed. In the Oxford prologues, on the other hand, the audience furnished by that seat of the Muses, as of more competent judgment, are addressed with more respectful deference. . . . In another respect, the reader may remark a pleasing difference between the London prologues and epilogues, and those spoken at Oxford. The licence of the times permitted, and even exacted from an author, in these compositions, the indulgence of an indelicate vein of humour; which, however humiliating, is, in general, successful in a vulgar or mixed audience, as turning upon subjects adapted to the meanest capacity. This continued even down to our times; for, till very lately, it was expected by the mobbish part of the audience, that they should be indemnified for the patience with which they had listened to the moral lessons of a tragedy, by the indecency of the epilogue. In Dryden's time, this coarse raillery was carried to great excess; but our author, however culpable in other compositions, is, generally speaking, more correct than his contemporaries in his prologues and epilogues. In the Oxford pieces, particularly, where the decorum of manners, suited to that mother of learning, required him to abstain from all licentious allusion, Dryden has given some excellent specimens of how little he needed to rely upon this obvious and vulgar aid, for the amusement of his audience. Upon the whole, it will be difficult to find pieces of this occasional nature so interesting and unexceptionable as those spoken at Oxford. They are, as they ought to be, by far the most laboured and correct which our author gave to the stage.' (x. 311–15.)

(j) *Mac Flecknoe*. 'In this satire, the shafts of the poet are directed with an aim acutely malignant. The inference drawn concerning Shadwell's talents is general and absolute; but in the proof, Dryden appeals with triumph to those parts only of his literary character which are obviously vulnerable. He reckons up among his titles to the throne of Flecnoe, his desperate and unsuccessful attempts at lyrical composition, in the opera of *Psyche*; the clumsy and coarse limning of those whom he designed to figure as fine gentlemen in his comedies; the false and florid taste of his dedications; his presumptuous imitation of Jonson in composition, and his absurd resemblance to him in person. But the satirist industriously keeps out of view those points, in which perhaps he internally felt some inferiority to the object of his wrath. He mentions nothing that could recal[l] to the reader's recollection that insight into human life, that acquaintance with the foibles and absurdities displayed in individual pursuits, that bold though coarse delineation of character, which gave fame to Shadwell's comedies in the last century, and renders them amusing even at the present day. This discrimination is an excellent proof of the exquisite address with which Dryden wielded the satirical weapon, and managed the feelings of his readers. We never find him attempting a desperate or impossible task; at least in a way which seems, in the moment of perusal, desperate or impossible. He never wastes his powder against the impregnable part of a fortress, but directs all his battery against some weaker spot, where a breach may be rendered practicable. In short, by convincing his reader that he is right in the examples which he quotes, he puts the question at issue upon the ground most disadvantageous for his antagonist, and renders it very difficult for one who has been proved a dunce in one instance to establish his credit in any other.

... The mock heroic may be said to have owed its rise to our author, and ... there is hardly any poem, before *Mac-Flecnoe*, in which it has been employed with all its qualities of grave and pompous irony, expressed in solemn and sounding verse.

It is no inconsiderable part of the merit of *Mac-Flecnoe*, that it led the way to the *Dunciad*: yet, while we acknowledge the more copious and variegated flow of Pope's satire, we must not forget, that, independent of the merit of originality, always inestimable, Dryden's poem claims that of a close and more compact fable, of a single and undisturbed aim. Pope's ridicule and sarcasm is scattered so wide, and among such a number of authors, that it resembles small shot discharged at random among a crowd; while that of Dryden, like a single well-directed bullet, prostrates the individual object against whom it was directed. Besides, the reader is apt to sympathise with the degree of the satirist's provocation, which, in Dryden's case, cannot be disputed; whereas Pope sometimes confounds those, from whom he had received gross incivility, with others who had given him no offence, and with some whose characters were above his accusation. To posterity, the *Mac-Flecnoe* possesses a decided superiority over the *Dunciad*, for a very few facts make us master of the argument; while that of the latter poem, excepting the Sixth Book,[1] where the satire is more general, requires a note at every tenth line to render it even intelligible.' (x. 429–31.)

84. Teutonic strictures

1808

Extract from Augustus William von Schlegel, *Lectures on Dramatic Art* (1809), 1846, translated by John Black and revised by A. J. W. Morrison, pp. 477–9 (Lecture xxviii). Schlegel (1767–1845) delivered his lectures in Vienna in 1808.

Dryden soon became and long remained the hero of the stage. This man, from his influence in fixing the laws of versification and poetical language, especially in rhyme, has acquired a reputation altogether disproportionate to his true merit. We shall not here inquire whether his translations of the Latin poets are not manneristical paraphrases, whether his political allegories (now that party interest is dead) can be read without the greatest weariness; but confine ourselves to his plays, which considered relatively to his great reputation, are incredibly bad. Dryden had a gift of flowing and easy versification; the knowledge which he possessed was considerable, but undigested; and all this was coupled with the talent of giving a certain appearance of

[1] Presumably the fourth and last book.

novelty to what however was borrowed from all quarters; his serviceable muse was the resource of an irregular life. He had besides an
immeasurable vanity; he frequently disguises it under humble
prologues; on other occasions he speaks out boldly and confidently,
avowing his opinion that he has done better than Shakespeare,
Fletcher, and Jonson (whom he places nearly on the same level); all
the merit of this he is, however, willing to ascribe to the refinement
and advances of the age. The age, indeed! as if that of Elizabeth compared with the one in which Dryden lived, were not in every respect
'Hyperion to a Satyr!'[1] Dryden played also the part of the critic: he
furnished his pieces richly with prefaces and treatises on dramatic
poetry, in which he chatters most confusedly about the genius of
Shakespeare and Fletcher, and about the entirely opposite example of
Corneille; of the original boldness of the British stage, and of the
rules of Aristotle and Horace.—He imagined that he had invented a
new species, namely the Heroic Drama; as if Tragedy had not from
its very nature been always heroical! If we are, however, to seek for
a heroic drama which is not peculiarly tragic, we shall find it among
the Spaniards, who had long possessed it in the greatest perfection.
From the uncommon facility of rhyming which Dryden possessed, it
cost him little labour to compose the most of his serious pieces entirely
in rhyme. With the English, the rhymed verse of ten syllables supplies
the place of the Alexandrine; it has more freedom in its pauses, but
on the other hand it wants the alternation of male and female rhymes;
it proceeds in pairs exactly like the French Alexandrine, and in point
of syllabic measure it is still more uniformly symmetrical. It therefore
unavoidably communicates a great stiffness to the dialogue. . . .

Dryden's plans are improbable, even to silliness; the incidents are
all thrown out without forethought; the most wonderful theatrical
strokes fall incessantly from the clouds. He cannot be said to have
drawn a single character; for there is not a spark of nature in his
dramatic personages. Passions, criminal and magnanimous sentiments,
flow with indifferent levity from their lips, without ever having
dwelt in the heart: their chief delight is in heroical boasting. The
tone of expression is by turns flat or madly bombastical; not infre-
quently both at the same time: in short, this poet resembles a man
who walks upon stilts in a morass. His wit is displayed in far-fetched
sophistries; his imagination in long-spun similes, awkwardly introduced. All these faults have been ridiculed by the Duke of Buckingham

[1] Shakespeare, *Hamlet* I. ii. 140.

in his comedy of *The Rehearsal*. . . . The vehicle of this critical satire
might have been more artificial and diversified; the matter, however,
is admirable, and the separate parodies are very amusing and ingenious. The taste for this depraved manner was, however, too
prevalent to be restrained by the efforts of so witty a critic. . . .

85. Blake against journeymen

c. 1810

Extracts from William Blake's Note-book, pp. 60–1 and 39.
(*Complete Writings* (1966), ed. Geoffrey Keynes, pp. 595 and 602.)

(*a*) 'While the Works of Pope and Dryden are look'd upon as the
same Art with those of Milton and Shakespeare, while the works of
Strange and Woollett are look'd upon as the same Art with those of
Rafael and Albert Durer, there can be no Art in a Nation but such as
is Subservient to the interest of the Monopolizing Trader who Manu-
factures Art by the Hands of Ignorant Journeymen till at length
Christian Charity is held out as a Motive to encourage a Blockhead,
and he is Counted the Greatest Genius who can sell a Good-for-
Nothing Commodity for a Great Price. . . .

> Dryden in Rhyme cries, 'Milton only Planned.'
> Every Fool shook his bells throughout the Land.

(*b*) 'I do not condemn Rubens, Rembrandt or Titian because they did
not understand drawing, but because they did not Understand
Colouring; . . . I do not condemn Strange or Woollett because they
did not understand drawing, but because they did not understand
Graving. I do not condemn Pope or Dryden because they did not
understand Imagination, but because they did not understand Verse.
Their Colouring, Graving and Verse can never be applied to Art—

That is not either Colouring, Graving or Verse which is Unappropriate to the Subject.'

86. Lord Monboddo on Dryden's *Odes*

(n.d.)

From Dr Emily Cloyd's transcripts of undated autographs of Lord Monboddo (1714-99): (*a*) National Library of Scotland MS A54b, p. 62; (*b*) Monboddo papers in Aberdeen. James Burnett, Lord Monboddo, was a Scottish judge, philosopher, and eccentric; a pioneer in anthropology; and author of *Of the Origin and Progress of Language* (1773-6, 1774-92). (*a*) is apparently a draft for the projected seventh volume of that work.

(*a*) 'Of Dryden's ode on St. Cecilias day—The finest piece of Rhyming Poetry in English—A wonderfull variety of verse in it—not only different in Length and Shortness, but in the Measure of the Verse—He has used feet different from any of those hitherto mentioned, as belonging to English verse—Analysis of the versification of this Poem—All the variety of Measure to be found in it that can be imagined in English Verse ... Mr. Pope's Ode on *St. Cecilias Day*, much inferior to Mr. Dryden's ... The Italian Language capable of all the variety of verse that is in English—But no one Poem in Italian of such variety as Dryden's ode. ...'

(*b*) '*Alexander's Feast* ... for the Beauty of the Sentiments and Diction, and the Variety of the versification, is the finest piece of Lyric Poetry in English ... the Measure of the Verse, which is most agreeably changed in different parts of the Ode, [is] exceedingly well suited to the different Sentiments. As the Beauty of this versification has not

I think been sufficiently attended to, I will beg leave to go thro' it with that view. . . .

The first Stanza is all in common Iambic measure, with great variety however of Long and short vers, to the last four Lines, beginning *Happy, happy, happy pair*, where the measure is very happily changed for the Trochaic and the Repetitions of *happy*, and *none but the brave*, are I think exceedingly fine, and very well suited to the Subject, being as it were the Acclamation of the People. . . .

The [third] Stanza contains the praise of Bacchus: It begins like wise with Iambics, the common foot in English Verse; and goes on for three Verses till the description becomes more animated; and then he changes the verse to Trochaic, with a Variety which he has not hitherto used, such as that of a residuous Syllable after the conclusion of the last foot, a variety which as I have shown has been practiced by other Poets. The verse I mean is

Sound the Trumpets, beat the Drums.

In the next verse he has a variety very uncommon in English verse; for the first foot is a Dactyle; the next is a Trochaic, and after it a Residuous Syllable accented or half a foot. The verse is

Flushed with a purple Grace.

Then he has the Common Iambic Line,

He showes his honest face,

which may seem Prosaic, but I think makes a very agreeable Variety intermixed with the other Lines. The Line after that is a Trochaic with a residuous Syllable: And it has a very fine break of the Sense in the Middle which if [it] be well imitated by the Music, should produce an excellent effect.

Now give the Haut boys breath; he comes, he comes. . . .

These Seven last Lines beginning with *Bacchus ever fair* [54–60], are of that kind of Poetry which the Greeks call *orchestic* such as we are told some of Pindars Odes were; and indeed the measure is altogether Saltant, and might I am persuaded be danced to with great propriety.

The next Stanza [IV] begins with a Dactyle; then two Trochees and a Residuous Syllable . . . then follows a Line all Iambics,

Fought all his Battles o'er again.

Then follows a very long Iambic line, which expresses wonderfully well the thing it describes,

> And thrice he routed all his foes and thrice he slew the slain,

being the longest verse in the whole Poem and in that way imitating very well the vain teadeous boasting of the King. . . .

[Monboddo continues a metrical analysis without critical comment for eight pages.]

These Observations will I am persuaded be thought by many of my Readers very trifling; and they will say that their Ear perceives all that variety of Measure, which I have described, without frittering and breaking it down as I have done: but such Readers will excuse me for telling them that they are not men of Science; otherwise they would know that there can be no Science without accurate division into parts. . . .

I had another reason for insisting so much upon the variety of measure in this ode, that I wanted to supply the Defects of my System of English Versification, which I have given in the Second volume of the Origin of Language. . . . I think I have not only made a System of English Versification, but shown that it is a compleat System. . . . It is such that the English ought to be very fond of it: as it sets their Poetry much above the French, and that of any Language now living, the Italian only excepted, which having accents as well as the English, employes them to give that variety to their Poetry, without which, as I have more than once observed, there can be nothing perfect in any of the Arts: But tho' the Italian has all that Variety of feet which the English has . . . I do not know that there is any one Poem in Italian of so small a compass as *Alexander's feast* which has the same variety of measure, and of long and short verse, that is to be found in Mr. Dryden's Ode.[1]

---

[1] Dr Cloyd comments that for Monboddo 'the great, over-riding excellence in any literature was *reasoned* variety'.

Appendix: early editions
of the works of Dryden

Some account of the contemporary publishing history of the main works is given in the Introduction, pp. 2–7.

'Upon the death of the Lord Hastings', in *Lachrymæ Musarum; The Tears of the Muses: Exprest in Elegies,* 1649, 1650.

'To his friend [John Hoddesdon], on his divine Epigrams', in Hoddesdon's *Sion and Parnassus,* 1650.

Lines to Honor Dryden (?1653), first printed in the *Gentleman's Magazine,* lv (1785), i. 337.

'Heroique Stanza's', in *Three Poems upon the Death of his late Highnesse Oliver Lord Protector of England, Scotland, and Ireland,* 1659, 1681, 1682 (Dublin), 1682 (London), 1687, '1659' (*c.* 1691).

'To my Honored Friend, Sʳ Robert Howard', in Howard's *Poems,* 1660, 1696, and *Collection of Poems by Several Hands,* 1693.

Astræa Redux. A Poem on the Happy Restoration & Return of His Sacred Majesty Charles the Second, 1660, 1688.

To His Sacred Maiesty, A Panegyrick on his Coronation, 1661, 1688, and in *Complementum Fortunatarum Insularum,* 1662.

To My Lord Chancellor, 1662, 1688.

'To my Honor'd Friend, Dʳ Charleton', in Walter Charleton's *Chorea Gigantum, or . . . Stone-Heng,* 1662.

The Rival Ladies. A Tragi-Comedy, 1664, 1669, 1675, 1693.

The Indian-Queen, A Tragedy, by Dryden and Sir Robert Howard, in Howard's *Four New Plays,* 1665, and *Five New Plays,* 1692, 1700.

The Indian Emperour, or, The Conquest of Mexico by the Spaniards. Being the Sequel of the Indian Queen, 1667, 1668, 1670, 1670, 1681, 1686, 1692, 1694, 1696, 1696.

Annus Mirabilis: The Year of Wonders, 1666, 1667, 1668, 1688 (with *Astræa Redux* and *To My Lord Chancellor*).

Secret-Love, or The Maiden-Queen, 1668, 1669, 1679, 1691, 1698.

Of Dramatick Poesie, An Essay, 1667, 1684, 1693.

St *Martin Mar-all, or The Feign'd Innocence: A Comedy*, by Dryden and the Duke of Newcastle, 1668, 1668, 1678, 1691, 1697.

The Wild Gallant: A Comedy, 1669, 1669, 1684, 1686, 1694.

The Tempest, or The Enchanted Island. A Comedy, by Dryden and Davenant, 1670; operatic version, 1674, 1676, 1690.

Tyrannick Love, or The Royal Martyr. A Tragedy, 1670, 1672, 1677, 1686, 1695.

An Evening's Love, or The Mock-Astrologer, 1671, 1671, 1675, 1691.

Prologues, Epilogues and Songs in *Westminster-Drollery*, 1671; *Westminster Drollery, The Second Part*, 1672; *New Court-Songs, and Poems. By R. V[eel]*, 1672; and *Covent Garden Drolery*, 1672 (3 edns.).

The Conquest of Granada by the Spaniards: in Two Parts, 1672, 1673, 1678, 1687, 1695.

Marriage A-la-Mode. A Comedy, 1673, 1684, 1691, 1698.

The Assignation: or, Love in a Nunnery, 1673, 1678, 1692.

Amboyna: A Tragedy, 1673, 1691.

'To the Lady Castlemain, Upon Her encouraging his first Play', in John Bulteel's *A New Collection of Poems and Songs*, 1674.

Notes and Observations on The Empress of Morocco, by Dryden, Shadwell, and Crowne, 1674.

Aureng-Zebe: A Tragedy, 1676, 1685, 1690, 1692, 1694, 1699.

Epilogue to Sir George Etherege's comedy, *The Man of Mode*, 1676, 1684, 1693.

The State of Innocence, and Fall of Man: An Opera, Written in Heroique Verse, 1677, 1678, 1684 (3 edns.), 1690, 1692, 1695, 1695.

Prologue to Charles Davenant's *Circe, A Tragedy*, 1677, 1685.

'To Mr. Lee, on his *Alexander*', in Nathaniel Lee's *The Rival Queens*, 1677, 1684, 1694, 1699.

All for Love: or, The World Well Lost. A Tragedy, 1678, 1692, 1696.

Epilogue to Lee's *Mithridates King of Pontus*, 1678, 1685, 1693, 1697.

Prologue to Shadwell's *A True Widow*, 1679; the Prologue later printed with Mrs. Behn's *The Widdow Ranter*, 1690.

Oedipus: A Tragedy, by Dryden and Lee, 1679, 1682, 1687, 1692, 1696 (n.d.).

Troilus and Cressida, or, Truth Found too Late. A Tragedy, 1679, '1679' (?1692), 1695.

.The Kind Keeper; or, Mr. Limberham: A Comedy, 1680, 1690.

Prologue to Lee's *Cæsar Borgia*, 1680, 1696.

Prologue to Nahum Tate's *The Loyal General*, 1680.

Ovid's Epistles, Translated by Several Hands, 1680, 1681; preface and three epistles by Dryden.

The Spanish Fryar or, The Double Discovery, 1681, 1686, 1690, 1695.

Epilogue to Charles Saunders's *Tamerlane the Great*, 1681.

The Epilogue Spoken to the King ... at Oxford on ... March the Nineteenth 1681, 1681 (2 edns.; half-sheets).

'Prologue to the University of Oxford', in Lee's *Sophonisba*, 1681; reprinted in *Miscellany Poems*, 1684, with changes.

A Prologue spoken at Mithridates King of Pontus, 1681 (half-sheet).

His Majesties Declaration Defended: In a Letter to a Friend, 1681.

Absalom and Achitophel. A Poem, 1681, 1681 (Dublin; 2 edns.), 1681 (bibliographically the second London edn.), 1681 ('The Second Edition; Augmented and Revised'), 1682 (3 edns.); reprinted in *Miscellany Poems*, 1684 and 1692, and with *Mac Flecknoe* and *The Medall*, 1692.

Prologue and Epilogue to John Banks's *The Unhappy Favourite*, 1681; the Prologue reprinted in *Miscellany Poems*, 1684, as 'An Epilogue for the Kings House'.

A Prologue ... to ... The Loyal Brother (half-sheet); Prologue and Epilogue to Southerne's *The Loyal Brother*, 1682.

The Medall. A Satyre against Sedition, 1682 (London), 1682 (Edinburgh), 1682 (Dublin); reprinted in *Miscellany Poems*, 1684 and 1692, and with *Absalom and Achitophel* and *Mac Flecknoe*, 1692.

Mac Flecknoe, or A Satyr upon the True-Blew-Protestant Poet, T.S., 1682 (a bad and unauthorized text 'Printed for D. Green'); in *Miscellany Poems*, 1684, 1692; reprinted with *Absalom and Achitophel* and *Mac Flecknoe*, 1692.

Prologue to His Royal Highness, Upon His first appearance ... since his Return from Scotland, 1682 (half-sheet).

Prologue to The Dutchess, On Her Return from Scotland, 1682 (half-sheet).

The Second Part of Absalom and Achitophel. A Poem, by Tate and Dryden, 1682 (2 edns., London), 1682 (Dublin).

Religio Laici or A Laymans Faith. A Poem, 1682 (3 issues), 1682, 1683.

The Art of Poetry, Written in French by the Sieur de Boileau, Made English, 1683, by Sir William Soame and Dryden.

Prologue. To the King and Queen, 1683, with an Epilogue.

The Duke of Guise. A Tragedy, by Dryden and Lee, 1683, 1687, 1699. Prologue and Epilogue, with a second Epilogue 'Intended to have been Spoken', separately published, 1683.

Epilogue to Lee's *Constantine the Great*, published with the Prologue (by Otway) in 1683 and with the play in 1684.

The Vindication: or The Parallel of The French Holy-League, and The English League and Covenant . . ., 1683.

Plutarchs Lives. Translated . . . *by Several Hands* (Life of Plutarch and Epistle Dedicatory by Dryden), vol. i, 1683; ii, iii, 1684; iv, 1685; v, 1686; 5 vols., 1688, 1693, 1700.

Miscellany Poems, 1684, containing 26 items by Dryden, 18 of them here first published.

Prologue to Southerne's *The Disappointment*, 1684; published separately and with the play.

'To the Earl of Roscomon', in Roscommon's *An Essay on Translated Verse*, 1684, 1685.

The History of the League. . . . *By Monsieur Maimbourg. Translated*, 1684.

'To the Memory of Mr. Oldham', in John Oldham's *Remains*, 1684, 1687, 1693, 1694, 1697.

Sylvæ: or, The Second Part of Poetical Miscellanies, 1685, 1692; Preface and 17 new pieces of verse by Dryden.

Threnodia Augustalis: A Funeral-Pindarique Poem Sacred to the Happy Memory of King Charles II, 1685 (London, 3 edns.), 1685 (Dublin).

Albion and Albanius: An Opera, 1685 (Prologue and Epilogue also printed separately), 1687 (words and music), 1691.

'To my Friend Mr. J. Northleigh', in John Northleigh, *The Triumph of our Monarchy*, 1685.

'To the Pious Memory of the Accomplisht Young Lady Mrs Anne Killigrew . . . An Ode', in her *Poems*, 1686; revised for *Examen Poeticum*, 1693.

A Defence of the Papers Written by the Late King . . . *and Duchess of York*, in part by Dryden, 1686.

'To my Ingenious Friend, Mr. Henry Higden', in Higden's *A Modern Essay on the Tenth Satyr of Juvenal*, 1687.

The Hind and the Panther. A Poem, In Three Parts, 1687 (London; 3 edns.), 1687 (Edinburgh), 1687 (Dublin).

A Song for St Cecilia's Day, 1687; reprinted in *Examen Poeticum*, 1693.

Lines on Milton in *Paradise Lost*, fourth edn., 1688, frontispiece.

Britannia Rediviva: A Poem on the Birth of the Prince, 1688 (London), 1688 (Edinburgh), '1688' (c. 1691).

The Life of St. Francis Xavier, of the Society of Jesus. . . . *Translated*, 1688.

The Prologue and Epilogue to The History of Bacon in Virginia, 1689.

Don Sebastian, King of Portugal: A Tragedy, 1690, 1692.

Prologue to *The Prophetess*, 1690; Beaumont and Fletcher turned into opera. *The Vocal and Instrumental Musick*, 1691.

Amphitryon; or, The Two Socia's. A Comedy, 1690, 1694.

Preface to William Walsh's *A Dialogue concerning Women*, 1691.

Prologue to Joseph Harris's *The Mistakes*, 1691.

To Sir George Etherege: 'Mr D— Answer', in *The History of Adolphus. . . . By a Person of Quality*, 1691.

King Arthur: or, The British Worthy. A Dramatick Opera, 1691, 1695.

'To Mr. Southerne', in Southerne's *The Wives Excuse*, 1692.

Eleonora: A Panegyrical Poem: Dedicated to the Memory of the Late Countess of Abingdon, 1692.

Cleomenes, The Spartan Heroe. A Tragedy, 1692.

'Character' of Saint-Evremond, prefixed to his *Miscellaneous Essays . . . Translated*, 1692; vol. ii, 1694.

The Satires of Decimus Junius Juvenalis. Translated into English Verse. By Mr. Dryden, and Several other Eminent Hands. Together with the Satires of Aulus Persius Flaccus made English by Mr. Dryden, 1693, 1697.

Examen Poeticum: Being the Third Part of Miscellany Poems, 1693, containing a Dedication and 10 new pieces of verse by Dryden.

'Character' of Polybius in Sir Henry Sheeres's translation of *The History of Polybius the Megalopolitan*, 1693, 1698.

Epilogue to the anonymous tragedy, *Henry the Second*, 1693.

'To My Dear Friend Mr. Congreve', in Congreve, *The Double-Dealer*, 1694.

Love Triumphant; or, Nature will Prevail. A Tragi-Comedy, 1694.

'To Sir Godfrey Kneller' and a version of *Georgics* iii in *The Annual Miscellany: For the Year 1694. Being the Fourth Part of Miscellany Poems*, 1694.

De Arte Graphica. The Art of Painting, By C. A. Du Fresnoy. . . . Translated . . . Together with an Original Preface by Dryden, 1695.

An Ode, on the Death of Mr. Henry Purcell, 1696; reprinted in Purcell's *Orpheus Britannicus*, 1698.

Epilogue to *The Husband his own Cuckold* by John Dryden Jun., 1696.

The Works of Virgil . . . Translated into English Verse, 1697, 1698.

Alexander's Feast; or The Power of Musique. An Ode, in Honour of St. Cecilia's Day, 1697; reprinted in *Fables*, 1700.

'To Mr. Granville', in George Granville's *Heroick Love*, 1698.

'To my Friend, the Author', in Peter Motteux's *Beauty in Distress*, 1698.

The Annals and History of Cornelius Tacitus translated in part by Dryden, 3 vols., 1698.

Fables Ancient and Modern; Translated into Verse, From Homer, Ovid, Boccace, & Chaucer: With Original Poems, 1700.

Prologue, Epilogue, and Secular Masque in Fletcher's *The Pilgrim* ('very much Alter'd, with several Additions'), 1700, 1701.

Collections of Dryden's plays made up in quarto with varying title pages appeared during the 1690s. *The Comedies, Tragedies, and Operas . . . Now first Collected together, and Corrected from the Originals* appeared in two folio volumes in 1701. With two more volumes—*Poems on Various Occasions; and Translations* together with the *Fables*, and the 1698 edition of the *Virgil*—they made up a collected edition of the *Works*.

Posthumously published poems include:

Lines on Tonson in William Shippen's *Faction Display'd*, 1704.

10 pieces of verse in *Poetical Miscellanies: The Fifth Part*, 1704.

The first book of *Ovid's Art of Love . . . Translated*, 1709.

The Life in *The Works of Lucian, Translated*, 4 vols., 1711.

'Æsacus transform'd into a Cormorant' in *Ovid's Metamorphoses . . . Translated*, 1717.

Minor verse in Lintott's *Miscellaneous Poems*, 1712.

The Ode on the marriage of Anastasia Stafford and George Holman in Arthur Clifford's *Tixall Poetry*, 1813.

Index

II. WORKS OF DRYDEN DISCUSSED IN THE TEXT

THE CRITICAL HERITAGE SERIES

GENERAL EDITOR: B. C. SOUTHAM